TOWARD A THEORY OF CULTURAL LINGUISTICS

GARY B. PALMER

TOWARD A
THEORY OF
CULTURAL
LINGUISTICS

University of Texas Press
AUSTIN

First edition, 1996

Requests for permission to reproduce material from this work should be sent to Permissions, University of Texas Press, Box 7819, Austin, TX 78713-7819.

LIBRARY OF CONGRESS CATALOGING-IN-PUBLICATION DATA

Palmer, Gary B., 1942–
   Toward a theory of cultural linguistics / by Gary B. Palmer. —
1st ed.
      p.   cm.
   Includes bibliographical references (p.   ) and index.
   ISBN 0-292-76568-1. — ISBN 0-292-76569-X (pbk.)
    1. Anthropological linguistics. 2. Cognitive grammar. I. Title.
P35.P27   1996
306.4'4'089—dc20   95–47742

TO MY MOTHER AND FATHER,

MARIAN AND FRANK PALMER

CONTENTS

TABLES

FIGURES

ACKNOWLEDGMENTS

For reading and commenting on selected chapters of the manuscript I thank Keith Basso, Wenny Carstens, Zoltán Kövecses, Colin Loader, John Swetnam, George Urioste, Gary Witherspoon, and lay readers Pat and A. D. Hopkins and Keith Peterson. Elizabeth Brandt, René Dirven, Austin Hale, Ronald Langacker, Jacqueline Lindenfeld, Gunter Radden, and Ralf Reimann provided extensive comments and criticisms. The readers are not responsible for any residual foolishness, nor should Basso, Kövecses, and Witherspoon be held responsible for the uses to which I have put their data. Evan Blythin, Timothy Clow, and Scott Locicero, who is greatly missed, helped significantly by discussing many of the ideas with me. Hideki Kishimoto, Wendy Sanders, and Ester Waher engaged me in friendly adversarial discussions of generative grammar that forced me to reexamine my own very divergent premises. Don Diener, Terry Knapp, and Lori Temple answered my frequent pleas for references to pertinent findings in cognitive psychology and psycholinguistics, much of which I regretfully had to omit. Ondieki Kennedy outlined Kisii noun classes for me, Mohamed Kaseko helped with Swahili, and Rusandre Hendrikse provided information on *mhondoro* 'lion,' a key term in my analysis of Shona noun classes. The terrific initiative and research collaboration on Coeur d'Alene semantics of Debra Kendrick-Murdock, Debra Occhi, and Roy Ogawa, boosted my enthusiasm for the project. Dorothy Neal Arin contributed data on Shona noun classes.

Several elders of the Coeur d'Alene Indian Tribe have acted as my consultants as I studied their language, culture, and history over the past twenty years. My experience with the fascinating sounds and images of Coeur d'Alene is one of the main inspirations for this book. Those I called on most often are Lawrence Nicodemus, Felix and Lawrence Aripa, and Lavinia Felsman. Tom Connolly, Armando DaSilva, the late Bernard

LaSarte, the Coeur d'Alene Tribal Council, and many others, both Indian and non-Indian, on the reservation have contributed to my studies in one way or another. Some of my work with Coeur d'Alene was jointly supported by the tribe and the Association for the Humanities in Idaho through the Coeur d'Alene Language Preservation Project. Some of it was supported through Faculty Research Council Grant 4758 FP-6/30/81, "The Definition of Words in Coeur d'Alene."

This book has benefited immensely from the opportunity to attend courses and participate in discussions at the Linguistic Institutes at Stanford in 1987 and at Tucson in 1989. My attendance was supported financially by my department and college. Phyllis Margolis, Sherron Bell, Michael Geary, and Catherine Hoye provided unstinting secretarial assistance.

Even though more than two decades have passed since I received the Ph.D. in anthropology at the University of Minnesota, I would like to take this opportunity to thank my advisor, Luther P. Gerlach, and the other faculty there for their generous guidance and enthusiastic encouragement.

And to Evan, Alan, and especially Jeanne, thanks for your patience and encouragement.

PART ONE

GOALS AND CONCEPTS

CHAPTER 1

INTRODUCTION

Everyone is talking and writing about language these days, but there is little agreement on how it works. Some scholars regard the human capacity for language as a mechanical device, much like a digital computer. Others think of language as something that we do to other people, like handing them a book or clapping them on the back. In my own view, language is the play of verbal symbols that are based in imagery. Imagery is what we see in our mind's eye, but it is also the taste of a mango, the feel of walking in a tropical downpour, the music of *Mississippi Masala*. Our imaginations dwell on experiences obtained through all the sensory modes, and then we talk.

But what, exactly, does language have to do with imagery? Perhaps a metaphor will help. The Kaluli people of southern New Guinea regard birds of the forest as spirit reflections of deceased persons who inhabit a parallel world (Schiefflin 1976; Feld 1990). I believe that words are like the birds of Kaluli: they are fleeting vocalizations, symbolically linked to conceptual shades that inhabit the parallel world of our imaginations. This imagined world sometimes closely represents what we apprehend from direct daily experience, but it is not very reliable in that respect; much of the time it presents us with alternative realities and fantasy worlds based on mythology, or soap opera, or unproven theories. Nevertheless, in world views we find those stable representations and fleeting images that are the conventional meanings of linguistic expressions.

The notion that language evokes imagery and requires imagination for its interpretation may sound like a truism to poets, literary critics, and symbolic anthropologists (indeed, almost everybody), but, surprisingly enough, not everyone takes it for granted. Many linguists, perhaps even the majority, leave imagery out of their theories entirely, even when those theories attempt to consider linguistic meaning! These variously non-imagistic, formal, and generative theories have been challenged most effectively by George Lakoff (1987), who disparaged their "objectivism," and Ronald Langacker (1987, 1990a: v), who accused them of "narrowness" and "lack of naturalness." [1] Rather than adding another extended critique to the literature, I will instead attempt to make my case by marshaling cogent examples. Imagery does not explain everything about language, but an examination of its role illuminates many usages and domains of language of abiding interest to anthropologists.

This theme of imagery in language provides a basis for examining a surprisingly wide range of linguistic topics. It applies not only to narrative and figurative language, but also to the semantics of words and grammatical constructions, to discourse, and even to phonology. In the past, these linguistic domains have been subjected to disparate and mutually inconsistent theories as though they differed in kind, when they really only represent different points of view. I will argue that they can best be understood in terms of a single theory of culturally defined mental imagery—a cultural theory of linguistic meaning. In this *cultural linguistics*, phonemes are heard as verbal images arranged in complex categories; words acquire meanings that are relative to image-schemas, scenes, and scenarios; clauses are image-based constructions; discourse emerges as a process governed by the reflexive imagery of itself; and world view subsumes it all. The approach builds on older traditions as well as contemporary theories in anthropological linguistics, but it draws most heavily on new developments in cognitive linguistics, the most rapidly growing branch of linguistics.

Since the death of Benjamin Whorf in 1941, linguistic anthropology has paid little attention to imagery, even while interpretive and symbolic anthropologists have accorded it, or "experience," an important place in their theories (Turner 1967; Fernandez 1986; Bruner 1986b). Though "impoverishment" is certainly too strong a word to characterize the result, linguistic anthropology has nevertheless suffered a needless cognitive deprivation. Since good ethnography often requires close linguistic analysis, the effects of this neglect on anthropology are far reaching. In order to reawaken the interest of linguistic anthropologists in cultural imagery, I will show that cognitive linguistics, especially as defined by Langacker (1987, 1990a, 1991) and Lakoff (1987), can be applied directly to language and culture. Cognitive linguistics can be tied in to three traditional approaches that are central to anthropological linguistics: Boasian linguistics, ethnosemantics (ethnoscience), and the ethnography of speaking. To the synthesis that results I have given the name *cultural linguistics*.

Let us now consider an actual instance of how imagery governs a grammatical construction. The example is taken from my studies of Coeur d'Alene, an Amerindian language of northern Idaho and eastern Washington state.[2]

"The palm of the hand is 'the surface in the back of the hand'? What do you mean by that?" I prompted my distinguished elderly consultant as we sat in his living room in the old two-story frame house on the Coeur d'Alene Indian reservation in northern Idaho. He raised his right hand, cupped it slightly, and traced along the inside of the palm with his left index finger, saying, "It is the surface in the back of the hand," revealing clearly how the concave surface nestled within the convexity of the back of his hand. Having grasped the model, I had started to discover a conceptual world of space and form in which I could properly interpret the complex descriptive noun that had prompted my question: *snch'mích'ncht* 'surface in the back of the hand,' a word analyzable into no less than five morphemes: /s-n-č̕əm-íč̕ən̓-ɪčt/ NOM-IN-SURFACE-BACK-HAND.[3] I would later learn that the spatial models that demarcate the entire surface of the body (but not the organs inside the body) and define terms for hands, fingers, toes, and many other body-parts also apply to Coeur d'Alene place-names and even, metaphorically, to expressions for emotions and social relationships (Palmer 1990; Occhi, Palmer, and Ogawa 1992; Ogawa and Palmer 1994). But it was this expression for the palm that triggered my interest and impressed me with the importance of studying linguistic imagery.

The Coeur d'Alene example illustrates the role of imagery at just one level of language, that of the word or lexeme, albeit in this case quite a complex word, comparable in its parts to a typical spoken sentence of English. There are many other levels and dimensions to consider as well, ranging from the auditory imagery of phonemes to meaningful patterns of pragmatic effect and speaker participation in culturally defined genres of discourse; and there are the tropes of metaphor and metonymy, which themselves operate on multiple levels and dimensions.

As Charles Fillmore (1975: 114) wrote, evoking yet another image, "when you pick up a word, you drag along with it a whole scene," but what kind of scene? Words evoke mental images that range from sensory experiences as simple and concrete as a mouthful of hot buttered popcorn to conceptual structures as abstract and complex as the cultural postulates of true love. Some of the images called forth by words closely reflect the orientations, forces, and stuff of immediate experience. The Coeur d'Alene word for the palm of the hand is one of those that elaborate basic spatial schemas. Other images and imagistic cognitive models, still structured, but even more schematic or metaphorical, as of love, friendship, and marriage, make up the social contents of our world views (Quinn 1985; Kövecses 1988; Kövecses 1991b; Quinn 1991; Kövecses 1993). In some cases, the abstraction from imagery proceeds so far that it is more practical to speak of features, cultural axioms, or propositions, but these are best understood as deriving from prior experience and more concrete imagery. They are not alternatives to an imagistic theory of language, but part of it.

The Coeur d'Alene example of the palm of the hand may give the mistaken impression that languages merely express imagery given by experience and world view the way a Spandex body-suit reveals underlying muscles, bones, and sinews. It is better to say that discourse invokes conventional imagery and provokes the construction of new imagery. At the same time, imagery structures discourse; they are mutually constitutive. Through time and incessant patter, speakers in language communities collaborate and negotiate over the imagery of evolving world views. Old or new, unwanted ideas are filtered out. New imagery and language emerge together. This is what Edward Sapir called the "mountainous and anonymous work of unconscious generations." [4]

To study language is to hear the clamor of culture grappling with raw experience; it is the sound of tradition adjusting itself to absorb the inchoate (Fernandez 1986), the (sizzling) fusion of text and context (Werth n.d.). In the flux of context, it is the culturally constructed, conventional, and mutually presupposed imagery of world view that provides the stable points of reference for the interpretation of discourse. The tabloids and the cinema, for example, provide conventionalized images of space aliens as smooth, pale humanoids with immense, curious eyes, like the one who visited President George Bush in the *Weekly World News*, or as rapacious, carnivorous reptilians, maws dripping with green slime, that deposit their voracious larvae in human bodies, as in the popular film *Alien*. These images from pop culture provide us with a set of mutual presuppositions for conversations about space aliens. They belong to what T. Givon (1992: 12) called "the generically shared context, or cultural knowledge," to what Deborah Schiffrin (1987: 28) called the "information state," which concerns "what a speaker knows and what a hearer knows," and to what Deborah Tannen and Cynthia Wallat (1993: 60) called "knowledge schemas," which are "expectations about people, objects, events, and settings in the world." Together with the situation and history of a particular discourse, cultural knowledge provides the shared contexts that confer "referential accessibility" on discourse topics.[5]

Cultural knowledge is particularly important to the interpretation of conventional tropes (especially metaphors and metonyms), which are increasingly found to be situated in complex structures of "polytropes" (Friedrich 1991; Ohnuki-Tierney 1991). In a restudy of Fray Bernardo Sahagún's data on figures of speech in the Nahuatl language, I show how the historic Aztecs of Central Mexico constructed intricate couplets alluding to scenes of theocracy and human sacrifice. A single couplet, such as ALREADY AT THE EDGE OF THE FIRE, ALREADY AT THE STAIRWAY, may combine metaphor and metonymy in complex and provocative structures of allusion.

Cultural knowledge often takes the form of cognitive models or schemas that organize highly schematic knowledge of recurrent topical domains, such as the human body or the emotions of love and anger. Looking at Japanese metaphors of anger, we will examine the model that underlies the notion that heat rises to the head with a click. But, unlike Americans, the Japanese do not blow their figurative tops (Matsuki 1989). As in English, many Japanese metaphors of anger express the idea that anger is a hot substance confined in a container. Knowledge of the model is necessary for the interpretation of everyday expressions.

Similarly, the English words *love* and *lying* must be defined in terms of cognitive models. An emotion term, such as *love*, predicates not only feeling states, but also scenarios of discourse and social action. Lying may be a pragmatic speech act, but it is also defined relative to a folk model of communication in which people try to help, knowledge is beneficial, people do not purposefully misinform, and beliefs have adequate justification (Sweetser 1987). Since, in this model, adequately justified beliefs are true, then beliefs are true. Since, in this model, you do not say what you do not believe, a lie can simply be defined as a false statement. This may seem a long way around to get to a seemingly obvious statement, but without the folk model the definition of *lie* must be more elaborate, less coherent, and less clear in its implications.

Shared understandings embedded in conventional scenarios also govern the structure of traditional narratives. Examining myths of the Kuna Indians of Panama, we find that they are recited in a non-narrative fashion, that is, violating the natural order of events (Sherzer 1987). A boy who has died and become a spirit in a pepper plant seems to appear before his death to direct his sister to the pepper plant in which he already resides. An unnatural sequence may affect us with a sense of temporal disorientation, but it is no doubt quite transparent to the Kuna themselves, who know the underlying plot in advance and perhaps prefer to dramatize the spiritual significance of the vegetative growth of pepper, which is one of their important medicines. Our sense of narrative sequence is culture-bound.

Cultural linguistics is also concerned with folk ontologies that define the essential nature of things for each culture. Bantu languages, such as Kiswahili and Shona, reveal abstract worlds of shape and substance in their grammatical classifications of nouns (Creider 1975; Denny and Creider 1986); speakers of Western Apache in the American Southwest embed similar imagery not in nouns, but in verbs (Basso 1990b); while in the Dyirbal language of northeastern Australia noun classes appear to predicate mythical domains rather than schemas of shape and substance (Lakoff 1987). The Dyirbal case prompts a reexamination of Proto-Bantu noun classes, where there is some intriguing evidence for a governing domain of ancestral spirits. Our approach enables us to see how speakers may use classifiers strategically to highlight some aspect of shape, quality, or ritual significance (at the same time helping listeners to form expectations concerning the verbs to follow).

Meaning doesn't exist in a vacuum. In discourse, utterances acquire additional, situated meanings beyond their conventional imagery. We understand the expression *big dog* to mean something different when coming from breeders of Chihuahuas and mastiffs. The expression *power tie* makes sense only in the context of corporate competition. Every discourse event demands a situated reinterpretation of conventional forms. But even situated discourse requires framing with conventional linguistic symbols. Chapter 4, dealing with Apache stories, Bedouin songs, and Kuna snake-handling rituals, examines how meaning emerges from the confluence of conventional symbols, situated usages, and novel experiences.

Discourse itself is structured and governed by schematic imagery of sociolinguistic events, by its own metalinguistic or metadiscursive imagery. This reflexive imagery of discourse is as culturally defined as that of figurative language. Indeed, folk metalanguage may be metaphorical, as when we speak of "carrying on a conversation" or we say that words "contain" information, as though they were physical containers and information consisted of material objects (Reddy 1979). The Kaluli pattern their songs after birdcalls, describe their stories as hardening into clear images, and compare narratives to the murmur and splash of flowing and falling water (Feld 1990). The Apache use a hunting metaphor in which stories are arrows (Basso 1984, 1990b). What is less well understood is that metadiscursive imagery also governs the usage of polite forms, pronouns, indexicals, and linguistic "shifters" in general (Silverstein 1976). For example, the Japanese particle *yo*, meaning, roughly, 'I'm telling you,' is an indexical form that directs the listener to attend to portions of the speaker's previous utterances—to recall an image of the discourse itself (Cook 1991). Within cultural linguistics, discourse indexicals such as *yo* are simply a special case and require no separate theory of their own. For reasons that I will explain in Chapter 7, I refer to them as *pragmatic discursives* in preference to the terms *discourse marker* (Schiffrin 1987: 31) or *non-referential indexical* (Silverstein 1976).

This book builds on previous theories in linguistic anthropology and borrows heavily from the field of cognitive linguistics to construct a theory of cultural linguistics that can encompass the great range of linguistic phenomena that anthropologists commonly encounter in field-work. In it I discuss many specific cases that illustrate the cognitive designs of languages. These cases show that world views provide some of the basic models on which languages of the world are patterned.

You will find more research problems than answers in this book. There are two reasons for this. First, the approach is new; second, there are more interesting linguistic phenomena in the world than the available linguists and anthropologists can ever study with scientific rigor. The variety of cases considered in this book is sufficient to reveal a wide range of linguistic possibilities. They come from Europe, Asia, North America, Central America, Japan, the Middle East, Africa, and Australia. From this broad territory, I have elected to cast my conceptual net over a small sample of languages and linguistic forms, hoping to capture something of interest. The design of cultural linguistics will be the subject of several chapters, but first we should inspect some of the old nets to see where they are sound and where they may need mending.

CHAPTER 2

THREE TRADITIONS IN LINGUISTIC ANTHROPOLOGY

Contemporary linguistic anthropology has grown from at least three traditions that are somewhat intermingled, but sufficiently distinct to have developed their own followings: Boasian linguistics, ethnosemantics, and the ethnography of speaking (hereafter, ES). They are not the only traditions drawn upon by linguistic anthropologists, but they have in common a stance of linguistic relativity together with either a focal interest in meaning (Boasian linguistics and ethnosemantics) or an interest in discourse (ES). Boasian linguistics and ethnosemantics are regarded by many as obsolete, a view with which I disagree for reasons to be discussed. ES today casts the widest net for linguistic anthropology, but it is a net in need of some patching, for there is much of linguistic and anthropological interest that passes through its conceptual holes. Without in any way demeaning or discrediting the many important findings already accumulated in any of these subfields, I am advocating that linguistic anthropology explicitly incorporate the principles of cognitive linguistics, a new subfield that appears to offer a modern approach to Boasian linguistics (Lee 1993) and a framework that will subsume the findings of ethnosemantics and contribute an essential perspective to ES. If the theory of cognitive linguistics can be combined with that of ES, the result should be a useful new synthesis that merges linguistic theory, cultural theory, and sociolinguistic theory. The purpose of this chapter is to review the previous approaches to linguistic anthropology in order to determine how cognitive linguistics might best fit into the synthesis that I call cultural linguistics. This review will pay special attention to the role of imagery in the three traditions. We will see that imagery played the most important role in Boasian linguistics and plays almost no role at all in ethnosemantics and ES, though in the latter case it may play a greater role in practice than in theory.

BOASIAN LINGUISTICS

The Boasian approach, which flourished from the first decade of the 1900s through the 1940s, was primarily concerned with describing the grammars of languages in their own terms rather than framing them in terms of categories previously developed for the study of Indo-European languages. Franz Boas (1966: 32) observed, for example, that classification of nouns by sex, such as occurs in Spanish and in English pronouns, is only one of "a great many possible classifications of this kind" and that other languages may classify by such principles as animate/inanimate, human/non-human, tribal member/non-member, and a variety of other principles that were not then, and are still not, well understood. Boas was also concerned with discovering the psychological bases of languages and cultures (Boas 1966; Stocking 1974: 476–478). It is therefore not surprising that he also saw that language is relative to mental imagery: ". . . it will be recognized that in each language only a part of the complete concept that we have in mind is expressed, and that each language has a peculiar tendency to select this or that aspect of the mental image which is conveyed by the expression of the thought" (1966: 39).

Boas (1966: 59) wrote in 1911 that language was one of the most important manifestations of mental life, so that "the purely linguistic inquiry is part and parcel of a thorough investigation of the psychology of the peoples of the world." In his view, language studies belonged to ethnology because it was "the science dealing with the mental phenomena of the life of the peoples of the world." In sum, Boas observed that languages delineate underlying classifications of experience, that various languages classify experience differently, and that such classifications need not rise to conscious awareness (Lucy 1992a: 12–13).[1] Nevertheless, classifications that surface in grammar do reflect a selective expression of mental imagery. While Boas in 1911 emphasized the way in which languages reflect the thought or psychology of their speakers, in later years he also considered the possibility that linguistic categories might impose themselves on the thoughts of their speakers (Lucy 1992a: 15).

Boasian linguistic relativity was taken further by Boas's own student Edward Sapir and his contemporary, the exceptional self-taught linguist Benjamin Whorf. One of Sapir's main contributions to Boasian linguistic relativity was the notion that linguistic classifications of experience are "arranged into formally complete yet incommensurate systems" (Sapir 1964; Lucy 1992a: 18). Sapir (1949 [1921]: 12–13) also noted that any linguistic classification of experience had to be "tacitly accepted by the community as an identity." Were he writing today, he might have described linguistic classifications as "socially constructed." But Sapir is perhaps best known for his advancement of the strong form of the linguistic relativity hypothesis: that linguistic classifications fix the boundaries of thoughts or "channel" thoughts, as illustrated with a famous and dramatic quote from a 1931 issue of *Science*:

> Such categories as number, gender, case, tense, mode, voice, "aspect" and a host of others, many of which are not recognized systematically in our Indo-European languages, are, of course, derivative of experience at last analysis, but, once abstracted from experience, they are systematically elaborated in language and are not so much discovered in experience as imposed upon it because of the tyrannical hold that linguistic form has upon our orientation in the world. (1964)

While Sapir and Boas defined the problem of language and culture for American linguistics, it was Whorf who made it the focus of his investigations. Like Sapir, Whorf seemed to assign to grammar an important role in constraining our perceptions of the world. He argued that the "automatic, involuntary patterns of language are not the same for all men but are specific for each language and constitute the formalized side of language, or its 'grammar' " (1956b: 221). He continued:

> From this fact proceeds what I have called the "linguistic relativity principle," which means, in informal terms, that users of markedly different grammars are pointed by their grammars toward different types of observations and different evaluations of externally similar acts of observation, and hence are not equivalent as observers but must arrive at somewhat different views of the world.

Determining exactly what Whorf believed concerning the channeling influence of grammatical categories on culture and world view has become a small industry within anthropology and linguistics, as has criticism of his specific characterizations of the Hopi language and world view, so I refer the reader to other sources (Hoijer 1954a; Whorf 1956b; Malotki 1983; Lakoff 1987; Schultz 1990; Ridington 1991; Hill and Mannheim 1992; Lucy 1992a; Lee 1993). For our purposes, it is important to note that Whorf pursued interests in gestalt psychology that led him to study such topics as alternative construals of visual scenes, configurations of grammar and meaning, figure and ground relations in complex Amerindian words, and covert categories, thereby anticipating much of the modern theory of cognitive linguistics (Lee 1993).

To give just one example, Whorf explicitly applied principles of gestalt psychology to grammar in his 1940 analysis of figure and ground
relationships in complex Shawnee words. He proposed for Shawnee
grammar that "figure precedes external field, the more figural precedes
the less figural," listing as prototypical figures such linguistic stems as
pap- 'roomy configuration,' *teepwe-* 'truth,' and *kiš-* 'warm, hot' and as
prototypical grounds *-peewe* 'hair, feathers,' *-aapo* 'liquid,' and *tepki*
'swampy, marshy terrain' (1956a: 167–168). From this perspective, he
analyzed the term *ni-peekw-aalak-h-a*, meaning 'I clean or dry gun by
running ramrod in it,' that has as its figure *peekw* 'dry or clean spot' and
its ground *aalak* 'hole' (1956a: 168–169). This interpretation clearly anticipated recent work on grammatical figures and grounds in English and
American Indian languages (Talmy 1983; Casad and Langacker 1985;
Lakoff 1987; Brugman 1988; Palmer 1990; Langacker 1990a; Occhi,
Palmer, and Ogawa 1992). Whorf also proposed that words fit together in
(semantic) relational networks, which he called *rapport*: "It is not words
mumbled, but RAPPORT between words that enables them to work together
at all to any semantic result" (1956b: 67); and he postulated the existence
of abstract concepts—*cryptotypes*—that influence the morphology of
words, but are not realized overtly as words or morphemes (Whorf 1956b:
70). Example cryptotypes include "dispersion without a boundary," "os-
cillation without agitation of parts," "nondurative impact," and "directed
motion." Today cognitive linguists and anthropologists might call such
cryptotypes by the term *schema* or *image-schema* and realize that, once
again, Whorf got there first. J. R. Martin (1988) recently applied Whorf's
concept of cryptotypes to an analysis of Tagalog.

The Boasian program of seeking cultural and psychological configurations of meaning in language had few active followers during the thirty-
year period from 1950 to 1980, a time when formal and mathematical
approaches grabbed everyone's attention. Some Americanist linguists and
anthropologists did continue to work in the relativistic framework and
scholars in other fields maintained an interest in what came to be known
as "the Sapir-Whorf hypothesis." From the late 1930s through the 1940s,
Dorothy Lee attempted to discover the world view of the Wintun of northern California through the close study of their grammar and mythology.
She wrote that "grammar contains in crystallized form the accumulated
and accumulating experience, the Weltanschauung of a people" (Lee
1938: 89, cited in Lucy 1992a: 71). Perhaps her most interesting observation was that, in their unmarked state, Wintun nouns refer to generic
substances and require modification with a derivational suffix to give

them particularity and specific reference. By comparison, English nouns are ordinarily specific, as evidenced by the fact that they are either singular or plural and definite or indefinite (Lee 1940, 1944, 1959). The following passage illustrates the usage:

> We take the word for *deer* for example. In the instances I give, I shall use only the objective case, nop for the generic, and nopum for the particular. A hunter went out but saw no *deer*, nop; another killed a *deer*, nopum. A woman carried *deer*, nop, to her mother; a hunter brought home *deer*, nopum. Now the woman's deer was cut in pieces and carried, a formless mass, in her back-basket; but the man carried his two deer slung whole from his shoulder. Some brothers were about to eat venison; they called, "Old man, come and eat *venison*, (nop)." The old man replied, "You can eat that stinking *venison*, (nopum) yourselves." The brothers saw it just as deer meat; to the old man it was the flesh of a particular deer, one which had been killed near human habitation, fed on human offal. (1959: 123)

Lee's studies led her to characterize the Wintun world view as one in which a reality or ultimate truth "exists irrespective of man," but "outside man's experience, this reality is unbounded, undifferentiated, timeless." In this apparent generic sea, somehow "matter and relationships, essence, quality are all given." The speaker of Wintu may impose shape on this generic reality or "actualize" a design, giving it temporality or form, but "he neither creates nor changes" it (Lee 1959: 121). Thus, Wintu lexemes may refer generically to "unpartitioned masses" (matter), relationships, or qualities of things, but they must be modified to express particularities of time and shape. John A. Lucy (1992a: 72) pointed out that Lee's work is all internal to language and rests on "strong, untested assumptions about the relation of language to thought," but does not itself test or establish the validity of those relations.

In 1953, Harry Hoijer and Robert Redfield convened a conference at the University of Chicago to consider the interrelations of language and culture. Hoijer (1954a: ix) reported "little agreement among the members of the Conference on what Whorf actually said," but indicated that some progress was made in defining problems. Hoijer, who studied linguistics under Sapir, made explicit use of Whorfian concepts in his studies of Navajo (1953, 1954b, 1964a, 1964b). He argued that, if language rigidly channels thought, the reason might be found in the fact that language "interpenetrates all other systems within the culture." While Hoijer, unlike Lee, attempted to establish connections between language and culture, he was criticized by Lucy for the weakness of the proposed linkages. For example, Hoijer argued that an emphasis on reporting motion in Navajo verbs could be explained by parallels in Navajo culture, specifically in the nomadic lifestyle and the journeys of culture heroes in mythology. We see this emphasis on reporting motion in, for example, the variety of active verb bases (a "base" in this context is "any verb segment to which paradigmatic prefixes may be added to form a free verb construction"). He noted that "the numerous verb bases employing the theme 'a round object moves' are divided into no less than seven aspectival categories, each with a distinctive set of stems" (1964a: 144). The aspectival categories, each with its own paradigm, are imperfective, perfective, progressive, future, iterative, customary, and optative.

Lucy criticized Hoijer's conclusions on several grounds. He questioned his characterization of Navajo verbs as showing exceptional concern with motion, noting that other verbs also classify their nominal arguments; he regarded the evidence of mythology as just another kind of linguistic evidence; and he considered the link between verbs of motion and nomadic lifestyle a weak one that fails to establish that motion is "a common or habitual focus of individual Navajo thought patterns in daily life or that it underlies a wide variety of specific Navajo cultural institutions" (1992a: 79).

In 1979, Madeleine Mathiot edited a collection of then recent findings in "empirical semantics" titled *Ethnolinguistics: Boas, Sapir, and Whorf Revisited*. In the overview, she praised ethnosemanticists for adding "the systematic investigation of lexical meaning to empirical semantics" (1979: 316). Distinguishing between lexical and grammatical meaning, she concluded that the two types "lend themselves equally well to an investigation of the relation of language both to world view and to the rest of the culture" (1979: 317), but she did not commit herself to the strong relativist position. She did distinguish between "referential meaning" (by which I take it that she meant lexical and grammatical meaning) and world view, theorizing that world view is more inclusive than referential meaning, because "referential meaning is 'the *specific* information about the world that is *directly* communicated through linguistic behavior.' World view is 'the general way of thinking about the world that *underlies* all of cultural behavior, including linguistic behavior' " (1979: 318). She saw a mutual influence of the medium (language) and world view in which language would exert some specific, but unspecified influences on world view.

Mathiot proposed that the semantic domain of language is that aspect of world view that is bound to and discernible only through linguistic behavior, while the cognitive domain of language is that aspect of world view that may also be expressed in other media. This view of semantics seems to cut it off from cognition and much of world view and turn it into an autonomous domain; it would omit from semantics those elements of linguistic meaning that govern linguistic forms *if and only if* they also govern other forms. Conversely, the fact that semantic structures govern language is insufficient reason to exclude them from the domain of cognition. This book provides ample evidence that elements of meaning that we regard as semantic are themselves elements of world view, or have parallel conceptual structures to those of world view, or are closely linked to elements of world view that govern non-linguistic behaviors. While language may display some special features, language and world view are part of the same cognitive network. The discussion in a later chapter of Dyirbal, Bantu, and Apache noun classifiers that are organized along culturally significant dimensions provides an illustration of this point, as does the discussion of Navajo object prefixes, which are governed by a culturally defined hierarchy of control. A paper in Mathiot's own edited volume argued that hunter-gatherer societies that live in open treeless environments express the distinction "in view/not in view" and the "distal" notion of verticality in their noun-classes, while those that live in closed forest environments express notions of hardness and flexibility, presumably because these distinctions are both cultural and semantic (Denny 1979). Lucy (1992a: 73) criticized Mathiot for "lingua-centrism" and for treating grammatical structure as "linguistic" and lexical content as "essentially nonlinguistic."

Lucy has written two books that explore the linguistic relativity hypothesis anew. One is an intellectual history that concludes by advocating more experimental rigor (1992a). The other applies the experimental approach to grammatical number in English and Yucatec Maya (1992b). Since experimental tests of the Sapir-Whorf hypothesis are fraught with difficulties, it will be interesting to examine Lucy's approach closely.

Lucy attempted a reformulation of the Whorfian hypothesis by narrowing the problem to the influence of language on thought, especially the influence of formally structured linguistic meanings of "morphosyntactic categories" on the habitual thought of non-specialists. The critical question for Lucy is "whether or not there is or can be solid empirical evidence linking distinctive language patterns to distinctive habitual behavior or belief at the level of the aggregable individual social actors" (1992a: 7). Whether or not the habitual thoughts of the aggregate add up to world view is a problem that he explicitly chose to leave aside. In Lucy's view, research on linguistic relativity must follow four methodological principles: (1) it must compare two or more languages (e.g., English and Yucatec Maya), (2) it should provide some common stimulus condition ("external non-linguistic reality"; e.g., drawings, triad sorts), (3) it must include formal analysis (i.e., morphosyntactic analysis) pertaining to some semantic domain ("configuration of meaning," such as grammatical number), and (4) different habitual patterns of language usage should entail differences in thought.

The "external non-linguistic *reality*" in one set of his experiments is a series of test drawings depicting persons, animals, containers, tools, and substances (see Chapter 6). These were shown to a group of Mayan men aged eighteen to forty-five plus and a group of U.S. male college students aged nineteen to twenty-seven years. There was apparently a large disparity in education between the two groups; Lucy (1992b: 99) reported that ten of the Mayan men had "at least one year of formal education and some ability to read." To minimize the importance of educational disparities (which might militate against his desire to compare non-specialists), Lucy designed the cognitive tasks to be "relatively simple." In one test, he showed the subjects a set of line drawings and asked them to "describe what they see in each picture" (1992b: 100). He then scored responses according to whether they mentioned certain objects and whether they indicated the number of objects. In other tasks, the subjects were shown line drawings and after varying lengths of time were asked to pick the originals from arrays containing the original and similar alternate drawings. This was to assess non-verbally the salience of number in short- and longer-term recognition memory (1992b: 122, 130). Subjects were also asked to make similarity judgments among triads of objects with the goal of assessing "the relative cognitive salience of shape versus material" (1992b: 136).

In interpreting his results, Lucy postulated no specific intervening imagery, schemas, or cognitive models, but he did speak of "cognitive dispositions," "cognitive performance," "cognitive entailments," differential construals of "a common reality," and a rather broad notion of attention to number (1992b: 156). Perhaps he came closest to considering imagery when he proposed the investigation of "a whole configuration of meaning" (1992b: 2). Still, the primary problem as he defined it is to relate linguistic behavior to non-linguistic behavior and "the contextual surround" under controlled circumstances.

So what are the cognitive dispositions by means of which language might be found to exert its influence on thought? These are to be found in Lucy's hypotheses, where they are phrased as the tendency of speakers habitually to attend to number:

> First, English speakers should habitually attend to the number of various objects of reference more than should Yucatec speakers. In particular, they should habitually attend to number for a wider array of referent types for which they obligatorily mark number. Second, English speakers should attend relatively more to the shape of objects and Yucatec speakers should attend relatively more to the material composition of objects. (1992b: 156)

Lucy concluded that "the results of the cognitive assessment were consistently in line with these expectations." Finally, he answered the general question that he had posed concerning the influence of language on thought by concluding that "the frequency of pluralization in each language influences both the verbal and nonverbal interpretation of pictures" and that "the underlying lexical structures associated with the number marking in the two languages have an influence on the nonverbal interpretation of objects" (1992b: 157).

While there are problems in proceeding from the stimulus testing methods to these conclusions, the purpose of this section is not to provide a full critique of Boasian theories, but rather to characterize the conceptual background of linguistic anthropology. I will therefore leave that critique and a detailed summary of his specific comparisons and findings concerning the expression of number in Yucatec Maya and English for Chapter 6, on connecting languages to world view.

During the three decades from the 1950s through the 1970s, American structural linguists all but defined meaning out of their field of view, while many linguistic anthropologists writing under the rubric of *ethnosemantics* or *ethnoscience* pursued the study of culturally organized domains of meaning with the feature-based methods of componential analysis and taxonomic classification. The Boasian approach as pursued by Lee, Hoijer, Mathiot, Lucy, and a few others became only a minority and non-representative part of that enterprise. Perhaps the publication of Lucy's two volumes heralds a revival of interest in the Boasian perspective.

ETHNOSEMANTICS

Ethnosemantics emerged as the favored mode of linguistic analysis in anthropology during the 1960s and remained a popular mode of interpretation in the 1970s. Many of its most seminal, representative, and note-worthy articles are collected in Stephen A. Tyler (1969a) and Ronald W. Casson (1981). In 1969, Tyler wrote of the ferment in anthropology that gave rise to ethnosemantics: "The journals are full of articles on *formal analysis, componential analysis, folk taxonomy, ethnoscience, ethnosemantics,* and *sociolinguistics,* to list but a few. Nearly all of these topics have appeared in the brief span of approximately ten years, with increasing frequency in the last three or four years" (1969b: 1).

Ethnosemantics, or ethnoscience, is the study of the ways in which different cultures organize and categorize domains of knowledge, such as those of plants, animals, and kin. Tyler (1969b: 3) viewed ethnosemantics as a part of cognitive anthropology, which was concerned with "discovering how different peoples organize and use their cultures" and with the search for "the organizing principles underlying behavior." He regarded cognitive anthropology as a reaction against theories that sought categories of description in the native language of the anthropological researchers rather than in the languages of the natives. In its fascination with native categories of thought, ethnosemantics had a Boasian flavor, but its methods of investigation and analysis were quite different, at least from those of the early Boasians.

Though ethnosemantics was driven by a strong interest in cognition, its practitioners have not, for the most part, developed, or even utilized, a theory of imagery. Rather, they have focused primarily on describing systems of folk taxonomic classification and analyzing atomistic features of meaning, often producing componential analyses of lexicons or folk taxonomies projecting over significant semantic domains.

A componential analysis is a collation of terms in a semantic feature matrix. All terms that share the same feature or combination of features are assigned the same position in the matrix. The result is a paradigm (Tyler 1969b). In one approach, the investigator assumes that cultures differently classify entities with similar objective characteristics (such as similar biological kinship status) by assigning them to different positions in a universal feature matrix (such as one based on dimensions of sex, generation, lineality, collaterality, and relative age). Alternatively, the investigator assumes that various cultures classify entities (such as kin) differently by assigning terms to positions on matrices composed of culturally distinctive sets of features that constitute their denotative meanings. Anthony F. C. Wallace (1969 [1965]), for example, showed that a psychologically valid analysis of a set of Japanese kinship terms required a distinction between *nikushin* 'flesh relatives' and *kinshin* 'non-flesh relatives,' a distinction that is, in its particular Japanese definition, absent from English and probably from most other languages.

A taxonomy is an arrangement of terms in a hierarchy from most inclusive to least inclusive, as when we classify dogs, wolves, and foxes as types, or kinds, of canines, and cocker spaniels and collies as types of dogs. Ideally, each class possesses all the features of its superordinate class and contrasts in one or more features with other classes at the same level. Anthropologists frequently returned from the field with folk taxonomies of plants and animals, but they also looked at illnesses, kinds of spirits, anatomical nomenclature, and even kinds of tramps (Frake 1961; Berlin, Breedlove, and Raven 1966; Frake 1969; Spradley 1970; Berlin, Breedlove, and Raven 1973; Berlin, Breedlove, and Raven 1974; Saunders and Davis 1974; Turner 1974; Brown 1984; Berlin 1992).

Some ethnosemanticists devoted a great deal of effort to determining the distribution across languages of terms for basic colors (white, yellow, red, green, blue, black, and a few others) (Conklin 1964; Berlin and Kay 1969; Berlin 1970; Kay and McDaniel 1978; Kay, Berlin, and Merrifield 1991; MacLaury 1991; Lucy 1992a). Some of them attempted to establish evolutionary sequences by which new basic color terms or terms for plants and animals enter languages (Berlin and Kay 1969; Berlin 1970; Brown 1977; Brown 1979; Brown and Witkowski 1981; Brown and Witkowski 1983; Brown 1984a, 1984b; Kay, Berlin, and Merrifield 1991). Basic color terms are discussed in more detail in Chapter 5, on concepts of cognitive linguistics.

Ethnosemantics has typically focused almost exclusively on lexical semantics. To gather data on lexical domains ethnosemanticists typically use a question-frame method of elicitation that Tyler (1969b) termed "controlled elicitation." This involves learning to ask appropriate questions in the native language. A typical question frame is "What is this?" If the answer happened to be "A broccoli dicer," we might then ask of another item "Is that a broccoli dicer, too?" and "Is a broccoli dicer a kind of widget?" The question "What other kinds of X are there?" could be asked recursively on its own answers to elicit a taxonomy. Carefully constructed questions developed in consultation with native consultants can remain almost entirely within native frames of reference. The ethnographer thereby avoids biasing the results with questions and categories from her own frame of reference.

While feature-based analysis imposes a major limitation on ethnosemantics by abstracting too severely from the rich imagery of human categorization, the method of controlled elicitation may be its greatest strength. However, controlled elicitation carries its own risks. Applied too narrowly, it may exclude important dimensions of native thought from elicitation, if, for example, the researcher were single-mindedly to pursue the semantic relation of inclusion without regard for similarity, contiguity, partibility (part/whole), functionality, or other considerations suggested by native speakers themselves, such as the kinship of one kind of plant to another. For example, in the Thompson and Lillooet languages of British Columbia, all berries have kin relations (Turner 1989).

In spite of the predominant interest in feature-based paradigms and taxonomies, there were developments within ethnosemantics that foreshadowed or paralleled the emergence of cognitive linguistics. Mathiot studied cognition and world view, but she utilized a methodology that proceeded from the discovery of semantic oppositions to postulation of distinctive features (1985: 136). Robert A. Randall (1976) introduced the notions of "memory association model" and "vegetative image" to explain why the Samal of the Philippines did not store information about plants in taxonomies. A few researchers utilized prototype theory (Bright and Bright 1969; Berlin 1992) or defined native categories in terms of the perceived utility of their referents as opposed to relying solely upon attributes of physical form (Hunn 1985; Turner 1989; Turner 1992). Prior to these, Floyd G. Lounsbury (1964) had argued that kinship terms for distant relatives in Crow-Omaha type systems could be viewed as systematic semantic extensions of the terms for focal or prototypical near relatives. This approach to kinship terminology, termed the "extensionist hypothesis," is discussed in more detail in a section on "generative categories" in Chapter 5. John A. Lucy and Richard A. Shweder (1981 [1979]) defended Whorf's linguistic relativity as it pertains to color terminology, arguing that color memory is determined more by culturally defined terms and meanings than by innately given focal color perceptions. In the chapter on concepts I will describe a very similar recent cognitive linguistic argument advanced by Anna Wierzbicka (1990).

Michael Agar (1973) theorized that words from the drug culture, such as *hustle* 'obtain money illegally,' *cop* 'buy heroin,' and *get-off* 'inject heroin,' were defined in terms of events. Each event was prerequisite to the succeeding one, and each had other prerequisites as well. A careful reading of his work suggests that he intended that the linked events in his theory were cognized or imagined by speakers; they were not events recorded by independent observers. Unfortunately, from our perspective, rather than asking how the cognition of events relates to word meanings, he asked two questions that drew him away from language *per se* and toward culture and performance: "how is this cognitive structure related to actual performances?" and "how does a *junkie* select among possible prerequisites?" (1973: 24). In a recent popular work, Agar (1994) again took up these same data on the drug culture and worked the other way, toward language.

Charles O. Frake, whose work on the ethnosemantics of disease terminology of the Subanun was particularly influential, advocated in 1977 that we regard culture as "a set of principles for creating dramas, for writing *scripts*, and, of course, for recruiting players and audiences [emphasis added]" (1981: 375–376). He regarded this new direction not as a surrender to symbolic and interpretive approaches, but as an expansion of the cognitive perspective of ethnoscience. Keith Basso (1976) found that Apache metaphors can only be understood if we understand the Apache classification of animate beings; and Gary Witherspoon (1980) outlined the hierarchy of control in the Navajo world view in order to explain the use of passive and active constructions.

But in spite of these parallel experiments with prototype and perceptual analysis, rear-guard defenses of Whorf, and the discovery of cultural scripts, ethnosemantics never turned to imagery or image-schemas. In fact, the methods of analysis often obscured the imagistic bases of semantic domains. Ethnosemantics and cognitive anthropology failed, until quite recently, to follow up on the implications of cultural scripts for interpreting language and for unifying the study of language and culture.

Not all linguistic anthropologists were happy with the state of theory during this period. Paul Friedrich (1975: 235), for example, bemoaned the inadequacy of "the current choice between logico-transformational syntax, statistically oriented sociolinguistics, and the taxonomies of the anthropologist." He called for acknowledgment of the non-arbitrariness of lexical symbols so that linguistics could be applied to the creative use of language, especially to poetic creativity, and to the "relations of phonetic and lexical structure with the real world and with the deeper systems of meaning in the semantic and cultural codes" (1975: 235–236). The influence of ethnosemantics on anthropology waned in the 1980s as symbolic and interpretive approaches gained in popularity. Linguistic anthropology turned away from lexical semantics to ES and to sociolinguistics with a focus on discourse.

THE ETHNOGRAPHY OF SPEAKING

Developed during the 1960s and 1970s, ES assumes that purposeful speakers apply linguistic resources toward social ends in culturally defined situations. ES provides a needed dimension of social context and a dynamic perspective that is largely missing in the relatively static studies of native vocabularies typical of ethnosemantic approaches. But ES is little better than ethnosemantics at conceptualizing the role of culturally defined imagery in language. Social ends, styles of speaking, speech acts, and situations are sometimes taken as the content of folk (emic) constructs, but seemingly more often as fundamental analytical (etic) categories of the theory. This emic/etic ambiguity surfaces in the writings of Dell Hymes and his followers.

The ES approach was first articulated by Hymes in a series of influential articles written in the 1960s and 1970s (1962, 1970, 1971, 1972, 1974a, 1974b). Here Hymes made explicit the connection between language and culture, but, unlike Boas, he seemed not to regard "mental phenomena" (i.e., cognition) as a central concern. Hymes (1971: 340) treated speech as a system of cultural behavior, but he did not himself pursue the study of language and culture as psychology or cognition. He instead emphasized the importance of studying speech acts, discourse, and performance (as the enactment of poetic forms), all situated in social contexts. It is precisely this program that has come to dominate linguistic anthropology.

Hymes argued that the linguistic competence of speakers includes not only the ability to produce appropriate syntax, as the generativist Noam Chomsky had proposed, but also the ability to use language pragmatically in specific social and cultural contexts. He stressed "the priority of the functional perspective" and the role of speech in "mediating between persons and their situations," as opposed to a view in which language would mediate only between vocal sound and meaning (1971: 65). Scholars using Hymes's approach have recorded and documented many speech phenomena that typically fall outside the purview of mainstream linguistics, such as speaking to stones in Ojibwa culture, Indian time, black street talk, ritual language, wailing, and many other genres (Hymes 1974a, 1974b; Sherzer and Urban 1986; Sherzer 1987; Abrahams 1989; Philips 1989). Hymes himself (1981) examined performance and poetic forms in Chinookan narratives.

Hymes never denied the importance of cognition, or "knowledge," in language. In fact, he included Boasian and ethnosemantic works in his widely read anthology and credited Boas himself with defining "almost the total scope of American linguistic anthropology until the present time" (1964a). He commented favorably on the structural descriptions and contrastive analyses of ethnoscientists such Harold Conklin and

Charles Frake and raised the question of "the extent to which the cognitive categories of a people find overt expression in linguistic forms" (1964b: 97; see also 1974: 11–12). But he left the cognitive study of language to the ethnoscientists,[2] who never articulated their theories to ES. For the most part, they stuck to the contrastive and componential analyses of nomenclatural systems (kinship, colors, botany, illnesses) and produced no cognitive theories of grammar, discourse, or speaking, though Frake (1969a), at least, as noted above, did speak of culture as "a set of principles for creating dramas, for writing scripts, and, of course, for recruiting players and audiences." While ethnoscientists focused heavily on componential and taxonomic analyses of nomenclatures and Hymes raised our awareness of speech as social action, the cognitive study of most aspects of language was overlooked in anthropology.

Rather than presenting an explanatory theory, Hymes advocated a "descriptive theory" aimed at producing a taxonomy of languages. The descriptive theory is essentially a linguistic checklist; the ethnographer should record *settings, participants, ends, act sequences, keys, instrumentalities, norms,* and *genres. Setting,* which refers to "time and place, or culturally defined scene," appears to be equivalent to *situation* in Hymes's framework (1971: 64). *Instrumentalities* is a complex category including channels (oral, written, etc.) and forms of speech (language, dialect, code, variety, register). *Keys* refers, a bit vaguely, to tone, manner, or spirit.

As these categories do not connote a strong interest in representations, ideas, images, schemas, frames, or gestalts, it is unclear exactly where cognitive linguistics would fit in Hymes's approach. So if we accept the validity of Boas's linkage of language and mental phenomena, then it must be admitted that ES as defined by Hymes was an incomplete approach that might benefit from cognitive theory. In Chapter 7 I will show how cognitive linguistics contributes to the study of speech acts, ends, act sequences, and genres by giving each a definition that is relative to the concept of discourse scenario.

I don't wish to imply that students of ES and the broader field of the ethnography of communication have shown no interest in cognition, because such an interest is implicit in the notion of communicative competence. Muriel Saville-Troike (1989: 21) presented a definition of communicative competence as extending to

> both knowledge and expectation of who may or may not speak in certain settings, when to speak and when to remain silent, whom one may

speak to, how one may talk to persons of different statuses and roles, what appropriate nonverbal behaviors are in various contexts, what the routines for turn-taking are in conversation, how to ask for and give information, how to request, how to offer or decline assistance or cooperation, how to give commands, how to enforce discipline, and the like—in short, everything involving the use of language and other communicative dimensions in particular social settings.

This definition suggests a strong cognitive orientation. Saville-Troike (1989: 24) also provided an outline of components of "shared knowledge that speakers must have in order to communicate appropriately." The outline is as follows:

1 Linguistic knowledge
  (a) Verbal elements
  (b) Nonverbal elements
  (c) Patterns of elements in particular speech events
  (d) Range of possible variants (in all elements and their organization)
  (e) Meaning of variants in particular situations
2 Interaction skills
  (a) Perception of salient features in communicative situations
  (b) Selection and interpretation of forms appropriate to specific situations, roles, and relationships (rules for the use of speech)
  (c) Discourse organization and processes
  (d) Norms of interaction and interpretation
  (e) Strategies for achieving goals
3 Cultural knowledge
  (a) Social structure
  (b) Values and attitudes
  (c) Cognitive maps/schemata
  (d) Enculturation processes (transmission of knowledge and skills)

In spite of Saville-Troike's explicit recognition of the need for the description of communicative competence as knowledge or expectations, she, too, defined her units of analysis not in terms of cognitive theory or even in terms of folk theory, but rather in terms of Hymes's more pragmatic and behavioral categories. In her case studies and examples, communicative competence is conflated with behavioral descriptions. However, she did discuss the problem of trying to arrive at native interpretations from ethnographic data (1989: 133).

Like cultural linguistics, ES is concerned with intentions, sociocultural context, and cultural conceptions of discourse itself. For example, Alessandro Duranti (1988: 210) said that the theoretical contributions of ES "are centered around the study of *situated discourse*, that is, linguistic performance as the locus of the relationship between language and the socio-cultural order." Charles Goodwin and Duranti (1992: 25) asserted that the ES approach to studying speech events is grounded in culturally defined categories. Like cultural linguistics, ES rejects fixed universal categories (Duranti 1988: 219).

While Duranti was correct that contemporary theory rejects fixed universal categories, he might overstate the case for Hymes, who was clearly interested in developing universal descriptive categories and generalizations based upon them. For example, Hymes (1972: 51–52) wrote of the need for "a general theory of the interaction of language and social life" and the need for "etics . . . of terms and types, as an input to description," and he asserted that "just as a theory of grammar must have its universal terms, so must a theory of language use." On the other hand, Hymes (1972: 49) also proposed that it would be "these features and dimensions, more than particular constellations of them," that would be found to be universal.

While studies conducted within Hymes's framework have undeniable value as linguistic ethnographies, ES is not yet a tightly articulated theory of language. It is better described as a comprehensive and eclectic approach, borrowing its methods from structural linguistics and ethnography and its theory somewhat diffusely from linguistics, cultural anthropology, philosophy, and sociology.[3] I believe that ES would gain in coherence by explicitly incorporating the principles of cognitive linguistics. I will therefore try to forge some conceptual links between them. Principle among these links will be the concepts of *discourse scenario* and *situation model* (defined in Chapter 7).

In summary, the traditions of Boasian linguistics, ethnosemantics, and ES share an interest in the native's point of view. The problem is to advance the program of Whorf, avoid the objectivism of ethnosemantics, and add precision to ES. A cultural linguistic synthesis is possible. It is based on integrating these three approaches with contemporary cognitive linguistics. But first let us try to gain a better understanding of what cognitive linguistics holds in store for cultural linguistics.

CHAPTER 3

THE EMERGENCE OF COGNITIVE LINGUISTICS

The premise that language analysis should begin with conventional imagery has emerged most clearly in the new field of cognitive linguistics (often termed cognitive grammar). The field shares the psychological interests of Boasian linguistics and could be regarded as a modern revival of that approach, except that it has not so far shown the same broad interest in culture that we find in Boasian linguistics or, for that matter, in the ethnography of speaking. But a more direct way to understand cognitive linguistics is to situate it within the field of cognitive science.

COGNITIVE SCIENCE

Traditionally, theories of language, reasoning, culture, imagery, and world view have been distributed among the academic disciplines, but with the advent of cognitive science the various topics have begun to merge into one. During the three decades from 1960 to 1990, scholars in several disciplines have constructed a theory of cognition that has strongly influenced the study of language. Researchers in anthropology, artificial intelligence, linguistics, neuroscience, philosophy, psychology, and rhetoric have all contributed to the emerging theory.[1] Their common enterprise is most often referred to as cognitive science, but with such broad participation from the humanities and sciences the common field of interest might better be termed cognitive studies. Nevertheless, in each of these fields, at least a few scholars are applying the new insights to language. But what do they mean by the terms *cognition* and *cognitive science*?

One branch of cognitive science emphasizes computation in its definition of the field. For example, Herbert A. Simon and Craig A. Kaplan (1989: 2) defined cognitive science as "the study of intelligence and its computational processes." This view leads researchers to search for intel-

ligent processes, a term that could describe such diverse models of thinking as the operation of sets of production rules or of neural networks.
According to Simon and Kaplan (1989: 9), the "standard model" of
cognition includes short-term memory, characterized by rapid access and
limited capacity, and long-term memory, characterized by "associative
organization and a virtually unlimited capacity." Some versions of the
standard model include in long-term memory such specialized components as declarative information, procedural information (operators), and
an "index" to the memory, sometimes referred to as a "discrimination
net." Declarative information may be organized as schemas, which may
be "propositionlike, picturelike, or both" (1989: 10). Models of symbolic associations, that is, those that "designate or 'point to' structures
outside themselves," may incorporate either serial or parallel processing
(1989: 11).

While the standard model still governs most research in cognitive science, some cognitive scientists have become dissatisfied with its limitations. For example, Raymond W. Gibbs (1994: 443) criticized cognitive
psychologists and psycholinguists for their undue emphasis on the general
architecture of the language processor as opposed to investigation of "the
contents of the mind in terms of the actual beliefs and conceptions that
people have of themselves and the world around them or how such knowledge specifically motivates linguistic behavior." Howard Gardner (1985:
6) outlined an approach to cognitive science that seems to satisfy Gibbs's
concern for content.

In *The Mind's New Science: A History of the Cognitive Revolution*,
Gardner (1985: 6) defined cognitive science as "a contemporary, empiri-
cally based effort to answer long-standing epistemological questions—
particularly those concerned with the nature of knowledge, its components, its sources, its development, and its deployment." His definition is
useful in its ability to provide an umbrella for a great variety of disciplines
and theoretical approaches. For example, it would admit studies of reasoning, imagery, perception, language, culture, and world view. Within
language itself, it would admit both syntax and semantics.

While Gardner's definition of cognitive science casts a very wide net,
it is too general to capture the sense of the term *cognition* as it is typically
used in cognitive linguistics. Gardner himself narrowed it down by proposing that the central characteristic of cognitive science is an interest in
mental representations. According to Gardner (1985: 38–39), "cognitive
science is predicated on the belief that it is legitimate—in fact, necessary—to posit a separate level of analysis which can be called the 'level

of representation.' " [2] "Human cognitive activity at this level must be described in terms of symbols, schemas, images, ideas, and other forms of mental representation." [3] Gardner asserted that behavioral sciences other than cognitive science may avoid positing mental representations in their explanations: neurologists, for example, explain the behavior of the brain in terms of nerve cells and anthropologists explain human behavior in terms of culture. (He seemed to overlook the possibility of using the terms *culture* or *world view* to refer to the aggregate representations of whole communities and societies.)

COGNITIVE LINGUISTICS

Representations are also important to cognitive linguistics, a fact that places this new discipline squarely on the conceptual ground that Gardner mapped out for cognitive science. Wallace Chafe (1990: 80) noted that the human organism is able to deal with its environment by means of its ability to imagine, that is, "to create elaborate *representations* of the world around it, to represent within itself its own view of what the world surrounding the organism is like [italics added]." Both Langacker's and Lakoff's versions of cognitive linguistics proposed that language expresses mental representations or coherent ideas, whether these be called *gestalts*, *schemas*, *images*, or *Idealized Cognitive Models (ICMs)*. Ronald W. Langacker (1987: 1) proposed in his difficult, but important work *Foundations of Cognitive Grammar* that cognitive grammar "speaks of imagery at a time when meaning is generally pursued with apparatus derived from formal logic." He made extensive use of the concept of "schema," which he described as a concept that is "abstract relative to its nonzero elaborations in the sense of providing less information and being compatible with a broader range of options" (1987: 132).

In *Metaphors We Live By*, George Lakoff and Mark Johnson (1980: 81) used the phrase "experiential gestalts," by which they meant "ways of organizing [multidimensional] experiences into *structured wholes*." For example, the experiential gestalt for the experience of conversation includes the dimensions of participants, parts, stages, linear sequence, causation, and purpose. Lakoff (1987) later developed the term "Idealized Cognitive Models (ICMs)" for the complex mental representations that figure prominently in his theory of cognitive linguistics. An ICM is "a complex structured whole, a gestalt, which uses four kinds of structuring principles" (1987: 68). The structuring principles include propositional structure, image-schematic structure, metaphoric mappings, and metonymic mappings.

Thus, Gardner's view of cognitive science as a science of representations seems well borne out within cognitive linguistics as developed by Lakoff and Langacker in particular. Neither of these scholars would argue that images, schemas, or Idealized Cognitive Models are mirror images of phenomena or perceptual experience. What they have in common is an interest in imagistic representations—coherent, structured concepts that may have complex internal relations and find symbolic expression in language. The representations of interest to cognitive linguistics are more than mere collections of features; they are gestalts, which are unified concepts deriving from principles of grouping and connection, in which "the whole is conceptually simpler than the sum of the parts" (Lakoff 1987: 486–487, 489–490).

The use of gestalt theory in linguistic analysis is by no means new. Benjamin Whorf (1956a), for example, made explicit use of gestalt principles in his 1940 analysis of figure-and-ground relationships in Shawnee stems. Penny Lee (1993: 4) suggested that "the figurative application of the figure/ground concept to construal activity which is the active concern of cognitive linguists may perhaps be regarded as a further stage [of Whorf's research program] that is already underway."

Cognitive grammar has been characterized as "the most rapidly expanding linguistic approach of the last decade" (Harris 1993). Perhaps it is growing so rapidly because it holds important advantages over rival theories that represent all meaning as arising from a separate module of the language-producing apparatus, as a purely linguistic level of conceptualization, or as a system constructed of discrete categories operating at discrete levels of integration. Cognitive linguistics unifies the study of seemingly disparate realms of language as phonology, syntax, semantics, and discourse by treating them all in terms of the same set of principles. This means that researchers who explore these various levels of language can more readily track one another's progress and contribute to a general science of language. Accordingly, cognitive linguistics treats language not as a set of discrete levels (e.g., morpheme > lexeme > phrase > clause), but as a smooth continuum of categories.[4] It offers a synthetic approach that easily accommodates intermediate categories, linguistic continua, prototype phenomena, and irregular lexical semantic networks such as those typically found in the nomenclatural domains of plants, place-names, and anatomical terms (Bright and Bright 1969; Tyler 1969a; Berlin 1992; Palmer n.d.b). It provides for both analogic and categorical variation within complex linguistic systems, such as verb paradigms that display both regular and irregular forms (Bybee 1985). This perspective results in an account of language that is both natural and realistic.

Langacker (1990a: 343) claimed for cognitive grammar the attributes of "naturalness, conceptual unification, and theoretical austerity." Justifying this claim, he wrote:

> Cognitive grammar is natural in the sense that it relies only on well-established or easily demonstrable cognitive abilities (e.g. to categorize, to establish correspondences, to form complex conceptual and phonological structures, to forge symbolic links between the two, to impose figure/ground organization, to conceive of a situation at different levels of specificity, and so on). It is conceptually unified because it posits only semantic structures, phonological structures, and symbolic relationships between them. Lexicon, morphology, and syntax thus form a seamless whole consisting exclusively of symbolic structures, and semantics constitutes an inherent and indissociable aspect of grammar.

Cognitive linguistics uses the metaphor of connectionism and parallel distributed processing (McClelland and Rumelhart 1986; Varela, Thompson, and Rosch 1991: 85–103). In this approach, the mind is viewed as a network of neurons all engaged in reciprocal interactions via their connections with neighboring neurons and neuronal layers. A node in the network may take its input either from another node or from the environment, or from both. Neural networks have emergent or self-organizing properties in that they seek certain attractor states that may represent periodicities in time or space. A mental state is a global configuration that is a function of both environmental patterns and emergent patterns, including those that direct perceptual processes.

Because meanings are defined as global states of the network rather than as combinations of symbols, the relation of the connectionist model to symbolic processes is somewhat problematic. One solution is to see symbols as "higher level properties that are ultimately imbedded in an underlying distributed system," so that the subsymbolic system includes the symbolic system (Varela, Thompson, and Rosch 1991: 101). It follows, then, that symbols and their meanings would be relative to global states of mind. From this, it follows that meanings of symbols would be stabilized to the extent that they satisfy attractor states of neural nets, but, since biological neural networks undergo continual change, no two usages of a symbol would be strictly identical.

In linguistics and linguistic anthropology, the influence of the connectionist metaphor appears most clearly in non-linear or autosegmental phonology (Halle 1988; Lakoff 1989; Pulleyblank 1989; Clark and Yallop 1990; Goldsmith 1990), but cognitive anthropologists Claudia Strauss and Naomi Quinn (1994) recently advocated a connectionist approach to culture itself. In a connectionist approach, such traditional linguistic domains as phonology and semantics operate not as separate modular processes activated serially, but concurrently and in parallel, each subject to its own constraints (rules) and to other constraints arising from related dimensions. These patterns of linkage may or may not correspond to traditional levels of analysis. The connectionist approach to culture can be seen as the hypothesis that significant dimensions of human thought, emotion, language, and non-verbal behavior are globally and inextricably correlated and that global mental states pertain to all of these at once.

Cultural linguistics draws heavily upon cognitive linguistics. Consequently, it assumes neither arbitrary conceptual boundaries nor sequentially applied algorithms. Rather than neatly inclusive categories, discrete levels of language, and modular processes for phonology, morphology, syntax, and semantics, it more often structures linguistic concepts as complex and gradient and as parallel and interrelated processes constituted by patterns of mutual activations in conceptual networks.

Charles Fillmore (1984: 74) wrote a trenchant passage intended to warn us against arbitrary categories of analysis:

> Using a different image, we need to distinguish the perspective of a butcher from that of an anatomy student, each confronting a pig's carcass. The anatomy student, in disassembling the pig, traces a muscle from one of its moorings to the other, because he is interested in how the animal is put together. The butcher, by contrast, makes his segmentations of the animal in accordance with the prevailing practices of local meat-eaters and his own inner urges.

Fillmore implied that cognitive linguistics is really discovering "how the animal is put together"; we are anatomy students, not butchers.

Cognitive linguists have devoted a great deal of effort to examining the musculature of categorization, but we shouldn't conclude from this that cognitive grammar ignores process. Langacker (1990a: 15), for example, characterized a linguistic unit as "a cognitive routine," that is, "a thoroughly mastered structure, i.e. one that a speaker can activate as a preassembled whole without attending to the specifics of its internal composition." [5] In this view, listeners evaluate novel expressions by comparison and by bringing to bear "appreciation of context," "communicative objectives," "esthetic sensibilities," and "any aspect of general knowledge that might prove relevant" (1990a: 16). "Communicative objectives" and "esthetic sensibilities" call to mind Hymes's stress on the priority of the functional perspective and his interest in poetics. In cultural anthropology, the concern with communicative objectives fits with the current interest in "internalized motives" of cultural actors (Strauss and Quinn 1994). Communicative objectives govern discourse itself, including both clause-level grammar and cultural rules for the appropriate usage of language in various contexts, as in family arguments, conversations with acquaintances, and religious ceremonies. Every time we hear someone say "ain't," or use double negatives (negative concord), or assume a first name familiarity in a formal situation we are reminded by our own reactions of how motives and emotions govern grammar and discourse.

Cognitive linguists have so far largely confined themselves to the explanation of grammatical patterns, only occasionally grappling with such wider notions as culture, discourse, narrative, and world view. Cognitive linguistics has so far produced few studies of discourse. The fact that a conference on "Conceptual Structure, Discourse, and Language" was held at the University of California in San Diego in November 1994 suggests that more will be forthcoming, but the titles of the papers reveal that their forays into discourse are closely tied to lexical and clause level grammar, with nothing approaching the global interests of the ethnography of speaking. Formerly, the implications of cognitive linguistics for a theory of culture could only be inferred from the use of such concepts as "conventional expressions" (Langacker 1987: 35) and "cultural schemas" (Lakoff 1988: 135). Nevertheless, cognitive linguists have made important implicit contributions to our understanding of cultures and world views, particularly as they can be inferred from systems of metaphor. Cognitive linguists have studied metaphorical systems pertaining to love, anger, argument, time, and many other topics (Lakoff and Johnson 1980; Kövecses 1987; Lakoff 1987; Kövecses 1988; Matsuki 1989; Kövecses 1990; Kövecses 1991a; Kövecses 1991b; Kövecses 1993).

Finally, cognitive linguistics also illuminates the elusive connections between language and reasoning. In this view, reasoning is an imaginative process, based upon the mental manipulation of imagistic cognitive models and schemas of space, force, perspective, and social action, as well as the mechanistic logic of verbal postulates, formal propositions, and syllogisms (Lakoff 1988: 120, 142). Reasoning in this sense does not proceed entirely through language, but it may be evoked by linguistic frames.

Since world view consists of such conceptual materials as cognitive models and schemas, both language and world view are mutually implicated in reasoning processes. Where linguistic reasoning pertaining to social relationships can be shown to be based upon apparently non-imagistic concepts, on linguistic formulas or "proposition schemas," for example (Quinn 1991), it can still be argued that these concepts are best regarded as merely the most abstract pole of a schematic continuum that has very specific and concrete imagery at the opposite pole.

To conclude, anthropologists will see most clearly the usefulness of cognitive linguistics to the study of nomenclatural domains, the interpenetration of language and culture, and the relation between language and reasoning, but to limit the applications to only these topics would be a mistake. Traditional linguistic topics, such as phonology, morphology, syntax, sociolinguistics, and discourse, can also be studied within the framework of cognitive linguistics in ways that have new relevance to anthropology.

CHAPTER 4

THE SYNTHESIS OF CULTURAL LINGUISTICS

This chapter proposes the general terms of a synthesis of cognitive linguistics with Boasian linguistics, ethnosemantics, and the ethnography of speaking (ES). To some extent, these disciplines already stem from common roots and share assumptions, goals, and methods, so a synthesis may lie latent in their existing formulations. All embrace some degree of cultural relativity and empiricism. Researchers with Boasian goals have sometimes used ethnosemantic methods, as seen, for example, in the work of Mathiot. Ethnosemantics shares the Boasian interest in the psychologies of native speakers. Like the Boasian approach, ES strives to record native categories of language, especially those genres manifested naturally in actual discourse and performance as opposed to controlled elicitation or the recording of texts in artificial circumstances (Sherzer 1983). Like Boasian linguistics, ES builds upon the analysis of native categories of grammar, and, like ethnosemantics, it may pursue the analysis of lexical domains (Sherzer 1983; Saville-Troike 1989). Hymes (1964a: 9), the main exponent and formulator of ES, wrote that "with Boas almost the total scope of American linguistic anthropology until the present time became defined or adumbrated."

So to some extent, a synthesis has already occurred and perhaps ES represents it best. Yet there is still a need in anthropological linguistics for a more systematic cognitive approach that would embrace the goals of grasping the native point of view and of studying language use in its social and cultural context. Where appropriate, it should utilize the methods of controlled elicitation, participant observation, and systematic ethnography in natural contexts. Having incorporated these aspects of previous approaches, the synthesis should redefine their conceptual categories with those of cognitive linguistics. That is, they should be redefined as folk categories whose native conceptualizations are unknown prior to investigation. If this restriction were applied to ES, notions of speech community, speech genre, settings, participants, purposes, linguistic varieties and styles, modes and manners of performance, speech acts, and norms of interaction should all be analyzed *as folk cognitive models*, that is, "emically," as models in the minds of speakers rather than in the minds of ethnographers. It is no doubt true that some followers of ES have focused on discovering native categories, but the distinction is not built into the theory and some have clearly ignored it.

With Hymes's ideas subsumed under the umbrella of cognition, the repertoire of concepts drawn from cognitive linguistics and anthropology (discussed in detail in the following chapter) can be brought to bear on the analysis of native or folk patterns and categories of speech. We can, for example, treat speech genres as culturally defined cognitive models; we can examine linguistic varieties and norms of interaction as governed by sociolinguistic schemas; we can study speech acts as minimal discourse schemas; and we can gain greater insight into the semantics of lexical domains, polysemy, figurative language, and grammatical structures.

This synthesis may be termed *cultural linguistics*, a label that is intended to connote a broad interest in language and culture, a concern with folk knowledge, and a reliance on both ethnographic and linguistic methods. Cultural linguistics is concerned with most of the same domains of language and culture that interest Boasians, ethnosemanticists, and those following the program of ES, but it assumes a perspective on those phenomena that is essentially cognitive. It treats as cognitive not only the structure of the lexical domain of kinship terms, but also the plots of Coyote stories, not only the abstract structure of the phoneme [a], but also the phrasing of intonation in songs for the dead (Feld 1990), not only the abstract agents and patients of case grammar, but also the roles of participants in traditional discourse among chiefs (Sherzer 1983). Insofar as settings, participants, and situations are regarded as givens in the environment or the community under study and described according to the ethnographer's own categories, as often seems to be the case in linguistic ethnographies, they would be treated as background information that may or may not figure into native understandings. Cultural linguistics is primarily concerned not with how people talk about some objective reality, but with how they talk about the world that they themselves imagine. However, even this restricted formulation raises the interesting questions of how people frame experiences and abstract meanings from them.[1]

Since contemporary linguistic anthropology is firmly committed to the understanding of language through discourse, a synthesis must deal directly with that concern. The purpose of the following section, then, is to explain how the cognitive perspective of cultural linguistics bears on the important anthropological problem of delineating emergent and situated meaning in discourse.

THE PROBLEM OF EMERGENT AND SITUATED MEANING

An important trend in language and culture studies of the 1970s and 1980s has been to recognize that meaning emerges in discourse itself as participants interpret one another's speech performances. Meanings are contingent on events rather than entirely fixed in conventional word glosses and grammatical structures (Clifford 1986; Sherzer 1987; Brody 1991). Listeners frame situations and construe meaning in them. If language expresses cognition, it is cognition in interaction and process, not the apparently frozen cognitive structures of taxonomies and componential analyses. Wherever conventional and literal meanings alone are insufficient to encompass events and experiences, we find at work the human cognitive ability to construct meaning in discourse.

The contingency of meaning is not a new discovery, for all human speakers have probably had the conscious experience of creating or discovering new meanings. Even simple, everyday expressions take on new meanings according to situations. "He's a real sweetheart" may connote affection when spoken by a new girlfriend, or hostility when spoken sarcastically by the long-suffering wife of an abusive husband. Of course, such emergent usages themselves often become popular and conventionalized. New social meanings may emerge in speech performances that reconstitute existing social statuses, as when I say something in a manner which normally can only be adopted with a close friend, such as "I rely on you." Said to an old friend, it reaffirms our relationship. But the same expression may also create new or temporary social statuses: said to a new acquaintance, it may, under the proper circumstances, establish a new bond of friendship. Discourse creates meanings out of situations, thereby becoming "the essence of culture" and constitutive of language, culture, and society (Sherzer 1987).

Whether conventional or emergent, meaning is relative to society and politics and subject to disputation by interlocutors coming from different backgrounds and social statuses. Mutually understood meanings must often be negotiated. For example, the word *tribe* may mean a traditional band when used by an Indian tribe seeking fishing rights in federal court, but its usage may be restricted to a particular reservation when used by the judge, as happened in a recent decision involving the Moses Columbia Indians and several related bands in the Northwest. The effect of the restriction was to exclude the Moses Columbia from traditional fishing places on the Columbia River. This occurred in spite of testimony that the Moses Columbia and others had maintained their tribal identities from 1855 to the present day. The testimony itself was based upon historical evidence and linguistic evidence of family names.[2] Because of the importance of power and social context in negotiating meanings, it is always the case that meanings are not only relative, as in the meaning of *tribe*, but also situated in the discourse among interlocutors who bear historical and sociopolitical identities.

Cultural linguistics may require "thick description" (Geertz 1973; Sherzer 1983). Determining the meaning of discourse requires attention to the identities and histories of discourse participants, as well as to the immediate previous history of the discourse under interpretation, *especially as these are construed by the participants*. But determining what is sufficient, pertinent, and meaningful is often a matter of perspective and social position. Therefore, the determination of meaning must be interpretive, taking into account speakers' and listeners' own construals. Langacker, in fact, always maintained that "a crucial part of the meaning of any expression includes the speaker's apprehension of the total context (linguistic, social, cultural, and interactional)."[3] William F. Hanks (1993) used the term *framework* to stand for the immediate discourse situation in all its concrete remembered detail. Paul Werth (1993: 82) used the term *common ground* to encompass not only the immediate framework as defined by Hanks, but also interlocutors' world models. All these formulations suggest convergence on an interpretive approach.[4]

Robin Ridington (1991: 252) said that "the words we pass between us bring into being the densely interactive weavings of a world we hold in common." This metaphor of connections can be formulated in cognitive terms using the notion of discourse scenario, a kind of conventional cognitive model that entails human participants and interactions. World view is constituted of myriads of these connected scenarios, together with a host of other culturally defined entities and processes. Speakers and listeners implicate one another in connected scenarios by instantiating them with images of self and interlocutors. Thus, meaning is not only relative to scenarios, it is also relational and contingent in its weaving together of discourse scenarios.

If meaning is always relative to context and situated in social relations, how is it that people come to understand one another? One popular model of communication, still found in textbooks of communications, has failed to solve this problem. This is the conduit metaphor for language, a folk model found in both English and Japanese (Reddy 1979; Lakoff 1987: 108). The conduit metaphor, by now something of a straw man, construes linguistic meaning as consisting of discrete, stable objects contained in words and sent from speaker to hearer. But the model is surely wrong, because, as Langacker (1987: 162) pointed out, "nothing travels from speaker to hearer except sound waves." It is therefore the task of the listener to construct "a reasonable hypothesis about the nature of the conceptualization that prompted the speaker's utterance." As Fillmore (1975: 80) put it, "At any point in the discourse the interpreter needs to be aware of scenes or images or memories that are, so to speak, 'currently activated.' "

The paradigm of emergent meaning offers a dynamic and indispensable perspective, but taken to the extreme it becomes untenable, for if all meaning were to emerge only through discourse, then all meaning would be inchoative or momentaneous (Ellis 1991). In practice, words would have no dependable utility and dictionaries would be irrelevant and entirely useless. The stable, consensual meanings and patterns evident in cultures, traditions, and natural languages would never come into play. In fact, language and culture would not exist. There would be only communication and flux.

Since our experience of discourse is not quite this inchoate, there must be a middle ground, a nexus where consensual conventional meanings interact with conventional situations to frame meanings that are both conventional and relative to various discourse situations. This is what is meant by *situated meaning*. I contrast the term with *emergent meaning*, which involves the schematization of relatively novel and unfamiliar experiences and their framing or interpretation in terms of conventional categories. Languages contain large stocks of expressions and structures with stable imagery (e.g., morphemes, words, idiomatic phrases, metaphors, traditional narratives), but each usage of a conventional expression implicates it in a particular social and linguistic situation or requires the framing of a novel experience.

Langacker dealt with the problems of situated and emergent meaning by defining cognitive grammar as "a 'usage based' model of language structure," by which he seemed to have two things in mind: an inductive approach and a context-based approach that is "maximalist, nonreductive, and bottom-up" as opposed to the generative tradition, which is "minimalist, reductive, and top-down," at least in spirit (1990a: 260–266, 280–

281). That he regarded cognitive grammar as inductive is not particularly relevant to the problem of emergent meaning, but I present it here to avoid presenting a partial and distorted view of his idea. More relevant to our problem is his assertion that "usage-based" also implies that all linguistic structure emerges from context, which includes, among other things, "recurrent cultural knowledge."[5] He asserted that "language use (and the basis for language acquisition) consists of **usage events**, in which full, contextually grounded understandings are paired with phonological occurrences in all their phonetic detail." This seems to mean that symbols, as pairings of sound and meaning, emerge, or evolve, in usage events, that is, in discourse itself.

Given this understanding of "usage events" as encompassing the context of discourse, conventional meanings become established by the "entrenchment of recurring commonalities":

> To the extent that usage events are similar, schematization comes about through the reinforcing and progressive entrenchment of recurring commonalities, as well as the "cancellation" (non-reinforcement) of features that do not recur. This abstraction can be carried to any degree, as more usage events are taken into account and the discernible commonalities become more tenuous. While semantically this usually involves substantial decontextualization, any facet of the context that consistently recurs across a set of usage events can be retained as a specification of the schema that emerges from them.[6]

Note that Langacker treated "any facet of the context that consistently recurs" as potential conventionalized meaning. This is very significant because it establishes a basis for the understanding of discourse and pragmatics. Because the processes of discourse and pragmatics constitute part of the meaningful context of all usage events, perceptions and understandings of them are likely to be abstracted and incorporated into the meanings of terms that we might not otherwise think of as pragmatic. In fact, any expression that seems to require no pragmatic interpretation whatsoever is treated as a special case![7]

One of the points of difference between cognitive linguistics and ES is that the latter stresses the pragmatic aspects of speech as social action as though this were a dimension apart from referential meaning. Langacker's approach showed that the boundary is arbitrary. I will argue further that speech acts, such as questioning, describing, and demanding, can be seen as enactments of minimal discourse scenarios, which come complete with intentions, affective values, and existential modal values (contingency probabilities).

STALKING WITH STORIES IN APACHE: A CASE OF EMERGENT MEANING

I will provide just one example of how meaning can be created by applying conventional understandings to novel situations. In one of the most enlightening and entertaining articles to be found anywhere in ethnographic literature, Basso (1990b) described the Western Apache discourse of *stalking with stories*, which refers to the practice of telling a moralistic historical narrative (*'agodzaahi*) in the presence of an offender against community morals without directly mentioning or addressing the target of this verbal sanction. Among the cases which he described was that of a seventeen-year-old Apache woman who returned home from boarding school to attend a girls' puberty ceremony, but inappropriately left her hair done up in pink plastic curlers, a violation of the expectation that at puberty ceremonies the hair should be worn loose to show respect for Apache customs. Here is Basso's description of what happened to this girl at a birthday party, two weeks later:

> When the meal was over casual conversation began to flow, and the young woman seated herself on the ground next to her younger sister. And then—quietly, deftly, and totally without warning—her grandmother narrated a version of the historical tale about the forgetful Apache policeman who behaved too much like a white man. Shortly after the story was finished, the young woman stood up, turned away wordlessly, and walked off in the direction of her home. Uncertain of what had happened, I asked her grandmother why she had departed. Had the young woman suddenly become ill? "No," her grandmother replied. "I shot her with an arrow." (1990b: 122)

Of course, the "arrow" of which she spoke was the story itself. The full moral meaning of the story can only be inferred by the offender and other listeners from parallels between the story and the context in which it is told. The offender is aware that the story represents a moral principle and that all of the listeners present at the telling may understand who it is that stands in violation. The investment of historical stories with such contemporary meanings requires acts of imagination by both speakers and listeners.

A similar process operates in other linguistic genres: listeners extract normative scenarios from specific narratives and use the scenarios to

frame specific events. Lakoff (1990: 71) noted that "the metaphoric interpretation of such discourse forms as proverbs, fables, allegories, and so
on seems to depend on our ability to extract generic-level structure from
a specific knowledge structure." He proposed a mapping of specific schemas from proverbs to general schemas and the remapping of the general
schemas to specific schemas, so as to arrive at a mapping of source to
target. The process depends upon the two-way application of a single
metaphor, which he termed GENERIC IS SPECIFIC.

SENTIMENTS AND SITUATIONS VEILED IN BEDOUIN SONG

Lila Abu-Lughod (1986: 173) described the local interpretations of poetic
songs of the Awlad 'Ali, an Arabic-speaking, patrilineal Bedouin society
of the North African littoral, a society in which people value "improvi-
sational talent and the ability to play with linguistic forms." This is a society in which ordinary discourse expresses a code of honor and morality
that safeguards the integrity of the patrilineage, but the genre of song
known as the *ghinnawa* expresses otherwise disparaged personal sentiments of love, longing, loss, and despair that, given free rein, would
threaten the patrilineal social organization. People attend closely to the
songs to discover the repressed feelings of the singers. The following
(Arabic omitted) is a poem sung by a woman named 'Aziza (Abu-Lughod
1986: 172):

> Patience brought no fulfilled wishes
> I wearied and hope's door closed . . .

Her friend answered with a poem implying that it was better to replace
love with patience. 'Aziza rejoined with a poem about the persistence of
memories; her friend countered with an exhortation to forget those who
cause pain. 'Aziza then resumed her original theme of patience with the
following poem:

> If patience availed her in despair
> the self would commit no offense, even small . . .

The friend responded with a poem warning of the ill effects of bringing
up tales of old loves. Abu-Lughod (1986: 173) reported that when she
played the songs for other women, they looked "solemn and pained,"
commenting "Her luck is bad!" or "This is news that makes you cry,"
and some even wept.

There are several points to keep in mind in trying to understand how
this genre communicates sentiments, that is, conventional feelings. First,

as mentioned, people are expected to express their personal feelings in the songs. Second, there is a large corpus of the poetic songs, and it appears that most people are familiar with many songs. Third, the people hearing the songs are familiar with the personal history of the singer, so they have expectations concerning the feelings revealed in song. Fourth, singers and audience share a cultural tradition of interpretation. They have heard others interpret many similar songs. Abu-Lughod (1986: 173) noted that "by drawing images and experiences from the shared world of a small, culturally homogeneous community, poems gain meaning." Fifth, the songs express sentiments abstractly: despair, weariness, unfulfilled longings, and hope. They are vague. Were they more specific or concrete the bereaved, for example, might sing of physical weakness, loss of hunger, or the draining of blood from the face rather than despair. Instead, the sentiments predicated by the songs are feeling-schemas.

What was it that the Bedouin women knew about 'Aziza that enabled them to interpret the songs and moved them to sympathy and tears? 'Aziza had indeed had a very difficult life that would move most women to despair: having married an abusive husband (Bedouins insist on arranged marriages), she escaped home to live with her father, but the father soon died; her brother, who should have supported her, was moody and poverty stricken; she returned to her husband's household, where his other wife mistreated her and got her into trouble with her husband, who divorced her; she then refused to remarry and raised her son alone, but since the husband's family has full rights in any children, she lived in fear that they would take her son away from her; to top it all off, she had a hideous and painful skin disease that flared up in times of stress.

The Bedouin women who listened to the tapes made by Abu-Lughod understood this history. Thus, the songs, "so seemingly impersonal," predicating conventional abstract sentiments with which the Bedouin frame situations, also predicate specific aspects of those situations that best elaborate the sentiment schemas. The interpretive task of the audience is to guess the intended meaning in the shared understanding of the context. Even were the guesses to be in error, the songs would still engender appreciation by evoking other similar songs in the corpus and evoking listeners' memories of their own experiences that would fit the schematic sentiments expressed in song. The understanding of context is crucial to the interpretation of the songs. Abu-Lughod (1986: 175) reported that "Awlad 'Ali are in fact hard-pressed to interpret poems without contextual information—whenever I asked anyone the meaning of a particular poem, their first question was 'Who said it?'" Thus, in seeking to discover the meaning of a song, Abu-Lughod (1986: 177) would ask "what people are saying about their experiences through their poems, what their goals are in reciting them, and to whom they are addressing the poems."

In some discourse genres, such as the Bedouin songs, generic structure is explicitly profiled and the interpretive problem is to find the specific content in the understood context that it frames. Discourse may occur in social contexts that have evolved in the course of weeks or years into recognizable situations that are widely understood within a community. While unique in some respects, community understandings of historically evolved social situations are patterned according to the possibilities afforded by the social structures in which they are embedded. Their understandings of generic discourses are socially, culturally, and historically situated.

SITUATING SPATIAL MORPHEMES IN A KUNA SNAKE-HANDLING CEREMONY

The example of Apache "stalking with stories" illustrated the construction of meaning in a novel situation, while that of Bedouin song showed how general sentiments acquired meaning in historically evolved situations that are well understood by members of the discourse community. A final example of situated meaning comes from an article by Sherzer (1987: 297) that has become a point of reference in the study of discourse in anthropology. The example, from the language of the Kuna Indians of Panama, shows how conventional meanings may vary with highly conventional situations. Sherzer described how Kuna verbal suffixes with conventional meanings may take on magical meanings in ceremonial uses. The positional suffixes -*mai* (lying, in a horizontal position) and -*nai* (perched, in a hanging position) are used in magical chants which are spoken while raising a snake from the ground (where it is described with -*mai*) into the air (where it is described with -*nai*). The ostensible purpose of the ritual is to address a spiritual snake, commanding it to rise from the ground, where it is in a horizontal, lying position, and turn over, while it is in a hanging position. Sherzer said, "The spirit, on hearing the chant addressed to it in its special language, immediately does what the narrative of the chant describes and, at the same time, the real, actual snake does so as well." The poetic use of the positional suffixes in parallel couplets contributes to the magical effect of the ritual. The Kuna practice of verbally describing ritual acts while performing them is typical of the ritual use of language in the Americas. Sherzer's point is that the grammatical category of position registered in the suffixes takes on special meanings in discourse.

The Kuna example is instructive because it lies toward the conventional pole of the continuum from emergent to conventional meaning. The imagery of the positional suffixes is conventional and their descriptive use in the ritual of raising the snake makes literal use of the conventional meanings. The ritual, with the chants, is itself a conventional practice in that it means essentially the same thing every time that it is performed. Yet the suffixes acquire magical meanings by their usage in magical speech acts. These magical meanings, while conventional, are specific to the ritual setting. They can be described as situated meanings. It is true that this is a very conventionalized performance of ritual discourse in which the snake is the direct addressee, but observers of the ritual, as additional, indirect, participants in the discourse, must also make the assignment of appropriate meanings to the ritual utterances, and they can only do this if they understand the snake ceremony.

Apache stalking with stories, Bedouin songs, and Kuna snake-handling rituals have shown us three culturally patterned ways to construct meaning in discourse. In the Bedouin songs, generic meanings are explicit, but the generic meanings of the Apache stories require extraction from specific narratives. The constructed meanings of Apache sayings are emergent, applying to novel events, but the meanings of Bedouin songs derive from situations that have a longer community history and structure. The meanings of the Kuna snake-handling formulas are highly conventionalized. None of these distinctions is intended to be absolute, but they indicate some of the ways that cultural linguistics may apply to discourse events.

CHAPTER 5

CONCEPTS

Cultural linguistics and cognitive linguistics are fundamentally theories of mental imagery. They seek to understand how speakers deploy speech and listeners understand it relative to various kinds of imagery. Some of these kinds are cognitive models, symbols, image-schemas, prototypes, basic categories, complex categories, metaphor, metonymy, and social scenarios. Often the selection and understanding of linguistic expressions seem to depend upon speakers' and listeners' construals of more fleeting kinds of imagery involving the distribution of attention, such as figures and grounds, profiles and bases, levels of specificity, and perspectives involving orientations and points of view. All of these have been given technical definitions. In this chapter, I will present the definitions that have been advanced in linguistics and anthropology.

DEFINING IMAGERY

An image-based theory of language requires a comprehensive definition of the term *image*. The definition should accommodate imagery that is both specific and schematic. It should allow for imagery that arises from all of the sensory modes. Besides visual imagery, it should also allow for auditory, kinesthetic, olfactory, and temperature imagery. There is also the complex imagery that arises from the emotions—the affective imagery of feeling states.[1] The term *imagery* highlights the fact that concepts originate as representations of sensory experiences, even though they may subsequently undergo complex processes of formation and recombination. The prototypic function of imagery is to represent the environment, even though images seldom correspond directly to all the objectively definable features to be found there. This use of the term corresponds closely to the following definition from the *Oxford English Dictionary*:

image . . . 5.a. A mental representation of something (esp. a visible object), not by direct perception, but by memory or imagination; a mental picture or impression; an idea, conception. Also, with qualifying adj.: a mental representation due to any of the senses (not only sight) and to organic sensations.[2]

Images are mental representations that begin as conceptual analogs of immediate, perceptual experience from the peripheral sensory organs. Because they are the analogs of peripheral experience, they are also, therefore, indirect conceptual analogs of the environment, broadly construed to include society, natural phenomena, our own bodies and their organic (and mental) processes, and the rest of what is often called "reality" or "the world out there."

But the traces of perceptual experiences may undergo so much cognitive processing as to become only very indirect or distorted representations. In saying that images are only indirect conceptual analogs of peripheral experiences, I mean two things. First, I mean that conceptual schemas prime our senses to respond to a limited range of sensory experience, as when we scan a book looking only for certain topics. Images based on such filtered experience can only partially and incompletely reflect the environment, and often they greatly distort it, as when the shadow of a bush in the moonlight appears to be a lurking mugger. None of our experiences come to us as pristine sensations without context or interpretation.

Second, I mean that immediate, peripheral perceptions of experience (low-level, concrete, detailed, specific images), once registered by the mind, provide grist for the cognitive mill, which subsequently subjects them to a variety of normal, or in some cases abnormal, processes. They undergo gestalt formation, abstraction, framing, comparison, amplification or suppression, and analysis. Once resolved with related images and composed into cognitive models, they may undergo reconstruals of figure and ground, scope, orientation, and point of view. These terms are defined in this chapter and their application to language is explained. The point is that images, except for those closest to immediate peripheral experiences, are largely derivative, reflecting the environment only indirectly.

Lakoff (1987: 444) believed it is important to distinguish mental images from perceptions, which are much richer in detail. Certainly we can in most cases clearly separate perceptions given by the ongoing operation of the sense organs from the imagery that is retained after the experience, but there is a continuum here from immediate experience to that more removed in time, and the confounding influence of top-down framing of experience makes it hard to sustain such a clear distinction in every case. We have all seen referees of sports events make bad calls because their preconceptions conspired with concrete events to give the illusion of a violation where none actually occurred, as demonstrated by instant replay. Even in such very concrete situations, referees often see what they are primed to see, especially when the actual event is fleeting and resembles the frame of anticipation. Conceptualization and imagination interact with perception.

Langacker (1987: 112) provided a slightly different perspective on this theme of perception versus imagery. He distinguished between peripherally connected cognitive events, which are "induced by stimulating a sense organ," and autonomous cognitive events, which evoke the corresponding sensory image in the absence of such stimulation. Autonomous events may or may not have equivalent events that are peripherally connected. For example, emotions and abstract concepts are autonomous events that have no peripheral equivalents. Peripherally connected cognitive events include not only sensations from the eyes, ears, nose, and other sense organs, but also those cognitive events that are "directly responsible for eliciting motor actions."

Langacker (1987: 112) defined a *motor image* as "an event equivalent to one which elicits a motor response but which in fact actually fails to do so." Motor images are important to linguistics in at least two ways. First, the motor images of verbal sounds constitute articulatory routines that we can either imagine or implement as speech (in which case it does not actually fail to elicit a motor response). Together with auditory images, motor images constitute part of our knowledge of speech sounds. Second, he proposed that "the motor images corresponding to walking, kicking, or throwing figure prominently in our conceptions of these activities and are consequently included in the meanings of the verbs *walk*, *kick*, and *throw*."

Ronald A. Finke (1989: 41) reviewed much of the psychological research on mental imagery conducted during the 1970s and 1980s. The five general principles of imagery that he derived from recent and current research are useful as a basic foundation for understanding imagery. His *principle of perceptual equivalence* has a bearing on Lakoff's distinction between mental images and perceptions and Langacker's distinction between autonomous and peripheral events. The effect of the principle is to reduce the importance of this distinction:

The Principle of Perceptual Equivalence
Imagery is functionally equivalent to perception to the extent that
similar mechanisms in the visual system are activated when objects or
events are imagined as when the same objects or events are actually
perceived. (Finke 1989: 41)

Finke limited this principle to the visual system, but it probably applies
as well to other modalities. This unifying principle seems basic to an understanding of language and world view. It means that a single cognitive
system is responsible both for imagination and for any imagery that is
evoked by more immediate and direct perception, enabling us to describe
immediate experience, tell stories about what happened long ago, speculate about what might occur, appreciate myths and novels, and give cre-
dence to religious experiences. It also suggests that it may require special
conventions to distinguish the real from the unreal, to separate empiri-
cally verifiable events from prevarications and other products of imagination. In languages we find such empirical safeguards in evidential
markers. In the Papago language of Arizona, for instance, it is obligatory
to use the little word *ş* whenever you are describing something not seen
firsthand.[3]

To summarize these perspectives on imagery, Lakoff distinguished between mental images and perceptions. Langacker distinguished between
autonomous events and peripherally connected events. Motor images
constitute one class of autonomous events. Since perceptions are framed
and filtered by imagery (mental images or autonomous events) that is culturally constructed, it follows, then, that *virtually all imagery is structured by culture and personal history.* Imagery is either socially constructed or embedded in social constructions. Even the very immediate
image of a hot piece of pizza burning the roof of your mouth reflects your
understanding that the pizza is food and not the first touch of an instrument of torture.

Let me make this even more clear by stating the obvious, that conventional fantasy, for example, is not a mirror image of reality. Fantasies that constitute folklore, mythology, comic books, and great literature are socially motivated cultural constructions. Fantasies of mythology
such as stories of Bigfoot and Santa Claus consist of complex images
that are the end result of processing by many narrators and audiences.
Each consideration and telling of a story subjects it to cognitive processes that select, compose, reconstruct, abstract, distort, and reframe

its content in culturally defined narrative schemas, so that with each telling, perhaps over generations, it grows almost imperceptibly further from the more concrete images, that are closer to perceptual analogs of the environment.

Fantasies are often difficult to distinguish from ordinary reality precisely because they become so entrenched in cultures, so detailed, and so easy to generate that each consideration or telling may actually require minimal creative interpretation. Marcia K. Johnson (1991) conducted a series of experiments whose results suggest that the images that are easiest to generate are also the most difficult to separate from perceived events or everyday reality. This is particularly true when imaginations closely resemble perceptions in detail. To test this idea, Johnson and collaborators presented subjects with pictures, varying the number of times subjects saw each picture and the number of times they imagined each picture. Then they asked each subject how many times he or she had seen each picture. Subjects judged that they had seen a picture more times if they had actually seen the picture more times and if they had more often imagined that they had seen the picture. In my view, Johnson's findings help to explain the widespread occurrence of theatrical rituals and public spectacles underwritten by belief systems that lack empirical validation, such as those of religions, mythologies, and political ideologies. By dramatizing, evoking, and reinforcing highly detailed images, rituals make it easier for their participants to generate that imagery and correspondingly more difficult to separate it from perceptual experience. Such socially constructed non-empirical systems of thought constitute the cognitive models by which raw experience is interpreted.

As in the dictionary definition, my use of the word *imagery* includes non-visual imagery. In this usage I follow Lakoff (1987: 444), who said, "The term *image* is not intended here to be limited to visual images. We also have auditory images, olfactory images, and images of how forces act upon us." In this respect it is interesting to note that psychologist Albert Bregman (1990) studied "auditory scene analysis," the process by which people recover descriptions of each separate thing in their auditory environments. But while the imagery of all sensory modalities should be considered in the study of language, Lakoff noted that most linguistic research has concentrated upon visual imagery.

In a similar attempt to broaden the concept of imagery, Langacker (1987: 110–111) used the terms "**sensory imagery, visual imagery, auditory imagery**, etc.," but he limited his use of these terms to "the occurrence of a perceptual sensation in the absence of the corresponding perceptual input," the kind of imagery that we evoke by closing our eyes and imagining a scene.

Langacker proposed a much narrower technical definition of *image*, which is distinguished from both metaphor and perceptual imagery. In his framework, the term describes "our ability to construe a conceived situation in alternate ways—by means of alternate images—for purposes of thought or expression" (1987: 110). Our construals of a given situation may vary in figure-ground organization, level of specificity, scope, or perspective. Even though they may describe the same objective situation, the expression *the table is supporting the clock* differs from *the clock is on the table* in its figure-ground organization. *The clock is lying on the table* is more specific than *the clock is on the table*. The verb *lie* "calls attention to the alignment of the clock along the horizontal axis of the table," but if we said *the clock is resting on the table* we would be emphasizing "the static character of the locative relationship." Each of these sentences represents a different image of the same scene. This kind of imagery is conventional, but nevertheless "a fleeting thing that neither defines nor constrains the contents of our thoughts" (1986: 12).

Thus, Langacker distinguished between metaphor (or figurative language), sensory imagery, and the various conventional, but transient, images evoked by alternate construals of some background scene. In my opinion, it would be difficult to demonstrate a difference in kind between what Langacker called "imagery" in the sense of alternative construals of scenes and what he called "sensory imagery." Where it is necessary to make the distinction, I will distinguish between a source image or peripheral event obtaining immediately and in real time from sensory experience, a cognitive model or scene, and a particular image or construal of a model or scene in terms of level of abstraction (or, conversely, of specific detail), relative salience of its components or relations, its figure and ground organization, or the perspective from which it is viewed. These are easier to distinguish in theory than in practice because perception is guided by cognition. Either a construed image or a model may serve as the frame of interpretation for a source image. A source image may add specific content to a construed image on the one hand but lose some of its content through filtering on the other, as, for example, when we see only the shine and glamour of a new model car on the showroom floor, ignoring obvious defects of workmanship and safety. This is why the sales manager can say "Don't sell the steak; sell the sizzle."

THE ADAPTIVE FUNCTIONS OF LANGUAGE AND IMAGERY

The fact that humans have a well-developed capacity for imagery raises important questions. Why did this capacity develop? And why should it be so closely linked to language and culture? It is a basic premise of anthropology that culture is adaptive (though not all cultures in all times and places). One way to relate language and imagery to culture is to propose that they contribute to the effectiveness of cultural adaptations. Language has come to serve many functions in human affairs, but perhaps the most fundamental reason for its emergence in human evolution is that it provides a means by which speakers can evoke and reinforce adaptive imagery in one another. Imagery is adaptive if it guides or promotes adaptive behaviors, such as organizing for effective hunting and gathering or for defense, cooperation in child-raising, or avoidance of manipulative exploitation. Of course, distasteful though it may be, increased capacity for social imagery must have enabled some early humans to gain advantage by manipulating and exploiting others. Nevertheless, by communicating with language, gestures, and other symbolic media, humans collaborate to construct shared worlds of imagery that model the physical and social phenomena of the world around them and motivate them to cooperate. It is by means of symbolic discourse that humans construct adaptive cultures and world views.

While imagery is adaptive, it is often abstract, metaphorical, partial, illusory, and phantasmagoric. For example, many American Indian stories tell of hunters who marry deer, buffalo, or other game. How could such fantasies be adaptive? It may be that their only function is to bring people together around dramatic and pleasurable stories, but there may also be a cognitive payoff. If the world of hunter-gatherers is modeled in such transformations, it is perhaps only at an abstract level that models the social world after the patterns of hunting, so that a suitor is likened to a hunter and the object of his attentions to the creature hunted. But, by evoking scenarios of both hunting and mating, often in great detail, such tales induce the audience to reflect upon both domains, to remember their features, and to compare them to one another so that essential scenarios from both domains become more salient and readily available for reasoning. Megan Biesele (1986), commenting on the equation of women to meat animals among the !Kung hunter-gatherers, theorized that the stories reinforce lessons concerning the correct attitudes toward women and animals and create provocative and dramatic situations for the exploration of social and economic issues and pleasurable contexts for learning. Often it is only indirectly that we communicate about the so-called real world outside or about the experience of living in a physical body; mostly we communicate about mental images.

Language enables us to do this rapidly. In inventing language, our ancestors hit upon a very efficient way to communicate about imagery. The vocal apparatus, much improved by human biological evolution, supports the dense packing of information into rapid speech, averaging, in English, 900 phonemes per minute (Tartter 1986). Our vocal and auditory apparatus is specialized for producing and hearing the rapid segmentations of sounds that we hear as vowels and consonants. These occur in normal speech at a rate of 10 to 20 per second. Minimal meaningful segments of speech range in length from a single phoneme, as in the English word *a*, to a more normal length of 3 to 5 segments, as in the words *dog* [dɔg], *write* [rayt], and *widgit* [wɪjɪt]. If each word or morpheme evokes a basic image, as in *dog*, or an abstract image, as in the article *a* (which I would take to evoke the abstract image of a countable thing), then by means of language we could theoretically express complexes of several basic and abstract images per second. The ability to communicate images so rapidly should convey a tremendous adaptive advantage over creatures who lack it. This ability rapidly to combine and interpret morphemes with conventional meanings according to grammatical conventions is peculiarly human.

Language is not only rapid; it is also complex. In the course of human evolution, emergence of the ability to discuss complex ideas created a social and linguistic environment that must, in turn, have selected for the mental capacities to conceive and consider such ideas. Language and imagination must have developed interdependently in a process of mutual reinforcement. Each would facilitate the use of the other and confer additional advantages.

Evolution of the ability to conceptualize complex social and sociolinguistic patterns must have been, to a significant degree, language-driven. Cognitive specialization for social and sociolinguistic organization gives humans the capacity to imagine some of the more complex schemas involved in kinship, marriage, trade, treachery, revenge, and discourse. The social schemas constituting matrilineal kinship, generalized economic exchange, or any other social form are not necessarily innate, but the ability to conceptualize complex social scenarios and incorporate them into cognitive models is most likely uniquely human.[4] Evolving along with the capacity for social cognition, human language provided the means of communicating about it. While language enabled our ancestors to build more elaborate, more schematic, and more adaptive cognitive models, it also drove them to do it in order to keep up with their neighbors.

LINGUISTIC SYMBOLS

In cognitive linguistics, the term *symbol* is given a very simple, but specific meaning. According to Langacker (1987: 81–82), "a linguistic symbol is bipolar, defined by a semantic structure standing in correspondence to a phonological structure." Units such as affixes, roots, and words are verbal symbols because they are conventional phonological units having conventional meanings. In the section defining imagery, I presented evidence that both the phonological and semantic poles of this structure may be regarded as imagery. In Langacker's framework, basic grammatical classes and grammatical constructions are also symbols: "grammatical classes are defined by schematic symbolic units. The class of nouns, for example is defined by a schema that we can represent as [[THING]/[. . .]], where [THING] is a schematic semantic unit . . . and [. . .] a schematic phonological unit." Grammatical constructions are formed from "the syntagmatic combination of morphemes and larger expressions." Constructions are complex symbols that contain less complex symbols as components.

Smaller phonological units, such as consonants, vowels, and syllables of one or two segments, are non-symbolic to the extent that they pattern independently of meaning. There are no consistent direct links between the majority of these minimal phonological images on the one hand and semantic images or pragmatic outcomes of speech acts on the other. But in many cases a morpheme or word does consist of a single segment or a short syllable at its phonological pole, as in the English articles *a* and *the*. These are also symbols. In a discussion of Ipai sound symbolism taken up in Chapter 10, we will see that single segments may have important semantic content even where they do not constitute morphemes in the usual sense.

This definition of the symbol is a direct descendant of Ferdinand de Saussure's definition of the linguistic *sign*. In a course of lectures given from 1906 to 1911 at the University of Geneva, Saussure (1966: 66) defined the *linguistic sign* as that which "unites, not a thing and a name, but a concept and a sound-image. The latter is not the material sound, a purely physical thing, but *the psychological imprint of the sound*, the impression that it makes on our senses [italics added]." It is clear that the sign was central to Saussure's theory, because he located language itself at the place in the mind "where the *auditory image* becomes associated with a concept [italics added]" (1966: 14). He believed that the concept and the sound image were "intimately united" and that "the one recalls the other" (1966: 66). Saussure assigned the terms *signified* and *signifier* to the concept and the sound image, respectively.

While I have accepted Saussure's construction of the sign (symbol), he held other opinions that have to be rejected in the light of modern research findings. These pertain to the concreteness of the sound image and the completely arbitrary nature of signs. For example, he said, "The sound-image is sensory, and if I happen to call it 'material,' it is only in that sense, and by way of opposing it to the other term of the association, the concept, which is generally more abstract" (1966: 66). But, if abstraction or schematization is a basic cognitive process affecting imagery, then it should also apply to phonological imagery. In fact, we find it in the phoneme itself and in the many phonological rules found in languages, for example, in phenomena such as assimilations of neighboring segments (consonants or vowels) to one another, so that only one is realized, because they share some phonetic feature. For two segments to be recognized as similar, there must be some schema that unites or relates them. We find abstraction also in dissimilation, in vowel harmonies, in allophonic variations, and in rules for the assignment of stress to syllables. Schematization is as pervasive in phonology as it is in semantics. Consequently, symbols often link a phonological schema to a semantic schema, each requiring instantiation by some more specific form in an actual utterance. Such schematic symbols function as grammatical classes or the templates of constructions. This chapter looks at some of the general principles of cognition that govern symbolic activity.

COGNITIVE MODELS

That humans build imagistic cognitive models is a proposition that finds proponents in cognitive psychology, cognitive linguistics, and linguistic anthropology. However, there is less agreement on just how cognitive or mental models relate to such notions as proposition, schema, and reasoning. Do propositions belong to mental models or do they instead constitute an alternative type of conceptualization? Are propositions linguistic or are they somehow specified in a mental language of their own? Are models and the imagery within them specific or abstract? And should metaphor and metonymy be regarded as operations on models or as cognitive structures that themselves define types of models? These are some of the questions that this section attempts to answer. It seems vital to do so for two reasons: because mental models govern the use of language and because mental models are cultural models; world views consist entirely of mental models. Thus, their study provides the main access to an understanding of the interrelation of language and culture.

JOHNSON-LAIRD'S LAYER-CAKE MODEL

P. N. Johnson-Laird proposed that three kinds of representations are necessary for understanding the role of language in human reasoning: models, images, and propositions. Since models provide the basis for defining the other two types, I will start with them. It is clear from the following quote that mental models lie at the heart of Johnson-Laird's theory of human behavior (page numbers in parentheses are from Johnson-Laird [1983]):

> Mental models play a central role in representing objects, states of affairs, sequences of events, and the way the world is, and the social and psychological actions of daily life. They enable individuals to make inferences and predictions, to understand phenomena, to decide what action to take and to control its execution, and above all to experience events by proxy; they allow language to be used to create representations comparable to those deriving from direct acquaintance with the world; and they relate words to the world by way of conception and perception. (397)

Thus we learn that models represent, that they enable reasoning, that they control actions, and that they are necessary for linguistic representation, but the passage does not tell us exactly what models are. Johnson-Laird (1983: 11) defined a model, in a first approximation, as "an inner mental replica that has the same 'relation structure' as the phenomenon that it represents." This definition finds support in psychological research on mental imagery conducted during the 1970s and 1980s, as summarized in Finke (1989). Principles 2 through 5 seem particularly relevant. Principle 2, the *principle of perceptual equivalence*, was discussed above. I will discuss the remaining principles in turn.

The Principle of Spatial Equivalence
The spatial arrangement of the elements of a mental image corresponds to the way objects or their parts are arranged on actual physical surfaces or in the actual physical space. (1989: 61)

This principle is useful to keep in mind when discussing vocabularies and verbal descriptions of such important schematic images as abstract human faces, bodies, landscapes, pathways, links, and containers.

The Principle of Transformational Equivalence
Imagined transformations and physical transformations exhibit corresponding dynamic characteristics and are governed by the same laws of motion. (1989: 93)

This principle has particular relevance to verbal descriptions of physical and social processes, objects in motion, and acceleration, and to the ways that we reason about them, often metaphorically. Thus, we commonly speak of social inertia and momentum as though we were describing physical events (Lakoff 1987; Talmy 1988). An interesting, but hypothetical, corollary to this principle would be *The targets of spatial metaphors obey the Principle of Transformational Equivalence as it applies to the corresponding sources.*

The Principle of Structural Equivalence
The structure of mental images corresponds to that of actual perceived objects, in the sense that the structure is coherent, well organized, and can be reorganized and reinterpreted. (1989: 120)

This principle appears to subsume the principle of spatial equivalence.[5] It enables us to reason about mental images in the same way that we would reason about, or even manipulate, perceived objects. It helps to explain the creativity of language, because images are at least as susceptible to reorganization as the physical or social phenomena from which they are ultimately derived.

Johnson-Laird (1983: 423) implied that models may derive from perception and, like Fink (principle 2), he concluded (1983: 126–145) that it is possible to reason validly without logic. He also said that models are specific, but even so they can be used to represent a general class of entities by means of "interpretive processes," which treat the model as "no more than a representative sample from a larger set" (157–158). Models may be artificial, as in those "governing domains of pure mathematics," or natural, "acquired without explicit instruction" (11). Finally, models may be constructed in discourse, as when a listener attempts to build a mental model corresponding to the verbal description of a room (163).

Johnson-Laird (1983: 423) defined an *image* as a part of a model: an *image* is "a viewer-centered representation of the visible characteristics of an underlying three-dimensional spatial or kinematic model." Thus, images have inherent perspective and they are limited to visual representation of three-dimensional objects. An image "corresponds to a view of (or a projection from)" the underlying model (423). Since models "underlie" images, a model may be used to "recover a representation" of an object (157). The notion that "images correspond to *views* of models" (157) resembles Langacker's (1987: 110) definition of an *image* as "our ability to construe a conceived situation in alternate ways—by means of alternate images—for purposes of thought or expression." Langacker's framework may be aligned with that of Johnson-Laird by equating the "conceived situation" or, elsewhere, "scene" with an evoked or activated "mental model." In Johnson-Laird's view, images are specific—"you cannot form an image of a triangle in general, but only of a specific triangle" (157). Images may result from either perception or imagination, but "they represent perceptible features of the corresponding real-world objects" (157).

Propositions, in Johnson-Laird's framework, are a bit more difficult to delineate than models and images. A "propositional representation" is "a mental representation of a verbally expressible proposition" (155). The phrase "mental representation" is very general, but he seems to have had something more specific in mind. His theory appears to involve three levels of representation: verbal, propositional/semantic, and mental model. He said that propositions are "superficial" (162), that is, distant from models; they require less processing to construct than models (162); they "encode the linguistic form of sentences" (162); and they involve "expressions in a mental language" (164). Most revealing of all, "discourse can be represented in a proposition form close to the linguistic structure of the discourse" as opposed to "a mental model that is closer to a representation of a state of affairs" (160). The phrasing suggests that, for Johnson-Laird, propositions are at least very similar to linguistic entities. Finally, he said that "the semantics of the mental language maps these propositional representations into mental models" (164), suggesting that propositional representations are not the same as mental models, that propositions are ultimately interpretable only in terms of mental models, and that he has in mind a middle or semantic level, which he calls "the mental language."

While Johnson-Laird developed his ideas in terms of model-theoretic semantics, I would like to pursue his insights in a different direction by suggesting how models come into being. I propose that images have ontological priority and that a *model* represents the resolution of a group of images that are functionally related by virtue of representing diverse perspectives on a single process or thing. A model can be constructed from a collection of images only if the images overlap. Thus, a model is imagery of a more complex kind than an image given by peripheral perceptual experience. Perceptual images and analogous autonomous events of mental imagery always presume a particular perspective (Langacker 1990a: 12). But perceptual images must always be incomplete or fragmentary because they can only provide partial representations of complex entities, which are always presented to the mind's eye in particular orientations seen from particular points of view. When two or more images are resolved into a single more comprehensive imagistic entity, the result is a model. Because models are more complete than images, they can provide a more comprehensive basis for reasoning. So models are essentially imagistic and analogical; they are a relatively complex and complete kind of imagery. This formulation also sanctions creativity, play, and fantasy. This is because the images from which we construct models may come from autonomous mental events as well as from peripheral experience, though the latter may have developmental primacy.

This definition of model specifies no particular level of abstraction. Models themselves may undergo abstraction, so that some kind of functional skeleton or image-schema crystallizes within a rich imagistic matrix. For example, we probably form a concrete model of one or more human bodies prior to abstracting a schema of the body as a vertical tubular object with top and bottom, front and back, interior and exterior, with head, arms, and legs. The abstract body-schema may then coexist with, or within, the concrete model.

Perspective does not disappear from a model; rather a model potentially subsumes all of the perspectives provided by its contributing images. Multiple perspectives are available as part of the structure of the model. This formulation explains the findings of Stephen M. Kosslyn (1980: 43; also Finke 1989: 65) and R. N. Shepard and J. Metzler (1971) that we are able mentally to scan maps or pictures and to rotate objects in our minds. As we mentally scan or rotate a model, changing its orientation with respect to our viewing angle, we successively activate different perspectives provided by the model. Given sufficient experience with particular models and perspectives, we develop abstract perspectives that enable us to resolve neighboring or contiguous perspectives into smooth continua, so that we can rotate or scan a model without flickers or jerks, as we move from one image to the next. Similarly, we are able to construe a scene in terms of smoothly changing different points of view, walking around that vision of a new car in order to kick all four tires mentally.

This formulation of models as incorporating both concrete and abstract

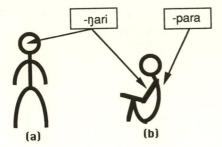

FIGURE 1. Frontal (*a*) and lateral (*b*) schematic images of human body. Frontal image is schematically vertical and lateral image is schematically concave in front and convex in rear.

imagery has important implications for language. As an example, consider the complex polysemy in body-part suffixes of the Tarascan language spoken in the state of Michoacán in southwest Mexico as described by Paul Friedrich (1979). The Tarascan suffix -*ŋari* can refer to the face and facial parts—its corporeal meanings—but it can also refer more abstractly to all kinds of flat, interior, and vertical surfaces. For example, it can refer to flat parts of the body, the inner wall of a house, the inner surface of a pot, or the face of a cliff. The suffix -*para* can refer to the back of a human or animal, but it also refers to exterior and convex surfaces such as the shaft of a penis, the exterior of a roof, and the belly of a pot (Friedrich 1979: 394–395).

Much of the polysemy in Tarascan suffixes of space can be explained if we posit the coexistence of concrete (corporeal) and abstract models of the body. In their corporeal senses of 'face' and 'back' the prefixes refer to the concrete model of the body. But an abstract model of the body as a vertical object with frontal concavity and posterior convexity (both transverse and longitudinal) provides a sense for each of the extensions away from the corporeal face and back. Such a schematic model can be derived from a prototypical image of a person leaning forward slightly, as though sitting, talking, or carrying a burden. Viewing this image from the side, we see inner concavity and exterior convexity (Figure 1). But from the front the most salient feature is verticality. It is the schematic model, with its still inherent multiple perspectives, that provides the basis for extensions of the suffixes to any interior, exterior, flat, concave, or convex surfaces. In effect, every metaphorical usage says that its target resembles some part of the body-schema taken from a particular perspective. The Tarascan example illustrates how image-schemas can be derived from models.

LAKOFF'S IDEALIZED COGNITIVE MODELS

We are now in a position to compare and evaluate linguist George Lakoff's formulation of Idealized Cognitive Models. Recall that Lakoff (1987: 68) proposed a four-part model consisting of propositional structure, image-schematic structure, metaphoric mappings, and metonymic mappings. He referred to the components of the model as "structuring principles," but in a subsequent discussion of the structure of categories underlying noun classes in the Australian Dyirbal language he seemed to raise the status of the four principles to that of "cognitive models" as follows (1987: 113–114):

> *Propositional Models* specify elements, their properties, and the relations holding among them. . . .
> *Image-schematic models* specify schematic images, such as trajectories or long, thin shapes or containers. . . .
> *Metaphoric models* are mappings from a propositional or image-schematic model in one domain to a corresponding structure in another domain. . . .
> *Metonymic models* are models of one or more of the above types, together with a function from one element of the model to another. . . .

There seems to be a rough correspondence between Lakoff's and Johnson-Laird's frameworks in that both contain imagery and propositions. Lakoff included propositions as part of idealized cognitive models, an arrangement with which I concur, while Johnson-Laird treated them as a separate kind of conceptualization from mental models.

FILLMORE'S TEXT MODELS

Charles J. Fillmore's concept of model or "text model" resembles Johnson-Laird's transitory model that is constructed out of schemas for the purpose of interpretation. His notion of schema seems to correspond more closely to the notion of a stable model such as the Idealized Cognitive Model of Lakoff. His view of text models emerged in the context of his definition of the *frame* as "the specific lexico-grammatical provisions in a given language for naming and describing the categories and relations found in schemata" (1975: 127).[6] Fillmore's full statement of frame semantics defined the relationship between linguistic frames, cognitive schemas, and models as follows:

> from experiences with real-world scenes, people acquire conceptual schemata; in the acquisition of schemata, sometimes items from

language frames are learned for labeling these and their parts; words from a language frame activate in the mind of the user the whole frame and the associated schema; the schemata can be used as tools or building blocks for assembling, on the basis of the words in a text, a text model—i.e., a model of the world that is compatible with the text. (1975: 127)

In Johnson-Laird's view, models underlie schemas and stable models can be used to construct complex models of situations. Lakoff's view of models is quite catholic in the elements that it includes (image-schemas, propositions, metaphor, metonymy), but it seems to refer mainly to stable models. In Fillmore's view, complex models of situations are composed of schemas. These differences should not bother us much, because these concepts are relative. Both models and schemas may be more or less complex and more or less abstract, so that the distinctions between them tend to blur. Images may encompass more or less of a scene/model, so that the distinction between image and model may also be hard to establish clearly. And people may possess stable cognitive models that lie dormant and unspoken for months or years, only to be remembered and deployed in appropriate situations, as when we talk about protest marches in the 1960s and the music of Bob Dylan and the Beatles, and we use our models of events to construct a picture (complex model) of a generation. So the distinctions among stable cognitive models, evoked text models, and constructed models may also be difficult to maintain.

SCHEMAS AND IMAGE-SCHEMAS

> Catch salmon. Get dollar. Go drug store. Buy first reader. Read first reader.
> Catch salmon. Get dollar. Go drug store. Buy second reader. Read second reader.
> Catch salmon. Get dollar. Go drug store. Buy third reader. Read third reader.
> Catch salmon. Get dollar. Go drug store. Buy fourth reader. Read fourth reader.
> Catch salmon. Get dollar. Go drug store. Buy typewriter.
> (attributed to Okanogan Indian C. B. Susan, in "The Juice Bringers," *Okanogan County Heritage* [Summer 1974]: 9)

The Indian joke about education above evokes by repetition a self-deprecating schema of [*catch/get/go/buy/read*]. The joke depends upon breaking the pattern, which simultaneously shatters both the schema and the ethnic stereotype. This little narrative structure is just one of many kinds of schemas (i.e., abstract conceptual patterns or images) that underlie our every word.[7] It is likely that all native knowledge of language and culture belongs to cultural schemas and that the living of culture and the speaking of language consist of schemas in action. Both cognitive linguists and cognitive anthropologists have placed great reliance on schemas, so it will be useful to see just what is commonly meant by the term (Quinn and Holland 1987; Lakoff 1988: 136).

Albert S. Bregman (1990: 43) said simply that "a schema is a mental representation of some regularity in our experience." George Lakoff (1988: 136) pointed out that "culturally defined schemas are a product of human imaginative capacities. . . ." Wallace Chafe (1990: 80–81) described schemas as "ready made models" and "prepackaged expectations and ways of interpreting," which are, for the most part, supplied by our cultures. Schemas have been defined as knowledge structures or "structured ideational kernel[s]" (Schank and Abelson 1977).

In an influential early treatment, Charles J. Fillmore (1975: 127) defined schemas quite loosely as "conceptual schemata or frameworks that are linked together in the categorization of actions, institutions, and objects. . . . as well as any of the various repertoires of categories found in contrast sets, prototypic objects, and so on." They are "conceptual frameworks" that characterize "ideal or prototypical instances of some category." By this formulation, the term *schema* would seem to cover almost any unified abstraction or conceptual prototype. Having used the term *schema* for what amount to abstract, though often complex, conceptual scenes, Fillmore (1975: 127) then used the term *frame* for "the specific lexico-grammatical provisions in a given language for naming and describing the categories and relations found in schemata." By this, I take it that he means that a frame consists of a set of words and conventional grammatical constructions that a speaker might use to evoke various aspects of a schema.

In an extensive review of the literature on schema theory, Ronald W. Casson (1983: 430) determined that schemas are "conceptual abstractions that mediate between stimuli received by the sense organs and behavioral responses" and that they "serve as the basis for all human information processing, e.g. perception and comprehension, categorization and planning, recognition and recall, and problem-solving and decision-making." He noted that schemas occur at differing levels of abstraction and that they are "organic wholes comprised of parts that are oriented both to the whole and to other parts" and characterized them as autonomous, automatic, generally unconscious, non-purposive, and irreflexive. Contrary to Casson, others have argued that schemas may be purposive, in the sense of having, as part of their conceptualization, processes and end states with affective values and motivations (D'Andrade 1984; Strauss 1992a; Strauss and Quinn 1994); and they may be reflexive, in the sense of involving operations that can only be defined by reference to their own initial states, as in the motion implied in the expression "fall over" (Lakoff 1987: 442–443, 1988: 147).

For Langacker (1990a), the term *schema* seemed to refer to any abstraction, including abstract symbols. For example, he said that grammatical categories such as noun, verb, adjective, and adverb are "maximally schematic" both phonologically and semantically: "A noun, for instance, is claimed to instantiate the schema [[THING]/[X]], and a verb the schema [[PROCESS]/[Y]], where [THING] and [PROCESS] are abstract notions [described elsewhere], and [X] and [Y] are highly schematic phonological structures . . ." (1990a: 17).

While others have presented definitions of schemas, Leonard Talmy (1983: 225) developed a somewhat more complex notion of *schematization*, which he defined as "a process that involves the systematic selection of certain aspects of a referent scene to represent the whole, while disregarding the remaining aspects." The process has "little recognized generic properties," which include "idealization, abstraction, and a topological type of plasticity, as well as a disjunct character, which permits alternative schematizations of a single scene" (1983: 226). Like Langacker, he contrasted schematization with specificity and noted that a speaker must decide at which level of schematization to represent a scene, while a listener must deploy an "image-constructing process" that interacts with speaker's selection. Talmy's notion of schematization seems to include Langacker's notion of construal. *Idealization* refers to the process by which a particular schema is associated with or "applied to" a "full, repletely detailed referent" (1983: 258). It includes "the process by which familiar objects, in all their bulk and physicality, are differentially 'boiled down' to match ascribed schemas." My use of *frame* as a verb is equivalent to Talmy's *idealization*. He noted that idealization as a cognitive process was not well understood, but it would probably turn out to resemble "processes of Gestalt-psychological functioning or those operative in the drawing of stick-figures by children" (1983: 259).

Talmy regarded abstraction as a complementary process to idealization: "While idealization involves finding within a physical object the delineations that correspond to a particular schema, abstraction involves ignoring the rest of the object" (1983: 261). To illustrate this point, he contrasted two expressions containing the preposition *across*: *across the river* and *across the tennis court*. Both expressions presuppose a schema that transverses two opposite edges. The fact that a tennis court has two additional side boundaries, while a river is unbounded in the up- and downstream directions is ignored in the schema that governs the usage of *across*, thus allowing the same term to characterize both scenes.

Claudia Strauss (1992a: 3), who studied career orientations and other units of behavior and discourse that are more comprehensive than those normally taken up by linguists such as Talmy, proposed a very broad interpretation of schemas as "learned, internalized patterns of thought-feeling that mediate both the interpretation of ongoing experience and the reconstruction of memories." She noted that schemas organize our perceptions, provide bases for interpreting discourse, and have "directive force" and "embedded goals" (1992b: 198). Schemas are organized in hierarchies, so that love and success, for example, are higher than "joining a dating service or attending a job fair" (1992a: 3). And schemas, including those that constitute self-concepts, are "energized by memories of powerful life experiences" (1992a: 14). Similarly, Stephen Tyler (1978: 245–246, 248) opined that our understandings of the world "are always unities of fact and feeling," though for Tyler schemas are nothing more than commonplace knowledge.[8]

A narrower interpretation of schemas was proposed over a decade ago by Robert de Beaugrande and Wolfgang Dressler (1981: 90–91). They distinguished among *frames* as "global patterns that contain common-sense knowledge about some central concept, e.g. 'piggy banks,' 'birthday parties,' etc.," *schemas* as "global patterns of events and states in ordered sequences linked by time proximity and causality," *plans* as goal-directed patterns of events and states, and *scripts* as "stabilized plans called up very frequently to specify the roles of participants and their expected actions." Thus, their notion of schema is more restrictive than those linguistic and anthropological notions that would include some image-schemas and proposition-schemas that are either static or telic and not necessarily linked in ordered sequences.

Schemas may or may not be imageable and available to conscious inspection. For Mark Johnson (1987: 103), image-schemas are "structures of embodied understanding" that are neither rich images (mental pictures) nor abstract propositional networks. Lakoff (1987: 420) spoke of image-schemas that structure images but "cannot [themselves] be imaged concretely"; however, Naomi Quinn (1991), citing Lakoff in personal communication, reported that he intended for image-schemas to be imageable. Quinn (1991: 70) held that schemas underlying the use of metaphor may be "non-imagic."

Given these diverse, and somewhat inconsistent, constructions of the schema concept, I propose that we regard schemas as organic (in Casson's sense) abstractions that subsume conceptualizations that are more specific and more readily imagined as projections into consciousness (whatever that ineffable entity may ultimately prove to be). Those schemas of inter-mediate abstraction that are readily imagined, perhaps as iconic images, and clearly related to physical (embodied) or social experiences may be termed image-schemas. Schemas in general are units of relatively abstract imagery. Schemas of human behavior, and models built from them, may have intrinsic goal direction and affective content, and, like other kinds of schemas, they may be organized in networks or conceptual hierarchies.

Vocabularies relate to schemas, so that in a particular instance of us-age each word corresponds to a part of some schema or a perspective on a schema. A word must be defined relative to its schema. For ex-ample, while *ground* and *land* may be used to describe a piece of dry earth, *ground* belongs to a vertical schema that divides *sky* from *ground*, whereas *land* belongs to a horizontal schema that divides *land* from *sea*. The example is from Fillmore (1984: 89), who argued that "to know the meaning of a word is necessarily to have access to at least some of the details of the associated schematization."

To understand a word as its speaker intended or to use it appropriately, it is necessary to know the schema or schemas to which it belongs in a particular context of use. Words evoke systems of meaning, and often, as in metaphor, they evoke two or more systems at once. Whole vocabularies pertaining to the landscape, the body, kinship, and other topics all have their own underlying schemas. Along such schemas, words and idiomatic phrases are distributed more or less systematically.

In many languages, kinship terms can be neatly organized on schemas structured by generation, parental versus filial relations, relative age of siblings, or side of the family. During the 1950s and 1960s, anthropolo-gists made great efforts to describe kinship terminologies in hopes of find-ing the rules by which native speakers used their vocabularies appropri-ately.[9] These findings were presented in elaborate diagrams that students in introductory anthropology classes typically found painfully tedious and obscure. Nevertheless, some of these researchers were concerned that the systems that they described should have psychological reality. They were seeking not merely to find order in data and reduce kinship to formal logic, but to discover underlying native cognitive schemas. They showed that the meaning of a term such as *brother* cannot be understood apart from the meaning of *sister*, which has the same values on the dimensions of generation and parental affiliation but differs on the dimension of sex. In this respect their work should be regarded as an important and early contribution to cognitive linguistics.

Johnson (1987: 13) argued that certain very fundamental *image-schemas*, such as that of the *container* and that of *force*, originate in the structure of bodily experiences received early in life. That is, they are preconceptual, kinesthetic, and embodied. The container schema, for example, originates in our understanding of our own bodies as physical containers and is subsequently extended to interpret much of our daily experience metaphorically. For example, when you awaken, "You gradually emerge *out* of your stupor, pull yourself *out* from under the covers, climb *into* your robe, stretch *out* your limbs, and walk in a daze *out* of your bedroom and *into* your bathroom" (Johnson 1987: 30–31). The force schema originates in our bodily experiences with the movement of objects through space. To the container and force schemas, Lakoff (1987, 1988) added the schemas of *part-whole*, *link*, and *source-path-goal*. These physically grounded and embodied schemas may integrate imagery from both visual and kinesthetic modalities and from both perceptual and motor systems.

There are other kinds of imagery that might lay claim to something like the importance of the image-schemas already mentioned, though they may lack the element of physical embodiment through repetitive experience. Perhaps *animacy* itself, or *animate being*, should also be regarded as a fundamental image-schema. Certainly the animacy of persons and animals around them is something that all humans encounter in earliest infancy. Many languages, such as those of the Athabascan and Bantu language families discussed in Chapter 6, have grammatical forms whose proper use requires determination of whether a subject is animate.

Another candidate for the status of image-schema is the human face. Research is currently being conducted to determine whether the human face can be regarded as conceptually innate (Ellis 1986). Researchers at Carnegie Mellon University found evidence that higher visual centers in the brain are specialized for the recognition of faces and of living things in general (Farah, McMullen, and Meyer 1991: 191). They speculated that faces and living things may require more configurational or holistic encoding than non-living things. Whether or not one accepts the innateness of the human face as a cognitive schema, the face is such a pervasive part of our daily experience that it would seem a good candidate for the status of an image-schema.[10] The use of the face, and other body-parts, in metaphorical expressions is widespread, perhaps universal, among the languages of the world. In many American Indian languages it would be difficult to express yourself without using anatomical metaphors because they occupy well-entrenched frames in the grammar (Friedrich 1979: 341–401; Brugman 1983; Palmer 1990).

Event-schemas constitute a specific type. J. Mandler (1984: 14) found little agreement in how scholars define the term *schema*, but she defined an event-schema as generalized knowledge about "what will happen in a given situation and often the order in which the individual events will take place." Event-schemas are organized in hierarchies from the general to the specific. In her view, event-schemas underlie scripts and stories. Their hierarchical structure is constructed of part-whole relations rather than kind-of relations. It is therefore a collection rather than an instance of class-inclusion. The parts within a unit are connected in temporal relations, which may be causal, enabling, conventional, or arbitrary (optional). Mandler noted the similarity of event-schemas to scene-schemas, which are also collections having part-whole hierarchical structure, and the conflation of scene with event in the restaurant script of Roger Schank and Robert Abelson (1977). In one instance, Mandler appeared to assimilate configurational visual schemas to event-schemas, as when she gave as an example of an event-schema: "a face will almost surely have a pair of eyes." This would make sense from a subjective stance, because a complex visual presentation may, in some contexts, be perceived sequentially and thus constitute a sequential perceptual event. However, Mandler's definition seems to say little more than that event-schemas are abstractions having constituent structures linked in time or in space. This seems compatible with previously mentioned formulations, that schemas are "mental representations of some regularity in our experience," "prepackaged expectations and ways of interpreting," "frameworks that are linked together," or "units of relatively abstract imagery which constitute cognitive models." I will use the term *scenario* for what Mandler calls an event-schema.

IMAGE-SCHEMA TRANSFORMATIONS AND POLYSEMY

We have the cognitive ability selectively to focus attention on different components of complex mental images, to consider them from different perspectives, to zoom in and zoom out mentally, to trace paths through them, to turn them over in our minds, and to experience them as pro-

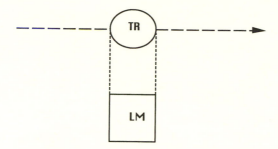

FIGURE 2. *The plane flew over.* From George Lakoff, *Women, Fire and Dangerous Things* (1987: 422). © 1987 by The University of Chicago. Reprinted with the permission of the University of Chicago Press.

cesses, that is, to play them back in our minds and view them at different phases. This sort of construal and reconstrual probably applies to all kinds of imagery, from complex social scenarios to elementary spatial schemas, such as *container*, *link*, and *source-path-goal*. The relations that arise between various construals of image-schemas have been called "Image-schema Transformations" (Lakoff 1987: 440–444, 1988: 144–149).

Lakoff argued that image-schema transformation plays an important role in polysemy, that is, the process by which words acquire multiple meanings. The example of the English preposition *over*, researched by Claudia Brugman (1988) and summarized by Lakoff (1987: 418–440), is instructive. According to Lakoff, the central sense of *over* combines elements of both *above* and *across*, as shown in Figure 2, which represents a plane (TR = trajector), whatever the plane is flying over (LM = landmark), and the path along which it moves (arrow).[11]

The figure appears to be quite elementary, but it actually contains a number of features that are important to consider from the standpoint of image-transformations. Lakoff (1987: 419) pointed out that the landmark is unspecified and that the path extends all the way across the landmark. Thus, PATH, TRAJECTOR, and LANDMARK are all important elements of this schema. This is a particularly schematic image, in part because it is left unspecified as to whether there is contact between trajector and landmark. In Lakoff's (1987: 420) view, because contact is left unspecified, this is a schema "that can not itself be imaged concretely, but which structures images." In my view, whether or not the schema for *over* can be imaged concretely is an empirical question; it is possible that either the contact schema or the non-contact schema could serve as an imageable prototype.

In one more specific variant of the *over* schema, the landmark may be

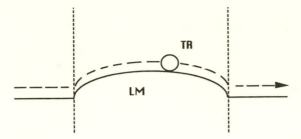

FIGURE 3. *Sam walked over the hill.* From Lakoff (1987: 422). © 1987 by The University of Chicago. Reprinted with the permission of the University of Chicago Press.

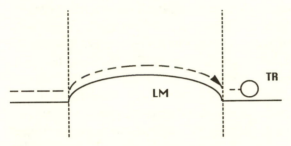

FIGURE 4. *Sam lives over the hill.* From Lakoff (1987: 423). © 1987 by The University of Chicago. Reprinted with the permission of the University of Chicago Press.

both a vertical and an extended obstacle with the trajector in contact with the landmark, as in Figure 3. Another variant (Figure 4) shows how the sense of *over* can undergo an image-schema transformation, that is, a different construal, by narrowing focus and profiling just the end point of the *source-path-goal* schema. Lakoff (1987: 442) explained that the *path focus ↔ end-point focus* transformation is natural because "it is a common experience to follow the path of a moving object until it comes to rest, and then to focus on where it is." Johnson (1987: 26) covered much the same ground, listing the following transformations:

a) *Path-focus to end-point-focus.* Follow, in imagination, the path of a moving object, and then focus on the point where it comes to rest, or where it will come to rest.

b) *Multiplex to mass.* Imagine a group of several objects. Move away (in your mind) from the group until the cluster of individuals starts to become a single homogeneous mass. Now move back down to the point where the mass turns once again into a cluster.

c) *Following a trajectory*. As we perceive a continuously moving object, we can mentally trace the path it has traversed or the trajectory it is about to traverse.

d) *Superimposition*. Imagine a large sphere and a small cube. Increase the size of the sphere until the cube can fit inside it. Now reduce the size of the cube and put it inside the sphere.

Lakoff (1987: 442–443, 1988: 147) listed the following four image-schema transformations, which do not include Johnson's category of superimposition:

path-focus ↔ *end-point focus*,
multiplex ↔ *mass*,
zero-dimensional trajector ↔ *one-dimensional trajector* [same as
  Johnson's *following a trajectory*],
non-reflexive ↔ *reflexive* [not listed by Johnson].

Image-schema transformations can result in categories of considerable complexity. The image-schemas in Figures 3 and 4 are linked to the even more schematic concept in Figure 2. Lakoff listed and diagramed many other fascinating variations of *over*, including the following:

The guards were posted *all over* the hill. (multiplex)
I walked *all over* the hill. (multiplex-path)
Roll the log *over*. (reflexive)
I *over*ate. (excess)

Lakoff raised a crucial question regarding the significance of linked schemas and image-schema transformations: whether the information necessary to interpret a word like *over* in its various schematic senses is part of the meaning of *over* itself or is instead contributed by the context of usage. Consider the sentence *Sam walked over the hill* diagramed in Figure 3. By one interpretation of this sentence, the word *over* contributes only the very schematic sense diagramed in Figure 2. The additional information that the landmark is both vertical and extended is contributed by the indirect object, *hill*. The additional information that there is contact with the landmark is contributed by the verb, *walked*. Since walking requires an extended landmark, that information may also be contributed by the verb. Because, by this interpretation, little of the information necessary to interpret this sentence is contributed by the word *over*, Lakoff called this the *minimal specification interpretation*.

But Lakoff argued that the minimal specification interpretation of *over* is incorrect. In his view, all of the related schematic senses of *over* are part of its conventional meaning and together they form a chain of meanings. He called this the *maximal specification interpretation.* As shown in Figure 4, the example *Sam lives over the hill* has end-point focus. Lakoff (1987: 420) argued that "the end-point focus is not added by anything in the sentence, neither *hill*, nor *lives*, nor *Sam.*" This sense of *over* with end-point focus is one step in the chain of meaning away from that of the *over* in *Sam walked over the hill*, which lacks end-point focus. Since end-point focus can only be added to senses of the preposition that have extended landmarks, then *over* must have this as one of its senses. The chain of meaning goes from (1) to (2) to (3) to (4) in the following expressions:

(1) over (most schematic sense)
   The plane flew over.
(2) over, extended landmark, contact
   Sam drove over the bridge.
(3) over, vertical extended landmark, contact
   Sam walked over the hill.
(4) over, vertical extended landmark, contact, end-point focus
   Sam lives over the hill.

The schematic of *over* in the first line of each of the expressions (2) through (4) adds detail to the schematic information in the expression that precedes it. Logically, the schema for each is an instance of the preceding, fully compatible with it. Such a linkage is called an *instance link.* Links in which elements of meaning are shared, but there is a conflict in one or more specifications, could then be termed *similarity links.*[12] Thus, there would be a similarity link between (2) and (5), where the difference occurs on the dimension of contact:

(2) over, extended landmark, contact
   Sam drove over the bridge.
(5) over, extended landmark, no contact
   The bird flew over the yard.

The instance link corresponds to what Langacker (1987: 66–71, 81) called a "schematic relationship," in which the "schematic semantic unit" is specified in greater detail by "instantiations" or "elaborations." The instance link would be one of "full schematicity." The similarity link would be one of "partial schematicity," which "involves conflicting specifications" (1987: 92). Partial schematicity underlies semantic extension and prototype categorization in which "a speaker judges class membership through a perception of similarity that permits him to construe a [conceptual] structure as an extension from the prototype" (1987: 69).[13] It corresponds to what Robert A. Randall (1976) termed the "memory association model" (explained below).

If we accept the full specification interpretation of the meaning of *over*, then it is clear that the preposition can have many conventional meanings. *Over* provides an example of polysemy, which is "the fact that individual words and morphemes typically have many meanings that are systematically related to one another" (Lakoff 1988: 140). From this we can conclude that the conceptual processes and entities that explain polysemy must include instance links, similarity links, and image-schema transformations, to use Lakoff's terminology, or complex categories and image construal, to use Langacker's.

Lakoff's formulation of the problem was criticized by Hoyt Alverson (1991), who objected to what he saw as Lakoff's characterization of image-schemas as "schematic diagrams of actualistically conceived geometric configurations." Alverson argued instead that they should be seen as "intentional-significance bestowing devices." Such devices carve out portions of a pan-humanly experienced scene that contains "(1) propinquity; (2) distance; (3) demarcation or spatial relationship; (4) the dial, orbit, or trajectory of sun and moon, whose light is both a point and a sweep or array; (5) cloud cover; (6) altitude; (7) courses of movement/travel through the trajectory; (8) barriers to sensory or locomotor access; and (9) behavior of entities occupying this scene" (1991: 112). The portion carved out by the English preposition *over* is "the experience of viewing a point from below that radiates out and covers a surface and is in motion such as to describe a course, part of the trajectory of which is an arc" (1991: 113–114). Alverson (1991: 114) argued that "beholding this scene can generate all the components-of-schemas that Lakoff's diagrams can generate, and many more."

Apparently unaware of Alverson's criticism, Robert B. Dewell (1993: abstract) also reanalyzed *over*, concluding that the key to its analysis is "a curved arc-trajectory in the central schema, replacing the flat 'across' trajectory presumed by Brugman and Lakoff." He asserted that "the arc-path schema provides the basis for explaining all of the variants of OVER using natural image-schema transformations (and metaphors)." So Alverson's formulation based on universal experience of the sun's arc is independently supported by Dewell's findings that usage of *over* is governed by an arc-path schema.

If Alverson's formulation is to be accepted, however, it may need some qualification. Given a primal scene, probably no language provides conventional expressions for all possible construals or transformations that could be generated from it. The various usages associated with the schema tend to cluster around a few image-schemas or transformations. Describing the grammar of spatial relations, then, requires the description of culturally specific image-schemas (Langacker 1990a; Occhi, Palmer, and Ogawa 1992). In the case of *over*, these would include such notions as *central region of arc* (*flying over*), *downward trajectory* (*Sam fell over the cliff*), *upward trajectory* (*The sun came up over the mountains*), *resulting state* (*Where is Sam?—He went over the bridge*), *subjective path* (*Sam lives over the bridge*), and so on (Dewell 1993). While the converging approaches of Alverson and Dewell represent significant modifications to Lakoff's and Brugman's theory of *over*, they are essentially refinements rather than refutations.

FEATURES VERSUS IMAGE-SCHEMAS IN NAVAJO SPATIAL TERMS

The distinction between feature and image-schema may, like much else in language, be a matter of degree (Langacker 1987: 14). The problem of distinguishing between them can be illustrated by Rik Pinxten et al.'s (1983) study of spatial concepts in Navajo. He defined a "Universal Frame of Reference (UFOR)," which includes 145 entries pertaining to spatial concepts. Many entries, such as "Near, separate, contiguous," "Part/whole," and "Bordering, bounding," have the look of features.

I suspect that native speakers may, consciously or unconsciously, arrive at some of the same abstractions, which may constitute real semantic connections within schematic domains of expression such as "nearness." Even so, Pinxten may have been striving to establish categories at a level of conceptualization that holds minimal significance for ordinary language. If the simple, but highly general, abstractions that he discovered are in fact abstractions from richer image-schemas having shape and dynamism, then we might learn more about language and cognition by investigating image-schemas, such as *pathway* and *container*, rather than highly abstract features, such as *part/whole*. Langacker (1990a: 55) argued that, even if a fully schematic sense of a complex category should be found, it would not suffice as a definition, because "it would also be schematic for indefinitely many values that [the category] happen[s] not to have" and "it would fail to provide an explicit account of the facts of the language, in particular the range of conventionally established senses and usages characteristic of these morphemes." In fact, many of the minimal units that Pinxten identified in Navajo appear to relate to spatial image-schemas. For example, the feature distinctions *internal/external* and *center/periphery* could subsume the container image-schema. As with other fuzzy or gradient categories in cognitive linguistics, it is not necessary to hold that there is a clear demarcation between unitary concepts (features) on the one hand and image-schemas with abstract shapes or forms on the other. There are likely to be intermediate levels of conceptualization.

It may be that both the discrete unitary (feature) and the image-schematic levels of abstraction are important to our understanding of language. They may in fact be complementary rather than opposed. Features may function to enable speakers to connect image-schemas and establish dimensions of contrast between categories, such as the contrast on the dimension of sex in Dyirbal Australian noun classes *bayi* and *balan* (Lakoff 1987). The full set of Navajo spatial units may represent a kind of metaschema or a metacognitive model of space in Navajo. Such a model might be useful, perhaps even necessary, for understanding the Navajo use of spatial language, but it is very likely insufficient. The Navajo language of space probably also requires elaboration of the metamodel by well-formed spatial image-schemas.

SCENARIOS AND SCRIPTS

On March 8, 1991, Army Specialist Anthony Riggs of Las Vegas was murdered while visiting his wife in Detroit shortly after his return from the Persian Gulf. His death, at first attributed to random street violence, caused a public outcry, but it was later alleged that Riggs was shot by his brother-in-law. His son, Mason, made the following statement: "I just couldn't see someone killing a man over a Nissan Sentra. I could maybe see it if it was an expensive luxury car. . . . If someone wanted a car like that they would have stuck a gun up to him and drove off. They wouldn't have killed him. And when they found the car about a mile away, nothing was gone. It wasn't even stripped." [14]

The quote describes two scenarios, one believable, one doubtful. The doubtful scenario goes *someone wants an inexpensive car, sticks gun up to owner, drives off, strips car*. The believable one goes *someone wants an expensive luxury car, shoots owner, drives off, strips car*. Fortunately or not, the evidence of such conventional behavioral sequences is all around us. Scenarios arouse our expectations, pattern our days, and provide the frameworks for interpreting experiences. A *scenario* is a culturally defined sequence of actions, a story-schema. I will treat the terms *scenario* and *script* as synonyms. In their famous book *Scripts, Plans, Goals and Understanding: An Inquiry into Human Knowledge Structures*, which first called the attention of psychologists and computer scientists to the scriptlike quality of thought, Roger Schank and Robert Abelson (1977: 41) defined a script as "a predetermined, stereotyped sequence of actions that defines a well-known situation." A script may be a song, a prayer, a dinner, a wedding, a manual technique, a robbery-murder, or any other frame where a sequence of ideas is well defined. According to these authors, "A human understander comes equipped with thousands of scripts. He uses these scripts almost without thinking" (1977: 68). Scenarios are like this.

Besides a temporal dimension, scenarios have something that most image-schemas lack: contingency relations with other schemas. Michael Agar and Jerry R. Hobbs (1985) described "schemata" for hustling that fit what I have called a scenario. The hustling schemata represent a burglar's understanding of how to avoid arrest by avoiding events that would lead to arrest: "to maintain his goal of avoiding arrest, a hustler can avoid talking about or doing hustles. If he hustles or talks about it, then he can try to avoid observation. If he is observed, he can try to prevent the information from reaching the police" (1985: 428). A hierarchy of simple scenarios is embedded in a causal chain. Two simple scenarios, (1) *let a do x* and (2) *a talk about x*, are "chunked" into a third, (3) *a draw attention to x*. Scenario (3) belongs to a causal scenario (4), which consists of the chain (3) *a draw attention to x* and (5) *b observe x* and (6) *b inform police [about]* and (7) *a cause police arrest a*.[15] Thus, (7) is contingent on (6), which is contingent on (5), which is contingent on (3) which may be realized as (1), (2), or both.

Scenarios, then, are simply social schemas and models that come with action imagery, contingencies, and intrinsic emotional values. Like other concepts, they may belong to complex categories, including hierarchies and category chains.

BASIC CATEGORIES

If there exists a scale of abstraction from immediately and peripherally perceived, concrete images to image-schemas, then somewhere in between lies a level that has been called *basic*. Lakoff (1987: 269) pointed out that this level is defined by functions; it is the level at which "people function most efficiently and successfully in dealing with discontinuities in the natural environment." It is the level of *physical experience* at which "we accurately distinguish tigers from elephants, chairs from tables, roses from daffodils, asparagus from broccoli, copper from lead, etc."

Lower-level categories are harder to distinguish, and, moving to a higher level, say that of a bird compared to the basic-level categories robin and ostrich, it is harder to form a concrete image. Linguistically, the basic level of categorization is represented by names for basic colors, qualities, plants, animals, substances, objects and actions—red, white, and blue; tall, short, and hard; lily, rose, and spruce; dog, cat, and horse; running, walking, and eating (Rosch 1978: 45; Lakoff 1987: 269–271).

But what of categories in the social domain, such as mother, father, brother, sister, student, teacher, team, gang, and ghost? All of these social and fantasy categories seem intuitively and by virtue of common usage to be just as conceptually basic as the foregoing physical objects and qualities. The categories dog and cat clearly correspond to structures or discontinuities present in nature. Priests, teams, gangs, and ghosts are just as clearly cultural constructs. Eleanor Rosch (1978: 30) defined "the most basic level of categorization" as "the most inclusive (abstract) level at which the categories can mirror the structure of attributes perceived in the world." If we are to accept the social constructs as basic, then we must put the emphasis upon "perceived," because such categories as ghosts do not have corresponding entities in the empirical world. But, then, Rosch did not say the "real world," so perhaps we can stretch her definition enough to include objects and their attributes in fantasy worlds. Lakoff (1988: 133) provided a useful list of properties of the basic level of categorization:

—It is the level at which category members have similarly perceived overall shapes.
—It is the highest level at which a single mental image can reflect the entire category.
—It is the highest level at which a person uses similar motor programs for interacting with category members.
—It is the level at which subjects are fastest at identifying category members.
—It is the level with the most commonly used labels for category members.
—It is the level first named and understood by children.
—It is the first level to enter the lexicon of a language in the course of history.

—It is the level with the shortest primary lexemes.
—It is the level at which terms are used in neutral contexts.
—It is the level at which most of our knowledge is organized.
—It is the level at which most culturally-determined functions for objects are defined.[16]

Notice that Lakoff's final criterion, which depends upon "culturally-determined functions," seems to provide a means of including social and fantasy categories.

Where I originally posited a scale of abstraction, we now have four candidates for distinct levels: concrete images (immediately perceived, peripheral, rich in detail), basic-level images (possessing detail sufficient to characterize a functional complex), image-schemas (relatively abstract, but retaining important patterns and often still imageable), and features (highly abstract and probably not imageable). While all of these concepts are useful for characterizing images, there is yet insufficient research to conclude that basic categories segregate out discontinuously from image-schemas as a distinct basic level in all human languages and cultures and in all conceptual domains. It is quite possible that, in some domains in all languages, there is a smooth continuum from basic images to image-schemas, or that the pattern of discontinuity varies among cultures and domains of culture.

PROTOTYPES

The modern usage of the term *prototype* owes much to the work of Eleanor Rosch (1978: 36), who defined the prototypes of categories as "the clearest cases of category membership defined operationally by people's judgements of goodness of membership in the category." [17] The theoretical notion of prototype is designed to account for the fact that humans easily classify a large number of things into categories that have no clear boundaries. Rosch (1978: 36) pointed out that even though categories often lack clear boundaries two categories can be clearly distinguished if the viewer emphasizes their structure, by which she meant the cluster of attributes that correlate most strongly. Thus, "two neighbors know on whose property they are standing without exact demarcation of the boundary line" (1978: 36). In her view, this special cluster of attributes does not, apparently, constitute the prototype, but it provides a standard for identifying prototypes. Thus, categories have family resemblances among members rather than discrete boundaries with precisely defined membership. Rosch (1978: 44) concluded that abstract superordinate categories such as furniture "may not be imageable per se apart from imaging individual items in the category." Of course, this leaves open the possibility that some categories, such as *bird*, may have a schema that is imageable apart from the image of its prototype.[18]

Donald A. Norman (1988: 188) defined a prototype as an image, more or less abstract, that averages similar experiences and "governs interpretations and actions related to any other event that seems similar." He pointed out that, even if there are a thousand similar events, "we would tend to remember them as one composite prototype" (1988: 188). The end result is that instead of a thousand memories or images we have only one, to which we may compare all subsequent experiences and ideas from other domains of thinking. Since the objects that we experience most frequently or saliently are coded as basic categories and since the objects that we experience most frequently are likely to emerge as prototypes through the process of averaging, it should come as no surprise that basic categories may serve as prototypes for their superordinate categories. Where no dominant form is available to evoke the formation of a prototype, the average will serve. The prototype may be thought of as a relatively salient and entrenched member of a family of images. It may denote either a very typical form or an average of the family.

Our interest in prototypes goes beyond the task of naming the clearest cases. The notion of prototype is central to Langacker's theory of complex categories (discussed in a subsequent section). Langacker (1990a: 3) pointed out that the meaning of a lexical item cannot be reduced to its prototype and that "not every lexical item has a single, clearly determined prototype."

GRADIENT IMAGERY AND BASIC COLOR TERMS

Basic color terms illustrate basic categories and prototype categorization, but they illustrate something new as well: a kind of category whose instances are all located somewhere on a gradient, which is a dimension that has scalar values. Studies of basic color terms have paid most attention to gradients of hue and brightness because the achromatic colors of white and black plus the unique hues of yellow, red, blue, and green are thought to be fixed in value by the biology of color perception.[19] These fixed perceptual categories provide a model for understanding how linguistic categories may be limited or governed by biological constants. Experiments that use basic color terms to demonstrate universals of color naming offer a challenge to cultural linguistics, which sees linguistic categories as largely, though not entirely, culturally defined. In this section I will show how cultural linguistics accommodates universals of color naming.

THE EVOLUTION OF BASIC COLOR TERMS

During the late 1960s and the 1970s, anthropologists made a concerted effort to discover semantic universals in the naming of colors, plants, and animals.[20] For example, Brent Berlin and Paul Kay proposed the existence of eleven basic color categories (Berlin and Kay 1969; Berlin 1970). After comparing over one hundred languages, they stated a series of generalizations that govern the order of appearance of color terms in an evolutionary sequence. These same generalizations also govern the possibility of a particular language having terms for certain basic colors. For example, they proposed that "all languages have color terms for black and white," and "if a language has 3 terms, the terms will be black, white and red" (Berlin 1970: 8). Eventually, they and their colleagues reconstructed two possible evolutionary sequences through which, they theorized, all languages must pass. Although a language need not have all the terms, it must not skip terms that lie along the pathway. At the next stage, a language would add either green or yellow, which was then followed by yellow or green, respectively. Thus, there are two branches to the evolutionary pathway: green --> yellow and yellow --> green. Next would come blue, followed by brown. Finally, a language might add purple, pink, orange, or gray.

The sequence fails to account for a few languages that name a composite category of YELLOW-GREEN (all of YELLOW plus all of GREEN), but it does describe the patterns occurring in the majority of languages studied. The predictable appearance of combinations of basic color terms in many of the world's languages was thought to reflect evolutionary sequences by which categories come to be named.

Examination of their theory must start with their definition of "basic color terms," which is worth examining for its linguistic limitations:

> Basic color terms were defined as those (a) which are monolexemic (unlike *reddish-blue*); (b) whose signification is not included in that of any other term (unlike *crimson* and *vermilion*, both of which are kinds of *red*); (c) whose application is not restricted to a narrow class of objects (unlike *blond* and *roan*); and (d) which are relatively salient as evidenced in frequent and general use (unlike *puce* and *mauve*). (Kay and McDaniel 1978: 612)

The definition excludes much of what might be regarded as normal color vocabulary, particularly the compound terms, such as *reddish-blue*.

Thus, our understanding of basic color term evolution does not provide a very comprehensive account of color term patterning or evolution.

In the literature of neurophysiology Kay and McDaniel found strong evidence for four categories of neural response: red, green, yellow, and blue. Notice that these are the four colors that succeed black and white in the proposed evolutionary sequence of color terms. Terms that occur late in the evolutionary sequence are found at wavelengths where primary colors overlap in category membership. "Brown is found in the region where *yellow* and *black* overlap, pink where *red* and *white* overlap, purple where *red* and *blue* overlap, orange where *red* and *yellow* overlap, and gray where *black* and *white* overlap" (Kay and McDaniel 1978: 632). Many languages have a basic color term that can be translated as blue-green. The blue-green color image is commonly assigned the symbol GRUE by researchers in this field. One of Kay and McDaniel's most interesting findings is that such terms may have two color foci—green and blue—which are both regarded by native consultants as better instances of blue-green than is the color region in between them.

Kay and McDaniel emphasized that basic color categories should not be regarded as discrete features with reliable and precise boundaries. Instead they found that consultants could select "best examples" of color terms that represented color foci, eleven in all, which they regarded as the primary referents of the basic terms. Otherwise, color categories behave like "fuzzy sets" with continuously graded degrees of membership. Consultants can reliably place color foci on a color chart such as the one included in this book but they are less reliable in placing the boundaries of color categories. Thus, it seems fair to regard the color foci as prototypes of the basic color categories.

Kay, Berlin, and Merrifield (1991) published additional observations on color naming systems based upon the testing of 25 speakers in each of 111 languages in the World Color Survey. They found that where basic color terms name composite categories ([RED + YELLOW], [RED + YELLOW + WHITE], etc.) only certain combinations are possible and these are distributed in an orderly fashion involving only contiguous categories on a two-dimensional continuum of hues and lightness (Figure 5). Note that a composite category such as [RED + YELLOW] extends over the entire color space occupied by both RED and YELLOW. It is not the same as ORANGE, which Kay suggested calling a "compromise category."[21] In Figure 5, the diagonal dashed line indicates a boundary that cannot be crossed in forming composite categories named with basic color terms. Composite categories include only components connected by

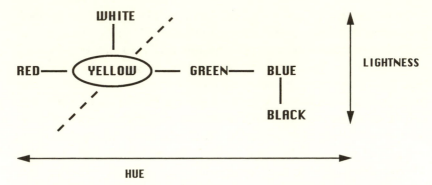

FIGURE 5. Visual and linguistic relations among FNR [Fundamental Neural Response] categories. From Paul Kay, Brent Berlin, and William Merrifield, "Biocultural Implications of Systems of Color Naming." Reproduced by permission of the American Anthropological Association from *Journal of Linguistic Anthropology* 1: 1, June 1991. Not for sale or further reproduction.

unbroken associational chains. Thus, [RED + YELLOW] and [WHITE + YELLOW] are possible, but not [RED + WHITE], because the components are non-contiguous, nor [RED + YELLOW + GREEN], because the union crosses the diagonal line. Category [GREEN + BLUE] is possible, but not [GREEN + BLACK], because the components are non-contiguous. The authors formalized this observation as the *Composite Category Rule*. In data from 111 languages, they found eight of the possible nine combinations and no exceptions to the rule. Although the rule would permit it, they found no instances in which a basic color term designated the four-part composite category [YELLOW + GREEN + BLUE + BLACK]. They were unable to explain why this composite has not been found.

These scholars appear to have discovered universal constraints on the naming of colors with basic terms. These basic terms symbolize very basic images: the focal categories, presumably the same as the neural response perceptual categories, and some of their combinations. Their findings suggest that basic terms for composite categories based on gradients are restricted in their semantic content to images that reside near one another on perceptual or cognitive continua.

THE CULTURAL CONSTRUCTION OF COLOR CATEGORIES: CONKLIN AND WIERZBICKA

Kay, Berlin, and Merrifield (1991) treated basic color terms as though they involve only the attributes of brightness, hue (the spectral value), and saturation (intensity), but Harold C. Conklin (1964) pointed out as early as 1955 that basic color categories may not be reducible to such a simple schema. In a study of the folk botany of the Hanunóo, who speak a Malayo-Polynesian language, he found that basic color terms, which he termed "Level I," also had "correlates beyond what is usually considered the range of chromatic differentiation, and that are associated with non-linguistic phenomena in the external environment" (1964: 191). His Level I terms included the following, where *ma-* 'exhibiting or having' is an attribute formative (1964: 190):

1. *(ma)bi:ru* 'relative darkness (of shade of color); blackness' (black)
2. *(ma)lagti?* 'relative lightness (or tint of color); whiteness' (white)
3. *(ma)rara?* 'relative presence of red; redness' (red)
4. *(ma)latuy* 'relative presence of light greenness; greenness' (green)

These four terms contrasted not only on the dimension of light and dark, but also on a dimension of wetness and dryness (or freshness and desiccation), and a third dimension of "deep, unfading, indelible, and hence often more desired material as against pale, weak, faded, bleached, or 'colorless' substance" (1964: 191). Thus, he argued that we should acquire knowledge of the "internal structure of a color system" and that we should "distinguish sharply between sensory reception on the one hand and perceptual categorization on the other" (1964: 192). Similarly, Varela, Thompson, and Rosch (1991: 171) argued that basic color categories are "experiential, *consensual*, and embodied: they depend upon our biological and *cultural history* . . . [italics added]."

Anna Wierzbicka (1990) recently raised a very similar challenge to Kay and McDaniel's idea that semantic categories, such as the eleven basic color categories and the composite color categories, should be defined in terms of fundamental neural response categories, or even in terms of fuzzy set theory. In a statement that reads like an echo of Conklin, whose work she cited, she asserted that "the question of mechanics of color PERCEPTION has very little to do with color CONCEPTUALIZATION" (1990: 102). Wierzbicka (1990: 112) observed that "the distinction between basic and non-basic color terms is not always clear-cut" and listed three terms in Polish—"*kremowy* (roughly, off white), *beżowy* (beige) and *bordo* or *bordowy* (roughly, maroon)"—that fit all the criteria for basic terms and yet are not as deeply entrenched in the Polish lexicon as *niebieski* 'blue,' *szary* 'gray,' or *brązowy* 'brown.'

As an alternative to defining color terms simply in terms of neurophysiological color foci, Wierzbicka proposed that the color foci must be projected onto concepts that are defined by experiences acquired through living in the world. Thus, for her, color categories are rather like what Lakoff and Johnson (1980: 81) called "emergent" categories. For example, Wierzbicka noted that, in English, *red* and *yellow* are both warm colors, but the association arises from different experiences. *Yellow* is associated with the sun, while *red* is associated with fire. Thus, she proposed the following "partial" definitions or "explications" of *red* and *yellow* (1990: 127):

X is *red*
when one sees things like X one can think of fire
when one sees things like X one can think of blood

X is *yellow*
when one sees things like X one can think of the sun

Wierzbicka's method allows for complex and symbolically rich definitions that accord with our intuitive and poetic understanding of words. Thus, yellow and red also have connotations of light and dark, which can be accounted for by expanding the formulas:

X is *yellow*
when one sees things like X one can think of the sun
at some times people can see everything
when one sees things like X one can think of times of this kind

X is *red*
when one sees things like X one can think of fire
when one sees things like X one can think of blood
one can see things like X at times when one cannot see other things

Wierzbicka appeared to raise a simple argument: color foci or neurophysiological perceptual attributes are insufficient to define color terms; definitions must be given in accordance with all the salient associations of terms; the English term *yellow* is associated in a common domain of experience with the sun, warmth, and light, while *red* is associated in a common domain of experience with fire, warmth, and darkness. In order to communicate about our universal neurophysiological percepts, we "project them onto something in our shared environment" (1990: 140–141). By this, she apparently meant that perceptual categories become associated with categories emerging from experience. Thus, color terms would refer at once to both perceptual and "conceptual" categories or attributes, though Wierzbicka would apparently assign priority to conceptual categories, because they are shared, whereas perceptual categories are private. The distinction is not without problems: first, because perceptual categories are necessarily shared to the extent that human beings share similar eyes and brains, and, second, because we experience perceptual categories simultaneously with conceptual categories and it can only be through some kind of ostension that we connect them.

Wierzbicka's statement appears to leave little role for culture in defining either the categories or the kind of experiences that determine concept formation. In a subsequent statement (1990: 142) she seemed to qualify this position by stating that it is only the foci that are "relatively stable across languages and cultures, not simply because our neural responses are the same, but because we share our fundamental conceptual models, which we base on our common human experience." Thus, her approach would also allow for linguistic and cultural variation in the definition of names for non-basic colors in terms of color experiences that are culturally relative and culturally defined.

Wierzbicka redefined the universal evolutionary sequence according to colors defined in terms of universal experiences and presented the results as in Figure 6. The final stage in her analysis contains eight basic color terms defined in terms of "colors which can make one think of X," where X is daylight, nighttime, fire, the sun, things growing out of the ground, the sky, and "two other colors."

Thus, if basic color terms refer to gradient categories, they are also complex, socially constructed, shared, and therefore conventional, categories that project not only over the foci and neighboring regions of color sensations, but also over correlated perceptions of natural phenomena. Not all color terms can be neatly pigeonholed as either basic or non-basic, but as we move along a continuum away from the basic terms it is likely that culturally defined experience plays a larger role in the definition of color terminology while common environmental experience plays a lesser role. By the same reasoning, it seems unlikely that culturally determined experiences can ever be completely disregarded, even in the definitions of basic color terms. To say that culture plays no role at all in determining common experiences and defining basic color terms would be to indulge in the fallacy of exclusion.

MACLAURY'S FRAMEWORK OF COLOR COORDINATES

Robert E. MacLaury (1992) tried to combine the perceptual approach and the cultural approach by examining how color categories are influenced

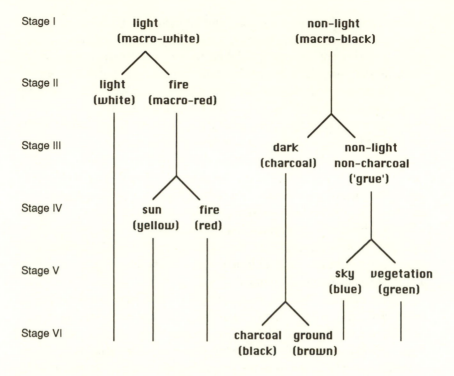

Stage I — light (macro-white) / non-light (macro-black)

Stage II — light (white) / fire (macro-red)

Stage III — dark (charcoal) / non-light non-charcoal ('grue')

Stage IV — sun (yellow) / fire (red)

Stage V — sky (blue) / vegetation (green)

Stage VI — charcoal (black) / ground (brown)

Stage VII ["mixed colors" added to those above]

FIGURE 6. The universal evolutionary sequence of basic color terms. From Anna Wierzbicka, "The Meaning of Color Terms: Semantics, Culture, and Cognition," *Cognitive Linguistics* 1 (1990): 144. Reprinted by permission of Mouton de Gruyter and Anna Wierzbicka.

by cognitive processes. In light of the concepts developed in this book, his suggestion raises the question of what cognitive processes people might apply as they categorize colors. Would they apply image-schema transformations, schematizations, or extensions from prototypes? Or perhaps they would apply some conventional construals of figure and ground, scope, and specificity. Perhaps the perception of focal colors or unique hues provides the stimulus for formation of emergent and named image-schemas of color. Perhaps observers schematize color perceptions by finding what is common to several neighboring colors and then name the schema. Perhaps they judge color perceptions to be more or less similar to focal prototypes and therefore assign them the same name. Perhaps they prefer to place some colors in the foreground and others in the background, providing different names for each type. Perhaps some color terms have scope over only the hues, while others have scope over brightness, and yet others have scope over hue and moisture. Perhaps they have terms that characterize the same ranges of hue and brightness at different levels of specificity. Perhaps all of these processes or some combination of them are operative in the color-naming behavior of every culture.

MacLaury's approach (1992: 138) is something like this, but before I explain his theory, I should explain his three methods. The first was the same as followed by earlier researchers: "the interviewer laid acetate over the array [see color chart] and asked native consultants to 'draw a fence' around the various color terms with a grease pencil and to mark the best example [focus] of each term." The second method was to request consultants to name loose chips from an array of 330 and to choose foci from the array. In the third method, "for each term in turn, consultants were asked to put a grain of rice on every color of the array that they could name with that term." Wherever possible, more than one consultant was tested.

MacLaury proposed that the dynamics of color categorization are analogous to spatial orientation, so that people determine their position in color space by adopting a point of view or "vantage." This vantage point is defined by reference to two coordinates, one "fixed" and the other "mobile" or "mutable." The fixed coordinate is a location with respect to the unique hues: white, yellow, red, blue, green, and black. It is fixed by the biology of color perception. I take this to mean that a person asked to categorize a color chip must determine its value relative to one of the unique hues.[22]

The mutable coordinate has two values: perception of similarity and perception of difference. Thus, presented with two chips that vary in color, we might choose to see them as similar or as different. It is a matter of construal. Individuals and cultures may vary in their tendency to construe two chips as belonging to one or two categories. Thus, MacLaury's theory seems to resemble Langacker's notion that people construct complex categories by making two kinds of judgments: (1) extension by judgment of similarity to prototypes and (2) schematization (or, conversely, elaboration of schemas). A color category turns out to be a complex category, but a special kind in which all the variants away from the prototype lie along gradients of hue, brightness, and saturation.

MacLaury used his approach to discuss several common relations between adjacent pairs of color terms on the Munsell color chart. The types of relations are as follows (1992: 141–142):

near synonymy: "two terms name one category; they are mapped in almost the same way over most of the same colors, and their foci are placed in close proximity to each other";

coextensivity: "the range of one term is slightly larger and evenly distributed [dominant], whereas the other is smaller and skewed" [recessive];

inclusion: "the skewed range has contracted to the colors surrounding only its focus, whereas the larger range retains its size and continues to cover both foci";

complementation: "both ranges have retracted to separate foci and neither range encompasses the other's focus."

In MacLaury's view, these relations are explained by how people assign focal colors in relation to unique hues and by how they construe similarities and differences in colors. For example, coextensivity results from "linking attention to similarity with one unique hue and attention to distinctiveness with the other" (1992: 144). "Attention to similarity" produces the "dominant" color category (because a large number of chips are judged to be similar) and "attention to distinctiveness" produces the "recessive" color category.

MacLaury's four categories of relations are useful for discussing overlapping color categories. Perceptual color coordinates and attention to similarity and difference may be useful in characterizing patterns of naming colors on the Munsell chart, but they do not adequately explain why those patterns differ from culture to culture or evolve according to fixed sequences. For those ultimate explanations, we must appeal to cultural models and social processes. MacLaury himself (1992: 176–178) appealed to novelty in the color environment to explain color term evolution and discussed some of the problems with cultural and historical explanations.

FOLK TAXONOMIC CLASSIFICATION

Native categories of plants, animals, and many other phenomena can sometimes be arranged into taxonomies resembling those so useful to the biological sciences. Taxonomies are hierarchical arrangements of classes based on the semantic relation "x is a *kind of* y." For example, Cecil Brown (1984a: 1) wrote, "For speakers of American English, white oaks, pin oaks, and post oaks are kinds of oak; oaks, walnuts, and maples are kinds of trees; and trees, vines, and bushes are kinds of plants. Such a system of inclusive relationships forms a *folk biological taxonomy*." Each class either includes two or more subclasses, or is included within some higher level class, or both. Since each subcategory in a taxonomy contrasts with others at the same level, the levels of inclusiveness are sometimes referred to as levels of contrast, as in Frake's (1961) well-known taxonomy of skin diseases of the Subanun of the Philippines. Frake showed, for example, that *nuka* 'skin disease' contrasted at the first level with *samad* 'wound.' At the next level, contrasting terms within *nuka* included *pugu* 'rash,' *nuka* 'eruption,' *meŋebag* 'inflammation,' *beldut* 'sore,' *buni* 'ringworm,' and *bugais* 'spreading itch.' At the third level of contrast, the term *beldut* 'sore' included terms for 'distal ulcer,' 'proximal ulcer,' 'simple sore,' and 'spreading sore.' At the fourth level of contrast, both distal and proximal ulcers were further divided into 'shallow' and 'deep.'

In taxonomic classification items at the same level of a taxonomy all contrast with one another on at least one dimension, but members of a single class must share one or more components of meaning (Frake 1962; Tyler 1969b: 7; Taylor 1991: 23). The essential conditions of taxonomic classification have variously been called *denotative meaning*, *sense*, and *core definition*, in contrast to *peripheral definition* or *connotative meaning* (Kövecses 1990). For example, primates constitute a taxonomic class because they have five digits on their limbs, clavicles, mobile and grasping thumbs and big toes, short snouts, binocular vision, poor smell, a simple cusp pattern on their molars, an expanded and elaborated cerebral cortex of the brain, and efficient processes for gestation of the fetus (Le Gros Clark 1959). Ideally, primates should have all of these characteristics, and possession of all of them is sufficient for membership in the order. Humans fit the pattern pretty well, except for the big toes, which are poorly suited, and consequently seldom used, for grasping tree limbs, thereby illustrating the need for flexibility in classification, folk or otherwise.

In the 1960s and 1970s, anthropologists harbored high hopes that taxonomic classification would provide a universally useful framework for analyzing native vocabularies.[23] They applied the model to folk nomenclatures for plants, animals, legal terms, illnesses, and many other topical domains (Frake 1961; Frake 1962; Berlin, Breedlove, and Raven 1966; Black and Metzger 1969; Berlin 1972; Berlin, Breedlove, and Raven 1973; Berlin, Breedlove, and Raven 1974; Brown 1984a; Berlin 1992). In his enthusiasm for the new semantic technology, Brent Berlin (1970: 4), much of whose research involved native classifications of plants, announced that "formal taxonomic structures and nomenclatural principles were found to be quite similar—if not totally identical—in many diverse and unrelated languages of the world."

But it has turned out that Berlin was mistaken and the taxonomic approach has limited application. Many subsequent studies by anthropologists and linguists have demonstrated that classification by similarity of forms and functions is more useful in explaining the shape of most folk nomenclatures than is taxonomic classification by form, and Berlin himself appears to have reached the same conclusion, as shown by his adoption of Venn diagrams rather than taxonomic trees or tables to represent classificatory relationships within nomenclatural domains (1992: 35–51).

One of the early critiques of the taxonomic approach was that of Jane D. Bright and William Bright (1969: 252), who, in a study of plant terms of the Yurok, Karok, and Smith River Indians of northern California, found "relatively few generic terms, and many terms which do not fall into any hierarchy." Their conclusions were questioned by Mary R. Haas (1967), who noted that plant and animal terms in these languages are classified by numeral classifiers (Yurok and Karok) and by classificatory verbs (Smith River). Thus, in Yurok, there is a basic dichotomy between Living Beings ("the animal kingdom") and Objects, with the animal kingdom divided into human beings and all other animals (except snakes). The plant kingdom is also divided into two categories: "(1) plants and bushes and (2) trees and ferns," but these were classified in terms of "a higher level of abstraction based on classification by shape" (1967: 359).

Haas showed that the Yurok classify, but she also showed just as clearly that the classification is not a taxonomy of the kind sought at that time by Berlin and others in which there are levels of taxonomic labels, each labeled taxon being subsumed within some higher-level labeled taxon until the zero level is reached. Yurok resolves into a dichotomy of living beings (humans and animals) and a dichotomy of plants which are cross-classified as objects. Furthermore, the classes are not set off by taxonomic labels. Instead, the nouns that belong to the classes are marked by suffixes (*-ɛɬ, -ɛyɬ* 'humans'; *-əʔəʔy, -əʔəyɬ* 'animals'; *-ɛk̓woʔn* 'bushlike'; *-ɛʔr* 'straight'; *-oh* 'round'; *-ɛk̓* 'ropelike'; *-ok̓s* 'flat'; *-əpiʔ* 'pointed'; *-ɛʔn* 'amorphous'; etc.), and these suffixes are rather flexible in their assignments to nouns. That is, in some cases, the same noun can be classified by more than one suffix, so that, for example, "*ci·sep'* means 'flower bush' when classified as Bushlike, but 'flower' when classified as Round: *kolitek̓woʔn ci·sep'* 'one flower bush (with flowers)' and *kohtoh weci·sep'* 'one flower' or 'one of its flowers' (*we-* is the third person possessive suffix)" (1967: 359). Thus, the Yurok classification of their world falls into the realm of grammatical classifiers rather than the realm of taxonomy, and this is probably true of most folk classification of living things and physical objects, if not of most folk classification in general. Classificatory systems are discussed in more detail in Chapter 6.

Robert A. Randall (1976) provided a cogent example illustrating both how and why native categorization may depart from strict taxonomic classification. He found that taxonomic trees deduced from interview data are not stored directly in memory and that taxonomy in the strict sense is not the normal way by which people categorize and name the features of their environments.[24] He proposed instead a "memory association model." Rather than storing large taxonomic trees directly in memory, people typically store only the perceptual characteristics of classes. When necessary, they can then use this knowledge purposefully to carry out their various activities, to name things, or even to provide classifications for anthropologists. He provided a fascinating example of how the memory association model works in an instance of classification from the Samal in the Philippines:

> In particular, I have often found that informants compared characteristics verbally when asked to provide a particular classification. For example, I have in my Samal field notes a justification for the belief that *lambakan* ('an edible mushroom'), a form of *sagbot* ('nonwoody vegetation'), is a kind of *tumbutumbuhan* ('vegetation'). . . . The informant did not claim that it was *sagbot* and then use this fact to argue that it must be vegetation. Rather, he merely pointed out that mushrooms, like other vegetation, have what he considers to be 'stems,' 'roots,' and 'leaves.' In effect, he claimed that mushrooms can be considered vegetation *because they have a vegetative image.* (1976: 552 [italics added])

It would greatly have simplified the work of anthropologists, linguists, and computer scientists if hierarchical taxonomic theory had prevailed, but speakers of other languages have time and again shown us more complicated and interesting ways to organize and name their stocks of images.

CLASSIFICATION BY CATEGORY CHAINING

The normal way by which humans categorize and name entities is by judging their similarity to the most typical members or to conceptual prototypes. The basic idea is not *x is a kind of y*, but *x is like y*. People do not typically group concepts into hierarchical taxonomies; instead, they connect them in associative networks, often assigning a single term to refer to a chain of concepts. Langacker (1987: 372) used the term *extension* to refer to a categorizing relationship based upon similarity. He contrasted extension with *elaboration*, which refers to categorization based upon full sanction by a superordinate schema.

Actually, to say that associative networks are based solely upon the relationship of similarity is an oversimplification. Other important relations, such as *part of x*, *connected to x*, *used for x*, *related to x* (in the sense of kinship), *older or younger than x*, *different from x*, *false x*, and *real x* also appear frequently in native schemes of classification. While these relations crop up commonly, the possibilities for the discrimination of new categorizing relationships are probably infinite. Nevertheless, J. B. Casagrande and K. L. Hale (1967) were able to identify thirteen types of semantic relations in a corpus of eight hundred Papago folk definitions. The thirteen relations are presented in Table 1 with example definitions in English translation.

Relations such as those listed by Casagrande and Hale may provide the basis for category chaining. For example, in the Thompson Indian language of British Columbia, some plant taxa establish conceptual links between otherwise unrelated taxa. Thus, black twinberry is "related to" mock-orange by common use as medicine for hemorrhoids, but it is also "related to" black huckleberry, presumably by the similar color of its berries. Black huckleberry is in turn "related to" flat-topped spirea, which is "related to" waxberry and to hardhack, which is "related to" sweet gale (Turner 1989: 95). Thus, a chain of links may develop, presumably involving mutually exclusive categories, but, in this instance, the chain is not itself named.

In some cases, the entire chain is named. Using data from R. M. W. Dixon (1982), Lakoff (1987) described an instance of category chaining in Dyirbal, a nearly extinct language of northeastern Australia. In ordinary speech, every instance of a noun must be preceded by one of four classifiers: *bayi*, *balan*, *balam*, and *bala*. Lakoff argued convincingly that the classes of nouns that are designated by these classifiers are best understood as category chains. Various principles of categorization account for classifications that have members sharing no common properties. Some typical members of the classes are as follows (Lakoff 1987: 92–93):

I. *Bayi*: men, kangaroos, possums, bats, most snakes, most fishes, some birds, most insects, the moon, storms, rainbows, boomerangs, some spears, etc.

TABLE 1.
SEMANTIC RELATIONS IN PAPAGO FOLK DEFINITIONS
ADAPTED FROM CASAGRANDE AND HALE (1967)[a]

1. *Attributive*:	X is defined with respect to one or more distinctive or characteristic attributes Y. *máihogi* 'centipede': "it has many legs."
2. *Contingency*:	X is defined with relation to a usual or necessary antecedent or concomitant Y. *wákon* 'to wash': "if a person gets dirty, he washes himself."
3. *Function*:	X is defined as the means of effecting Y. *ñí:ñ* 'tongue': "with which we speak."
4. *Spatial*:	X is oriented spatially with respect to Y. *ñí:ñ* 'tongue': "which stands in our mouth."
5. *Operational*:	X is defined with respect to an action Y of which it is a characteristic goal or recipient. *wátopi* 'fish': "which these white men catch and eat."
6. *Comparison*:	X is defined in terms of its similarity and/or contrast with Y. *ʔúwi* 'woman, female': "they wear different looking clothes."
7. *Exemplification*:	X is defined by citing an appropriate co-occurrent, Y. *tónalid* 'to shine on, give light': "as when the sun goes over and gives us light."
8. *Class Inclusion*:	X is defined with respect to its membership in a hierarchical class Y. *mó:mli* 'Mormon': "is supposed to be a white man."
9. *Synonymy*:	X is defined as being equivalent to Y. *mí:l* 'thousand': "ten hundreds."
10. *Antonymy*:	X is defined as the negation of Y, its opposite. *júmalk* 'low': "not high."
11. *Provenience*:	X is defined with respect to its source Y. *ʔó:la* 'gold': "it comes out of a mountain."
12. *Grading*:	X is defined with respect to its placement in a series or spectrum that also includes Y. *s-ʔúam* 'yellow': "when something is sort of white, but not very white."
13. *Circularity*:	X is defined as X. *mía* 'near, nearby': "when something is sitting nearby, we say 'near.'"

[a]Examples added.

II. *Balan*: women, bandicoots, dogs, platypus, echidna, some snakes, some fishes, most birds, fireflies, scorpions, crickets, the hairy mary grub, anything connected with water or fire, sun and stars, shields, some spears, some trees, etc.

III. *Balam*: all edible fruit and the plants that bear them, tubers, ferns, honey, cigarettes, wine, cake

IV. *Bala*: parts of the body, meat, bees, wind, yamsticks, some spears, most trees, grass, mud, stones, noises, and language, etc.

Lakoff recommended that we describe such systems in terms that I summarize as follows:

• a base model (the specification of the mutually exclusive categories, including the category which includes "everything else"; e.g., *bayi*, *balan*, *balam*, and *bala*),

• a specification of the central member(s) for each category (e.g., human male, human female, edible plants, everything else),

• a specification of important contrasts among the central members (e.g., male/female),

• chaining principles, together with a listing of predominant experiential domains (e.g., myth, fishing, danger),

• a short list of exceptions, which are given special treatment by being placed in a category other than where we might normally expect them.

Accordingly, Lakoff proposed the following schema by which, taken together with the principles of categorization, we can understand Dyirbal classification of nouns:

I. *Bayi*: human males
II. *Balan*: human females
III. *Balam*: nonflesh food
IV. *Bala*: everything not in the other classes

Focusing on class II, *balan*, from which Lakoff derived the title of his book, *Women, Fire and Dangerous Things*, there seem to be no features of meaning that are shared by all members, but if we examine the class in the context of Dyirbal culture, the assignments become understandable. The sun is *balan* because the sun is the wife of the moon in Dyirbal myth, and she is envisioned as a human female. Birds are *balan* because they "are believed to be the spirits of dead human females" (1987: 95). Crickets belong because in myth they are old ladies. The hairy mary grub belongs because its sting feels like sunburn, a fact that connects it to the sun, which myth establishes as a human female. The stonefish and garfish are harmful, as are the stinging trees and the stinging nettle vine. Their harmfulness causes them to be marked by putting them in a category that sets them apart from other animals, which appear in *bayi* (class I), and plants, which appear in *balam* (class III). Hawks appear not in *balan* with the other birds and dangerous animals, but in *bayi*, because hawks are dangerous, and therefore exceptional, birds.

Lakoff's argument is not entirely convincing. For example, he argued that dogs, platypuses, bandicoots, and echidnas belong to *balan* because they are exceptional animals, but it is not clear what makes them so. Dogs are the only aboriginal category of domestic animal, but platypuses, bandicoots, and echidnas are not domesticated. Lakoff argued that most animals belong to *bayi* with human males because animals are unmarked for gender, so animals generally go with the class whose central category, human males, is also unmarked. For example, you have to use *balan* to specify a female animal, as in *balan yuri* 'female kangaroo' (class II) but 'male dog' is *bayi guda* (class I). But Lakoff did not use Dyirbal data to demonstrate that human males are an unmarked category. Instead, he derived this premise from his knowledge of universal linguistic tendencies: "In most languages that have classification by gender, the male category is unmarked" (1987: 95).

Presumably, grammatical marking by gender represents a kind of linguistic experiential domain for the purpose of category chaining in Dyirbal class I, *bayi*. This is not impossible, but it seems inconsistent with the general theory that tends to rely upon such things as mythology and physical domains of experience whose imagery is more salient and obvious. The explanation by gender-marking seems *post hoc*. These are the weakest links in Lakoff's chain of reasoning, but given greater knowledge of Dyirbal culture and Dyirbal perceptions of category members, more cogent reasons in keeping with the general theory might be found to explain the distribution of animals in classes. For example, it might be significant that platypuses have poisonous spurs on their rear legs, echidnas have spines, and bandicoots are vicious little animals. All are *balan*.

Putting these reservations aside, a noun is likely to belong to a defined class, such as *balan*, if it typifies the salient cultural dimensions that define the class (male/female, nonflesh food), it is linked to a central (typical) member of the class by category chaining, or it names an unusual entity that would otherwise belong to a contrasting class. If a noun fails to meet any of these criteria for class membership, it is likely to be found in the "everything else" class, though this class and the unusual entity class may simply reflect our ignorance of Dyirbal culture. It is native speakers who make such assignments and it is up to us to discover them. They are not very predictable. The meaning of a class-name such as *balan* might be defined as the meaning of the central, most typical, member (human females) together with the meanings of all of its links and unusual members. It is only in discourse that the assignment of a classifier to a noun evokes and profiles a particular meaning among the many possibilities in the various chains of meaning.

Lakoff's elegant approach seems to me to be particularly useful to anthropologists. It provides the framework that I will use in Chapter 6 to examine the cases of Bantu noun classification and Apache verb classification. The interests of both linguists and linguistic anthropologists converge strongly on the principle of chaining for two reasons: first, because chaining is based on semantic linkages in experiential cognitive domains; and, second, because these experiential domains are structured by world views (including mythology, religion, beliefs, philosophy, core values, etc.) and by cultural traditions that dictate the rhythms of daily life. Anthropologists are also interested in discovering symbolic oppositions such as those that define contrasting categories such as Dyirbal *bayi* and *balan*. They are interested in symbolic webs of meaning, such as those that are constituted by noun classes and whole classifier systems. They are interested in determining what is typical and therefore central to complex categories. Finally, they are interested in knowing how classifiers serve discourse functions by evoking some entities and scenarios in preference to others.

COMPLEX CATEGORIES

It may seem that categories cannot get any more complex than category chains, but the term *complex category* has a technical meaning that, while it relates to these, is more restricted. Langacker (1987: 369) defined complex categories as "schematic networks," but his discussion made it clear that a complex category is a conceptual network containing both *schemas* and *prototypes*. Schemas are characterized by relations of *elaboration*. Prototypes are characterized by relations of *extension*.

The relation of extension is based upon a comparison of similarity or difference between two concepts. Given a comparison between a standard (S) and a target (T) we can represent extension with a broken arrow as

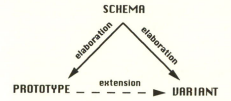

FIGURE 7. Complex category. Based on Figure 10.1 in Langacker (1987: 373).

S −-> T, where "S can be referred to as the **prototype**, in a generalized sense of the term" (1987: 371). Because a cluster of similar concepts will differ in their degree of similarity to the prototype, it can be said that membership in the prototype is a matter of degree.

The prototype and its variant provide the base for the abstraction of a schema that represents what they have in common. In Langacker's (1987: 372) view, "categorization by extension typically presupposes and incorporates schematic relationships." To see why this is so, consider what is actually involved in prototype categorization. In order to judge two concepts as similar or different, or even comparable, it is first necessary to perceive that they have something in common, but that something is nothing other than a schema. A schema is not merely a list of features; it is "an integrated structure," so categorization based on schematicity is not quite the same as taxonomic categorization. A schema is

> an abstract characterization that is fully compatible with all members of the category it defines (so membership is not a matter of degree); it is an integrated structure that embodies the commonality of its members, which are conceptions of greater specificity and detail that elaborate the schema in contrasting ways. (1987: 371)

The two relations of extension and schematicity holding between a standard, here labeled a prototype, and a target, here labeled a variant, can be diagramed as in Figure 7.

Langacker's formulation of categorization resolves a number of latent problems in our understanding of the category chains posited by Lakoff. It explains why some members appear to be taxonomic, meeting all the criteria for membership, while others are variants related by extensions. But relations that hold between central and peripheral members in the category chains described by Lakoff can also be viewed as metonymic, based on common domain of experience or contiguity. A *radial category* can be defined as a complex category containing a prototype or central member to which are attached conceptual chains based on extensions, metonymic relations, and metaphorical relations. In Chapter 10 we will see how Langacker's notion of a complex category applies to analysis of phonemes.

GENERATIVE CATEGORIES IN FOX KINSHIP TERMS

There is no set of rules by which we could generate all of the members of Dyirbal noun classes from the central members, but in some domains linguistic communities find it useful to establish more regular rules linking variants to their prototypes. This seems most likely to occur wherever well-entrenched institutions provide social statuses with clearly defined rights and duties. The most clearly defined statuses in the majority of the world's societies are those of kinship. Hence, it is not surprising that systems of kinship terminology are often highly regularized. In kinship systems it is often possible to assign names to all members of a complex category by a small set of rules.

Floyd G. Lounsbury (1964) formulated such a set of rules for kinship systems of the Crow-Omaha type. Crow systems are notable for naming father's sister's daughters by the same term as their mothers, who are ego's paternal aunts. *Ego* refers to the point of reference, the person whose kinsperson is being discussed or addressed by means of a kinship term. Omaha systems merge mother's brother's sons with their own fathers, who are ego's maternal uncles. For example, in the Omaha-type kinship terminological system of the Fox Indians, the term for mother's brother is *nehcihsähA*. Mother's brother is the focal category, but the term also applies to other kin of several generations, as in Table 2.

The Fox term for mother's brother also applies to kin of generations below the speaker. Lounsbury found that only three rules were needed to explain all the uses. To give just one example, his "skewing rule" states "*Let the kin type* FATHER'S SISTER, *whenever it occurs as a link between ego and any other relative, be regarded as structurally equivalent to the kin type* SISTER *in that context*" (1964: 220). If Lounsbury is correct, then the Fox have an abstract and tacit category that includes father's sister and sister. Successive applications of the appropriate rules to a kinsperson whose genealogy is known would enable the Fox to arrive at the appropriate term. Complex kinship relations can be thought of as schemas made up of linked categories, so derivation simply requires mentally scanning the logical kinship structure.

Lakoff (1987: 24) called the prototype or central member of regular formal categories a *generator*. He called the category itself, with all its

TABLE 2.
EXTENSIONS OF FOX KINSHIP TERMS

Generational Level	Kin Categories Covered by Term
grandparent	mother's mother's father's sister's son
parent	mother's father's brother's son; mother's mother's sister's son
ego	mother's brother's son; mother's father's brother's son's son; mother's mother's sister's son's son; mother's mother's brother's daughter's son

members, a *generative category*. A generative category is like a very regular chained category. It has a central member, dimensions of contrast with other comparable categories, and links based upon common participation in salient cultural domains: male and female, generation, side of family, etc. Where it differs from the chained categories found in such general classifications as the Dyirbal noun classes is that the admissible cognitive domains (dimensions) are relatively abstract, few, and closed. In formal systems, category chaining is relatively well bounded.

The view that sets of kinship categories can be generated by rules from focal categories has been called the *extensionist hypothesis*. That is, terms for prototypes are licensed to extend over just those categories of kinship status to which they have conventional semantic links (Lounsbury 1964; D'Andrade 1981; Casson 1983). The extensionist hypothesis is by no means a new idea. Jay Noricks (1987: 424) attributed the original formulation to Bronislaw Malinowski, who described how "a child growing up first learns the proper terms for elementary relationships such as mother and sister and is then taught to extend the terms to more distant relatives," "such usages always remaining 'an extension and a metaphor' for the prototypical relationships."

The extensionist hypothesis, then, refers to cases where linked categories of kin are called by the same term. Thus, the concepts of complex category and generative category provide us with a way of comparing classificatory schemes as diverse as noun classes and kinship terminologies. Generative categories will not be examined further in this book, but those interested in studying them further may consult Tyler (1969a).

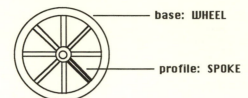

base: WHEEL

profile: SPOKE

FIGURE 8. Semantic profile and base for word *spoke.*

PROFILE AND BASE: IMAGES OF THE SAID AND THE UNSAID

Language can never designate all details of meanings. Words and other predications either may name the whole of an image, leaving the components implicit, or may evoke some component or components, leaving unspoken the fact that components belong to a larger image. Thus, every predication evokes at its semantic pole a basic, two-part structure, as follows (Langacker 1987: 183):

(1)   the *base*, or scope of predication;
(2)   the *profile*, a component of the base that has special prominence within a predication; the element of the base that is designated by a symbol.

Consider the meaning of the word *spoke*, as in the spoke of a wheel. The wheel is not explicitly mentioned, but without the wheel in the conceptual background there is no spoke, only a dowel. The base of *spoke* is the concept of a wheel with spokes. The profile, or designatum, is the spoke itself. The word for the part is only comprehensible in terms of its indispensable context: the concept of the whole wheel. Figure 8 illustrates the semantic profile and base of *spoke.* Table 3 presents other examples of profiles and their bases.

Profile and base designates just one aspect of how language symbolizes the distribution of attention. Others are *figure and ground*, *perspective*, and *specificity*.

TRAJECTORS AND LANDMARKS

One of the enduring concepts to emerge from gestalt psychology is that of figure and ground. The relationship of figure to ground appears in each of the sentences below:

A fly is sitting on *the butter plate.*
The waterfall seems pasted to *the face of the cliff.*
The hum of a mosquito disturbed *the quiet.*

The figures are *the fly*, *the waterfall*, and *the hum of a mosquito*. The grounds are *the butter plate*, *the face of the cliff*, and *the quiet*. Conceptually, the figure is that which draws the eye's focus or the ear's attention to a thing or an event within the ground. The ground provides background, points of reference, and relative stability. Figures are smaller, more compact, more clearly defined, less complex, more intense, and more likely to be in motion. Figures have more "liveliness" and "vividness"; they are more likely to have the character of a thing than a substance (Koffka 1961: 1161–1162; Talmy 1983: 230–231). In short, figures are more prominent and salient than grounds. Now consider rewritten versions of the first two sentences:

A fly is dive-bombing *the butter plate*.
The waterfall cascades down *the face of the cliff*.

In the imagery evoked by the modified sentences, figures are set in motion relative to their grounds. The fly and the falling water remain figures and their grounds are still the butter plate and the face of the cliff. Whether static or moving, figures and grounds in all of these examples are connected by relations (*is sitting on*, *seems pasted to*, *disturbed*, *is dive-bombing*, and *cascades down*).

In cognitive linguistics, the concepts have been given a grammatical interpretation. Langacker (1987: 217) defined a *trajector* as "the **figure within a relational profile**." A relational profile is an expression that designates a conceptual relation and the entities that it connects. That is, every relation connects a trajector and a landmark, either of which may or may not be further elaborated by a noun phrase or other term. By analogy, a *landmark* would be *the ground within a relational profile*. The terms *trajector* and *landmark* are abbreviated in Langacker's writings as *tr* and *lm*. Though it may seem more intuitive to limit the concept of

TABLE 3.
PROFILES AND BASES

Profiles	*Bases*
arc, diameter, radius, chord, etc.	circle
uncle, nephew, niece, etc.	family
painter, painted, painting	paint (process)
sin	morality
president	democratic government
lie	folk model of information exchange

trajector to figures in motion, Langacker's definition applies to both static and dynamic figures.

You might think that the terms *figure* and *ground* would have sufficed so that additional terms would be unnecessary, but there are advantages to the trajector/landmark terminology. For example, the term *landmark* connotes a point of reference for the conceptual scanning of a scene in search of a trajector, whether or not the trajector is moving (Langacker 1990: 18). The term *ground* lacks this important connotation. The convention has been adopted by Lakoff and others.[25]

Subjects and objects in English have a particular place in this scheme of trajectors and landmarks, as can be seen in the following sentences:

Debby actually read *the whole book.*
tr   lm
David skipped *too many classes.*
tr   lm

As Langacker (1990a: 10) put it, "The terms subject and object are generally reserved for overt noun phrases that elaborate a relational trajector and primary landmark at the clausal level." The regular patterning of trajectors and landmarks is found in other languages, too, but, as you would expect, the patterns vary from language to language. In Coeur d'Alene, a Salish language of northwestern North America, the roots of complex words often function as trajectors, while the suffixes function as landmarks, as in the word *stchchí'ntus* 'pupil of the eye,' analyzed as follows:

s-	*t-*	*chchí'nt*	*-us*
NOM[26]	ON	LITTLE PERSON	FACE/EYE
		tr	lm

'the little person on the eye, pupil'

Incidentally, the person metaphor for the pupil of the eye appears frequently in other languages (Brown and Witkowski 1981). Even in English, the term *pupil* is a dead metaphor for a figure reflected in the eye. To know why, you have only to peer into the pupils of the next person you encounter. In Coeur d'Alene it happens to coincide with our present interest in the trajectors and landmarks of relational predications. In this term, it is the prefix *t-* that designates the relational element of the predication. Many different kinds of grammatical entities can designate relations. In English these include verbs, prepositions, adjectives, and adverbs. Relational expressions can occur at every level of organization, including that of single morphemes (Langacker 1990: 11).

The conceptualization of figures and grounds is part of the imaging system by which we distribute our attention over domains and construe images, so it is relative to our shifting focus of attention, our perspective on a subject, and the scope of observation or construal. Consider the notions of trajector and landmark in terms of scope of predication. In looking at a housefly under a magnifier, if you zoom in to focus on the wing, you see the veins as figures against the wing. The wing provides a narrower scope than the fly itself. Zooming back out, the fly appears as a figure on the viewing platform. The scope of imagery has expanded. Maintaining resolution constant, you can select different figures against a single ground. Looking at your hand, you might see veins, hairs, freckles, wrinkles, and small cuts that stand out against the otherwise smooth, evenly colored surface. Turning your hand will change its orientation and thereby change your perspective, bringing different elements into the relationship of figure and ground. If your hand were not attached, you could walk around it, thereby changing perspective by changing your vantage point. Thus, figures and grounds arise from the ways in which we construe scenes as well as from the ways in which we experience them. The notions of trajector and landmark are applied to the understanding of place-names and anatomical nomenclature in Coeur d'Alene in Chapter 9. This sets the stage for a comparison of Coeur d'Alene place-names to those of Kwakiutl, recorded by Franz Boas (1939), and Apache, recorded by Keith Basso (1984).

METAPHOR AND METONYMY

Figurative language is central to cultural linguistics, as it is to much of symbolic anthropology (Sapir 1977; Fernandez 1986). The topic appears late in this chapter not because it is unimportant, but because it follows most easily from a prior understanding of such topics as cognitive models, schemas, and prototypes. Since the concepts of metaphor and metonymy are discussed at considerable length in Chapter 8, I will only introduce them here. This discussion draws heavily upon Lakoff and Johnson (1980).

In cognitive linguistics, metaphor is regarded as a cognitive process as well as a figure of speech. It is the process by which a concept (model or schema) from one conceptual domain is mapped to a concept from another domain. If both concepts are complex and there are systematic mappings from one to the other, the complex is termed a structural metaphor, as when we map the idea of an academic theory onto the schematized structure of a building, so that we can build a theory with a solid foundation, spacious rooms, and a fancy superstructure. Often, it is only one of the concepts (the academic theory in the previous example) that provides the immediate topic of discussion. This topic is commonly labeled the *target* of the metaphor. The other concept, normally more concrete or physical in its content, is labeled the *source*. Lakoff argued that our image-schematic understandings of concrete source domains emerge from common experiences. Because we build our thinking about less concrete domains on these formative and widely shared physical domains, almost all thought and language are metaphorical. Physical metaphors that organize whole systems of concepts with respect to one another are termed *orientational metaphors*. An example is the spatial orientation up-down, which organizes feelings (HAPPY IS UP; SAD IS DOWN), consciousness (CONSCIOUS IS UP; UNCONSCIOUSNESS IS DOWN), health (HEALTH AND LIFE ARE UP; SICKNESS AND DEATH ARE DOWN), and several other domains. Metaphors based upon our experience of physical objects and substances, especially our own bodies, are termed *ontological metaphors*. These include metaphors whose sources are entities and substances: *Grade inflation is ruining the university* (GRADE INFLATION IS AN ENTITY) and *I am getting a lot of satisfaction out of my anthropology course* (SATISFACTION IS A QUANTIFIABLE SUBSTANCE).

Lakoff and Johnson regarded metaphor as a fundamental aspect of human thinking. It is through metaphor that "understanding uses the primary resources of the imagination" (1980: 228). In their view, "metaphor is pervasive in everyday life, not just in language, but in thought and action. Our ordinary conceptual system, in terms of which we both think and act, is fundamentally metaphorical in nature" (1980: 3). This global view of metaphor has been challenged by Naomi Quinn (1991: 68), whose argument is taken up in the following section.

CULTURAL POSTULATES AND PROPOSITION-SCHEMAS

Emphasizing imagery in a theory of language leads to a useful definition of the term *postulate*. A *postulate* is simply a verbal predication with relatively abstract cultural imagery at its semantic pole. The kinds of postulates I am thinking about can be illustrated by such well-rehearsed expressions as the Christian fundamentalist slogan *Jesus saves*, or the Maasai African postulate that *the object of life is enkishon* (fertility), or the Swahili maxim *haraka haraka haina baraka* ('hurry, hurry, has no blessing,' i.e., haste makes waste), or the linguists' common assertion that *all languages are roughly equal in complexity* and the anthropologists' that *cultures should be understood in their own terms*. Postulates have verbal subjects and predicates that lend themselves to reasoning by propositional logic and syllogism. If Jesus saves, then a Christian should surrender herself to his mercy and his dictates. If the object of life is *enkishon*, then a Maasai man should strive to accumulate larger herds of cattle, more wives, and many children. Of course, behind the propositional logic you also find imagery, but people nevertheless use such deeply entrenched conventional expressions in discourse and everyday reasoning without necessarily activating the originating body of concrete imagery.

People use postulates much as mathematicians manipulate formal symbols. Postulates lie toward the abstract end of the abstraction continuum, which extends from the rich imagery of immediate experience to the abstract imagery of mathematics and formal logic. In anthropology, the study of postulates is closely tied to the study of cultural themes and axioms, core values, cultural configurations, and guiding premises (Opler 1946; Kluckhohn 1947; Hoebel 1966: 498; Williams 1990: 174–176). I would reserve the term *postulate* for those cultural premises that are entrenched in language, as in religious dogma, folk philosophy, folk law, and folk medicine, as expressed in slogans, aphorisms, rules, maxims, and incantations.

Similar to cultural postulates are nonverbal abstractions that may constitute cultural models and tacitly organize verbal statements, but are not themselves verbalized explicitly. Naomi Quinn (1987: 179) termed such abstractions *proposition-schemas*. Following E. Hutchins (1980: 51), she regarded such a schema as "a 'template' from which any number of propositions can be constructed." MARRIAGE IS ENDURING is such a proposition schema, inferred from such diverse metaphorical statements as those that have spouses "bound together" or "cemented together" (1987: 179–180) or engaged in a covenant with God (a "sacrament") (1991: 68). Quinn found that only eight such proposition-schemas were sufficient to organize the language that American spouses use to describe their marriages. They pertain to *sharedness*, *lastingness*, *mutual benefit*, *compatibility*, *difficulty*, *effort*, *failure*, and *risk*. Notice above that the proposition-schema *lastingness* (MARRIAGE IS ENDURING) governs the usage of the three very different metaphors of binding, cement, and covenant. Each of the eight was schematic for a variety of otherwise unrelated metaphors. Because a few proposition-schemas appear to govern a wide variety of metaphors, she argued that it is these culturally given proposition-schemas, and not metaphors *à la* Lakoff and Johnson, that constitute the cultural models that provide the basis for reasoning about marriage and that organize language about marriage.

Quinn's approach bears a strong similarity to the study of cultural themes and axioms, core values, and guiding premises that ethnographers sought to discover in the 1940s and 1950s, but it differs in that cognitive models built of proposition-schemas are not intended to be global. They govern limited domains of language and culture, such as the domain of marriage in America. Can proposition-schemas be regarded as imagery? Perhaps, but only in the most technical sense. Proposition-schemas and their constituent subjects (e.g., MARRIAGE) and predicates (e.g., IS ENDUR-ING) must be ultimately derived by abstraction from a variety of shared experiences that are gradually entrenched and refined as scenarios. Proposition schemas represent a level of abstraction from and beyond scenarios. Once formed, proposition-schemas may govern both practical reasoning and selections of verbal metaphors. A metaphor such as *we are cemented together* may be chosen as apt not because the permanent bond of cement provides a means of understanding marriage as a lasting institution, but because it instantiates and evokes the proposition-schema MARRIAGE IS ENDURING. On this account, understanding occurs when we activate cognitive models that consist of proposition-schemas and scenarios, not through reasoning from metaphor.

Quinn's proposal (and criticism of the constitutive view of metaphor) was challenged by Raymond W. Gibbs (1994), who argued that people's understandings of marriage may consist of complexes of a small number of frequently recurring metaphorical models (journeys, being in good locations, being balanced). It is significant that Americans do not typically model marriages in terms of other readily available models, such as "mowing the lawn, doing the laundry, reading books, going to the store, or mailing a letter" (1994: 206). He suggested that, by working only with relatively young couples with happy or successful marriages, Quinn had failed to discover the variety of cognitive models that other Americans have for their marriages, such as their models of ideal, typical, good, and bad marriages. In Quinn's defense on this point, it is not clear why an array of conflicting models would necessarily be constituted of metaphors rather than proposition-schemas, nor is it clear why the existence of more models in American society would invalidate the models formed by young, happy couples.

Gibbs (1994: 204) also argued that Americans use a variety of metaphors to talk about marriage because they "capture different aspects of our understanding of marriage, such as compatibility, mutual benefit, and lastingness." This, in itself, would only seem to strengthen Quinn's position, because "compatibility, mutual benefit, and lastingness" are just the sort of abstract notions that constitute proposition-schemas. Gibbs's advocacy of the constitutive view of metaphor appears to arise from a broader commitment to a poetic view of human cognition, but taken to the extreme it may be unduly romantic. To deny that Americans can generate useful abstract models from their experiences is reminiscent of Malinowski's Olympian pronouncement that "we cannot ask a native about abstract, general rules," [27] though in this case we are the natives and, rather than asking about their rules, we are inferring them. But, even if metaphorical models prove to be crucial in understanding talk about marriage, their importance would not necessarily rule out important roles for proposition-schemas and scenarios. At this early stage of research on cognitive and cultural models, we should avoid the fallacy of exclusion. Gibbs (1994: 206) was not dogmatic on the point. He suggested that rather than worrying about "whether the mind or culture is inherently metaphorical or non-metaphorical" we should instead examine various concepts to determine the ways in which these are constituted by both principles.

By the same token, just because people can reason with postulates or proposition-schemas does not mean that they forfeit their ability to reason with imagery that is more or less concrete and metaphorical. It is likely that people differ widely in their preferences for concrete or abstract modes of reasoning, which are, in any case, difficult to separate in practice. Most people probably mix them much of the time. Explicitly verbal postulates may predominate in highly ritualized social scenes, such as classrooms, courts of law, church services, marriage ceremonies, and funerals, while exerting less influence in less structured human affairs where tacit proposition-schemas or metaphorical thinking may hold sway.

One of the difficulties in much of contemporary writing about postulates in language, culture, and world view is that the authors fail to distinguish between non-verbal proposition-schemas and native speakers' explicitly verbalized postulates. Furthermore, it is not always clear whether the "postulates" or proposition-schemas are simply analysts' abstractions and verbal descriptions of what might better be described as scenarios. This topic is taken up again in the discussion of *love* (Chapter 6).

THE CULTURAL CONSTRUCTION OF EMOTIONS

All concepts are imbued, to varying degrees, with emotional values that constitute part of their imagery. This point is no doubt a controversial one, perhaps not widely accepted within cognitive linguistics, but it does have support in both cognitive science and anthropology. For example, Mark

Rollins (1989: 57–58) argued that "emotional effects can be systematically suffused," that "emotions and moods tend to be pervasive," and that "they affect the whole person's general outlook and behavior." While Rollins argued that emotion has a "physiological-cognitive character," I would also argue the converse, that cognition has an emotional character. Jerome Bruner (1986: 69) warned against *tripartism*: "the poverty that is bred by making too sharp a distinction between cognition, affect, and action." He said that "it is one of the functions of a culture to keep them related and together in those images, stories, and the like by which our experience is given coherence and cultural relevance." Roy G. D'Andrade (1981) presented a similar view.

Catherine A. Lutz (1988: 4–6) also argued against the prevailing Western emotional essentialism, the belief "that emotion is in essence a psychobiological structure and an aspect of the individual" apart from cognition and higher forms of rationality and social action. She proposed instead that emotion concepts are embedded in rich "pragmatic and associative networks of meaning," and so are "pre*eminently* cultural." Relating her theory of emotion to the theory of cognitive linguistics, she noted that "to understand the meaning of an emotion word is to be able to envisage (and perhaps to find oneself able to participate in) a complicated scene with actors, actions, interpersonal relationships in a particular state of repair, moral points of view, facial expressions, personal and social goals, and sequences of events" (1988: 10). Lutz used the term *scene* interchangeably with *scenario*.

The value of defining emotion words in terms of scenarios can be illustrated with interview data which Lutz recorded in the Solomon Islands among the Ifaluk people. The Ifaluk have a named emotion *rus* (panic/fright/surprise), which Lutz (1988: 186) defined as "freezing its victims in their tracks or causing them to run about in a confused and crazy way." One woman described to her the responses that people have to *rus*:

> Some people [who are *rus*] don't speak, even if we talk to them. [Others] become crazy and confused. I would ask what you are *rus* about. You would say something else [irrelevant]. Our eyes are not clear because of the *rus*. People sitting far away may have seen that *rus* thing and even though I was closer to it, I won't know or understand about it because I'm *rus*. My insides are random. Other people are still smart in their heads even though they are *rus*. People who are *rus* run around . . . and their eyes aren't the same. They hold themselves [wrapping their arms around themselves as if cold] and sometimes

their voices shake . . . We shake inside. Our legs tremble as we walk, and we think we'll fall. (1988: 186–187)

Note the variety of elements in the imagery of *rus*: discourse, cognitive states, physical feelings and behaviors, and lack of physical control. Discourse scenarios can be seen in the statements that "people [who are *rus*] don't speak, even if we talk to them" and "I would ask what you are *rus* about. You would say something else [irrelevant]." Cognitive states can be seen in the expressions "[Others] become crazy and confused," "Our eyes are not clear because of the *rus*," and "I won't know or understand about it because I'm *rus*." Physical feelings are evident in the expressions "my insides are random" and "we shake inside." Physical behaviors are described by "people who are *rus* run around," and "they hold themselves," and lack of physical control in "their voices shake. . . . Our legs tremble as we walk."

Having established the cognitive qualities of emotion, Lutz emphasized the pragmatic function of emotion concepts. Characterizing emotions as culturally constructed "elements of local ideological practice," she said that "the concepts of emotion can more profitably be viewed as serving complex communicative, moral, and cultural purposes rather than simply as labels for internal states whose nature or essence is presumed to be universal" (1988: 5). In her view, emotions are "a form of discourse" (1988: 7). In my view, emotions are complex configurations of goal-driven imagery that govern feeling states and scenarios, including discourse scenarios.

We can readily agree that the language of emotion is likely to have a strong pragmatic orientation, because emotions are strong motivators. Conversely, all pragmatic action, including discourse, is also emotional process. In my opinion, which is perhaps contrary to that of Lutz, the view that emotions are culturally constructed should not be taken as denying that there may be some irreducible biopsychological configurations of joy, rage, fear, or lust that are essentially universal, just as there are irreducible unique hues that anchor the complex color nomenclatures of all languages. But the dance of culture and biology is delicate, and there appears to be no scientific justification for making sharp analytical distinctions among emotions, cognitions, and discourse.

PART TWO

INTERPRETATIONS AND APPLICATIONS

CHAPTER 6

CONNECTING LANGUAGES TO WORLD VIEWS

Other sculptors, other statues from the same stone! Other minds, other worlds from the same monotonous and inexpressive chaos! My world is but one in a million alike embedded, alike real to those who may abstract them.
— WILLIAM JAMES, "PRINCIPLES OF PSYCHOLOGY"

Where does world view fit into cultural linguistics? Robin Ridington (1991: 249) claimed that "world view cannot be understood without language. It is fundamentally produced by linguistically mediated human thought." But this seems to ignore the active and vital role in human communication played by other symbolic and largely non-linguistic performances and productions of culture, such as sculpture, architecture, painting, cooking, gesture, music, dance, sport, ritual, and economic production. All of these essentially non-linguistic kinds of performances and productions are, like language, governed by world view. True, all are linguistically mediated in the sense that we talk about them. Furthermore, in certain phases successful performance may require the pragmatic use of language, but in many forms and instances they do well without language. Conversely, language itself may be mediated by other symbolic forms; ideas first expressed crudely in language appear in non-linguistic productions, as when suburban Americans build schools that look like fortresses or prisons from the outside, apparently giving concrete expression to the same physical insecurities that drive much of contemporary political rhetoric. The evidence suggests that language and world view are mutually constitutive.

Within anthropology there have been many approaches to the definition of world view (Dundes 1972). As I use the term, it refers to the fundamental cognitive orientation of a society, a subgroup, or even an individual. It encompasses natural philosophy (Pinxten, van Dooren, and Harvey 1983), fundamental existential and normative postulates or themes (Opler 1946; Hoebel 1966), values (often conflicting), emotions, and ethics; it includes conventional cognitive models of persons, spirits, and things in the world, and of sequences of actions and events; it includes social scenarios and situations, together with their affective values, contingencies, and feeling states (Spradley and McCurdy 1972; Hill 1988: 25; Ridington 1991). It includes, as well, the metaphorical and metonymical structuring of thought (Lakoff and Johnson 1980). World view as defined here may be taken as including *ethos* and *cultural configuration*, where these are defined as the "unconscious assumptions" or "unstated premises" of a culture (Kluckhohn 1947: 218) or as "evaluative" (Geertz 1957: 421).

My treatment of world view is more inclusive than that of Geertz (1957: 421–422), who set it up in opposition to ethos. Geertz defined ethos as "the moral (and aesthetic) aspects of a given culture, the evaluative elements," "the tone, character, and quality of their life, its moral and aesthetic style and mood; . . . the underlying attitude toward themselves and their world that life reflects"; he defined world view as "their picture of the way things, in sheer actuality are, their concept of nature, of self, of society. . . . their most comprehensive ideas of order." Unlike Geertz, I would include ethos within world view, because I want to avoid any arbitrary surgical extraction of emotion and value from cognition.

In short, a world view has all the complexity of life itself. To the extent that it subsumes the schematic imagery of linguistic semantics, world view can be seen as an important determinant of grammar; and the study of grammar can be regarded as the study of world view constrained to linguistic symbols. Perhaps the best formal treatment of this topic is that of Roger Keesing (1979), who showed how the semantics of nonphysical senses of words in Kwaio, a language spoken on Malaita Island in the Solomons, depends crucially upon knowledge of such cultural distinctions as PHENOMENAL/NOUMENAL, and POLLUTED/ORDINARY/SACRED. For example, the knowledge that human affairs "depend on spiritual potency infused by ancestors into objects and events" is necessary to understand many utterances in Kwaio, as is the knowledge that "the ancestors . . . are preoccupied with preservation of proper boundaries between the realms of the sacred, the mundane, and the polluted." One such utterance, if glossed literally, means 'cause to sink below the ground,' but if glossed figuratively means 'cause [a person] to waste away,' as through sorcery (1979: 20–22). Keesing regarded linguistic knowledge as "part of, and on the same epistemological plane as, cultural knowledge" (1979: 15).

Two paragraphs of a Coeur d'Alene Indian Coyote story may further illustrate why, in studying language, it is necessary to take world view into account:

> Coyote went off. He saw a man throwing up his eyes. He ran and said, "My eyes, come back again!" Then they dropped into his sockets again. Coyote said, "My gr-gr-gr-grandfather knew that trick too. Do you think you are the only one who knows it?"
>
> He took out his eyes and threw them up. "Come drop back, my eyes!" But the man ran and caught them and Coyote had no eyes. (Reichard 1969: 91)[1]

The eye juggler story is a wisdom tale illustrating the folly of pretension; Coyote should be satisfied with his own eyes and keep them in his head. The words are English, of course, but the translation preserves at least an outline of the native imagery. Though the meaning of this simple tale may seem transparent, we can enhance our understanding by considering the American Indian imagery that lies behind it.

The image of mythical Coyote losing his eyes springs from a scenario in which the body parts of mythical persons retain their functions when they become detached; and body products of mythical humans and animals, or even of plants, may gain human functions. Thus, losing his eyes disorients Coyote but causes him no pain. Accepting the premises enables us to follow the story as Coyote steals another man's eyes and puts them in his own sockets, where they prove to be too small, but still functional. When his new eyes are plucked out by a buzzard, Coyote replaces them with pitch from a tree. Finally he recovers his own eyes from four bird spirits and leaves his spittle to sing in his place as he makes his escape. In stories from other tribes, Coyote has even been known to seek the advice of his own feces.

Among other things, the story shows us that language does not necessarily refer to the external sensory world. It refers instead to images in the minds of speakers and listeners, images that may be given by a culture in its literature, its arts, or its daily discourse. If understanding this brief episode requires reflections on native Coeur d'Alene imagery, it is clear that much more knowledge would be required to interpret a complete story or a conversation with mere allusions to mythology narrated in the native language.

We need some independent understanding of other cultures in order to grasp the imagery and philosophies conveyed in texts such as the Coyote story, but knowledge of world views is also necessary for the more fine-grained activities of grammatical analysis and precise translation. World views provide the most entrenched and enduring semantic imagery that underlies both grammatical constructions and figurative expressions.

The linguist Ferdinand de Saussure (1966: 13–15) long ago pointed out that the patterns of language are social conventions (Dinneen 1967). Saussure called linguistic signs, such as words, "associations which bear the stamp of collective approval." And Edward Sapir (1949 [1921]: 12–13) stated that any linguistic classification of experience had to be "tacitly accepted by the community as an identity." Languages and world views have this in common. Building metaphorically on emergent image-schemas, people create their world views through performance, practice, and discourse and abstract a distillation of world view for presentation in the frames of language.

With the introduction of deconstructive postmodernist theory into anthropology, it has become popular to challenge concepts that seem to denote enduring, shared configurations of culture. The concept of world view is clearly subject to this criticism (Hill and Mannheim 1992). Cultural linguistics does not hinge on the existence of stable world views that are shared by all members of a culture or even a language community; nor does it rest on the premise that the world views of any pair of interlocutors are identical or that the world views of speakers are necessarily internally consistent. But it does assume that speakers and listeners have some understanding, however rudimentary, of one another's world views; that however many world views there may be in a culture they are nevertheless culturally defined with elements that are shared by friends, families, and larger language communities; and that language is relative to images drawn from world views.

WORLD VIEW AS CULTURALLY DEFINED IMAGERY

If we emphasize stability, we see world view as a part of culture, and culture—including language—is a society's entire stock of traditional knowledge, an ever-accumulating social edifice of partially shared imagery. Keesing (1979) termed this the "coral reef" image that reifies and essentializes culture while romanticizing the exotic other (Keesing 1989, 1992a, 1992b, 1994). He warned that it requires balancing with the understanding that cultures are also rife with contradictions, conflicts, and cleavages of class and gender and are characterized by diffuse or nonexistent boundaries, impinged upon by dynamic global social forces. At the same time, he warned that anthropologists tend to indulge in radical alterity, an extreme form of cultural relativism that treats languages and cultures as incommensurable to one another. This made him skeptical of the idea that personhood, agency, and emotion are culturally constructed. He believed that the approach of cognitive linguistics would eventually reveal the extent to which peoples' understandings are everywhere grounded in the same universal cognitive processes and bodily experiences (1992a, 1994).

There is plenty of evidence on both sides of this question. Cognitive linguists and anthropologists have amassed evidence for universal processes by which humans build cognitive models, schematize experience, categorize concepts, and construe scenes. At the same time, they have demonstrated that there is immense variation in the ways that people build, schematize, link, and construe, as seen in the marvelous variety of world languages and cultures. Even in the contemporary postmodern climate of academia there should be room for a concept of world view that highlights the framework of tradition without arguing that it is all there is, or that all traditions are old, unchanging, and shared by all within a culture, or that any culture is entirely localized in a single tribe, community, or society, or that cultures are entirely incommensurable.

The concept of world view presented here is very much like Anthony Wallace's (1970: 14) famous concept of *mazeway*, which he defined as a "mental image," consisting of "cognitive residues of perception . . . used by its holder as a true and more or less complete representation of the operating characteristics of a 'real' world." Wallace's mazeway concept includes representations of values, objects (both animate and inanimate), the self (both psychological and physical), the human (social) environment, the non-human environment (life, material culture, and natural systems), and techniques. In Wallace's formulation, mazeway is to the individual what world view is to culture. Wallace theorized that cultures could function even though individuals within them held widely divergent mazeways.

If world views are not entirely incommensurable between cultures, in what sense are they universal? Over generations, communities and individuals operating under normal conditions construct their world views gradually by integrating experiences. New experiences are always measured against traditional frameworks of our culture. But beneath the coral reef of every culture may lie a universal foundation consisting of a few innate human ideas, or ideas that derive from universal experiences, things as fundamental as abstract images of human faces and speech (apart from mere sound), animate entities, attribution of intentions to actors, basic colors, boundary phenomena, image-schemas, and understandings of figure-ground relations, perspective, and scope of observation. If so, then in every culture people first begin to construct a world view by comparing personal experiences to the set of universal ideas. Our first experiences are very basic: maternal nurturing, gravity and orientation, colors and shapes, sounds and human voices, external constraints on bodily movements, fatigue, hunger, thirst, cold and heat. As experience accumulates, our memory of it undergoes abstractions and associations that transform it into knowledge and provide a more elaborate framework for interpretation of subsequent experiences. The process accelerates as children learn to share traditions and personal experiences through speech and gestures, to involve others in their own scenarios, and to define their concepts of self relative to scenarios. As they mature into adults, they learn oral and gestural arts and plastic arts, and they learn to appreciate elaborate cultural performances and participate in complex productions.

Each of us builds, carries, and lives out a world view, but it is not just a frozen family portrait, a still life, or a static landscape. It is more like a theater of expectations with actors, roles, sets, and scenes. The playwright in the mind is continually at work abstracting situations from worldly experience and giving them significance. Inside the noggin of even the most inert couch potato watching reruns of the Three Stooges or the afternoon soaps there plays a lively inner theater. Paul Werth (n.d.) observed that our imaginations generate self-similar fractal subworlds in which "the characters are sentient beings, usually humans, having the same kinds of motivations, knowledge, beliefs, wishes and intentions as you or me." In the mental matinee, events may unfold according to well-entrenched, conventional plots, but sometimes the inner director creates her own narratives by reworking old cultural scripts, cutting and splicing, and adding some new material. True innovations may spring to mind unpredictably, summoned by contemplation or whimsy, by stress or excitement, by trances induced by rhythms of music and dance, by mind-altering drugs, or by neuropeptides produced naturally in organs of the body remote from the brain stem itself. Innovations distort and reorganize. They may amplify or dampen ideas, sever old connections, and forge new ones. In various institutional settings, they produce new gods, new ideologies, and scientific and technological inventions. They also work on the phonology and semantics of language itself. The resulting

"languaculture" (Agar 1994) may have far-reaching effects that are marvelous or horrifying.

MYTHOLOGIZING THE GULF WAR OF 1991

Though many would probably disagree, the world view of a majority of
Americans must be characterized as militaristic, or at least vulnerable
to militaristic rhetoric that frames significant international conflicts in
mythical terms. Beginning in October 1991, in response to the Iraqi in-
vasion of Kuwait, the president of the United States sent nearly 500,000
troops to Iraq, placing them at considerable risk of death by poison gas,
agents of biological warfare, and the usual mechanical hazards of war in
the twentieth century. The early stages of the campaign, designed to protect Saudi Arabia from a further Iraqi advance, were called "Desert
Shield." For the purpose of regaining control over Kuwait, President
George Bush, with the support of both houses of Congress, soon autho-
rized a massive air attack, sending over 2,000 sorties per day against Iraqi
military targets. The original defensive operation suddenly became a war,
dubbed "Desert Storm." Compared to later stage protests during the Viet-
nam War, protest by American citizens was minimal. Support for the
president, as measured by public opinion polls, reached a historic high.
Most Americans, even supporters of the war, openly admitted that the
primary purpose of the military presence was not to restore democracy or
self-government to Kuwait, but to protect American access to Middle
Eastern oil.[2]

One important source of American enthusiasm for a military campaign
was easy to find: President Bush framed the campaign in rhetoric designed to rally support for punishing the Iraqi president. Couching the
conflict as an apocalyptic battle between good and evil,[3] the president
painted the undeniably ruthless and often cruel Iraqi president, Saddam
Hussein, as the evil aggressor, as "Hitler revisited" with "a brutality that
is unprecedented." In an apparent show of disrespect, Bush typically
used Hussein's first name, mispronouncing it as [sǽdm], rather than the
Arabic [sadám], so that the first syllable rhymed with *sad*; with the accent fronted, the name evoked the phonologically similar terms *sadism*,
Sodom, and *Satan*, all of which conjure up the worst sort of depravity.
Whether the pun of address was deliberate or just interference from
Bush's acquired Texas accent is not clear.

While deliberately and repeatedly denigrating Saddam Hussein, the
president offered little or no informative commentary on the history of

American involvement with Iraq, the desperate state of the pre-invasion Iraqi economy, or the role of Kuwait and other Arab states in blocking Iraqi economic recovery by depressing the price of oil. Instead, he personalized the war in his rhetoric by placing the script of Saddam Hussein the evil and brutal aggressor in high relief against a background of good and evil in Kuwait. In this pragmatic rhetoric, a larger historical background of regional political and economic conflicts was ignored, apparently because only the rhetoric of good and evil could rally support for a military campaign.

The president's rhetorical strategy of demonizing Saddam Hussein was hugely successful. During the 1980s, we Americans wondered at Iranians for hysterically following the demagoguery of the Ayatollah Khomeini, but we seem equally susceptible to similar propaganda directed against a Middle Eastern personality by our own president. In the window of a dog-grooming shop in Las Vegas, for example, at a time when some 60,000 bombing sorties had been flown over Iraq, appeared the words "Give in to world peace, Saddam Hussein." Most Americans in the president's audience appeared to fear or hate Hussein, to seek his death or punishment, to resent alien control of oil, to regard the Gulf campaign as a "just war," and to regard military force as a legitimate means of maintaining American lifestyles, in preference to such alternatives as economic sanctions against Iraq and supporting a significant program of energy conservation and self-denial in the United States.

Lakoff (1992) argued that underlying the rhetoric of the Gulf conflict we find systems of metaphorical and metonymical thinking. One of these systems consists of the metaphors WAR IS POLITICS PURSUED BY OTHER MEANS (from Karl von Clausewitz) and POLITICS IS BUSINESS. These master tropes lead people to discuss war in terms of a cost-benefit analysis, "defining beneficial 'objectives,' tallying the 'costs,' and deciding whether achieving the objectives is 'worth' the costs" (1992: 464). According to Lakoff, the cost-benefit analysis provided the framework for much of the discussion in the Foreign Relations Committee, but President Bush resorted to another framework in order to justify the war to the American people. For that rhetorical work, the most influential trope involved the metonymical notion that the state is a person, with the related notion that the person-state stays strong by developing military power. This reminds me of a pseudoquote that comedian Will Durst attributed to George Bush in a fictitious scenario in which the president contemplates declining popularity in the polls just prior to the elections of 1992: "Coming next Fall, it's Desert Storm II, and this time it's personal!" [4] By equating the state to a person, the United States and Iraq could be inserted into what Lakoff (1992: 466) termed "The Fairy Tale of the Just War," which he described as follows:

> Cast of characters: A villain, a victim, and a hero. The victim and the hero may be the same person. The scenario: A crime is committed by the villain against an innocent victim (typically an assault, theft, or kidnapping). The offense occurs due to an imbalance of power and creates a moral imbalance. The hero either gathers helpers or decides to go it alone. The hero makes sacrifices; he undergoes difficulties, typically making an arduous heroic journey, sometimes across the sea to a treacherous terrain. The villain is inherently evil, perhaps even a monster, and thus reasoning with him is out of the question. The hero is left with no choice but to engage the villain in battle. The hero defeats the villain and rescues the victim. The moral balance is restored. Victory is achieved. The hero, who always acts honorably, has proved his manhood and achieved glory. The sacrifice was worthwhile. The hero receives acclaim, along with the gratitude of the victim and the community.

Lakoff's fairy tale scenario is apt. In the Gulf version of the Just War Fairy Tale, Saddam Hussein (not the Iraqi state) is clearly the villain, while President Bush, General Norman Schwartzkopf, and American soldiers are cast as the heroes. Kuwait assumes the character of the innocent victim of assault and theft. Bush sends the secretary of state to gather the help of the United Nations. Television news programs daily run clips of American soldiers (men and women) reluctantly leaving families and friends to journey to the hostile Arabian desert. Hussein is demonized as a modern Hitler. By not withdrawing from Kuwait, he leaves no choice but to engage him in battle. Our heroes prove their valor by defeating Hussein and rescuing Kuwait, so the sacrifice is worthwhile; they return home to considerable acclaim and the Kuwaitis show their gratitude by helping to pay for the war.

The Gulf campaign as a Just War shows the importance of understanding the role of imagery in language, but to characterize a part of the American world view as militaristic by observing reactions to Desert Storm is no doubt too facile. Americans vary greatly in their thinking about the conflict in the Persian Gulf. A protest march in San Francisco on January 26, 1991, for example, attracted an estimated 50,000 persons. But on the same day, 600 Hell's Angels rode their motorcycles in a parade to demonstrate their approval of the campaign. War supporters around the country either waved flags or wrapped themselves in them. Clearly, on this issue, there is no single American view. Concepts like world view and national character will probably always remain somewhat imprecise and subject to the criticism that they create unwarranted stereotypes, so they should be qualified as far as possible by adequate description of social and historical contexts, which are bound to be complex and confusing. World view is clearly a complex phenomenon, not an overriding pattern of the kind sought by configural anthropologists of the 1940s and 1950s. But if world view were nothing more than an unsystematic aggregate of partially shared and partially integrated cognitive models found in a community, then at least we would have a name for that aggregate. It would still provide us with an approach to understanding language and culture.

Another cognitive model that is fundamental to the American world view is that of romantic love. The next section presents a cognitive definition of the word that makes the world go around and drives the afternoon soaps. The topic shifts now, from war to love.

TRUE LOVE COMES ALONG

Some words, such as *anger*, *love*, and *lie*, seem to require complex cognitive models for their definition. Thus, much of our world view is embodied in such concepts. Definitions proposed for terms for emotions may include behavioral norms, maxims for appropriate behavior, and descriptions of emotional feelings and attitudes. Zoltán Kövecses (1988: 58–59; see also 1990: 36) published an idealized and prototypical love scenario that represents an English folk definition of love (see Table 4). This prototype is thought to be part of our "ordinary conceptual system," by virtue of which we assume a "simplified or idealized world" (1990: 37). When set out like this, it is hard to deny that the model has propositional content. There are entities: *I*, *the object of love*, and *true love*. There are propositions expressing relations between entities: *love gives me extra energy* and *the other attracts me*. And there are propositions describing the properties of entities: *the object of love is beautiful* and *love lasts forever*. Kövecses (1990: 36) said, "What I am suggesting then is that a cognitive model, like that of love, is composed primarily of knowledge that consists of combinations of entities and predicates (i.e. propositions)." These propositions appear to correspond closely to what Quinn (1991) would call proposition-schemas.

At first reading, such a definition appears to lack images. Yet the fact that Kövecses used only propositions to describe the prototypical scenario

TABLE 4.
IDEALIZED SCENARIO OF LOVE IN ENGLISH
FROM KÖVECSES (1988: 58–59)

---

1. True love comes along.
   The other attracts me irresistibly.
   The attraction reaches the limit point on the intensity scale at once.
2. The intensity of the attraction goes beyond the limit point.
3. I am in a state of lack of control.
   Love's intensity is maximal.
   I feel that my love gives me extra energy.
   I view myself and the other as forming a unity.
   I experience the relationship as a state of perfect harmony.
   I see love as something that guarantees the stability of the relationship.
   I believe that love is a need, that this love is my true love, that the object of love is
     irreplaceable, and that love lasts forever.
   Love is mutual.
   I experience certain physiological effects: increase in body heat, increase in heart
     rate, blushing, and interference with accurate perception.
   I exhibit certain behavioral reactions: physical closeness, intimate sexual
     behavior, sex, and loving visual behavior.
   I experience love as something pleasant.
   I define my attitude to the object of love through a number of emotions and
     emotional attitudes: liking, sexual desire, respect, devotion, self-sacrifice,
     enthusiasm, admiration, kindness, affection, care, attachment, intimacy, pride,
     longing, friendship, and interest.
   I am happy.

---

of love cannot in itself be taken as evidence that the idealized English concept of love lacks imagery. Even in this scenario we can apprehend such obvious images as *I, the other, the limit point, love's intensity, feelings of extra energy, unity, experiences of physiological effects, physical closeness, intimate sexual behavior,* and *sexual desire.* Of course, terms like *I* and *the other* do not necessarily stand for simple visual images. *I,* for example, I take to be the conception of the self, which, in American culture, would include speaker's subjective point of view, inner autobiography, kinesthetic and visual image of the body, knowledge, voice, and emotions, all conceived at varying levels of abstraction and activation depending upon the situation. In fact, the whole love scenario is laden with visual, physical, and emotional imagery and may be taken as a single complex cognitive model, some aspects of which are more abstract than others. Words and phrases that describe abstract qualities of imagery include *irresistibly*, *lack of control*, *harmony*, *stability of the relationship*, *true love*, *irreplaceable*, *forever*, *mutual*, *liking*, *respect*, and other words describing attitudes.

In fact, Kövecses (1990: 31) agreed with my general point, saying, "The study of emotional meaning cannot be confined to the study of propositional knowledge," though he would not necessarily agree that everything that I have called imagery should be so designated (personal communication, 1994). Elsewhere in the same work that contains the cognitive ideal of American love, he examined the object of romantic love as it is found in metaphor. For example, the object of romantic love is often spoken of in one or more of the following metaphors from Kövecses (1990: 129–133):

THE OBJECT OF LOVE IS (APPETIZING) FOOD
> Hi, *sweetheart*.
> Hi, *sugar*!
> *Honey*, you look great today.
> Hello, *sweetie-pie*.

THE OBJECT OF LOVE IS BEAUTIFUL
> Let's go, *beautiful*.
> Hi, *cutie*!
> Well, *gorgeous*?
> Shall we go, *angel-face*?

BEAUTY IS A FORCE (PHYSICAL AND PSYCHOLOGICAL);
LIKING IS A REACTION TO THAT FORCE
> She *bowled* me over.
> Who's that *attractive* man over there?
> She's a *dazzling* beauty.
> I was *hypnotized* by her beauty.
> What a *bombshell*!

THE OBJECT OF SEXUAL DESIRE IS (APPETIZING) FOOD;
SEXUAL DESIRE IS HUNGER
> She had him *drooling*.
> He's *sex-starved*.
> You have a remarkable *sexual appetite*.
> You look *luscious*.

INTIMATE SEXUAL BEHAVIOR STANDS FOR LOVE
> She showered him with *kisses*.
> It was a fond *embrace*.

He *caressed* her gently.
She *held him to her bosom.*

Kövecses presented more metaphors and more examples of these metaphors, but this is enough to convey the idea. He concluded that emotion concepts have a complex structure with at least the following parts:

1. a system of conceptual metonymies;
2. a system of conceptual metaphors;
3. a set of related concepts; and
4. a category of cognitive models, one or some of which are prototypical.[5]

Item 4, *cognitive models*, is regarded by Kövecses as exemplified by the propositional description presented above. THE OBJECT OF LOVE IS (APPETIZING) FOOD and the other metaphors provide an example of item 2. Item 3, *related concepts*, can refer to any linked concepts not treated under the other three items on the list. *Metonymies* (item 1) are discussed in Chapter 8.[6]

Quinn (1985) studied the cognitive structure of a social relationship closely related to love in the American world view. She investigated couples' understandings of their own marriages by interviewing eleven couples, spending fifteen to sixteen hours with each person. One of her significant findings from this research concerns their frequent use of the word *commitment*, which Quinn called a *scenario word.* In Quinn's usage, a scenario is a social schema that serves as the base concept for a set or frame of related words. In this case, the scenario governs the marital relationship itself.

Quinn found that couples redefined the word *commitment* differently as they discussed stages of courtship and marriage. The three senses of commitment define a marital scenario that progresses from mutual promises, to dedication, to attachment. What is even more striking is that commitment also assumes the syntactic roles of its closest paraphrase terms. Summarizing her findings, she wrote:

> Thus, to restate the claim being made, when interviewees offer such statements as "We made the commitment to get married" and "We were making a commitment together, that we were going to stay together," they are using "commitment" in the sense of PROMISE. When they say, "We are deeply committed to marriage and family" or "It's a commitment to wanting to make our marriage work," they

are using the word in the sense of DEDICATION. And when they say such things as "We were really committed to each other" and "Was I willing to commit myself to her?" they are using "commitment" in the sense of ATTACHMENT. (1985: 301)

Quinn framed her study as a lesson in polysemy (multiple word meanings), as well as a lesson in the attachment of words to scenarios. The meaning of *commitment* in any particular instance of usage depends upon the context defined in terms of stages in the marital relationship, much as allophones of phonemes appear in complementary distribution. Quinn also pointed out that scenarios contain goals. Scenario words, such as *commitment*, serve to constrain those goals to important general goals that are "long-range and effortful" (1985: 315). Let us turn now from the realm of social scenarios to what the world is made of, as this is apprehended in language.

LONG THINGS, STICKY THINGS, LUMPY THINGS, AND THE REAL LION-CHIEFS IN BANTU

Certain kinds of grammatical structures offer the most obvious promise for the investigation of world views in grammars because they seem to predicate the most salient and fundamental shapes and qualities of natural phenomena. Among the most intriguing of these are the noun classes and classifiers, which are found in many languages.[7] A type called numeral classifiers is found in Chinese, Japanese, Mayan, Ojibway, and many languages of southeast Asia (Burling 1970; Adams and Conklin 1973; Creider 1975). These languages have constructions that resemble English phrases for measures, such as "6 *sheets* of paper" and "5 *gallons* of gas" [italics added] (Adams and Conklin 1973: 1). Here the terms *sheets* and *gallons* are analogous to numeral classifiers in other languages. But systematic numeral classifiers are often more schematic, with translations such as "8 *round-things* of oranges" or "52 *long-things* of pine trees." And because they are more universally applied to the nouns of the classifying languages, they are more revealing of particularly salient schemas in their speakers' world views.

Bantu languages of Africa south of the Sahara have a system of noun classes that resemble in some respects the masculine-feminine-neuter genders of German or the masculine-feminine classes of Spanish. Some scholars refer to Bantu noun classes as gender systems, but Bantu languages classify nouns by characteristics other than sexual gender *per se*. The noun classes of Bantu pertain to shapes, animacy, control, and physical consistencies of substances. The segregation is a little untidy with its apparent mix of apples and oranges, but, then, so is the world that it sorts out. The Bantu themselves no doubt find the classes to be intuitively satisfactory.

Kiswahili is a Bantu language that is spoken as a first language by peoples living on islands lying along the coast of East Africa. It serves as a *lingua franca* for many coastal and inland peoples and it contains a large number of loan words from Arabic and other languages. A popular Kiswahili textbook, which I carried with me on an anthropological field trip to East Africa in 1968, lists six noun classes, not counting plurals (Perrott 1965). These classes are sometimes given semantic labels, such as *person*, *tree*, or *thing*, but they are more accurately labeled by their obligatory noun prefixes or numbers. A class of singular and plural forms is designated by a pair of numbers (e.g., 1/2, 3/4, 5/6, 7/8, 9/10, to name just those with which we will be most concerned).

Most classes have both singular and plural prefixes. For example, the prefixes *m-/wa-* (person class, 1/2) applied to the root *toto* 'child' give *m-toto* 'child' and *wa-toto* 'children.' The prefixes *ki-/vi* (thing class, 7/8) applied to the root *tu* 'thing' give *ki-tu* 'thing' and *vi-tu* 'things.' The following expression shows how the prefixes of adjectives and verbs depend upon the classification of the noun and show concord with the noun prefix:

vi-su   *vi-wili*   *vi-me-potea*
pl.-knife   pl.-two   pl. subj.-perf.-lose
'Two knives are lost.'

Concord is not always as regular as that shown in these three prefixes of the *vi-* class, but the general pattern is the same. A more complicated example from the back cover of Jomo Kenyatta's famous book *Naushangilia Mlima wa Kenya* (*Facing Mount Kenya*) (1966) follows, with concord elements for the *ki-* (thing) class in boldface:

Kitabu hi**ki cha** *Facing Mount Kenya* **ki**mesaidia elimu kwa njia nyingi.
book DEM Prep. *Facing* . . . has.helped knowledge Prep. ways many
'This book, *Facing Mount Kenya*, has advanced knowledge in many ways.'

Since classifying affixes appear in so many locations in the clause, it seems likely that they heighten the salience of the class. In spite of this obvious clue that noun classes are semantically important, some scholars have regarded the assignment of nouns to classes as largely arbitrary, once you get beyond a few obvious prototypes. That interpretation was rejected by Denny and Creider (1986), who attempted instead to discover the semantic basis of the noun classes of Proto-Bantu, the language that was ancestral to all the modern Bantu languages. In their view, apparently arbitrary members of noun classes can be semantically linked.

Table 5 lists some of the semantic categories that Denny and Creider identified, together with just a few glosses for root nouns belonging to each.[8] The Proto-Bantu categories of meaning do not correspond exactly to grammatical classes based upon prefix assignments. Some classes appear to contain more than one semantic category. Class 3, for example, contains "extended, long" and "dispersive." Different classes may contain nouns characterized by the same feature. Both class 6 and class 3, for example, contain nouns for liquids and viscous substances.

It is not entirely clear whether the distinctions identified by Denny and Creider operate at the level of the schema or the feature. Whatever the level, they reflect Denny and Creider's interest in semantic distinctions. The authors distinguished between nouns with concrete, "concrete-problematic," and abstract meanings. For the sake of clarity, I have omitted the problematic terms, which are much less numerous than the concrete ones in all classes. In any case, the same sorts of arguments would apply to the problematic terms. The main distinctions, then, are as follows:

non-extended (round, protruded, bunched)
extended (long)
non-extended, outline figure
extended, outline figure
differentiated internal structure
person
animal
utilitarian artifacts, (by extension) despised objects and beings
dispersive substances (separate particles, infusions)
liquids, viscous substances, aggregates
substances which stick together
differentiated substances, abstracts
unclear

Class 3, dispersive substances (separate particles, infusions), is further differentiated as:

dry particulate substances
liquids and viscous substances
solids
abstracts

Denny and Creider presented the classes in a tree diagram in which the first distinction is by count and mass (see Figure 9). Only count nouns take plurals. The count nouns are then discriminated by "configurations" that look very much like image-schemas. The main spatial configurations are non-extended, solid figures; extended, solid figures; non-extended, outline figures; and extended, outline figures. Both solid figure configurations have plural forms (collections). Only singular forms of outline figures are distinguished by extendedness, and the existence of a plural outline form seems in some doubt as the data are scarce (1986: 239).

Notice that body-parts appear in various of the semantic categories and classes. This is quite different from the Native American Salish languages such as Coeur d'Alene, for example, in which terms for body-parts segregate grammatically according to whether they refer to internal or external organs, and, if external, where they occur on the surface of the body. The different grammatical treatment of body-parts demonstrates that folk anatomical domains are culturally structured. However, there are also striking similarities in that certain suffixes predicating external body-parts in Salish languages also have abstract meanings that resemble the spatial categories of Bantu noun classes. Coeur d'Alene, for example, has body-part suffixes for head (CONTAINER), ear (DISTRIBUTED ALL OVER), back (SOLID, FLAT OBJECT), hand (BRANCH), belly (VERTICAL FLAT SURFACE), and skin, blanket, or hide (FLAT, FLEXIBLE OBJECT). Suffixes for tree (LONG, RIGID, CYLINDRICAL OBJECT) and canoe (OPEN OR CLOSED CONTAINER) are also in common use.[9] Another Salish language, Bella Coola, has a similar assemblage of anatomical suffixes, plus a group of lexical suffixes that appear to function solely as noun classifiers (Saunders and Davis 1975a, 1975b, 1975c; Denny 1979). Talmy (1983) observed that in closed classes of lexemes (such as English prepositions, Coeur d'Alene anatomical suffixes, or Bantu noun-class prefixes) spatial schemas such as these show very little overlap in meaning within a language. Perhaps they are disjunctive because closed classes, being small almost by definition, function to symbolize gross distinctions that are refined by further specification in discourse.

Surprisingly, the Proto-Bantu terms for chief, medicine man, and blind

TABLE 5.
SEMANTIC CATEGORIES OF PROTO-BANTU NOUN CLASSES
(ENGLISH GLOSSES ONLY)
ABBREVIATED AND REORDERED FROM DENNY AND CREIDER
(1986: 232–239)

Class 1/2: person

> person, husband, man, wife, woman, stranger, relative by marriage, old person, dead person

Class 3/4: extended (long)

concrete

> body, stream, leech, root, bark-fiber string, lip, river, line of objects, back of body, leg, arrow, tail

abstract

> work, load, spirit, footfall, year, month, moon, daytime

Class 3: dispersive substances (separate particles, infusions)

concrete

> sand, broth, gravy, ordeal poison, rain (continuous, misty), herbal remedy, smoke

abstract

> daylight, whistling, yawn, moonlight, darkness, life

Class 3: (Guthrie's) starred forms

dry particulate substances

> soot, sand, rain, chaff, salt, rice, sorghum, ashes, smoke, salt

liquids and viscous substances

> broth, gravy, ordeal poison

solids

> flesh, bread, metallic lead

abstracts

> pleasant flavor, whistling, evening, eight, smell, provisions, six, daylight, darkness, life

Class 5/6: non-extended (round, protruded, bunched)

concrete

> spot, freckle, breast, spider (bulbous body), stone, hair on body (circular), tear, fish hook, knee, egg, rubbish heap, sun, nose, ember, navel (often protruded), cooking stone, boil, stomach (protrusion), buttock, cheek, eye, tooth

abstract

> voice, ten, inheritance, twin

Class 5: substances which stick together

concrete

> clay for pottery, soil

abstract

> yesterday, top, sky

TABLE 5. (*continued*)

Class 6: liquids, viscous substances, aggregates
concrete
>   milk, excreta, urine, intestines (produce excreta), charcoal, pus, spittle

abstract
>   cold weather (wet)

Class 7/8: utilitarian artifacts, (by extension) despised objects and beings
>   thigh (deprecatory), lame person, sore, yam, pubes, mortar for pounding, platform (granary), well, frog, thing (belongings)

Class 9/10: animal
animal
>   animal, poisonous snake, buffalo, mosquito, dog, goat, leopard, cattle, bush pig, rat, civet cat, chicken

human
>   medicine man, chief, blind person

Class 9/10: non-extended, outline figure
concrete
>   pot (for storage), open space, seed, ground, country, calabash bottle, gall bladder, chief's house, drum, skin garment, outside, path, clearing, open way, eyebrow (surrounds the eye), neck (opening to stomach and lungs), tree hollow, fetish, charm (bundle), cooking pot

abstract
>   dream, cold wind

Class 9: Unclear
concrete
>   rain, mush, white clay, meat

abstract
>   shame, strength, hunger, famine

Class 11: extended, outline figure [category title added]
concrete
>   rib, side of body, spider's web, hill, crust, palm of hand, slap, fingernail, horn

abstract
>   bee-sting, journey, song (melodic duration)

Class 14/6: differentiated internal structure
concrete
>   bridge, bedstead, bow, canoe, face

abstract
>   night

Class 14: differentiated substances, abstracts
concrete
>   birdlime, iron-stone (iron-ore), grain, honey (honeycomb), mushroom

abstract
>   witchcraft, bitterness, medicine, fierceness, old age, shortness, fear

---

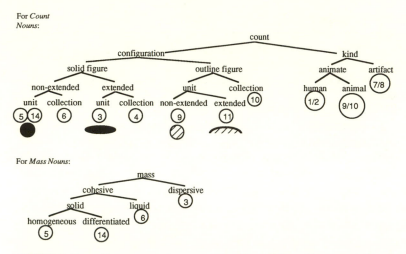

FIGURE 9. Proto-Bantu noun class semantics. From J. Peter Denny and Chet A. Creider, "The Semantics of Noun Classes in Proto-Bantu," in Colette Craig (ed.), *Noun Classes and Categorization* (1986), p. 219. Reprinted by permission of John Benjamins Publishing Company.

person appear in the animal rather than the human class (Table 5). Creider (1975) suggested that they fit there because Bantu symbolism makes a fundamental distinction between wild and tame. The animal class is "pre-eminently" the class of wild animals (though, oddly enough, it also contains the domesticates dog, goat, cattle, and chicken). Persons with special powers such as chiefs, medicine men, and possibly the blind group with wild animals. Is this because they are somehow more wild than normal persons or less subject to control by ordinary humans?

Other explanations may emerge as we gain a better understanding of Bantu cultures.[10] Perhaps Bantu noun classes are organized similarly to those of Japanese and Dyirbal, as described by Lakoff (1987: 91–114). Debra Spitulnik (1987: 25, 109–110) argued that Bantu noun classes have "central notional values," many of which "involve culturally situated and experientially based interpretations of the specific entities denoted by nouns." Each such set of central notional values constitutes a stereotype for the class, and each notional value is a sufficient, but not necessary, criterion for class membership (1987: 26). Thus, in ChiBemba, a language spoken in Zambia, the notional values for class 9/10 (*i*N-/*i*N-) are 'wild animal,' 'royalty/power,' 'hunted/edible animal,' 'deformity,' 'forest,' 'bounded space,' 'orifice-edge,' and 'round.' Almost all nouns in these classes will have at least one of these notions as part of their meaning. Spitulnik (1987: 37) characterized the stereotype for class 9/10 as "revolving around the notions of 'marginality,' 'exclusion,' and 'deformity'/'deficiency.' " Culture entered her interpretation as follows: "we have suggested that the noun *ímfumu* 'chief' occurs in the class dominated by nouns for wild animals (Cl. 9/10) because of the cultural association of the chief with the animal world. Specifically, the chief is of the crocodile clan (*íŋandú*; considered one of the most ferocious animals), and is often described through praise poetry and other imagery as a lion (*ínkalamo*)" (1987: 110). She also noted that domestic animals are kept by the ChiBemba primarily for gifts (often made to chiefs and other leaders) and sacrifices. She reported that "domestic animals such as cattle (*iŋómbé*) and chickens (*ínkoko*) are usually killed and eaten during certain rituals" (1987: 36).

Among the Shona of Zimbabwe there are close connections among mediums, animals of the forest, and ancestral chiefs (Lan 1985). The spirits of ancestral chiefs live in the bodies of lions. Mediums may be possessed by these ancestral chiefs or by other animal-ancestral spirits. Mediums work closely with living chiefs, so that there is a blurring of distinctions among chiefs, mediums, and possessing spirits (1985: 69). The chiefly ancestral spirits reign over both the things of the wild and human affairs: "All things that grow wild in the bush are under the protection of the *mhondoro* [spirits of ancestral chiefs]. Indeed, as their name implies, *mhondoro* are wild animals. They are lions. When an *mhondoro* is not in the body of its medium it lives in the body of a lion" (1985: 160). Michael Gelfand (1956: 23) said, "The *mhondoro* lions are not real lions, as they will not attack people, they are spirits and are called *mhondoro* (the word meaning "lion") because the lion is both a fearful and a powerful animal." One of the main functions of the *mhondoro* spirits is to bring rain and thereby confirm ownership of the land by their descendants, the living chiefs (Lan 1985: 59, 98; Bullock 1970: 130).

If Proto-Bantu beliefs were like those of contemporary Shona and ChiBemba, then what may appear to be a "wild" or "wild animal" class is perhaps better regarded as a class centering on ancestral spirits of chiefs, which possess both wild animals and human mediums. The salience of chiefly ancestral spirits in Proto-Bantu cultures would also explain the inclusion of domestic animals, other than dogs, in the same class with wild animals, because probably all Bantu peoples perform rituals in which they offer sacrifices of domestic animals to ancestors.

Let us see how category chaining might work for Shona and, therefore, for Proto-Bantu. For class 9/10, I will posit a domain of experience cen-

tering around possession by ancestral spirits of chiefs. Nouns may be attached to the category if the concepts that they predicate belong to or
participate in the same domain of experience, or if they are perceived as
somehow similar to a central member of the category. Chiefs, mediums,
ancestral spirits, and wild animals, especially lions, are salient participants in this domain and, therefore, central members. Chiefs and mediums also resemble each other in being cooperatively involved with
ancestral spirits. Mediums and wild animals resemble each other in that
ancestral spirits of chiefs may possess them both. Domestic animals belong because they are used in sacrificial rituals for the ancestors.

If we look at some members of class 9/10 in Shona, we find the
following:

mhondoro	'tribal ancestors, tribal spirits, lion'
ŋaŋga	'medicine men'
shumba	'lion'
ŋombe	'cattle'
ma-dzi-she	'chiefs'
ma-dzi-ɓaɓa	'several ancestors'

This looks like good evidence for the hypothesis, but what we actually
find is considerably more complicated than I predicted on the basis of a
single domain of experience. G. Fortune (1955: 88) explained that the *dzi-*
is a class 10 prefix that carries a distributive plural sense of various or
several. The *ma-* prefix on *ma-dzi-she* and *ma-dzi-ɓaɓa* indicates that
chiefs and ancestors properly belong to class 5/6, which includes persons who inspire fear. Looking more deeply into Shona culture, we find
that the *mhondoro* spirits possess *masvikiro* mediums of class 5/6 rather
than the expected *ŋaŋga* mediums in class 9/10 (Gelfand 1965: 132). The
masvikiro mediums may also be possessed by *vadzimu* 'lineage spirits'
of classes 1 and 2 (persons), which are themselves sometimes reclassified
as *midzimu* of class 3/4, which includes atmospheric phenomena. Note
that the class 10 distributive plural prefix *dzi-* also appears in *vadzimu* and
midzimu. The *ŋaŋga* mediums are possessed by *mashave* 'alien spirits'
of class 5/6 or by *vadzimu* of class 1/2 (Gelfand 1965: 58).

What do these data hold for the hypothesis of an ancestral spirit complex? The *mhondoro* spirits may belong to class 9/10 because they possess wild animals. Domestic animals may belong because they are used
in ritual sacrifices. This much appears to support the hypothesis of a
chiefly ancestral spirit complex. However, ancestors and lineage spirits
properly belong to other classes. Chiefs themselves appear to properly

belong to class 1a/2a (public personalities) and apparently only appear in class 10 because it provides the right sense of the plural. We are left without a clear reason for placing the *ŋaŋga* mediums in class 9/10, because they are not possessed by the *mhondoro*. However, the distinction between *mhondoro* and *vadzimu* spirits may be somewhat fuzzy or contingent on situations. Gelfand (1965: 129–131) reported the case of a boy who became an *ŋaŋga* when he was possessed by the spirit (*mudzimu*) of his grandfather, who appeared to him as a lion. If spirits of lions and other animals may possess *ŋaŋga* mediums, then there is motivation for the inclusion of *ŋaŋga* in class 9/10. Furthermore, *ŋaŋga* perform sacrifices of domestic animals.

The agents involved in the Shona spirit possession complex (chiefs, ancestor spirits of chiefs, lions, mediums, ancestors of ordinary people, lineage spirits, medicine men, alien spirits) fall into three different classes (see Table 6). Nevertheless, an interpretation much like Lakoff's (1987) explanation of the Dyirbal noun classes is still possible. Lions and chiefly spirits fall into class 9/10, as expected. Alien spirits, *masvikiro* spirit mediums, and ancestors may be regarded as prototypical for class 5/6, persons inspiring fear. This classification is consistent with their functions in the spirit possession scenario. Other persons in the class are there because they resemble the prototypes or are connected with them in some way. Chiefs and lineage spirits fall into class 1a/2a with public persons, which seems to leave their classification indifferent to the spirit possession scenario. However, ancestors, lineage spirits, and chiefs all contain a secondary class 10 plural prefix. Exactly how the term for ancestors (*madziɓaɓa*) differs in meaning from that for lineage spirits (*vadzimu* or *midzimu*) is not clear.

We can further pursue Lakoff's approach by delineating chains of connections based on common domains of experience and other relations. Medicine men and barren women are both in class 9/10. A major function of medicine men is to cure barren women and medicine men typically use drums in the curing ceremony. It is interesting that the terms for medicine men, barren women, and drums—*ŋaŋga*, *ŋgomŋa*, and *ŋgoma*, respectively—are phonologically very similar, sharing the abstract frame $[NV_{low}Na]$, where N is *ŋ*, *ŋg*, *mŋ*, or *m*, all of which include a nasal continuant and, except for *m*, a velar segment. The problem with this kind of reasoning is that other class 9/10 connections can readily be seen that may be salient to the Shona to an equal or greater degree: drums are covered with animal hide; mediums are likened to pockets that are filled with their spirits (Fry 1976: 30); since wild animals are also possessed by spir-

TABLE 6.

SOME SHONA NOUNS FOR CHIEFS, MEDIUMS, SPIRITS, LIONS, AND
RELATED CONCEPTS

Class 1/2 (*mu-/va-*), persons, members of tribes[a]

mudzimu,	'lineage spirit(s)'
vadzimu	
mucinda	'son of a chief'
muroyi, varoyi	'evil spirit(s),' 'witch(es)'
munhu, vanhu	'person(s)'

Class 1a/2a (∅/*va-*), relatives, public personalities, associates, personifications

ishe, madzishe	'chief(s)'[b]
mambo	'paramount chief'
nevanje	'heir to the chiefdom'

Class 3/4 (*mu-/mi-*), atmospheric phenomena, long things, some parts of body

mudzimu,	'lineage spirits,' 'shade of ancestor'
midzimu	
mŋea	'air, soul'
muti, miti	'tree(s)'

Class 5/6 (*ri-/ma-*),[c] persons and things inspiring fear, collections, augmentatives,
big size

shave, mashave	'alien spirit(s)'
svikiro,	'spirit medium(s)'
masvikiro	
madziɓaɓa	'ancestors'

Class 9/10 (*N-/N-*),[d] animals, birds, and reptiles; various kinds of people, everyday
objects

mhondoro	'tribal ancestors,' 'tribal spirits,' 'lion,' 'medium of tribal spirit'[e]
ngozi	'vengeful spirits'[e]
ŋaŋga	'medicine men, diviners'
ŋgoma	'drum'
ŋgomŋa	'barren women'
mhizha	'craftsman in iron'
mhuka	'animal'
shumba	'lion'
mbaɗa	'leopard'
nzou	'elephant'
nyati	'buffalo'
ŋguruve	'pig'
imbga	'dog'
ŋombe	'cattle'
mombe	'head of cattle'

TABLE 6. (*continued*)

nyama	'meat'
mŋeni	'stranger'
hari	'pot'

[a]The category designations and most of the terms are from Fortune (1955: 60–132). Other terms are from Fry (1976), Gelfand (1956, 1959, 1964, 1965, 1973), and Lan (1985).

[b]Compare Proto-Bantu -*kumu* 'chief,' (9/10) (Creider 1975).

[c]*ri-* is realized as voicing of some initial consonants.

[d]*N* represents a nasal consonant, but the system is too complex to describe here. See Fortune (1955: 83–84).

[e]Membership in this class is uncertain.

its, they, too, may be likened to containers, as may barren women and drums. The term for cattle, *ŋombe*, is phonologically similar to that for medicine men, barren women, and drums. Dogs are used to hunt wild animals. Strangers may be likened to the *ŋaŋga* mediums because they are possessed by alien spirits. It is possible that all of these connections enter into the determination of class membership, or that none do. There are undoubtedly myriads of other connections of which non-Shona are entirely unaware. That is why fieldwork that would inquire into the cultural basis of Shona categorization and classification is necessary to make this more than an attractive hypothesis.

To conclude this investigation, I can agree with Spitulnik (1987) that each noun class comprises a number of related notions involving cultural interpretations. I would prefer not to call each set of notions a "prototype" as she did. Rather, each of the notions in the set is itself a prototype or a schema. Some of the notions, such as that of possession by ancestral spirits of chiefs and by alien spirits or lesser ancestral spirits, are rich scenarios that are roughly equivalent to Lakoff's (1987) domains of experience. As with the Dyirbal, the agents and characters involved in the governing scenarios may assort into different classes. As with the Dyirbal and ChiBemba, for each class there seem to be central members or generic designations that subsume many members of each class: e.g., *-nhu* 'person' for 1/2, *-ti* 'tree' for 3/4, *-shave* 'alien spirit' for 5/6, *mhuka* 'animal' or *nyama* 'meat' for 9/10. It is not clear that a small set of contrasts is important in the organization of the generic and central members, but they are important to the assignments of the shape and substance schemas, as demonstrated in Figure 9. Certainly, there is nothing comparable to the obvious male/female contrast in Dyirbal, but in Bantu languages the number of classes is larger. Further research might explain why certain shape schemas and agents of prototype scenarios go together. It appears that category chaining is important to the organization of the classes, but much more research needs to be done.

Regarding Proto-Bantu, Denny and Creider (1986: 221) followed a similar line of reasoning when they said that "the problematic cases [in the extended solid figure class, 3/4] include two body parts, head and forehead, for which length may possibly have been culturally valued" (similarity) and "the other body part listed, heart, is certainly not extended in shape but is attached to the blood vessels which are in the extended classes 3/4 and 11/10" (contiguity, metonymy, or same domain of experience). Like Lakoff, they induced metaphor as an explanation for classification: "Looking briefly at the abstract nouns, we suggest that spatial extension may apply metaphorically to temporal extension, thereby including year, month and daytime."

While recognizing that a number of terms in each class share common features, linguists have often been puzzled by the exceptions, attributing them to arbitrary assignments or even to language degeneration. Thomas Hinnebusch (1979: 229), for example, argued that the ancestral Bantu language "followed consistent semantic parameters," but as the individual Bantu languages have developed separately, "the semantic basis of the classification system has been deteriorating." The theory is attractive because it is simple. A language develops a nice neat set of categories that are expressed in noun classes, but a dispersion of the language breaks them down. Unfortunately, things are probably not that simple. The theory does not explain, for example, why we never seem to find such a nice neat set of categories in contemporary classifying languages, Bantu or otherwise.

A cognitive perspective based on complex categories suggests that the language degeneration theory is wrong. It seems likely that Bantu noun classes have always been a bit fuzzy. To posit a pure Proto-Bantu with tidy noun classes from which the present Bantu languages have fallen seems a bit romantic and may remind us of nineteenth-century theories of cultural evolution which held that exotic forms of kinship, belief, and even human physical varieties must be survivals in societies that had degenerated from previous purer or higher forms. If, several centuries ago, there were any Proto-Bantu grammarians making conscious attempts to rationalize their system of noun classes, they would probably have found it equally hard to define the semantics of each class. Over the centuries Bantu speakers have no doubt added and subtracted many terms from the classes according to the principles of category chaining. Terms with meanings that most obviously fit the semantic categories have stable class membership, while those that fit poorly shift their membership more readily.

Why don't the Bantu simply create more classes for the hard-to-fit words? Perhaps because the world contains such infinitely variable phenomena that perfect rationality would require so many hundreds or thousands of classes as to be altogether impractical. Instead, they have found utilitarian value in having just a few classes to which nouns become linked by semantic relationships that are salient in Bantu cultures. There is an economics of classification that favors small numbers of classes in systems that are phonologically closed but semantically open. Nouns are assimilated to classes by (1) elaborating the classificatory schema in the case of central nouns and (2) extending central meanings by similarity or metonymical connection in the case of those whose meanings are peripheral to the class definition. Denny (1986: 302) theorized that classes express "sorts," which are "variables restricted as to the class of units that they range over." Their function is to "provide expectations about the verb predicate."

A second reason why the noun classifications of modern Bantu languages may differ from Proto-Bantu and from one another is that Bantu languages and cultures have evolved. As Bantu populations expanded in prehistoric and historic times and migrated from central Africa to eastern and southern Africa, villages and lineages dispersed into new landforms and exploited new resources. Dispersing Bantu peoples encountered new neighbors, making new enemies and allies and acquiring new domesticates and new ideas. As they settled and increased in new locations, old resources took on new meanings for them. Some of these events may have inspired or even required reclassifications of entities in their world views. Thus, modern classifications of nouns should be seen as symbolic systems that have evolved rather than deteriorated. Better understandings of the semantics of noun classes may be gained via linguistically focused studies of Bantu cultures, histories, and ecologies.

An alternative cognitive explanation of Bantu noun classes was advanced by A. P. Hendrikse and G. P. Poulos (1994). They agreed that one cannot identify any set of semantic features that are shared by all members of any one noun class and theorized that the semantics of nouns varies along a continuum from a prototype notion of concrete entities bounded in three-dimensional space to relations, such as locatives and infinitives. In their view, the Bantu noun classes predicate ("grammaticalize") segments of the concrete to relational continuum.

There are problems with the semantic continuum theory as an explanation for the noun classes of Bantu or any other language. It is likely that the nouns of all languages could be arranged on a similar semantic continuum from concrete to relational entities. Why, then, do the numbers of classes vary from language to language, and why do languages organize their classes around different sets of prototypes and central members? The semantic continuum theory does not explain why particular segments of the continuum are important enough to Bantu speakers to distinguish them in grammar. The theory of complex categories does. The problem with the semantic continuum theory is that it washes out the culture from the noun classes. As Michael Agar (1994) said, we need to put the culture back into the circle that is commonly drawn around grammar. Similarly, in a discussion of Burmese noun classifiers, Robbins Burling (1970: 61) concluded that "explicitly incorporating factors of the world outside of language may be more satisfying than an analysis that attempts to be purely grammatical."

If the complex category theory of noun classifiers is correct, we can predict that noun roots will sometimes vary in their class assignments as speakers variously attempt to categorize them by shape, personhood, wildness, or other abstract qualities of subjects that are subject to placement in different conceptual domains. In fact, we can see this in operation in Kiswahili terms based on the root *toto*: *m-toto* 'child' (person class), *ki-toto* 'childish' (thing class), and *u-toto* 'childhood' (abstract class). With the root *-ti* 'tree, pole,' use of the tree prefix produces *m-ti* 'tree,' but use of the thing prefix produces *ki-ti* 'chair,' that is, an inanimate object made from a tree or, more abstractly, from poles. Thus, the classifiers highlight certain features of their noun complements; they profile dimensions of the noun predicate that would otherwise remain tacit, or, as Denny (1986) put it, they set up expectations. In so doing, they narrow the range of felicitous correspondences with verbal complements.

Bantu noun classes function as symbolic complexes of prefixes that enter into constructions with roots of nouns, adjectives, and verbs, always governed by the *construal* of the noun. For those nouns that most obviously fit their classification, the noun class prefixes function (semantically) like schemas. For those terms that seem ill-suited to their classification, the noun classes function more like prototypes or, metonymically, as labels for domains of experience that include noun predicates. Since there is some latitude for assigning nouns to classes, speakers can use noun class prefixes to produce new words and to reschematize noun-roots.

This grammatical flexibility is not confined to Bantu languages. Burling (1970: 58–62) reported similar flexibility in assignments of Burmese numeral classifiers. Mary R. Haas (1967: 358–359) reported that different Yurok classifiers can be used with the same noun. In some cases this produces a clear difference in referential meaning ("Thus, ci.sep' means 'flower bush' when classified as Bushlike, but 'flower' when classified as Round"), but in other cases, she asserted, there was "no difference in referential meaning" and the different classification was "entirely taxonomic." This generalization is no doubt true if by "referential meaning" is meant only ostensive meaning: the assignment to some object or objectively available perceptual feature of the environment. However, it overlooks the notion that classifiers highlight selected features of their referents. The concept profiled by classifier plus noun varies with the classifier as well as the noun predicate.

RIGID THINGS, FLEXIBLE THINGS, AND MUSHY THINGS IN APACHE

We have so far encountered two grammatical devices by which languages classify nouns: the free morpheme noun classifiers of the Dyirbal and the concordial prefix frames of Bantu languages. In North America there is a family of languages native to Western Canada, Alaska, Arizona, and New Mexico that are collectively termed Athabascan. The most widely recognized of these are the closely related Apache and Navajo languages of the Southwest. Athabascan languages invest their verbs with the same basic kinds of information that the Bantu languages place in their concordial prefixes. All of the Athabascan languages contain classes of verb stems grouped according to the kinds of objects that undergo their verbal processes. Such stems therefore contain both nominal and verbal information.

The objects that Athabascan verb stems classify are figures in figure-and-ground schemas, which include path, motion, and manner (Talmy 1985: 60–76). Navajo and Apache thus belong to a type, along with Atsugewi, a Hokan language of northern California, in which verbs of motion typically conflate figure with fact-of-motion. That is, the verb predicates both the schematic shape of the figure object and the kind of motion that the figure undergoes. Typical glosses would be "long, slender rigid thing falls" or "round thing is lowered." By contrast, English (and

Chinese) verbs typically conflate fact-of-motion with manner (e.g., English *slide, roll, bounce*); Romance languages, along with Semitic, Polynesian, Nez Perce, and Caddo, more often conflate fact-of-motion with path (e.g., Spanish *entrar, salir, pasar*). As these examples show, the verbal schemas cross-cut major language families.

Western Apache verb stems function much like Bantu classifiers in that different classifications of the same argument selectively profile various dimensions of the argument. This can be seen clearly in Basso's description of how tobacco may be profiled as either elongated, like a cigarette, or squarish and compact, like a pack of cigarettes:

> For example, in Western Apache the stems *-tííh* and *-áh* are found in expressions such as *nátʼoh shantííh* and *nátʼoh shanʼáh*, both of which may be loosely interpreted as "Hand me the tobacco." The difference in meaning between the verbs in these expressions is signaled by their respective stems: *shantííh* specifies that a single elongated object is to be handled, while *shanʼáh* specifies that the object is squarish and compact. The two verb stems thus identify different referents of the noun *nátʼoh* ('tobacco'), indicating in this manner that the first expression is properly interpreted as "Hand me the cigarette" (or perhaps a cigar), the second as "Hand me the pack of cigarettes" (or perhaps a pouch of chewing tobacco). (1990b: 1)

I have used Basso's description to construct Table 7, which presents the Western Apache verb stem categories.[11] These stems reveal which physical dimensions of the trajector have salience for speakers of Apache. Basso presented the categories in Table 7 in the context of a formal analysis in which he found seven semantic dimensions to be necessary and sufficient to define all of the thirteen categories of Western Apache verb stems. The dimensions are ANIMAL/NONANIMAL, ENCLOSURE (IN CONTAINER), STATE (SOLID, PLASTIC, LIQUID), NUMBER, RIGIDITY, LENGTH, and PORTABILITY. A quick examination reveals that each dimension may enter into the definition of only one or a few of the schemas in Table 7. This partial occupancy of the semantic matrix implied by the seven semantic dimensions suggests that verb selections are governed by schemas rather than dimensions.

The semantic correspondences between Apache and Bantu classifiers are striking given that the two languages are separated by an ocean, belong to entirely different language families, and are spoken by peoples with vastly different physical environments and cultures. The classes are similar in number: ten Bantu versus thirteen Apache. Both systems can

TABLE 7.

SEMANTIC CATEGORIES OF WESTERN APACHE VERB CLASSES
BASED ON BASSO (1990b: 1–14)

I. *single, solid, long rigid objects (-tiih)*
   pencil, pen, hunting knife, crowbar, log

II. *single, solid, compact rigid objects (-'áh)*
   pail, coffee cup, frying pan, shoe, light bulb

III. *single, solid, flat flexible objects (-tsoos)*
   piece of paper, blanket, sleeping bag, trousers, tortilla

IV. *single, solid, long flexible objects and two objects from categories I, II, III, and IV (-léh)*
   lasso, shoestring, belt, electrical extension cord, plus two of any items in I–IV, as two pencils, pails, pieces of paper, or lassos

V. *more than two solid, long, rigid objects (-diił)*
   "more than two of any item in category I," as 3 pencils, 4 pens, 4 hunting knives

VI. *more than two solid, compact, rigid objects (-jáh)*
   "more than two of any item in category II," as 3 pails, 4 kerosene lanterns, 5 loaves of bread

VII. *more than two solid, flexible objects (-né')*
   "more than two of any item in category III, and more than two of any item which, when spoken of in the singular, belongs to category IV," as 3 pieces of paper, a stack of 6 tortillas, 8 T-shirts, a pile of blankets

VIII. *masses or conglomerates of plastic material (-tłééh)* mud, wet clay, oatmeal, ice cream

IX. *uncontained liquids (-ziig)*
   water, soda pop, beer, gasoline, soup

X. *objects enclosed in rigid containers (-kaah)*
   "any item (or items) in categories I, II, III, IV (singular component), VIII, and IX when these are contained in any of the following: a cup, a washbasin, a drinking glass," as a cup of nails, a cup of corn kernels, a glass containing cigarettes, a basket containing papers

XI. *objects enclosed in flexible containers (-deh)*
   "any item (or items) in categories I, II, III, IV (singular component), VIII, and IX when these are contained in any of the following: a paper bag, a burlap sack (feed sack), a plasticene bag," as a paper bag containing cigarettes, a buckskin bundle containing feathers

XII. *"animals that are light enough to be easily lifted and transported by one person" (-teeh)*
   puppy, mature dog, calf, trout, water snake, earthworm, bobcat, goat, human infant

XIII. *"animals that are too heavy to be easily lifted and carried by a single person" (-loos)*
   heifer, steer, cow, bull, horse, adult deer, adult human, mountain lion

be sorted on dimensions of animacy, length, and liquidity. The Apache class of *masses or conglomerates of plastic material* resembles the Bantu class of *substances which stick together*.

Beyond these remarkable similarities, Bantu categories reveal more interest in distinguishing humans from animals, in the curvatures of objects, in recognition of intangible substances, and in social valuation; Apache seems more focused on tangible, mechanical values: plurality, flexibility, containability, and portability. For reasons unknown, the Apache classes seem much more regular and predictable than those of Proto-Bantu. This difference could be real, or it could result from different methods of elicitation or analysis. The conflation of noun classifiers with the verb in Apache suggests that the class schemas are more relevant to verb selection than is true of systems where classifiers are free morphemes or prefixes on the noun. This seems somehow connected with the fact that the Apache system has evolved to describe the suitability of objects and animals for mechanical manipulation.

Why should some languages favor schemas conducive to manipulations of objects while others appear to keep their subjects at a distance? Denny (1979) theorized that noun classifier systems evolve to fit the environment. Languages spoken by hunter-gatherers living in open environments are more likely to contain grammatical forms suitable for classifying objects at a distance. Thus, Eskimo has a "distal style of classification" with an extended class that applies only to large objects, such as a broom or a gun, but not to a pencil. The classifiers of the Toba hunter-gatherers of the wide open spaces of the Argentinian Chaco are similar. Classifiers of languages spoken by hunter-gatherers living in forested environments are more likely to show a "proximal style" of classification that specifies kinds of objects, suggesting a concern with the close-range work of manipulating objects. Thus, in Cree and Ojibway, extended objects are subclassified as either rigid or flexible. We have already seen that Apache classifiers are organized by states of solid, plastic, and liquid and by rigidity and portability. The Athabascan classifier systems, including that of Apache, originated in the boreal forest.

Denny further theorized that classifier systems of languages spoken by people concerned with the boundaries of property and people who live a settled existence in houses are likely to add a dimension of "interioricity," often schematized as "ring" or "hole." Proto-Bantu, which we might expect to fit the pattern, actually departs from it in grouping these with the non-extended outline class, but within the class one finds "not only 1) rings and 2) holes but also 3) containers such as clay pots and gourd bottles 4) houses, and 5) geographical spaces such as clearing, ground, open space, village, lake and grassland" (Denny 1979: 111). Bella Coola, a Salish language of British Columbia, is included in the group of languages that have the distinction between ring and hole outline figures. Bella Coola has lexical suffixes that apparently function solely as classifiers. These include *-ał* 'container,' *-aX* 'long object,' *-aXikt* 'long, flat object,' *-ikt* 'flat object,' *-ł* 'hooplike object,' *-uł* 'house,' and *-ūł* 'three-dimensional objects' (Saunders and Davis 1975c). Citing H. E. Driver (1969), Denny (1979: 112) noted that "Salishan fishing, hunting, and gathering sites were owned by wealthy men with rights to use belonging to their relatives. Ownership could be bought and sold, and was inherited by the owner's son." Other languages besides Bella Coola and Proto-Bantu that classify for "interioricity" are Trukese, Tzeltal, and Burmese.

Denny's speculations seem plausible, but since he reasoned from only a few cases and language families, they are hardly proven and they are not without problems. Let us look at a possible counterexample. Coeur d'Alene is related to the Bella Coola language that Denny chose as an example. In former times the Coeur d'Alene were hunter-gatherers who lived much of the year in the wooded environment of the Rocky Mountains of northern Idaho, though some families also spent part of the year in the open grasslands of the Columbia Basin. The theory seems at first to work for Coeur d'Alene lexical suffixes.[12] Since they were hunter-gatherers ranging widely in a forested environment, we might expect a "proximal style" of classification. As we would expect, Coeur d'Alene has a variety of extended suffixes that are rigid or flexible:

extended rigid (1D) (*-ilqʷ* 'tree, pole')
extended rigid (2D) (*-ičənʼ* 'back')
extended flexible (2D) (*-ićəʔ* 'skin, hide'; *-ilxʷ* 'hide, mat, covering')

These appear to match the "proximal style" identified by Denny. However, Coeur d'Alene also has suffixes that refer to features such as a mountainside and a path on a spur of land, evidence of a "distal style":

extended vertical (2d) (*-inč* 'belly, bank, mountainside')
extended horizontal (*-ilqs* 'road, path, end')

Unlike the other hunter-gatherers cited by Denny, but like the coastal Bella Coola, Coeur d'Alene also has a variety of suffixes that suggest an interest in "interioricity." These include

-qən 'head, container, top'
-gʷəl 'canoe, wagon, abdomen' (open or closed container)
-iɫxʷ 'house'
-iɫ 'inside'
-cən 'mouth, interior surface' (2D edge)
-ilpq 'mouth'
-ilgʷis 'heart, stomach' (interior sense)
-iẃis 'between'

Of course, these are not all classifiers in the strict sense, because most also have specific lexical content, but in their abstract senses they function much like the classifier suffixes of Bella Coola cited by Denny. The boundary between classifier and lexical suffix is a fuzzy one in Salish languages, as it seems to be also in Yurok. Haas (1967: 359) observed that the Yurok classifier suffix *-ep'* 'tree, bush' is "perhaps . . . not strictly speaking, a classifier, but simply a concrete suffix that can be used with numeral as well as noun stems." This flexibility of function in Coeur d'Alene and Yurok lexical suffixes is no doubt a much more general phenomenon in which substantive nominal suffixes may undergo grammaticization processes that gradually transform some of them into classifiers. Perhaps a still better way of thinking about the phenomenon is that Coeur d'Alene and Yurok have a classifier gradient that extends from the very abstract to the very specific. The latter are more commonly known as lexical or substantive suffixes.

Incidentally, the verbal suffix classifiers of Coeur d'Alene, Bella Coola, and Yurok provide a degree of relevance to verbal predication that is less than the suppletive conflation of Athabascan verbs, but more than the free morphemes of Dyirbal. The scale of noun classifiers so far discussed could be represented, from least relevant to most relevant (to verbal predication), as follows: *free morpheme in noun phrase > affix on noun > affix on verb > verbal suppletion*. Bantu languages have classifying affixes on both the noun and the verb. In view of this scale, it is interesting that the free morpheme classifiers of Dyirbal noun phrases seem not at all concerned with shapes or substances, suggesting a greater degree of independence from verb predication and selection.

Why Coeur d'Alene should show evidence of "interioricity" is not clear. In former times, the Coeur d'Alene people probably lived in earth dwellings during the winter. Though families and bands did have areas of traditional use, they displayed little interest in ownership, purchase, or exclusive use of lands or resources (Palmer n.d.a). Their access to salmon fishing sites on the Spokane River was limited. Thus, they seem not to fit any of Denny's broad classifications of language and cultural ecology very well. While Denny's attempt to relate classifiers to patterns of cultural activities characteristic of various environments seems reasonable, the very broad categories of open versus closed environment, proximal versus distal style, and interioricity are probably inadequate to the task of describing the relevant features of all classifying languages. It is probable, for example, that the material cultures of many wide-ranging hunter gatherers give them a classificatory interest in containers and other manifestations of interioricity.

There is also evidence that broader cultural schemas, rather than mere material expediency, may be influencing the dimensions of noun and verb classification in ways that are still poorly understood. In the next section I will discuss the Navajo conception of an essentially animate world in the context of a linguistic framework for the study of animacy. Intelligent control over things and beings of various masses appears as another fundamental schema in the Navajo world view and determines the use of object prefixes on Navajo verbs. I will also discuss the relationship between this Navajo hierarchy of control and proposals for universal hierarchies of linguistic animacy and empathy.

LINGUISTIC ANIMACY

Bernard Comrie (1989: 186) argued that animacy is a universal conceptual category. You might think that animacy could be mentally represented as a scenario of living beings in action. However, Comrie appeared to define animacy not as a mental model, but as a hierarchy of entities arranged on the scale *human > animal > inanimate*. He asserted that "some languages in fact make use of less fine distinctions (e.g. human versus non-human, animate versus inanimate) or of finer distinctions" (1989: 185). So for Comrie it is not the structure of mental models of animacy that is primary, but the distinctions among levels. In my view, this is getting the cart before the horse, because the levels can only be properly interpreted after we have reached an understanding of the scenarios that lie behind them, whether these be universal or particular to each language community.

Comrie (1989: 188–194) discussed a variety of linguistic phenomena that appear to correlate with noun-phrases high in animacy: they may have special case marking; they are more likely to carry distinctions of number, that is, to be countable, to show pluralization in pronouns, and to require agreement on the verb. He also pointed out that animacy is a quality of noun-phrases and therefore differs from *control*, which is "a relation contracted between a noun-phrase and its predicate" (1989: 186–187).

Comrie may be correct about the universality of animacy as a conceptual category with grammatical significance, but cultures vary greatly in attributing life to natural phenomena. In American Indian cultures, plants, rocks, and mountains are nearly universally regarded as animate beings by virtue of indwelling spirits. Anthropologists have given the term *animism* to this way of thought (but not to any particular religion). It is distinguished from *animatism*, which postulates that the universe is animated by abstract and impersonal powers, such as the *yin* and *yang* in Chinese philosophy. The cosmological philosopher Chou Tun-Yi (1017–1073) explained, for example, that "the two Ethers [the *Yin* and *Yang*] by their interaction operate to produce all things, and these in turn produce and reproduce, so that transformation and change continue without end [brackets in original]" (Fung 1966: 270). Thus, while the *human* > *animal* > *inanimate* hierarchy may often structure linguistic categories, we might better seek some prototypical concept of animacy as the cognitive point of departure for linguistic analysis, a concept such as self-initiated movement characteristic of living beings or BEINGS IN SELF-INITIATED MOTION.

Some cultures may regard the world as essentially static or essentially animate. I encountered striking evidence of this among speakers of Yaqui, a Uto-Aztecan language of northern Mexico and southern Arizona. While conducting linguistic elicitation, I found that Yaqui speakers attribute dynamic qualities to pictures that I felt most inclined to describe as static.[13] I drew a crude picture of a stick figure and a house, which I would normally describe as "a man standing by a house," but the figure was described by Yaqui speakers, in Yaqui, as "a boy walking by a house." Other pictures of animate subjects appearing in what seemed to me to be static poses received the same treatment (see Figures 10 to 12). Regarding Figure 12, it was explained to me that the duck was being carried along on the current.[14] The elicitation session was too brief to make any conclusive statements about Yaqui imagery, but the experience does suggest that for Yaqui speakers animate images may have greater salience than static images, and in this respect they may differ from speakers of English.

FIGURE 10. *The boy is walking beside the house.*

u 'ili'ow kari-ta mak-u weeye
Det./boy/house-Acc./beside-Pp./walking
'The boy is walking beside the house.'

FIGURE 11. *The bee is crawling on the wall.*

u mumu sapti-t weama
Det./bee/wall-Pp./move
'The bee is crawling on the wall.'

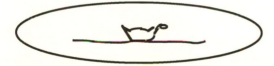

FIGURE 12. *The duck is moving in the middle of the water.*

u pato nasuk va'am-po weama
Det./duck/middle/water-Pp./move
'The duck is moving in the middle of the water.'

The evidence for an essentially dynamic construal of the world is firmer for Navajo, where several generations of researchers have reached similar conclusions. Harry Hoijer (1964a: 145) observed that the Navajo, who are neighbors to the Yaqui, but linguistically unrelated, have a "dominant conception of the universe in motion." Navajo verbs report movement "in painstaking detail, even to the extent of classifying as semantically different the movements of one, two, or several bodies, and sometimes distinguishing as well between the movements of bodies differentiated by their shape and distribution in space." He noted, too, that the "high degree of specificity in reporting movement . . . permeates the Navajo lexicon" and affects even those verbs that at first appear not to be expressive of movement (Hoijer 1964a: 145). Even substantive concepts are framed in terms of "some characteristic action or movement of an object or set of objects." For example, *hàní:bá̧:z* 'full moon' translates as 'a hoop-like object has rolled out,' *ʔàdìldìł* 'stave game' is 'several objects move repeatedly through space,' *nà:lcò:s* 'a paper, letter' is 'a fabric-like object is moved about,' and *cìnà:bá̧:s* 'wagon' is 'wood rolls about hoop-like' (Hoijer 1964a: 146). This conclusion has been supported by Gary Witherspoon (1977: 48–53) and by Rik Pinxten et al. (1983: 15), who stated that "a basic characteristic of the Navajo world view, inherent in all particular phenomena it distinguishes, is the fundamentally dynamic or active nature of the world and anything in it." The dynamic applies even to so-called inanimate objects. For example, *tsé si'á* is said to mean 'the rock is in place, it is in the process of being in place.' The Navajo world is a place in which all things have already been set in motion. This Navajo linguistic emphasis on motion has been questioned by John A. Lucy (1992a), who nevertheless observed that, if it is true of the Navajo, it is equally true of other American Indian languages.

WHY YOU CAN'T SAY *THE HORSE KICKED THE MAN* IN NAVAJO: YET ANOTHER VIEW

In a world view such as that of the Navajo, where all things were set in motion by spirits in mythical times, agents would no longer be needed to impel motion, but there would still be a need to control the inherent and characteristic or capricious actions of beings and the motions of objects and substances. In such a world, it would be control over the outcomes of interactions, rather than agency, that would be left to humans and animate beings. Schemas of control would assume greater salience, and consequently greater grammatical significance. In the language of a culture that presupposes an animate world, we would expect to find the marking of control as a prominent feature of the grammar. The Navajo language provides an illustration of this point. Navajo marks objects with pronominal prefixes on transitive verbs (Hale 1973; Witherspoon 1977). Navajo object prefixes are governed by a schema of control that also patterns other areas of the language and culture, such as the grouping of animate and inanimate beings, the classification of verbs, and even the names of deities. Let us see how it works.

Navajo transitive verbs have two prefixes for third person singular object pronouns, *yi-* and *bi-*, which can both be translated according to context as *him*, *her*, or *it*. A normal pattern for a transitive sentence uses *yi-* as follows:

> *łį́į́'*   *dzaanééz*   *yiztał*
> horse   mule   it-it-kicked
> 'The horse kicked the mule.'

Another pattern, using *bi-*, appears to parallel the English passive by inverting the subject and object and has commonly been translated as such, but, as Witherspoon pointed out, this is a serious misinterpretation. I have put a question mark before the English to flag the translation as questionable.

> *łį́į́'*   *dzaanééz*   *biztał*
> horse   mule   it-it-kicked
> ? 'The horse was kicked by the mule.'

Now, according to Witherspoon (1977: 64), this regular "subject-object inversion" fails with certain subjects and objects:

> However, when we change the mule to a man, something strange seems to occur. We find that the sentence 'the man kicked the horse'

> (3)   *Hastiin*   *łį́į́'*   *yiztał*
>   man   horse   it-it-kicked

is acceptable, but that the sentence 'the horse was kicked by the man'

> (4)   *łį́į́'*   *hastiin*   *biztał*
>   horse   man   it-it-kicked

is unacceptable. Sentence (4) is not just poor grammar; it is an impossibility in the Navajo world.

In order to understand what is going on, we must isolate the grammatical pattern, and in addition, as Witherspoon suggested, link this pattern to a schema in Navajo world view. But in the interest of simplicity and clarity I am going to depart somewhat from Witherspoon's approach by introducing terminology and concepts from semantics.

The terms *subject* and *object* are of dubious value here in that they commonly refer to both position and meaning. There is a subject position and an object position, which are, respectively, initial and final in English. But the terms also refer to subjects as actors and to objects as recipients of actions. The confusion arises in discussing passive constructions where the semantic object of the action occupies the subject position. For precise discussion of meaning apart from grammatical position, it is better to speak of agents and patients. Agents are initiators and controllers of actions. Patients are entities that are affected by the actions of agents or that themselves undergo some involuntary action, such as falling. In English the usual case is for the agent to occupy the subject position and the patient to occupy the object position: *The man* (AGENT and SUBJECT) *kicked the horse* (PATIENT and OBJECT). The passive voice in English functions to place the patient in subject position: *The man* (PATIENT and SUBJECT) *was kicked by the horse* (AGENT). Such a switch of agent and patient into subject position may operate on different principles in other languages, and the differences may follow from different cultural definitions of agents and patients, that is, from cultural schemas of control and action.

Navajo is best understood if we define two kinds of agents: those that control other agents and those that lack control. To strengthen the metaphor, we can think of the latter as helpless agents, unable to act on their intentions, if they have them, until allowed to do so by their controllers or impelled to do so by primary agents. Only animate beings may be controlling agents. Non-controlling or helpless agents may fall into any of the Navajo categories of entities in the world, as diagramed in Figure 13. That is, non-controlling agents may be animate speakers or callers, or they may be any of the inanimate types of entities. Let us see how these grammatical agents and patients derive from Navajo culture.

In the Navajo view of the world, nothing happens without the intention and control of some animate being, whether human or spirit. There is a hierarchy of control, so that animate beings may control inanimate beings, but not the reverse. Among the animate beings, the talkers, such as humans and certain spirits, control the callers, such as infants and animals. In comparing two talkers, or two callers, there is a tendency to attribute control to the agent with the higher intelligence and the greater mass. A cat would normally dominate a mouse. Hale (1973: 308) proposed a hierarchy of animacy or potency as an explanation for what he saw as "subject-object inversion," but he did not himself work out the cultural model, which he predicted would be "subtle and complex." Figure 14 depicts what may be a prototypical Navajo action schema. The non-controlling agent is optional, as shown in Figure 15, which depicts

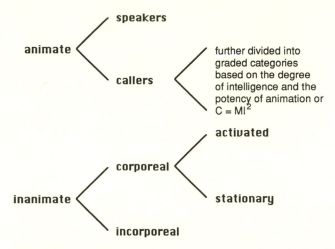

FIGURE 13. Navajo classification of control. The formula $C = MI^2$ refers to the relation between control, mass of participants, and intelligence of participants. From Gary Witherspoon, *Language and Art in the Navajo Universe,* p. 78. Copyright © by The University of Michigan 1977. Reprinted by permission of the University of Michigan Press.

FIGURE 14. Navajo action schema. A controlling agent causes or allows a non-controlling agent to do something to a patient.

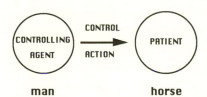

FIGURE 15. Action schema of clause *the man kicked the horse.*

only a controlling agent and a patient. The English clause *the man kicked the horse* represents such a schema.

Often a clause presupposes the three-part action schema depicted in Figure 14, but explicitly mentions only one of the agents, together with the patient. Figure 16 depicts the schema underlying the English clause

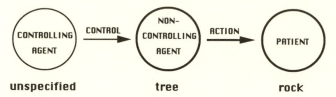

unspecified   tree   rock

FIGURE 16. Three-part action schema of clause *the tree rolled onto the rock*. Only the non-controlling agent and the patient are explicit. The controlling agent which set the tree in motion is implicit.

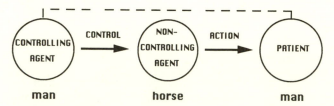

man   horse   man

FIGURE 17. Action schema of clause *the man let himself be kicked by the horse*. Dashed line shows identity of controlling agent and patient.

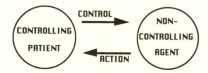

FIGURE 18. Action schema of controlling patient and non-controlling agent, as in clause *the man let himself be kicked by the horse*. Same as Figure 17.

the tree rolled onto the rock, which mentions only a non-controlling agent and a patient. Sometimes the controlling agent and the patient are one and the same, as in the English clause *the man let himself be kicked by the horse*. This situation is depicted in Figure 17. This schema is collapsed to give that in Figure 18.

Given the action schemas depicted in the figures, all we need say to account for Navajo clauses with transitive verbs is that Navajo normally marks the patient with a pronominal particle *yi-* prefixed to the verb, but in the case where the patient is also the controller, the prefix is *bi-*. To put it another way, the prefix *yi-* marks prototypical patients, that is, those that lack control. The prefix *bi-* marks just those special patients that control actions directed at themselves. This is why Witherspoon regards the *bi-* as more like a reflexive than a passive marker. I call it the *controlling patient marker*. Now look at some of the examples provided by Wither-spoon (1977: 63–81) in the light of the agent and patient distinctions developed here:

Controlling Agent/Non-Controlling Patient (yi-)

hastiin	*łíí'*	*yiztał*
man	horse	it-it-kicked

'The man kicked the horse.'

łíí'	*dzaanééz*	*yiztał*
horse	mule	it-it-kicked

'The horse kicked the mule.'

at'ééd	*tó*	*yoodláá'*
girl	water	it-it-drank

'The girl drank the water.'

awéé	*łíí'*	*yiztał*
baby	horse	it-it-kicked

'The baby kicked the horse.'

Non-controlling Agent/Patient (yi-)

tsé	*t'iis*	*yikich'ínímááz*
rock	tree	it-upon-horizontally-it-rolled

'The rock rolled upon the tree.'

t'iis	*tsé*	*yikiikééz*
tree	rock	it-upon-it-fell

'The tree fell upon the rock.'

tó	*tsin*	*'ayííł'éél*
water	stick	away-it-it-carried

'The water carried off the stick.'

yas	*abe'*	*yistin*
snow	milk	it-it-froze

'The snow froze the milk.'

Controlling Patient (bi-)

łíí'	*dzaanééz*	*biztał*
horse	mule	it-it-kicked

'The horse was (let himself be) kicked by the mule.'

hastiin	*łįį'*	*biztał*
man	horse	it-it-kicked

'The man was (let himself be) kicked by the horse.'

at'ééd	*tó*	*biisxí*
girl	water	it-it-killed

'The girl was (let herself be) drowned (killed) by the water.'

hastiin	*awéé*	*biztał*
man	baby	it-it-kicked

'The man let the baby kick him.'

So far, these have all been acceptable Navajo clauses, but we must know more than rules of grammar in order to produce correct Navajo clauses with this rule. While very similar to several of the clauses recorded above, the following are all unacceptable, though not necessarily grammatically incorrect. They are bad Navajo because they violate Navajo cultural knowledge of how entities control one another. Their unacceptability is indicated by the prefixed asterisk.

łįį'	*hastiin*	*yiztał*
horse	man	it-it-kicked

'The horse kicked the man.'

Men are talking beings and horses are calling beings. Since talking beings have control over calling beings, it is unacceptable to suggest that the horse has control over the man by using the non-controlling *yi-* object prefix to index the man.

łįį'	*hastiin*	*biztał*
horse	man	it-it-kicked

'The horse was (let itself be) kicked by the man.'

Use of the *bi-* prefix improperly, or perhaps humorously, suggests that the horse has control over the man.

awéé	*hastiin*	*yiztał*
baby	man	it-it-kicked

'The baby kicked the man.'

Men are talking beings and babies, like animals, are calling beings. Thus, this example suffers from the same contradiction of Navajo logic as *the horse kicked the man*.

*tó   at'ééd   boodláá
water   girl   it-it-drank
'The water was (let itself be) drunk by the girl.'

In Navajo thinking, water is inanimate and has no intelligence. Therefore, it cannot control another agent and the use of the *bi-* suffix, here
realized as *bo-*, is unacceptable.

*tsin   tó   'abííł'éél
stick   water   away-it-it-carried
'The stick let the water carry it off.'

The inanimate stick has no capacity for intelligence or control and
therefore cannot govern the *bi-* prefix. Now we can represent the grammatical schemas. The basic schema is

[ENTITY   ENTITY   OBJECT-VERB]

This breaks down into the following subtypes:

[AGENT   PATIENT   *YI*-VERB]

[CONTROLLING_PATIENT   NON_CONTROLLING_AGENT   *BI*-VERB]

The description of this system by Robert W. Young and William Morgan (1987) seems correct as far as it goes, but it leaves the meaning of
expressions with *yi-* and *bi-* somewhat obscure. They noted without explanation that the occurrence of *bi-* with two inanimate arguments (e.g., a
rock and a log) is uncommon, a fact also noticed by Hale (1973). In this
analysis, *bi-* requires a controlling patient, and since inanimate entities
cannot exert control it would be irrational to use *bi-*. The fact that *bi-*
sometimes does occur with two inanimate arguments suggests that the
subject argument may be metaphorically reconstrued as an animate controlling patient. This would be similar to English when we say something
like *the car just wanted to go off the road.*

Following Hale (1973), Witherspoon (1977) also referred to the rever-
sal of patient and agent positions occurring with the *bi-* marker as "subject-object inversion." It is true that we can think of the prefix as a marker
that shifts our search for the patient from the normal object/patient 2 position to the subject/agent 1 position, but calling the phenomenon S-O
inversion obscures the fact that the patient in the *bi-* expressions remains
something of a subject in that it controls action predicated by the verb and
the non-controlling agent becomes an object of control, though not the

object of the action itself. We could call it agent-patient inversion, but a more straightforward name for the construction is *marking the controlling patient*. The controller remains steady in initial (subject) position and only its role as a patient is marked by the prefix. This syntactic anchoring of the controller in subject position suggests that the relation of controller to non-controller is more salient to the Navajo than the relation of agent to patient. Taken as a whole, with the focus on semantics, the *yi-/bi-* system could be termed *patient control*. *yi-* marks non-controlling patients; *bi-* marks controlling patients. With the focus on syntax, the system could be called *subject control*, because the subject is always the controller.

But the important point here is that mastery of the grammatical pattern can only produce acceptable clauses and interpretations when it is linked to the Navajo world view, particularly to Navajo concepts of animacy, intelligence, and control. The relative control, potency, or intelligence of the agent and patient entities must be known, and these are culturally defined.

THE EMPATHY HIERARCHY

The Navajo hierarchy of control may not be as unique as it would seem to a speaker of English. Langacker (1991: 306–307) proposed that the status of nominals as subjects depends, in part, on their position in a universal *empathy hierarchy*. This hierarchy has the structure *speaker > hearer > human > animal > physical object > abstract entity*.

Langacker's empathy hierarchy looks very much like the Navajo hierarchy of control, which, in general outline, places humans above animals and the latter above inanimate objects. There is also a close similarity to the hierarchy of animacy (*human > animal > inanimate*) proposed by Comrie (1989: 185) and said to correlate with certain characteristics of nouns, such as special case marking, distinctions of number, that is, countability, pluralization in pronouns, and agreement on the verb. Jane H. Hill (1988) framed the Navajo *bi-/yi-* alternation in terms of the animacy hierarchy, suggesting that Navajo simply reflects universal tendencies. However, recall that Comrie pointed out that animacy is a quality of noun-phrases and therefore differs from *control*, which is "a relation contracted between a noun-phrase and its predicate" (1989: 186–187). It is the Navajo relation between the noun-phrase and its predicate with which we are concerned here. Still, it does look as though animacy, empathy, and control are closely related phenomena. Human speakers are likely to see more similarity in and find more common concerns with animate than inanimate entities and therefore to rank them higher on the scale of empathy. Furthermore, control requires a degree of animacy and no doubt evokes more empathy.

Thus, it might be best to say that animacy, empathy, and control are facets of a possibly universal interaction scenario. Each culture elaborates the universal scenario in its own way and ties in its own linguistic frames. While each culture defines its interaction model uniquely, most will align with the universal hierarchies proposed by Langacker and Comrie. Thus, the Navajo define adults as higher in control than infants, intelligent beings as higher than the less intelligent, and larger beings as higher than smaller. Both specific and general animacy scenarios may govern grammar and usage in discourse.

The empathy hierarchy is only one of the determinants of a nominal's status as subject in Langacker's framework. In his view, subjects, because of their special cognitive salience, have a strong tendency to assume "a pivotal role in grammatical structure" (1991: 306). This high salience of the subject can be called *topicality*. High *empathy* represents one kind of topicality. Other factors that impart topicality are *agency, definiteness,* and status as *figure within a profiled relationship*. Thus, the prototypical subject is "agentive, human, definite, and the figure within the profiled relationship" (1991: 308, 1995: 24). In Navajo, the *bi-* prefix marks a patient-subject that has lost its agency but retained its control. Thus, in Navajo, the control (or empathy) hierarchy takes precedence over the subject's status as an agent.

ATTENDING TO NUMBERS IN YUCATEC MAYA AND ENGLISH

The Sapir-Whorf hypothesis is the name that linguistics and anthropology have given to the problem of linguistic relativity. In its strong formulation, it is the proposition that grammatical categories both enable and limit their speakers' perceptions of the world. Our view of the world is channeled, for example, by systems of noun classifiers, case systems (e.g., conjugations), and paradigms of verbal tense, aspect, and mood. In Sapir's words, "the 'real world' is to a large extent unconsciously built up on the language habits of the group," in Whorf's, "we dissect nature along the lines laid down by our native languages." [15] In a weaker formulation, the hypothesis may be taken as the proposition that language somehow reflects world view. Attempts to test either the strong or the weak form of the hypothesis have had little success, but two recent ones deserve consideration: John A. Lucy's study of grammatical number in

Yucatec Maya and English and Alfred Bloom's study of counterfactual reasoning in Chinese. I will start with Lucy's (1992b) study of number.

Lucy skirted around the concept of world view, preferring to limit the scope of his investigations to that of habitual thought of non-specialists. Nevertheless, his problem falls within the scope of my conception of world view as culturally defined imagery. According to Lucy (1992b: 1), the first task in any investigation of cultural relativity is to obtain comparable data on two or more languages. Accordingly, he focused on grammatical number in English and Yucatec. English, as we know, marks number with plural inflection *-s* (~ *-es*), with determiners such as the indefinite article and similar forms *a* (~*an*), ordinal indicators (first, second, third, etc.), and cardinal indicators (one, two, three, etc.), with concord on the verb (usually suffix *-s*) in the present indicative, and with forms of pronouns that are singular (he/she/it, him/her/it) or plural (they/them). Yucatec optionally marks lexical nouns with a plural suffix (*-ó'ob'*), as in *pèek'* 'dog' and *pèek'-ó'ob'* 'dogs' (1992b: 46). Pronouns can also take the plural marker. An identical suffix marks third person plural complements on verbs. Lucy reported that "the suffix is optional or *facultative* in that it need not be used for correct reference when a multiplicity of referents does in fact exist, but it can be used to clarify or emphasize such multiplicity" (1992b: 46). The facultative is usual with animate nouns (Lucy, personal communication, 1995). Thus, "one can speak of *ǧéeǧek pèek'* 'few dog' without any need to attach the plural suffix to *pèek'* 'dog'" (1992b: 47).

Yucatec, like English, can also mark nouns with a modifier signifying a numeral, but in Yucatec the numeral modifier is bound to a morpheme that functions as a numeral classifier. These classifiers mark (or determine) their nouns as 'one dimensional shape,' 'two dimensional shape,' 'three dimensional shape,' 'self-segmenting shape,' 'agricultural or other socially significant plant,' 'pair,' 'stack' (usually of two-dimensional items), parts of wholes, including 'side, face' and 'corner, edge,' portions of wholes, including 'strand' and 'slice,' four classes of measures, and two irregular classes. Thus, *ká'a-túul 'úulum* (i.e., two + animal/person classifier + turkey) (Lucy 1992b: 49). Modern Yucatec has "somewhat fewer than 100" of these classifiers (50). Yucatec also has other quantitative markers with the senses of 'few,' 'another [one],' and 'which [one].' In everyday speech plural inflection and concord are limited to animate entities or to objects possessed by them, such as heads and houses (55). Lucy (1992b: 55–56) concluded that Yucatec shows little evidence of concern with number:

The basic Yucatec pattern is to disregard number, and most lexical noun phrases are Neutral in number. . . . Number distinctions as such simply do not have the general significance within Yucatec grammar that they do in English, and grammatical number is expressed very indifferently in comparison with English.

But the problem that Lucy set for himself was to compare and contrast English and Yucatec "as to how they differently construe a common reality" (2). Presenting a common reality to speakers of both languages is no easy matter, but it is an explicit part of his method: "such comparison should take an external non-linguistic *reality* as the metric or standard for calibrating the content of linguistic and cognitive categories" (2). In order to create a semblance of a common reality, Lucy presented his subjects with sets of line drawings of people working with implements in settings that contained buildings, vehicles, animals, trees, and fluids (see Figure 19). The drawings varied according to the numbers and amounts of their constituents. Subjects were asked to describe verbally what they saw in the drawings, sometimes with the drawing in view, sometimes not. A third task required the subjects to judge "which of five associated alternate pictures was most similar to an original" (97). In a fourth task, each subject was asked "to select an original he had seen from an array containing the original and its five alternates" (98). The subjects were twelve Yucatec men and twelve U.S. men for each task. Estimated ages of the Yucatec men ranged "from 18 to 45+ years" (99). The English speakers were all college students ranging in age from 19 to 27 years.

Given this elaborate research framework, Lucy (1992b: 156) was able to advance the following hypotheses:

First, English speakers should habitually attend to the number of various objects of reference more than should Yucatec speakers. In particular, they should habitually attend to number for the wider array of referent types for which they obligatorily mark number. Second, English speakers should attend relatively more to the shape of objects and Yucatec speakers should attend relatively more to the material composition of objects.

Lucy found his hypotheses to be confirmed, in that English speakers more frequently mentioned number of animal or implement referents compared to substance referents, while Yucatec speakers more frequently mentioned number only of animal referents compared to substance referents. In triad sorting tasks, "Yucatec speakers showed a greater ten-

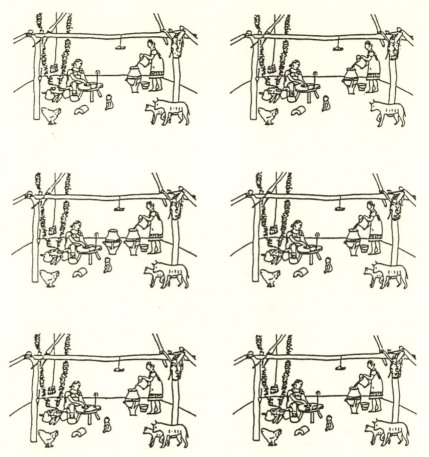

FIGURE 19. Drawing from stimulus presentation materials used in Lucy's comparison of English and Yucatec Maya grammatical number. From John A. Lucy, *Grammatical Categories and Cognition* (1992b: 170, Fig. 7). © Cambridge University Press 1992. Reprinted with the permission of Cambridge University Press.

dency to group objects on the basis of common material composition and English-speakers showed a strong tendency to group objects on the basis of common shape" (157).

What can we conclude from all this? Lucy had set himself the task of determining the "cognitive entailments" of language patterns that are used habitually: "Fourth, the implications of the language differences for *thought* must be articulated. This involves proposing plausible cognitive entailments of the habitual use of the language patterns at issue" (2).

Thus, it is not surprising that he concluded that language influences thought, or more specifically that "the frequency of pluralization in each language influences both the verbal and nonverbal interpretation of pictures" and "the underlying lexical structures associated with the number marking in the two languages have an influence on the nonverbal interpretation of objects" (157).

But these conclusions go too far. The fact that patterns of grammatical usage co-vary with the results of sorting tasks does not necessarily entail that the frequency of usage of grammatical forms or the existence of plural grammatical structures is influencing the nonverbal interpretations. We could as justifiably argue (1) that grammatical usages are influenced by non-verbal cultural categories (as discovered by triad sorting tasks), (2) that grammatical categories are, at their semantic poles, identical with abstract cultural categories, or (3) that both grammar and categorization are influenced by something else, such as some consistent differences in the socioeconomic and discourse environments of speakers of English and Yucatec. My own preference is for position (2), that semantic and cultural categories of number are epistemologically identical, or at least that the semantic categories of number are subsumed within some larger set of cultural categories of number. If so, then we could reasonably argue that category formation is influenced by both language usage and nonverbal cultural practices. We speak about what we think (and do), and we think about what we speak about. Speaking, thinking, and doing can all activate semantic schemas. On a subsequent page Lucy made a weaker claim: "In short, there is good preliminary evidence that diverse language forms bear a relationship to characteristic cognitive responses in speakers" (158). He also wrote of "the interplay of linguistic structure with the various psychological, cultural, and semiotic functions of language" (161). These positions seem more readily supportable by the data pertaining to grammatical number in English and Yucatec.

DISCUSSING THE UNREAL IN CHINESE

Since it is so difficult to prove that grammar constrains our perceptions of the real world, perhaps we can get a new perspective on the problem by examining how grammar structures our conception of the unreal. Perhaps there is a language out there somewhere which has no way of talking about what might be, as opposed to what is. One researcher has reported that Chinese is such a language, or at least that Chinese speakers are little inclined to discuss the possible as opposed to the actual. To be more specific, Alfred Bloom (1981: 13) found that speakers of "the Chinese language" experienced great difficulty in following statements of the type "If the Hong Kong government were to pass a law requiring that all citizens born outside of Hong Kong make weekly reports of their activities to the police, how would you react?" [16] He asserted that, unlike English, Chinese had no grammatical devices designed especially for expressing counterfactual ideas and nothing corresponding to English subjunctives such as *were to* and *would*. His attempts to get Chinese speakers to use counterfactual reasoning would elicit such reactions as: "We don't speak/ think that way"; "It's unnatural"; "It's unChinese" (1981: 13).

Bloom also found that the Chinese were generally reluctant to make nouns out of verbs and adjectives (sincere $\rightarrow$ sincerity; proliferate $\rightarrow$ proliferation). Actually, he spoke of "entification"—the construal of entities from qualities and processes. He asserted that, under the influence of English, they were acquiring linguistic resources to this end, but these were widely recognized as belonging to Westernized speech. More commonly, Chinese speakers faced with highly nominalized passages and counterfactuals would complain that they were too abstract and obscure.

Many speakers of English would probably agree with the Chinese on this point. Passages of English with numerous nominalizations and counterfactuals can be difficult to follow, though they are much used, especially in academic prose. But Bloom's point was this: since the Chinese language lacks common grammatical devices for expressing these cognitive schemas of counterfactuality and nominalization, the schemas themselves are relatively undeveloped. The schemas required to nominalize and speak counterfactually lie at a level of abstraction or complexity sufficiently removed from ordinary experience to require linguistic reinforcement for their survival as conceptual entities. Since Chinese provides no grammatical devices of counterfactuality or nominalization, the schemas receive no cognitive reinforcement. The Chinese appear to dislike thinking in these channels; hence, they lack motivation to maintain grammatical devices specialized to this purpose.

The counterfactual requires willingness to consider the influence of one unreal event upon another. Bloom concluded that because such abstract and complex concepts require frequent linguistic reinforcement they provide cases where language exerts strong influences over cognition. It is in the more rarefied fields of language, rather than in basic color terms and other basic experience and vocabulary, that the strong form of the Whorfian hypothesis may be valid. At the level of image-schemas representing embodied physical patterns, cognition influences language most strongly. At the level of complex syntax, there may be an opposite influence, as Bloom proposed.

T. K. Au (1983) reviewed Bloom's studies and tested his conclusions with studies of her own. In contradiction to Bloom, she claimed that "in the real world Chinese speakers use counterfactuals with little ambiguity" (1983: 157). The particular construction used depends upon whether the audience is familiar with the topic. If the audience knows whether a declaration is factual or not, then the if-then construction will serve to introduce a counterfactual implication. She claimed, "For instance, when a Chinese speaker remarks, 'If I am the U.S. President, then I will think before I speak,' everyone knows immediately that the remark is counterfactual because they all know that the speaker is not the U.S. President" (1983: 157). However, if the topic is not one that is familiar to the audience, the Chinese speaker must "first negate the premise and then use the 'if-then' construction for the premise and the implications," as follows:

> For instance, when talking about a "Mrs. Wong" whom the audience does not know, the speaker has to say, "Mrs. Wong not know English. If Mrs. Wong know English, she can then read the New York *Times*." Its English translation is: "Mrs. Wong does not know English. If Mrs. Wong knew English, she would be able to read the New York *Times*." (1983: 157)

If the Chinese version sounds quaint, it is only because Chinese verbs are unmarked for tense in the first and third person singular. Bloom had presented his Chinese and American subjects with a story that Au (1983: 158) nicely summarized as follows:

> The story was about an 18th century European philosopher, Bier, who could not read Chinese. At that time very few Chinese philosophical works had been translated into European languages, but if he had been able to read Chinese and so to learn about Chinese philosophy, he would have made various contributions to Western philosophy. The abstract form of the story was, "A was not the case. If A had been the case, B would have been the case; C would have been the case; D would have been the case; E would have been the case."

Au argued that the Chinese in Bloom's experiments had scored low in their ability to interpret counterfactual statements not because they lacked the ability, but because the Chinese language in Bloom's test story was not idiomatic. In her first experiments, she therefore introduced a new story about a Dutch explorer in central Africa who observed some natives cook a dead human body and drink the broth; seeing this, he fled from the scene. The story claims that if the explorer had been able to understand the language of the natives and had not fled so quickly, he would have learned that the deceased was a hero of the tribe who was killed in an accident, that the natives drank the broth of their hero only out of a desire to acquire his virtues, and that they were friendly.

The tastefulness of the topic aside, the Human Broth story clearly displays a talent for writing action drama that is lacking in the Bier story, and this is not entirely irrelevant to the argument over the interpretation of the results, as we will eventually see. Au found no significant differences in the ability of Chinese and American subjects to reason counterfactually. Both groups scored high under various experimental conditions. She concluded that her findings did not support Bloom's hypothesis.

Au also rewrote the Bier story in "simpler and more idiomatic Chinese" with similar results: the differences in performance between Chinese and American subjects disappeared. But perhaps her bilingual Chinese subjects had learned the counterfactual schema along with their English subjunctives and were able to use the schema in interpreting the story written in Chinese. To head off this criticism, she presented the Human Broth story to a group of twelve- to fifteen-year-olds who did not control the English subjunctive. She found that 98 percent of them were able to assign counterfactual interpretations.

Bloom countered that his argument applied only to complex reasoning and that the stories used by Au were too simple. He was not asserting that the Chinese do not have or understand counterfactual expressions, but that in intellectually demanding language their way of expressing them is more round about and provides more opportunity for confusion and distraction. His own paragraphs in the Bier story involved "rather abstract, intellectually demanding content," whereas Au's were "more concrete, less intellectually demanding content" (1984: 281). Furthermore, the Bier story and the Human Broth story were structured differently. In the Bier story, factual statements were limited to the original premise: "i.e., Bier was an Eighteenth Century Western philosopher who wanted . . . and who could not speak Chinese" (1984: 281). In the Human Broth story, factual content was introduced throughout the story, making it less intellectually demanding. Bloom countered Au's claim that his Chinese versions of the Bier story were non-idiomatic by asserting that they were written by native Chinese-speaking professors at the National Taiwan University. However, P. W. Cheng (1985) cited the judgment of five native speakers of Chinese that the Chinese version of the Bier story contained numerous errors, including systematic omission of the character *hui* in the implicational then-clause, where it would have had the effect of English *would* or *would have*.

To Bloom's riposte, Au responded with a variety of arguments concerning the nature of counterfactual language in Chinese that are too detailed to go into here. She did further experiments in which she tried to make the Chinese and English versions as comparable as possible. She found, for example, that adding hypothetical markers *jiu*, *hui*, and *yidan* to one of the Chinese versions of the Bier story to balance off against the incidence of subjunctives in the English version raised the counterfactual response rate from 23 percent to 81 percent. Once again, she concluded that the findings yield little support for the Sapir-Whorf hypothesis.

Cynthia Hsin-feng Wu (1991) argued that if Bloom's hypothesis were correct, speakers of Chinese would have great difficulty operating in the real world. She maintained that Chinese does indeed have several common counterfactual expressions, which translate as *if*, *in case*, *supposing*, and *were it not the case*. Lacking sufficient control of Mandarin Chinese, Bloom erred in omitting such expressions from the story and test questions that he presented to his subjects. For example, he translated *would have* into Chinese expressions meaning *it was*, *he was*, etc. Wu revised Bloom's test and compared a group of American students with 349 college students in Taipei. Much to her surprise, she found that the Chinese students were much less likely to register an understanding of counterfactual expressions.

It is not clear why Wu's Chinese subjects scored low on counterfactual interpretations, and there are many plausible explanations. For example, they may, to a greater degree than American students, regard every test as a serious evaluation of their academic skills and concrete knowledge. In such a performance-oriented context, a test of counterfactuality may be irritating and unwelcome, causing subjects to lose interest or even to subvert the test. It would help to know how the two groups of students interpreted the testing situation.

Thus, the question of the effect of language on counterfactual reasoning is still unsettled. Au's extensive experiments, similar experiments conducted by L. Liu (1985), and observations made by P. W. Cheng (1985) appear to contradict Bloom's conclusions, but Wu's findings lend support and D. K. Jordan (1982) found Bloom's conclusions plausible. After a very detailed and thorough review of the whole controversy, Lucy

(1992a: 251) rejected Bloom's conclusions because he failed to provide "evidence that the specific labels at issue had demonstrable effects on any pattern of everyday behavior and thought."

It may be impossible to control all the cultural and social variables that might impinge upon testing situations and significantly bias test results, but perhaps a commonsense interpretation of Bloom's findings will help to define their significance. Since, by his own insistence, his test instruments were intellectually demanding and representative of the writing style of Chinese intellectuals, it seems likely that the grammatical frames and their underlying semantic schemas were more complex than those in vernacular use. For example, a frame that allowed for a series of unmarked implications following a premise and the first "then" clause would be more complex than one that required every implication to be prefixed with an implication marker, if only because it would contain both marked and unmarked "then" clauses (for which the real marker would be their syntactic position). Perhaps the Chinese translators were writing over the heads of the intended subjects to a greater degree than was the case with the English version of the Bier story.

In this regard, it is interesting that Cheng (1985) noted that Chinese students receive much less practice than American students in answering questions based on essay comprehension because Chinese education places greater emphasis on memorization than on comprehension. Perhaps this bias is what Au was correcting with her rewrite of the Bier story to include more hypothetical markers. If Bloom limited the hypothesis to the intellectual realm, then it would appear that his claim is much like the rather obvious and uninteresting claim that those who understand mathematical symbols are more likely to understand the concepts that they represent. Few would deny that the frequent use of mathematical symbols and language helps to entrench mathematical concepts. But it is hard to argue from this analogy alone that most speakers of English and Chinese differ fundamentally in their ability or inclination to reason counterfactually. Similarly, G. Hatano (1982: 819) observed that "what Bloom demonstrates is that people may fail to comprehend discourse that includes 'unnatural,' seldom-used expressions" and that "Bloom does not prove that native speakers of Chinese tend to have difficulty in comprehending/ utilizing the counterfactual mode of processing even when it is appropriate in their own cultural context." Hatano worried that some ethnocentric Western scholars would be tempted to think that Chinese and native speakers of the language are less sophisticated than English and its native speakers.

On a more philosophical level, we could regard the counterfactual as an instance of the ability to entertain two opposing ideas. As we have seen, logical opposition is a fundamental theme of Chinese language and culture. It can be seen in the supernatural principles of *yin* and *yang*, which are both contradictory and complementary, connoting a balance of male and female, life and death, winter and summer (Fung 1966). It can also be seen in the common phrasing of questions as the negation of one possibility by its opposite, as in the greeting *ni hao bu hao?* 'you good not good?' It seems highly unlikely that people who habitually structure their thinking and grammar along lines of opposition would lack the ability or inclination for counterfactual reasoning. Perhaps a better way to approach this problem would be to study natural language and Chinese texts to try to discover how speakers of Chinese normally speak of possibilities and hypothetical ideas and how they structure these realms in their thinking. The various critiques of Bloom's work also testify to the importance of understanding the institutional culture in which language use is situated. An ethnography of speaking approach is a necessary preliminary wherever the purposes of language use may bias test results.

CHAPTER 7

DISCOURSE AND NARRATIVE

DISCOURSE SCENARIOS

One afternoon as I was walking my dog in the suburban residential neighborhood where I live in Las Vegas, two boys about ten years of age rode by me on their bikes. They were earnestly engaged in a conversation, of which I was able to catch only the following before they peddled out of earshot: "And when your dad says, 'Why did you beat him up?' you say, 'Because he called me a dick,' and then you say, 'Just ask John.' " Though short, the conversation is pithy. The boy proposing his friend's excuse in a pseudoquote ("Because he called me a dick") was imagining a dialogue based on a discourse scenario something like the following: *when a parent questions your bad behavior, justify it by describing the other kid's verbal abuse, and get a friend to verify it.* Discourse scenarios consist of abstract imagery of speakers and listeners. They are complex images of people speaking, listening, and replying, or otherwise responding and reacting as they play roles in social scenes. It is because discourse scenarios are imagistic that we can either talk about them, as did the boy quoted above, or act them out, as his companion may have done later. The study of discourse scenarios can be put to several uses: to discover why discourse is coherent or incoherent, to determine how talk *about* discourse can make sense, and to investigate how various cultures and subcultures may define discourse scenarios differently.

I propose to investigate the way in which discourse itself is represented in culturally defined scenarios. Typically, schema or frame theories of text and discourse propose that interpretations are constrained by listeners' or readers' preconceptions (Shakir and Farghal 1991). The proposal that schemas or cognitive models represent discourse events themselves, including their contextual relations and subjective groundings (i.e., "centering") and their sequentiality, intentionality, and intersubjectivity, provides a second avenue by which cognitive theory can be brought to bear on discourse. I am going to discuss a broad framework of analytical categories starting with discourse scenarios, which are cognitive (and cultural) models of discourse events. Like models of physical entities and non-linguistic events, they are complex entities that are activated and construed from different perspectives at different levels of specificity and scope. Discourse scenarios are comparable to cultural scripts (Wierzbicka 1992b, n.d.) and they are roughly equivalent to what Deborah Tannen and Cynthia Wallat (1993: 59–60) called "interactive frames": "a sense of what activity is being engaged in, how speakers mean what they say," or "a definition of what is going on in interaction." Deborah Schiffrin (1993: 233) defined interactive frames as "what people think they are doing when they talk to each other."

Discourse scenarios reside within *situation models*, which are more inclusive representations of social context. For example, in a Lebanese village, conventionalized lying (*kizb*) is something a young male villager does to an enemy or a rival at every opportunity (Gilsenan 1976). It is the established rivalries that provide the situations for *kizb*. To give an example closer to home, a scheduled university class session includes the verbal discourse of lectures and class discussions, but it may also include such non-verbal behavior as written testing and seating arrangements. Similarly, a law case includes verbal pretrial depositions, courtroom testimony by witnesses, and argument by lawyers, but it may also require non-verbal written depositions, assembly and conveyance of documentary and physical evidence by clerks, and general patterns of physical movement as permitted by the physical layout of the courtroom and required by the purposes of a trial. All of these elements belong to the situation model. Strictly speaking, it is only the representations of speaking that are discourse scenarios, but, in practice, separating discourse scenarios from situation models may be problematic.

The situation model corresponds roughly to what Schiffrin (1987: 28) called the "information state," which she defined somewhat diffusely as "the organization and management of knowledge and metaknowledge" and "what a speaker knows and what a hearer knows." It seems also to correspond loosely to Tannen and Wallat's (1993: 60) notion of "knowledge schemas," which are "participants' expectations about people, objects, events, and settings in the world, as distinct from alignments being negotiated in a particular interaction." However, the fit between "discourse scenario" and "interactive frame" on the one hand and "situation model" and "knowledge schema" on the other is only a loose one. Tannen and Wallat's distinction between interactive frame and knowledge schema seems to hinge on particular interactions versus general knowledge of interaction and situation. The distinction that I make here between discourse scenario and situation model hinges on the distinction between verbal discourse and the wider situations in which discourse is embedded, as these are cognized by interlocutors. Both types of knowledge (verbal and situational) enter into the active scenes of particular interactions.

A situation model is relatively stable and therefore not quite the same as a participant's built-up, negotiated, model of an ongoing discourse situation in all its concrete remembered detail. The latter has been termed the *text world* by Werth (n.d.). William F. Hanks (1993) called the built-up text world the *framework* of discourse in order to distinguish it from the *frame*, which is more abstract and comparable to a discourse scenario as defined here. To the extent that interlocutors share world views, discourse scenarios, situation models, and discourse frameworks, they have a *common ground* that enables discourse (Werth 1993: 82).

Common ground becomes important in explaining how even mundane conversations can be coherent. Schiffrin theorized that a linguistic expression can evoke "a number of potential frames (both institutional and interactional) within which a next utterance can be interpreted." Thus, when Henry says, "Want a piece of candy?" and Irene says, "No," Henry's next words (if I read Schriffrin correctly) may reveal his employment of any of several possible frames (models, schemas) for understanding or ignoring Irene's response: "There's nothing wrong with it" (*people refuse food if they suspect there is something wrong with it*), "Just testing you! I know you're on a diet" (*people on diets don't accept food*), "I didn't hear you" (*Henry has trouble hearing Irene*), or "What time did the teachers leave?" (shift of topic to unrelated frame) (1993: 256). Unless Irene also understood these frames, she would be unable to grasp Henry's meaning.

Discourse scenarios integrate a variety of schema types, including but not limited to schemas of (1) participation, (2) speech acts such as assertives, directives, commissives, expressives, and declarations, (3) sequencing (reciprocal and narrative), (4) perspective (e.g., subjective, objective, self-conscious, role-playing), and (5) ideation. Elements (2), (3), and (5) correspond to rhetorical, sequential, and ideational structures in Gisela Redeker's (1991: 1168) theory of discourse coherence. The five types constitute an "etic" framework of analytic categories intended only as a guide to the investigation of folk discourse scenarios.

PARTICIPATION SCHEMAS

Participation schemas define who speaks to whom. They often involve multiple participants whose roles are mutually interdependent and defined intersubjectively. For example, the English terms *speaker* and *listener* entail participation schemas defined so generally that they sanction anyone speaking to anyone else. If participation schemas are really crucial to understanding discourse, then we would expect them to influence grammar. In fact, much of the information on honorific terms of address can be understood as predicating culturally defined participation schemas.

Participants' roles in verbal discourse typically represent only part of their wider roles in institutions as teachers, secretaries, detectives, or parents. Folk participation schemas may emerge at various levels from simple speech acts to complex discourse events. Hanks treated what I am calling "participation schemas" under the somewhat more general rubric of voicing in text, which "subsumes the relation between the textual artifact and the framework of production and participation from which it arises." Voicing in text concerns "the distinctions among monologue, dialogue, direct, indirect, and quoted discourse . . . , dialogism . . . , collaborative . . . , cooperative . . . , and one-person productions [citations omitted]" (Hanks 1989: 102).

What I am calling "participation schemas" are related to what others have called "participant frameworks" (Goodwin 1990: 10) and "participation frameworks," which are "the way that speaker and hearer are related to their utterances and to one another" (Schiffrin 1993: 233). Within such participation frameworks are "participant alignments" that are "related to the way interactants position themselves relative to one another, e.g., their relationships of power and solidarity, their affective stances, their footing . . ." (Schiffrin 1993: 233). Such participant alignments must arise as interlocutors interpret ongoing discourse events and imagine themselves as participants.

Participation schema is a general analytic category that should be used as a kind of flashlight to discover folk categories that are similar or more specific. A recent study of children's discourse illustrates the difference between analytic and folk categories of participation. Observing the speech patterns of black children in southwest Philadelphia, Marjorie Goodwin (1990) identified "participant frameworks" in a particular type of gossip dispute, which she termed "he-said-she-said." This is an activity in which "one girl accuses another of a particular breach: having talked about her behind her back":

The utterances used to make such statements provide multiply embedded animations of *addressee, speaker*, and *third party*; indeed, a separate biography for each character as a relevant past culminating in the present accusation unfolds. He-said-she-said accusations thus provide an example of a participant framework that explicitly depicts relevant parties. (1990: 10)

Within the general framework of addressee/speaker/third party, she found a more specific framework of accuser/defendant, but "accuser" and "defendant" were not terms used by the children themselves. Goodwin determined the participant framework from biographical statements such as "And **Ar**thur said that **you** said that **I** was showin' off just because I had that **bl:ou**se on" (1990: 195). This example, and many others, suggest that accuser/defendant schemas held less cognitive salience for the children involved in he-said-she-said discourse events than did personal identities, such as "**Arthur**," "**you**," and "**I**," and categories of speech act and social action such as *saying* and *"showin' off."* Thus, Goodwin may have struck closer to the cognitive mark when she identified the participation schemas as *addressee, speaker*, and *third party*. In the children's descriptions of discourse, pronouns and personal names reveal highly specific participation schemas centered on personal identities. This pattern probably emerges from the special social concerns of these Afro-American children as opposed to an Afro-American cultural focus on the expression of personal identities (Kochman 1981).

Susan U. Philips (1989) described patterns of participation involved in the perception of "Indian time" on the Warm Springs Indian Reservation. The study, done under the rubric of the ethnography of speaking, is perceptive and the conclusions are quite interesting from the standpoint of ethnography and social action, but the method of presentation is such that we cannot be confident that observed patterns of participation represent folk cognitions. For example, she wrote:

There is a wide variety of ways in which the factors involved in participant regulation can be combined. An activity can involve participants who are committed or not committed in advance, or both. Whom the activity is open to can be defined in terms of a wide range of social criteria. The number of possible and/or necessary participants can be finite, or situation-determined. For any bounded activity, participants may be obliged to sustain their engagement in that activity, or they may be replaced by others at certain points. Warm Springs Indian activities involve the actualization of certain specific combinations of these dimensions from among the probably infinite possible combinations, and it is the range and frequency of what the Indians perceive as desirable combinations that distinguishes them from other groups of people. (1989: 107)

Philips probably obtained these data in a variety of ways, including personal observations, participation, and interviews, but since no native-language statements are presented it is not possible to determine how closely the analytic "factors" (commitment, social criteria, replacement) also reflect folk participation schemas. Philips (1989: 109) came closer to a cognitive approach when she wrote the following:

If the individual is to become an actual participant, and is to sustain his participation, he must at all times be able to recognize and identify the nature of the regulation of participation, know how it will alter, and recognize in what direction it is altering, as it is altering. . . .

This knowledge is knowledge of "social context" or "situation"; and it is knowledge which the individual must have merely to sustain his co-presence with other participants in ongoing activity, and thus be in a position to speak, let alone speak in a socially appropriate fashion.

But this is more a proposal for the investigation of folk situation models than a description of them; it refers more directly to knowledge inferred from social action than to discourse schemas inferred from language. Philips (1989: 94) came closest to what I have in mind when she said, "From the Indians' point of view, there are some activities on the reservation that run on Indian time, and other activities that run—or are supposed to run—on white time (for which there is no analogous term of reference, 'Indian time' being the marked category)." "Indian time" is clearly a folk-category, covering not only participation, but a whole range of discourse events and sequences. "Indian time" is a cognitive model, a significant chunk of the world view at Warm Springs.

One who comes analytically closer to what I have in mind by participation schema is Michael R. Walrod (1988: 29), who studied persuasive or normative discourse found in informal litigation among the Ga'dang people of the Philippines. Walrod's concept of the *litigation script* includes knowledge about who may participate, that is, "who should speak first, who should speak next, who should not speak" (1988: 29). It also includes knowledge of speech acts for initiating proceedings and getting the floor. Like Agar's burglar hustling schemas, Walrod's litigation script seems general enough to allow for contingencies.

SPEECH ACTS AS MINIMAL DISCOURSE SCENARIOS

Speech act scenarios represent the minimal units in the sequential structures of discourse events. Speech act scenarios may entail cognitively salient feeling states, as *scold* entails shame, *tease* entails frustration or embarrassment, and Black English *dis* entails humiliation and resentment. They may entail behavioral responses, as *telling a joke* typically entails laughter. Thus, even the most minimal of discourse scenarios integrate linguistic and non-linguistic domains of experience. It may ultimately make more sense to speak of cultural scenarios, which would be comparable to Wierzbicka's cultural scripts. A prototypical speech act scenario implicates, at a minimum, a participation schema that provides for both a speaker and a listener, though these may be one and the same (as in talking to yourself or promising yourself).

A point of reference for much of contemporary pragmatic language theory is the work of John B. Searle (1990: 410), who defined illocutionary speech acts according to what we *do* with propositions:

> In the illocutionary line of business there are five and only five basic things we can do with propositions: We tell people how things are (assertives), We try to get them to do things (directives), We commit ourselves to doing things (commissives), We express our feelings and attitudes (expressives), and We bring about changes in the world so that the world matches the proposition just in virtue of the utterance (declarations).

Searle's formulation is pragmatic and action-oriented. It seems to direct our attention away from speakers' and listeners' cognitive worlds to some relationship to an outside world. The categories are analytic and seem to provide no avenue for the discovery of folk categories. The analyst adopts the position of one watching the events and reading interlocutors' intentions into them. The question is whether Searle's speech acts can be reformulated in more cultural terms.

Let us suppose that discourse is partly governed by scenarios that include participants' intentions, actions, roles, and thoughts. Speech acts predicate these scenarios. To label them "speech acts" is simply to call attention to the pragmatic aspect of language, the intentions, motives, and goals that are inherent in all human discourse but may be defined more clearly in some kinds of expressions. Given this cognitive perspective, the five basic types of illocutionary acts defined by Searle can be regarded as minimal and highly schematic discourse scenarios in which interlocutors with various intentions interact to produce various cognitive and behavioral outcomes. I would redefine Searle's five basic illocutionary acts in terms of the following discourse scenarios:

Assertives predicate that speaker is thinking of something that speaker intends for listener to believe.
Directives predicate that speaker intends for listener to do something.
Commissives predicate speaker's intention to behave in a certain way under circumstances that are specified or presupposed.
Expressives predicate feeling states of speaker.
Declarations predicate that speaker intends for a particular ideational world-model or world-construal to be consensual.

But these are analytical categories. Searle believed them to be basic, and, therefore, presumably universal. I doubt that he was correct in this. The challenge for cultural linguists is to discover the configurations of native speech acts, which may comprise a variety of pragmatic intentions and feeling states within their culturally defined gestalts. For example, on the Micronesian atoll of Ifaluk, speech acts may be instances of *fago*, an emotion term related to compassion, love, and sadness. Catherine A. Lutz (1988: 119) reported, "*Fago* is uttered in recognition of the suffering that is everywhere and in the spirit of a vigorous optimism that human effort, most especially in the form of caring for others, can control its ravages." It is difficult to assimilate *fago* to any of Searle's categories, but a combination of them might get us close. Similarly, Jane H. Hill and Judith T. Irvine (1993: 8) argued that Searle's framework fails to account for a speech act of the Ilongot of the Philippines: "*tuydek* (roughly, 'command'), requires particular differences in social rank, which in turn derive from other qualities of persons achieved in social action, such as a knowledgeable heart." Thus, while Searle's classification of speech acts may provide some general questions to direct initial research, they are almost certainly culture-bound and should be abandoned when native language evidence leads in other directions.

SEQUENCING SCHEMAS

The sequencing of speech acts is important to most definitions of linguistic genres. It is perhaps in his analysis of sequence that Hymes came closest to developing an explicitly cognitive theory of discourse. His analyses, with Joel Sherzer, of an Abipon shaman's retribution and a girl's puberty rite include formal descriptions of sequences that represent Abipon knowledge of how to participate in speech acts (Hymes 1972: 66–67).

Sequencing involves directionality, which may be reflexive (as in talking to yourself), one-way (as in monologue and some narrative), or reciprocal with turn-taking (as in dialogue, conversation, and call-and-response). Narrative scenarios define narrative genres, story scripts, or story grammars (Bartlett 1932; Dundes 1964; Dundes 1965; Propp 1968; Colby 1973; Rumelhart 1975; Beaugrande 1979; Hymes and Cazden 1980; Palmer 1980; Mandler 1984; Bruner 1986a).

Some of this sequential structure may be innate: Edward M. Bruner (1990: 72) argued that humans have an " 'innate' and primitive predisposition to narrative organization," but that our culture "soon equips us with new powers of narration" through mythology, its tool kit of canonical scripts, and its "tradition of telling and interpreting." He noted that "to be a viable culture is to be bound in a set of connecting stories, connecting even though the stories may not represent a consensus" (1990: 96); and he argued for the innateness of turn-taking and mutual exchange.

Sequencing schemas, like speech act scenarios, may contain imagery of non-verbal behavior interspersed with or concurrent with verbal imagery. Thus, they belong to what Schiffrin (1987: 25) called the "action structure" of discourse, which includes "what action precedes, what action is intended, what action is intended to follow, and what action actually does follow," or at least they belong to the scenarios that govern the action structure.

Sequencing schemas also govern what Schiffrin (1987: 24) identified as the "exchange structure" of discourse, which includes turn-taking and such adjacency pairs as questions-and-answers and reciprocal greetings. She treated both action structures and exchange structures as pragmatic, "because of the central role which speakers and hearers play in negotiating their organization" (1987: 25). But, in her view, action and exchange structures are non-linguistic, emerging "through units (turns and acts) which are realized by the use of language but are not linguistic *per se* [italics in original]" (1987: 26). In my view, both action structures and exchange structures should be subsumed into sequencing schemas that integrate components that are variously linguistic and non-linguistic.

PERSPECTIVE SCHEMAS

Like other human transactional processes, such as society and human ecology, discourse involves the observer as a participant. We can conceptualize discourse as non-participants, but in order to be participants, we *must* conceptualize it. This fundamental fact of discourse raises a number of interesting questions. How, for example, can we have a point of view as observer/speaker or observer/hearer? How can we project ourselves into discourse patterns learned by observing others and execute them with competence? How can we take both sides of a conversation? How can we quote, pseudoquote, speak for others, and discuss the discourse of others? How can we be objective observers of our own discourse? What do we have in mind when we talk about speech in metalinguistic and metacommunicative acts? How can we project the outcomes of speech acts? And how can we fit all of these various perspectives together to swim freely in the stream of conversation? My approach to these problems involves posmiting a set of schemas with speakers and listeners serving as both interlocutors and observers.

Langacker's work on subjectification (1990a: 215–220, 1990b) has exerted a particularly strong influence on the ideas presented here. In his framework, the construal of entities is maximally objective when "they function solely and prominently as the object of perception, and not at all as part of the perceptual apparatus itself." The construal is maximally subjective when the entities function "exclusively as part of the subject of perception" as a "component of the perceiving apparatus, but are not themselves perceived." Thus, to apply this to discourse schemas, when a viewer is a participant in a conceptualized speech event, but is not part of that which is perceived as onstage, then viewer/participant's construal of the event is maximally subjective, but when all participants are solely the objects of perception, and viewer as the perceiving subject is not conceptualized as a participant, then viewer's construal of the event is maximally objective.

Langacker (1990b: 6) pointed out that his technical distinction between subjective and objective differs from that made "when speaking of a judgement being subjective vs. objective (i.e. 'personal, idiosyncratic' vs. 'impartial, based on solid evidence'), or even in referring to subjectivist vs. objectivist theories of meaning." In his framework, the contrast between subjective and objective refers to "the inherent asymmetry between a perceiving individual and the entity perceived" (1990b: 7). Given a viewer and a perceived object, the construal (image) of the viewer herself (by the viewer) is maximally subjective and the construal of the perceived object is maximally objective only when viewer stands completely outside the perceptual field. A viewer may be construed more objectively by being moved into the perceptual field. As Langacker (1990b: 8) put it, "Each step along the path toward focused self-examination increases the objectivity of V's [viewer's] construal and diminishes that of P [perceived object] [information in brackets added]." Langacker (1990b: 8) provided examples of how a subjectively construed viewer may come to be objectively construed:

> ... suppose I experience an emotion, such as fear, desire, or elation. If I merely undergo that experience non-reflectively, both the emotion and my role in feeling it are subjectively construed. But to the extent that I reflect on the emotional experience—by analyzing it, by comparing it to other experiences, or simply by noting that I am undergoing it—the emotion and my role therein receive a more objective construal. Or compare how I conceive of my house when mentally tracing the route I take in driving to work, and when drawing a map showing the location of my house in relation to the campus. In the former instance, the house's location is construed subjectively, serving only as the implicit point of origin for the mental path. In the latter, by contrast, it has an objective construal by virtue of being put onstage as an explicit focus of attention.

Langacker then showed how lexical meanings and grammatical constructions depend upon the speakers' construals along the axis of objectivity/subjectivity. My interest in Langacker's schema of objectivity/subjectivity lies in the observation of discourse itself and in the fact that observers may or may not participate in conceptualized speech acts. In what follows I will use the term *observer* rather than *viewer*, because discourse is perceived with more than the eyes.

These are the implications that I see for the understanding of discourse: observer's construal of her part in a discourse event is maximally subjective when she is part of the discourse but is focusing her observations on interlocutor, as often happens when we speak or listen to another person. I will refer to this situation as the subjective construal of a discourse event, diagramed as in Figure 20, with two speakers, one of whom (S1) is also the observer/conceptualizer (O). That part of the construed discourse event which observer places in the "onstage area" or general locus of attention is shaded, while the specific focus of attention is indicated by a bold outline. The more extensive area outlined by the box is what Langacker called "the full expanse of the viewer's perceptual field."[1] The dashed arrow represents the perceptual relationship between observer and perceived speaker. In the diagrams that follow, conceptualized speech and discourse events are bounded by rectangles. Consequently, the rectangles no longer necessarily represent what Langacker termed the perceptual field.

To illustrate these points, a relatively subjective construal of speaker/

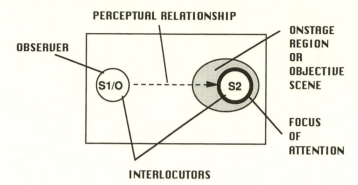

FIGURE 20. Subjective construal of discourse event (S = speaker; O = observer).

observer underlies the examples of metacommunication in (1) to (3) from Michael Stubbs (1983: 49), only if we omit the elements in parentheses. The utterances in (1) and (2) would then subjectively predicate, among other things, an intention to establish discourse. The utterances in (3) subjectively predicate acknowledgment and breaking off. However, if the elements in parentheses are retained, the utterances then symbolize a relatively objective construal of both interlocutors.

(1) Hello! Can you hear (me)? Oh, you're still there. (I thought you'd hung up.)
(2) Come in Z-Victor One! Do you read (me)?
(3) Roger! Out!

Observer's construal of discourse is maximally objective, in Langacker's sense, when observer lies entirely outside the speech event, that is, when the event is construed as involving only third parties, as in Figure 21. (In the objective construal of a discourse event, the nonparticipating observer may construe herself subjectively as an observer, but not as participant.) In most cases, it is likely that observer's attention alternates between interlocutors.

This perspective imagery can be used to characterize metalinguistic predications, that is, language about discourse itself. Interpreting metalinguistic predications is something we all do easily and naturally, though not without mistakes and misunderstandings. Nevertheless, the analysis will require some mental gymnastics, so please be forewarned. The following discussion is somewhat tricky.

Either subjective or objective construals could underlie the following italicized metalinguistic utterances from Stubbs (1983: 49): "*I'm sure he*

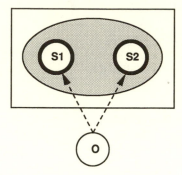

FIGURE 21. Objective construal of discourse event.

didn't mean what he said; or *He never says what he means*," "*She said it with such feeling*," and "*He always knows what to leave unsaid*." In the first sentence, observer predicates herself objectively in the commentary on the discourse ("I'm sure"), but not as part of the discourse under discussion ("He didn't mean what he said"). That is, it is not explicit, or even certain, that speaker ("he") was addressing observer. These would all predicate subjective construals of the actual speakers of these sentences if they referred to an event or events in which the *observed* speakers, predicated by "he" and "she," had addressed the unspecified speakers of *these* sentences. Only the speakers indexed as "he" or "she" are construed objectively. They would still be objective construals (of "he" or "she") if they predicated that the observed speaker had addressed the unspecified addressee-interlocutor of these sentences or a fourth party. In this sense, neither the actual speaker of these sentences nor the addressee is predicated, either subjectively or objectively, as might be indicated by the pronouns "me" or "you," for example. Perspective may be difficult to formalize, but the fact that the expressions cited above would be readily intelligible in either context in everyday conversation is testimony to our cognitive facility with shifting perspectives. Such an important faculty deserves more scientific attention.

Observer's construal of a discourse event *in which she is a participant* only becomes objective when observer herself is placed within the objective scene to become a second focus of attention, as in Figure 22. The diagram suggests that S1/O (Speaker 1/Observer) is self-consciously observing her own part in the discourse. The subjective/objective polarity of participants in the subjective construal is attenuated, as shown by the half-bold circle around S1/O. However, there is probably a continuum that starts with focus entirely on S2, passing through a stage where the focus on S1/O and S2 is equivalent, and finally reaching the point where the focus is entirely on S1/O, as shown in Figure 23 (compare Langacker [1990b: 7–8]).

By virtue of their common participation in the onstage region, the interlocutors in Figures 22 and 23 are construed as participants in a relation. The observation of the event by one participant constitutes a second relation, which is not diagramed. The connected entities in these relationships may be construed as trajectors and landmarks, which are manifested in descriptive clauses as subjects and objects. Self-conscious speech schemas (i.e., those in which speaker-observer is construed objectively) underlie the following metacommunicative and metalinguistic utterances from Stubbs (1983: 49, 51): *"I couldn't get through to him; I managed to get the idea across* [to someone]*; Do you follow me?; We don't seem to be on the same wavelength"*; *"How dare you talk to me like that?"*; *"Who do you think you are talking to?; Don't use that tone of voice with me!"*; *"I could do with a bit of silence"*; and *"What I'm trying to say is . . .* [brackets added]." Compare the subjective, non-self-conscious, predication of the metacommunicative utterance *"Do you want to say something at this point?"* and the objective, but not self-conscious *At this point, Sam said something to Alan.* Note also the importance of metaphor in characterizing discourse in the phrases *get through to, get the idea across, follow,* and *be on the same wavelength.*

Perspective schemas enter into larger constructions where they are activated fleetingly but crucially for intelligible communication about discourse itself. It is not just discourse scenarios, but also *construals* of them that become schematized and conventionalized. This entrenchment is

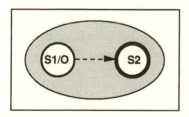

FIGURE 22. Schema of speech event with participant-observer emerging as part of objective scene with attenuated subjective/objective polarity.

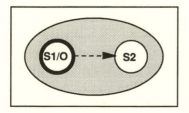

FIGURE 23. Schema of speech event with participant-observer construed as part of objective scene with extreme self-conscious focus of attention.

what gives us ready access to different perspectives, scopes of observation, and levels of specificity and thus provides participants with ready-made interpretive schemas. Perspective schemas are only the initial building blocks. Discourse can also be represented as composite schemas that specify how reciprocal acts of listening and speaking, as in conversations, can themselves be referred to in metaconversations.

These notions of perspective help to reveal the discourse functions of quotations and pseudoquotations. The boy quoted in the introduction constructing a pseudoquote had assumed the perspective of a boy responding to his father. Tannen (1989: 25) proposed that constructed dialogue, that is, "direct speech" or "direct quotation," functions to involve listeners and elicit emotional responses by "the creation of voices . . . [evoking] the imagination of a scene in which characters speak in those voices." But quotation can also be seen as a narrative device for activating subjective schemas in listeners' imaginations. It is the subjective perspective that induces personal involvement. Intensely involved listeners often want to speak along with narrators or to respond in their own voices. A good play induces the audience to forget their role as objective observers. Perspective shifts to the point of view of one or more actors, subjectively perceived. Perspective is also involved in the phenomenon of "speaking for another" (Schiffrin 1993).

The problem of perspective in discourse is one that continues to bedevil anthropologists who have come to think of anthropology itself as discourse and find themselves asked to consider their own involvement in the processes that shape the institutions and persons who they study or to choose between objective observation and subjective or self-conscious dialogue (Clifford 1986; Marcus and Fischer 1986; Marcus 1994). Some anthropologists describe conversion experiences that give them the perspective of a native (Kearney 1992), while others find the worlds of other cultures unfathomable. After eight fieldwork trips among the Kwaio of the Solomon Islands, Roger Keesing (1992b: 77) wrote: "I was still all I will ever be: an outsider who knows something of what it is to be an insider."

Anthropologists are caught in a dilemma. Anthropology's ideological commitment to participant observation by definition renders an objective perspective very difficult, or secondarily derived at best; but at the same time the one or two years of adult life as an outsider that most anthropologists spend in another culture are insufficient to provide the sheer multiplicity of experiences from different perspectives that may be required to construct complete and well-formed native discourse scenarios. Anthropologists attempt to compensate for their relative paucity of native experiences by entering into intense dialogues with "key informants," reconstructing life-histories, and participating in native activities.

IDEATIONAL SCHEMAS

Gisela Redeker proposed that ideation is one factor in discourse coherence. To the extent that a discourse describes or presupposes a "world" or scene, then ideation pertains to expected temporal sequences, elaborations, causes, reasons, and consequences, all more or less mutually understood by speakers and listeners. Unlike Searle, who defined speech acts according to their fit to "the world," Redeker (1991: 1169) referred to "the world the discourse describes," which makes her formulation more compatible with a cognitive approach.

I think that Redeker intended ideational coherence to be an analytic category, but it can also be applied metalinguistically to characterize folk representations of ideational coherence in discourse. Thus, in our English folk classification of speaker coherence we can imagine speakers who are "logical," "present ideas clearly," or "make sense," and those who "just don't make sense," are "schizy," "off the wall," or "out of it," or "babble incoherently." Furthermore, we can characterize some discourse events as "satisfying," "informative," or "useful," while others are "unsatisfying," "uninformative," or "incoherent," according to whether they are, among other things, ideationally coherent. Folk conceptualization of ideational coherence is important, but schemas of ideation need not be confined to evaluations of coherence. In terms of ideation, we may judge that a joke was clever or a story full of surprises. If we were characterizing the same events as speech acts, we might judge the joke to be funny or the story to be moving.

CONSTRUALS OF DISCOURSE SCENARIOS

If discourse scenarios are imagistic, then they must be subject to processes of construal in terms of figure and ground, scope, profile and base, specificity, and perspective (Langacker 1990a). The imagery of discourse events in this technical sense must govern how discourse is performed, interpreted, and talked about. For example, the discovery of figure and ground relationships in discourse scenes could involve the construal of one participant as a figure against the others or the identification of one kind of speech act as figure against other speech acts. It is the question of who sings lead and who sings backup in our image of a singing group. In our image of a complex conversation among several people, it is the question of which participants speak at normal volume while others speak softly. Part of our communicative competence is to recognize the schemas and participate appropriately.

Control of scope in discourse may involve drawing the boundaries of situations. A suggestion to a teenager to do her homework might be taken as a friendly reminder if the scope is limited to a single day, but it will almost certainly be taken as unfriendly criticism if interpreted to cover a long-standing pattern of poor study habits and failing grades. Part of communicative competence involves knowing how to construe the scope, either to follow the intended meaning or to create new fields of meaning.

The relationship of profile to base at the level of lexemes is that of *spoke* to *wheel*. A term is meaningless apart from the conception of its base. This distinction may also apply to discourse predications. Eve E. Sweetser (1987), for example, showed that a speech act can only be judged a lie (the conceptual profile) relative to a folk model of communication (the conceptual base). Thus, a speech act may only take on meaning in the context of a discourse scenario or in terms of some more general folk model of communication that is structured less like a time-bounded event and more like a set of interrelated principles.

Specificity is an important dimension of our representations of discourse in general and of pseudoquotations in particular. Here we can compare the archeologist who expounds at great length on glazes, colors, and impressions on pottery traditions to the elliptical Buddhist monk who poses conundrums such as the sound of one hand clapping. Tannen (1989: 26–27) argued that detailed imagery creates involvement in conversational discourse, but detail can also exceed conversational norms and bore listeners (Grice 1975). Very specific narratives and place-names may contain tacit schemas that acquire highly specific emergent meanings in social situations. Basso (1984) explained how Apache place-names evoke moralistic stories. The Apache speak these names in certain situations to "shoot" and discipline transgressors against traditional norms. Thus, in addition to their more general moralistic meanings, the names take on meanings specific to situations.

It is also important to consider the level of schematization/specificity at which interlocutors construe discourse participants, sequentiality, and speech acts. Thus, when someone predicts "if you do that, someone is going to come down hard on you" he or she is offering a schematic construal of the anticipated speech act. By contrast, the overheard discourse in the introduction to this chapter was very specific, even containing pseudoquotes. The dimension of specificity in discourse imagery can be seen in the following sentences arranged according to increasing specificity:

(1) He pleaded for mercy.
(2) The robbery victim pleaded for life in a whining voice.
(3) The robbery victim said, "Please don't kill me" in a whining voice.

On one level, the examples illustrate the potential for levels of specificity in lexical choice and grammatical construction, but the real purpose of presenting them here is to illustrate levels of specificity in speakers' imagery of discourse. In (3), it is the pseudoquote that adds the increment of specificity. That specificity can be an important dimension of folk discourse imagery is shown by the experience of Steven Feld in presenting portions of his ethnography to the Kaluli. They objected that he had not included enough specific detail and that he had left himself out of the stories. Feld (1990: 252) reported that "Kaluli prefer reports from direct experience. That desire to situate knowledge and experience with specific actors, agendas, and instances was most on their minds in any discussion of the book."

Discourse scenarios thus establish a theoretical framework that unifies some of these disparate areas of interest and opens up new questions for investigation with implications for the understanding of discourse as rhetoric, as communication, as social action, and as dramatic performance.

WIERZBICKA'S CULTURAL SCRIPTS

Anna Wierzbicka (1992b, n.d.) developed an approach similar to that advocated in this paper in that she related cultural differences in ways of communicating to "underlying differences" in ways of thinking. In her view, speech communities have characteristic ways of speaking that are governed by cultural scripts, which she defined as tacit systems of cultural rules (1992b). She described cultural scripts using a purportedly universal "natural semantic metalanguage" that allows us "to portray and compare culture-specific attitudes, assumptions, and norms from a neutral, culture independent point of view . . ." (n.d.: 4).[2] The scripts that she discerned are very general, such as those representing the Japanese tendency to avoid speech in favor of mutual empathy according to the ideal of *omoi-yari*. A few such scripts for Japanese are:

1. it is good not to say to other people all that I think
2. often it is good not to say anything to other people

3. when I want to say something to someone, it is good to think
   something like this before I say it:
     it is good not to say to other people all that I think
     something bad could happen because of this
4. if I say many things to people
     people may think something bad about me
     I may feel something bad because of this
5. when I want someone to know what I think
     I don't have to say it to this person
     I can do something else
6. when I want someone to know what I feel
     I don't have to say it to this person
     I can do something else
7. it is good if I can know what another person
     feels/thinks/wants
     this person doesn't have to say anything to me
   (1992b)

In my view, it is important to realize that, however succinct, precise, and useful for cross-cultural comparisons such scripts may be, they are not the cultural models themselves—the tacit knowledge of culturally appropriate ways of speaking—but metalinguistic representations of them. The social and linguistic scenarios that motivate speech and action consist of imagery that cannot be fully captured in a few words. Wierzbicka was not always clear on this point, seeming often to conflate the representations with the underlying thoughts.

Wierzbicka's cultural scripts conflate the types of discourse schemas that I have proposed with schemas for social action. This is not a criticism, because language cannot be neatly partitioned off from culture. The mixing of content that Wierzbicka found is probably found in all cultures and may in fact be the best representation of Japanese discourse models. In the Japanese scripts listed above, the schema of participation is very general, dealing only with *I*, *other people*, and *this person*. The only speech act that Wierzbicka introduced is *say*, by means of which speakers reveal their thoughts and evoke thoughts in others. These scripts involve no dialogue, so sequencing schemas would be irrelevant, other than the sequencing of thinking/speaking/thinking or speaking/feeling. The ethnographer's use of the first person conveys the impression that the holder of such a script is a self-conscious objective observer. Characterization of the ideation involved is also extremely abstract and general: people *may think something* or I may say *something* or *many things*. The emotional and modal values of the scripts are conveyed by the terms *feel*, *want*, *good*, and *bad*.

Wierzbicka's cultural scripts appear to lie at a level of abstraction comparable to or slightly below that of the proposition-schemas of marriage identified by Quinn and the postulates of love identified by Kövecses. Such highly abstract scripts seem useful for a general characterization of prototypical cultural patterns of discourse, but in a thorough ethnography of speaking they would have to be supplemented by many more specific and variant scripts.

COMPARING APPROACHES: CULTURAL LINGUISTICS AND THE ETHNOGRAPHY OF SPEAKING (ES)

Most readers will probably have noticed the overlap between the terms that I have used—scene, speech act, participation schema, situation—and those of Hymes's ethnography of speaking (ES), but I am using the terms in a more restricted sense. All of the analytical language presented here refers to mental representations of discourse as constructed and experienced by interlocutors, not to the discourse itself or to the external world prior to interlocutors' experience and conceptualization. Hymes's discussions of his analytical language appear not to discriminate between situations as they are defined by interlocutors on the one hand and by outside observers on the other. For example, Hymes (1972: 56) used the term *speech situation*, which is defined only by exemplification as "ceremonies, fights, hunts, meals, lovemaking, and the like." He proposed that "such situations may enter as contexts into the statement of rules of speaking as aspects of setting (or of genre)." Perhaps Hymes intended the phrase "enter as contexts" to be taken as a statement about discourse cognition, but we cannot be sure. John Gumperz (1982: 155) observed that ES had failed to deal with how members of social groups "themselves identify events" and "how social knowledge affects the interpretation of messages." By contrast to the ES approach, cultural linguistics explicitly defines the situation model as the *cognized* context of discourse scenarios.

Hymes's discussion of speech acts is similarly lacking in discussion of their status as cognitive events, but he was proposing a theory of speaking as social action with situated meanings, not a cognitive theory. He did speak of "the knowledge that speakers share as to the status of utterances as acts," but his overriding purpose was to differentiate ES from generative grammar and to establish speech acts as an autonomous level of competence apart from syntax and semantics:

> To some extent speech acts may be analyzable by extensions of syntactic and semantic structure. It seems certain, however, that much, if not most, of the knowledge that speakers share as to the status of utterances as acts is immediate and abstract, depending upon an autonomous system of signals from both the various levels of grammar and social settings. (1972: 57)

Apart from the difficulty of imagining the apparent contradiction of an "autonomous system of signals from both the various levels of grammar and social settings," one difficulty with reading Hymes is that he seems often to equivocate between treating speech as knowledge or as social action. For example, in a recent review of the status of the term *competence*, he said, "I am the first, so far as I know, to *define a speech community as involving knowledge*, not only of a variety of language, but also of its use," but on the same page he subsequently wrote that "the challenge of the notion of speech community, as a context for competence, is to see it as more than a locus, whether of grammar or dialectology, and to see it instead as *an organization of language-using persons . . .* [italics added]" (1992: 50). While Hymes's theory is somewhat indeterminate with respect to the role of cognition, he never denied the importance of cognition, or "knowledge," but rather, as noted previously, he took it for granted that others would pursue cognitive approaches while he pursued his interests in speech actions and poetics. While ethnoscientists focused on nomenclatures and Hymes raised our awareness of speech as social action, the systematic study of the cognition of discourse fell through the cracks.

Hymes's most explicitly cognitive (but also somewhat circular) definition is that of *scene* as "the 'psychological setting,' or cultural definition of an occasion as a certain type of scene." By "psychological setting" he had in mind such distinctions as "formal to informal, serious to festive, or the like" (1972: 60). He noted that "speech acts frequently are used to define scenes, and also frequently judged as appropriate or inappropriate in relation to scenes." Scene is contrasted with *setting*, by which Hymes meant "the time and place of a speech act and, in general, . . . the physical circumstances." Following the logic of the cognitive approach that I have been developing here, settings of time, place, and physical circumstances are regarded as aspects of discourse scenarios and situation models.

Hymes approximated a cognitive approach most closely in his treatment of *purposes* (*outcomes* and *goals*). For example, he said that "conventionally recognized and expected outcomes often enter into the definition of speech events," that "the conventionally expected or ascribed must be distinguished from the purely situational or personal, and from the latent and unintended," and that "the actual motives, or some portion of them, of participants may be quite varied" (1972: 61–62). However, his intent in this passage was not to show how purposes enter into the cognition of discourse events, but to distinguish expected outcomes from goals and individual goals from communal ones.

Hymes's descriptive theory is elaborate and contains other categories—speech styles, ways of speaking, message content, key, channels, forms of speech, norms of interaction, norms of interpretation, and rules of speaking. To deal with each of them would take us too far afield. Forms, codes, and norms of communication are the focus of a recent collection of articles (Carbaugh 1990a). Viewing communication as "the creation and affirmation of identities in social situations," Donal Carbaugh (1990b: 7) asked, "How does communication create senses of moral order, and in turn, how do moral orders influence communication?" The differences between the approaches of ES and cultural linguistics are largely differences in the cognitive and social action perspectives. Ideally, cultural and cognitive linguistics will remain as aware of social context as ES, while ES will make more explicit distinctions between folk and analytical categories.

GRICE'S MAXIMS OF SUCCESSFUL COMMUNICATION (IN A SIMPLIFIED WORLD)

One of the most influential frameworks in studies of discourse and pragmatics is that of H. P. Grice (1975), who attempted to formulate the most fundamental presuppositions of any communication, that is, what it would be necessary for the participants in *any* conversation to assume to be true. These he phrased as maxims. His most general maxim is simply to be cooperative.[3] This he dubbed the *cooperative principle*, which breaks down into four maxims. Since the maxims have been summarized somewhat more succinctly by Herbert H. Clark and Susan E. Haviland (1977: 1–2), I will quote their version, as follows:

Quantity: Make your contribution no more and no less informative than is required.

Quality: Say only that which you both believe and have adequate evidence for.

Relation: Be relevant.

Manner: Make your contribution easy to understand; avoid ambi-
           guity, obscurity, and prolixity.

Were I seeking directions to the magazine rack at the supermarket, I would keenly appreciate all of these. However, there are many more situations in which they seem less than fully applicable. A quantity of information required for a presentation to an audience of scholars often puts students to sleep. Who decides how much information is required? Two old college chums might discuss old times in great detail with interest, verbally caressing each well-worn memory that bores their wives to distraction. What is deemed adequate evidence is one thing for a scientist and another for an enthusiast on the topic of space aliens. As for belief, a listener may encourage a speaker to say something that they both know is believed by only the speaker in order to gain rapport or to escalate a dispute. An adult may lie to spare a child emotional pain. Michael Gilsenan (1976: 212) wrote of a Lebanese village that endemic lying, called *kizb*, "acts as a positive, 'enabling' element in the everyday world." Attempting to boost their social prestige, young men commonly concoct elaborate fantasies, which they purvey to their peers. Certainly in this village the maxim of quality is either limited in its scope of application or differently defined.

Being relevant is to honor the given-new contract, that is, to refer to an antecedent image or mutual understanding and to add some new bit of information. It is no doubt necessary for conversational coherence, but what is deemed relevant varies widely according to individual and cultural circumstances. When speaking in tongues in fundamentalist churches, speakers are being relevant, but non-believers may regard tongues as gibberish, irrelevant to any topic. Nevertheless, instances of tongues must be regarded as successful communications from the standpoint of the believers, because certain people with the gift of interpretation can render translations in English. Within the university, most academic subcultures cultivate styles that are wordy, while some are deliberately ambiguous and obscure. Each of Grice's maxims is subject to cultural and subcultural definition and ratification.

We can agree that information density, the nature of evidence, relevance, and manner are important aspects of discourse in all languages and cultures, but Grice's specific maxims seem valid only as descriptions of conversational norms in the more sober circles of Western society. Hill (1988: 21), however, argued that "it seems likely that [Grice's maxims] are everywhere applicable, even where some highly valued styles of speech depend on directness [*sic*] and elaboration." But cross-culturally, all we can say with any certitude is that each culture defines its own maxims of discourse. Rather than attempting to apply Grice's culture-bound maxims universally, we should seek to discover the distinctive maxims of non-Western or subcultural genres of discourse. Perhaps it is best to regard Grice's maxims as defining a simplified world of information exchange that speakers of English invoke only in special circumstances, such as an intellectual conversation (Sweetser 1987).

CHASTISING A NEPHEW IN HOPI

Much of what is called *joking* seems to violate Grice's maxim of quality: say only that which you both believe and have adequate evidence for. For example, in former times, Hopi Indians engaged in a form of rough sexual joking which included threats of castration directed at young boys by certain of their male in-laws and sexual provocations directed at them by their fathers' sisters. Here is a bit of testimony from the autobiography of Don Talayesva (Simmons 1942: 40), as quoted in Alice Schlegel (1975: 522):

> After I was four or five nearly all my grandfathers, father's sisters' and clan sisters' husbands, played very rough jokes on me, snatched at my penis, and threatened to castrate me, charging that I had been caught making love to their wives, who were my aunts. All these women took my part, called me their sweetheart, fondled my penis, and pretended to want it badly. . . . I liked to play with them but I was afraid of their rough husbands and thought they would castrate me. It was a long time before I could be sure that they meant only to tease.

Schlegel proposed a plausible explanation for the joking threats and sexual play. Hopi husbands live in their wives' houses, where they occupy a somewhat vulnerable position with respect to their male in-laws. An insecure, frustrated husband may accumulate hostile feelings against his wife and her family, which he can act out by threatening the sons of her brothers and sisters or other boys who stand in similar, but more distant, kinship relations. Hopi women, for their part, use sexual joking to play upon their husbands' insecurities by holding up their brothers' sons as future rivals for their affections. In Schlegel's opinion, Hopi men are particularly vulnerable to rejection by their wives because they have been raised as children to be dependent upon women.

Thus, Hopi joking about castration and sex provides a clear counterexample to Grice's maxim that successful communication requires saying only what you believe. Perhaps from the standpoint of the nephew, who was the butt of the joke, the communications would not be regarded as successful, but in some sense they must be so regarded because they are Hopi linguistic traditions. It would not be hard to find hundreds more counterexamples.

LYING IN A SIMPLIFIED WORLD

(VII) Two patients are waiting to be wheeled into the operating room. The doctor points to one and says, "Is Jones here the appendectomy or the tonsillectomy?" Nurse Braine has just read the charts. Although she is anxious to keep her job, she has nevertheless confused the charts in her mind and replies, "The appendectomy," when in fact poor Jones is the one scheduled for tonsillectomy. Did Nurse Braine lie?

(VIII) Superfan has got tickets for the championship game and is very proud of them. He shows them to his boss, who says, "Listen, Superfan, any day you don't come to work, you better have a better excuse than that." Superfan says, "I will." On the day of the game, Superfan calls in and says, "I can't come to work today, Boss, because I'm sick." Ironically, Superfan doesn't get to go to the game because the slight stomach ache he felt on arising turns out to be ptomaine poisoning. So Superfan was really sick when he said he was. Did Superfan lie? (Coleman and Kay 1981: 31–32)

Lying is a pragmatic speech act intended to create a false impression. Since there are many kinds of lies—white lies, social lies, bald-faced lies—perhaps there is also a prototypical cognitive model of a lie, an image of lying from which all other types depart in some respects, but resemble in other respects. In other words, perhaps lying is a complex category. As a first attempt at a solution to the problem, we might guess that the prototypical lie in the English language occurs when someone says something he or she does not believe, perhaps violating Grice's Maxim of Quality: Say only that which you both believe and have adequate evidence for. A similar approach has been pursued by Coleman and Kay (1981). Much as Paul Kay and Chad K. McDaniel (1978) had earlier determined that intermediate shades of the color spectrum can be judged as good or poor instances of focal colors, Coleman and Kay proposed that lies have varying degrees of membership in the category of lying. They suggested that lying, like a basic color term, is a "fuzzy" category and defined the concept of prototype as follows:

> Let us say, roughly, that a semantic prototype associates a word or phrase with a prelinguistic, *cognitive schema or image*; and that speakers are equipped with an ability to judge the degree to which an object (or, if you prefer, the internal representation thereof) matches this prototype schema or image [italics added]. (1981: 27)

I italicized the phrase *cognitive schema or image* in order to highlight the kinship of their approach to that of cultural linguistics.[4] Coleman and Kay then defined the prototype of lying, as "(a) falsehood, which is (b) deliberate and (c) intended to deceive." They reasoned that instances of lying which met all three criteria would be judged to be better examples, while those that matched only one would be regarded as poor examples. In social lying, for example, the speaker may tell a deliberate falsehood, but with no intent to deceive the listener (1981: 29):

(2) a. What a lovely party!
    b. The dinner was very good.
    c. Oh, you wrote that paper on lying? I found it extremely interesting.
    d. How nice to see you!
    e. Drop in any time.

Then there are cases where one intends, deliberately, to deceive by saying something that is literally true (but perhaps violates Grice's Maxims of Quantity and Manner):

> For example, if Mary is leaving the house to buy John's Christmas present, and John asks her where she is going, she might reply:
> (3) Oh, Shod's having a sale on shoes and mine are worn out.
> (4) We're out of paprika.
> (5) To the store.

The first two statements (3 and 4) misdirect without making false statements. The third (5) ignores the intent of John's question, which was doubtless to determine Mary's intended activities, as well as her whereabouts. Mary provides insufficient information.

In an experiment to test the prototype theory of lying, Coleman and Kay devised a questionnaire containing eight stories representing possible variations on the prototype. Stories VII and VIII appear under the heading on page 194. Each story contained an utterance, set off in quotation marks, that could be judged as a lie. Subjects were asked to rate the quoted utterances by circling answers in the following format (1981: 30): "It was {a lie / not a lie / I can't say}."

In my own folk theory of language, the utterance of nurse Braine in VII is unpremeditated, and therefore a mistake, but not a lie. The utterance of Superfan in VIII was a lie at the time of the call, but turned out to be true. I would have circled "a lie." The point is that in the "honest mistake" in VII, there was no intent to deceive. In VIII, even though the speaker believes his statement to be false, intent to deceive is again lacking. Because of its extra complications, this question produced results that were difficult to interpret.

Coleman and Kay gave their questionnaire to seventy-one native speakers of English, some fifty of whom were "students, faculty, or staff at Berkeley." Subjects varied in age from fifteen to seventy-two years with the sexes "about equally represented." Otherwise, they made no attempt at a systematic sample, nor, I believe, was one required to justify their conclusions.

The researchers predicted that examples with all three of the prototype elements would more often be judged as lies and that those lacking any of the elements would least often be so judged. Examples with only one or two elements of the prototype should fall at the appropriate places on a scale of judgment. In eighteen out of nineteen comparisons of judgments on pairs of stories the results confirmed their prediction to the .01 level of significance, which is substantially better than the .05 level normally required to establish the significance of experimental results. Furthermore, they found that the elements of the prototype were ranked in importance.

Let us restate the three elements of the prototype, ranked in order of their influence on the judgments of the subjects in Coleman and Kay's experiment:

1. Speaker believes statement to be false.
2. Speaker said it with intent to deceive.
3. The statement is false in fact.

It turned out that belief in falsity was the most important element in the prototype, while intent to deceive and actual falsity were respectively less important.

Sweetser (1987) took a different approach to the problem of understanding what people mean when they say someone is lying. She started with an exploration of the English model of informational exchange, which constitutes a simplified world in which lying can be clearly defined. This simplified world starts with a metamaxim, that is, a maxim about maxims, and a general rule. The metamaxim is People normally obey rules; the general rule is Try to help, not harm. Lakoff's maxims of politeness and Grice's maxims of communication also depend upon these same cultural postulates. The rest of the postulates in Sweetser's model of informational exchange for English follow:

Sweetser's Model of Informational Exchange for English (1987: 47; italics added)

(0) People normally obey rules (the default case).

(1) Rule: Try to help, not harm.

(2) Knowledge is beneficial, helpful. (Corollary: Misinformation is harmful.)

(3) Rule: Give knowledge (inform others); do not misinform.

(4) *Beliefs have adequate justification.*

(5) Adequately justified beliefs are knowledge (= are true).

(6) Therefore, beliefs are true (are knowledge).

(7) Rule: Say what you believe (since belief = knowledge); do not say what you do not believe (this = misinformation).

Within this simplified setting of informational exchange, which is an important part of the world view of American speakers of English, a lie can now be rather simply defined as *a false statement*. In any other setting, say one calling for a joke or a polite expression, the same statement might not be a lie, or it might be less than a prototypical lie. The reason that a lie can be defined so simply is that a false statement entails non-belief, and non-belief entails falsity in fact. The simplified world is a system whose statements follow from one another; they are all mutual entailments. Let me restate these entailments. If a person says something false, she must not believe it. If she doesn't believe it, it must be false in fact.

I italicized the fourth postulate—*Beliefs have adequate justification*—because this seems to be the most crucial one and the most difficult one for someone with any training in science or logic to accept. I would guess that most readers of this book have been trained to regard beliefs with deep suspicion until they can be subjected to rigorous validity testing by the scientific method or matched against rules of inference. But Sweetser's is a folk model, not a scientific model. The human race has communicated with language for many thousands of years, certainly at least

50,000, without modern science or formal logic. Our ancestors probably accepted without question a model of informational exchange something like that outlined by Sweetser, and most of us, for most purposes, still do today. Were it otherwise, we could hardly communicate because we would be forced to justify every belief before speaking. Indeed, some people we may regard as overly intellectual do have difficulty communicating for this very reason. It is only when engaging in intellectual or legal communications that we normally shift to a more elaborate and reliable model of informational exchange, rather like buckling our informational seatbelt.

How does the new one-line definition of lying within the simplified world of informational exchange accord with Coleman and Kay's definition of the prototypical lie as a statement believed by the speaker to be false, said with intent to deceive, and false in fact? In the simplified world, we say what we believe, so uttering a false statement immediately entails that we do not believe it. Therefore, we must be intending to deceive. In the simplified world, beliefs are adequately justified. Since a statement which is false is not believed, then it is not adequately justified in the speaker's mind, and it may be false in fact. Thus, the most directly entailed principle, belief, is the most diagnostic according to Coleman and Kay. The most indirectly entailed principle, factuality, is the least diagnostic.[5]

However, it is still not entirely clear that Sweetser formulated just the right description of the simplified world of informational exchange, or just the right definition of lying within this world. If a lie is a false statement, then what of Nurse Braine's honest mistake, which caused poor Jones to get an unnecessary appendectomy? Honest mistakes seem to fit Sweetser's definition of lying as a false statement, contrary to our commonsense understanding of both categories.

Sweetser's approach requires that words about language be defined relative to elaborate background models of communication, as lying is somehow embedded in the model of informational exchange. These background models vary with cultures. Ronald Scollon and Suzanne Wong-Scollon (1990) observed that in Athabascan communities it is assumed that the dominant person in a speaking relationship should do most of the speaking "as the exhibitionist." Basso (1990a) introduced "extralinguistic factors" of uncertainty and unpredictability to explain why the Western Apache keep silent, but certainly such a behavioral correlation must relate to Apache discourse scenarios. Such a model would also be linguistic, unless we hold a restricted view of what belongs in that category.

Indeed, the cultural model of communication could be said to constitute an essential part of the meaning of any communication.

Sweetser (1987: 56) viewed speaking and listening as an asymmetrical power relationship in which a cooperative listener grants a speaker license to alter her beliefs. Once granted a moment of linguistic power, a speaker assumes responsibility not to harm the listener by lying. Of course, the seriousness of a lie depends upon the circumstances; but generally the greater the authority of a speaker, the greater the vulnerability of the listener and the greater the potential for abuse of authority by lying.

Lying to people undermines their power of self-determination and violates one of the most fundamental values of an American speaker of English: rugged individualism. Since Americans are known for the degree to which they value personal autonomy, they are likely to be offended by any lying, even if intended to avoid harm or acted out in jest. In paternalistic cultures, such as the Japanese or Chinese, where individuals expect family elders or company seniors to take large measures of responsibility for their well-being, people might learn to appreciate lies by superiors if they are intended to avoid harm or embarrassment, but be grievously wounded when the same persons tell lies that are intended to harm.

This view of discourse as an asymmetrical power relationship helps to explain why people often avoid the appearance of lying by qualifying their statements with hedges specifying the nature of the evidence. They may say such things as "to the best of my knowledge; so far as I know; if I'm not mistaken; as far as I can tell; for all I know; as I understand it; my best guess is; speaking conservatively; at a conservative estimate; to put it mildly; beyond question" (Sweetser 1987: 56). Some languages even have evidential hedges built into the grammar, suggesting well-developed cultural models of informational exchange. For example, in the O'odham (Papago) language of southern Arizona, it is almost always necessary to use a small word, *ṣ*, to indicate that the narrator is merely reporting what she or he has been told. (The dot in *ṣ* indicates that the consonant is pronounced with the tongue curled toward the back of the mouth.) Conversely, in Hualapai, a Yuman language of northern Arizona, the fact that the speaker has actually seen what she is reporting can be specified by suffixing an *-o* to a verb. The Wintun use the verbal suffix *-ke* for hearsay information and the narration of myths, the suffixes *-da*, *-besken*, or *-be* (first, second, third person) for visual or unquestioned evidence, the suffixes *-ntida*, *-nterestken*, and *-nte* for nonvisual sensory evidence, and the suffix *-re* for information based on inference (Lee 1938). The nature of the evidence is therefore revealed by the grammar, and these constructions are called *evidentials*. What a lot of breath and ink this might save us in English if we had evidential suffixes that we could use in the courtroom. Using the Wintun suffix, we might say, for example, "The defendant shoplift-*be* the compact disc," thereby eliminating the need to ask the inevitable question, "Did you actually see her take it?"

Sweetser's strategy for defining the discourse category of lying bears a remarkable resemblance to Quinn's proposition-schema model of marriage and Kövecses's postulate model of love, a category with emotional and social dimensions. Both love and lying have verbal, emotional, and social dimensions. The topic of lying focuses attention on verbal behavior, whereas love may highlight social behavior and feeling states. Both Kövecses's and Sweetser's models represent simplified, prototypical worlds that are norms or distillations of social behavior. When we assemble and integrate the various simplified worlds of communication, love, power, and other areas of prevailing interest within a culture, we arrive at world view.

SELLING A SEWING MACHINE WITH
HONORIFIC LANGUAGE IN JAPANESE

The sales transaction is a genre of discourse in which pragmatic speech acts stand out clearly because the salesperson must maintain the flow of discourse while the potential customer would probably rather break it off. The salesperson must also attempt to motivate the victim to purchase a product. Aoi Tsuda (1984) provided us with the English translation of a delightful text of a Japanese sewing machine salesman making a pitch to a reluctant customer. I have reproduced the first twenty-two turns, with minor changes, below.[6]

In order to understand the text it is necessary to realize that schemas of social ranking and distance underlie most Japanese discourse, including sales transactions. The ranking schema can be seen in many features of speaking, but most obviously in the use of honorific expressions. In the sales transaction, the salesman uses humble forms for himself and honorific expressions that elevate the customer and her relatives. Generally, he uses polite or formal expressions wherever possible, invoking a status relationship that improves his chances of making a sale. Of course, salespersons in the United States may also elevate the status of the customer, but the honorific speech conventions of Japanese provide more tools for the job.

The use of expressions implying ranking is coded in the example text with (H) Honorific, and (F) Formal Style. Wherever one of these appears, it signals the use of a special term of address or reference or a special form of the verb. Here is how Tsuda (1984: 50–51) described the setting and participants: "S is a salesperson in his forties, selling a sewing machine. C [customer] is a housewife, mother of two daughters. The following conversation took place at the door of C's house in Tokyo."

S: Excuse me. (F)

C: Yes.

S: Excuse me (F). I'm from J (company's name) (F). Yes, J (company) (F).

C: What do you want of me?

S: Do you know, *Okusan* (H) (meaning housewife) about television commercial (F)? The one we can sew even very thick ones or even very thin ones . . .

C: Well, a sewing machine. We have one at home.

S: Is that so (F)?

C: Yes.

S: When did you buy (H) it (F)?

C: Well, let me think. Four or five years ago.

S: Four or five years ago. Is that for straight or for zigzag (F)?

C: It is for zigzag (F).

S: Hum, hum. Zigzag. Which (H) brand is that (F)?

C: J brand, I wonder.

S: Is that so (F)? Thank you very much (F). Is that one which we change *cam* (a part of the machine)?

C: What?

S: You know about *cam* which is so many attachments?

C: Yes.

S: About 10 things. I mean you change them. (F)

C: Hum.

S: The new sewing machine which began selling on May 1 does not need to change *cam* (F). We call it electronic sewing machine.

C: We already have one now. It's enough for my house.

From this text, it is a relatively simple task to parse out the pragmatic speech acts, or *moves* as they are called by Tsuda, and list them by category, as I have done for the first seventeen, in Table 8.

After introductions, the speech acts of the sales transaction fall into a pattern of questions posed by the salesman followed by answers from the

TABLE 8

SEVENTEEN OPENING MOVES IN A JAPANESE SALES TRANSACTION BY CATEGORY[a]

Requests:
  S: Excuse me. (F)
  C: Well, let me think.
Declaration–Self Introduction:
  S: I'm from J (company's name) (F). Yes, J (company) (F).
Reply to Request:
  C: Yes.
Questions:
  C: What do you want of me?
  S: Do you know, *Okusan* (H) (meaning housewife) about television commercial (F)? The one we can sew even very thick ones or even very thin ones . . .
  S: Is that so (F)?
  S: When did you buy (H) it (F)?
  S: Is that for straight or for zigzag (F)?
  S: Which (H) brand is that (F)?
Declarations–Replies to Questions:
  C: Yes.
  C: Well, a sewing machine. We have one at home.
  C: Four or five years ago.
  C: It is for zigzag (F).
  C: J brand, I wonder.
Echos and Acknowledgments of Replies:
  S: Four or five years ago.
  S: Hum, hum. Zigzag.

---

[a] S = Salesman, C = Customer; (H) Honorific; (F) Formal.

customer, who seems too polite to send the salesman away. After each reply by the customer, the salesman either echoes the answer or poses new questions in order to sustain the transaction. The basic sequence for the early part of the sales transaction, then, is [[Question-Reply-(Acknowledgment)] . . .], where the parentheses show that acknowledgment is optional and the ellipsis signifies an indefinite number of repetitions. Eventually the salesman offers more information about his products and financing and recommends a purchase. The customer acknowledges his declarations, questions his information, and explains why she is not in a position to buy. Much of the transaction consists of negotiation over whether the sewing machine being plugged by the salesman would fit into the life of the customer and her family. Salesman and customer negotiate a very specific image of the situation that could conceivably become a goal, and perhaps even motivate a sale.

But the salesman's speech predicates more than just the suitability of his product for this customer. Formal (F) and honorific (H) expressions appear in all five of the questions put by the salesman, while the five replies by the customer contain only one (F), and that one appears to echo an expression used by the salesman. The salesman asked, "Is that for straight or for zigzag (F)?" to which the customer replied, "It is for zigzag (F)." Perhaps changing the formality level in an echo reply would impolitely suggest that the questioner had spoken improperly. The salesman's use of formal language seems to predicate a status relationship that must invoke its own scenarios that lock into the sales scenario. By invoking a higher status for the customer, the salesman may be arousing the concern, sympathy, and generosity that duty requires people to show to social inferiors or dependents.

This analysis of the sales transaction shows that at least three kinds of imagery contribute to its structure. These include background knowledge, the participation schema of high-status customer and low-status salesperson, and the sequence schema for speech acts. Most of the content of the transaction involves building up a picture of the life of the customer with its possible place for a sewing machine with special attachments and financing arrangements. It is a constructed scene or text model, in W. F. Hanks's (1993) sense, a framework. This scene represents aspects of what are called the setting and the ends (or goals) by anthropologists who work within the ES tradition. Of course, the goal that drives the whole episode is the salesman's motivation to sell a machine, but that never appears explicitly in the text. For example, the salesman never says something to the effect that if the customer will just help him by purchasing a machine he will get a nice bonus from his boss.

The participation schema is that of customer and salesman, but honorific language also locks it into a schema of high and low status. The honorific language fits what Hymes called norms, that is, "culturally based rules for appropriate communicative behaviors," but the use of honorific language here is not only appropriate—it is a strategic deployment of contextual cues as well (Gumperz 1982, 1992).[7]

Speech act sequences such as the [[Question-Reply-(Acknowledgment)] . . .] frame sustain the flow of the sales transaction. At a higher

level, the whole sales transaction could be regarded as a complex intentional speech act (and thus it could be taken to subsume Hymes's category of *ends*), but the term *speech act* is usually reserved for smaller
acts encompassed by a clause or a phrase (greetings, questions, declarations, etc.).

In this analysis, I have posited only three basic types of imagery: the
constructed scene, situation, or text world, the temporarily invoked relative social ranking of the participants, and the sequence of speech acts.
The most dynamic of these is the situation, which undergoes intense negotiation, revelation, and elaboration in the course of the transaction. The
salesman's goal, of course, is to negotiate the customer's acceptance of a
text world in which she needs his merchandise and a social system in
which she feels responsible for the well-being of the salesperson or the
continuance of an amicable relationship. This would presumably motivate
her to the culminating speech act of the ideal sales transaction: a promise
to buy.

This example of the sales transaction provides a good prelude for a
more general discussion of Japanese honorific and polite language. Masayoshi Shibatani (1990: 374–380) presented a simple example in which
someone is speaking to some indefinite listener about a third person
named Taro. In plain speech, we can say *Taroo ga ki-ta* (*Taro came*), but
if we wish to be polite to our audience, we might add the polite verbal
suffix *-masi* and say *Taroo ga ki-masi-ta*. Thus, from the standpoint of
the speaker, use of the polite verb form is governed ("controlled") by the
addressee, who is not explicitly mentioned in this sentence. The full
analysis is given in expressions (1) and (2) below (1990: 375). NOM refers
to the nominative case marker; *ga* marks its head noun as a subject.

(1) *Taroo*   *ga*   *ki-ta.*   (plain)
     Taro   NOM   come-PAST
     'Taro came.'
(2) *Taroo*   *ga*   *ki-masi-ta.*   (polite)
     Taro   NOM   come-POLITE-PAST
     'Taro came.'

Honorifics may be controlled by referents other than addressees. Special prefixes and suffixes may be used to honor the subject of a sentence,
as in examples (4) and (5), below, or the object, as in (7). In examples (4),
(5), and (7) it is the teacher who is honored. HON flags an honorific prefix
or suffix. ADV refers to an *adverbializer*. ACC is accusative case; that is, it
marks the preceding noun as the object of the verb (1990: 376).

Subject honorific (referent-controlled)

(3)   *Sensei   ga   warat-ta.*   (plain)
      teacher   NOM   laugh-PAST
      'The teacher laughed.'

(4)   *Sensei   ga   o-warai   ni   nat-ta.*   (honorific)
      teacher   NOM   HON-laugh   ADV   become-PAST
      'The teacher laughed.'

(5)   *Sensei   ga   warawa-re-ta.*   (honorific)
      teacher   NOM   laugh-HON-PAST
      'The teacher laughed.'

Object honorific (referent-controlled)

(6)   *Taroo   ga   sensei   o   tasuke-ta.*   (plain)
      Taro   NOM   teacher   ACC   help-PAST
      'Taro assisted the teacher.'

(7)   *Taroo   ga   sensei   o   o-tasuke   si-ta.*   (honorific)
      Taro   NOM   teacher   ACC   HON-help   do-PAST
      'Taro assisted the teacher.'

The polite forms can be used independently of the honorific forms, but they are most often used in combination. What is done if the addressee is the subject or object controlling the honorific and also the object of polite language? In this case both forms would be used, as in example (8):

(8)   *Itu   o-kaeri   ni   nari-masu-ka?*
      when   HON-return   ADV   become-POLITE-Q
      'When are (you) coming back?'

In his explanation of these usages, Shibatani said that when polite language is used honorifics are usually also used "when the referent is appropriate," though honorifics may occur in the absence of polite verb forms. The use of the polite forms is governed by various dimensions of the situation, including the "nature of the addressee, the formality of the occasion, the nature of the topics of discussion, and the nature of the bystanders," but the underlying dimension that governs both honorifics and polite forms is relative psychological distance. For example, when a mother and daughter speak together about the father, they discuss him using honorifics, but using them when speaking about the father to someone outside the family would be inappropriate. In other words, in the triangle of speaker-listener-referent, honorifics are appropriately applied only to the outsider as either listener or referent, as the one who is the most psychologically distant of the three. The same principle holds in other settings.

Shibatani (1990: 379) provided an additional example of possible value to those interested in Japanese corporate protocol. In this example, a secretary is referring to the president of her company. Her use of the honorific form depends upon the status of the person to whom she is speaking. If the addressee is a colleague in the company, she uses the honorific (example a, below), but when speaking to someone from outside the company she continues to use the polite form, but no honorifics for the president (example b, below). TOP marks a topic (1990: 379):

   a. *Syatyoo-san   wa   ima   o-dekake   ni   natte   i-masu.*
       president-HON   TOP   now   HON-go   out   HON   be-POLITE
       'The president is gone out now.'

   b. *Syatyoo   wa   ima   dekake-te   ori-masu.*
       president   TOP   now   go out   be-POLITE
       (same as *a*)

The rules that use relative psychological distance are taught explicitly at school and in the home. The principle of psychological distance seems to work well enough when two people discuss a third, but when two people speak together and one addresses the other with honorifics they still require the social ranking schema. Of course, ranking itself can be regarded as a kind of psychological distance with the person of higher rank assigned the greatest distance by default. The important point to keep in mind is that the honorifics themselves are speech acts that predicate the participation of interlocutors in discourse scenarios with mutual obligations. By predicating a small range of scenarios that implicate the speakers, honorifics serve as "contextualization cues" that frame the discourse situation, and that framing may be strategic (Gumperz 1982, 1992).

YO 'I AM TELLING YOU': PRAGMATICS OF A JAPANESE DISCOURSE PARTICLE

Some words and grammatical particles seem on first inspection to lack conventional referential meanings, taking on meaning only in context. Because they point to some aspect of the context of discourse, they have been called *non-referential indexicals* (Silverstein 1976). Looking at such English words as *oh, well, and, but, or, so, because, now, then, I mean, y'know*, Schiffrin (1987: 31) called them *discourse markers*, which she defined as units of interaction, that is, "sequentially dependent elements which bracket units of talk." I propose to take a different approach that assumes that discourse markers and "non-referential" indexicals do in fact predicate conventional meanings and derive meaning from context, much as do other linguistic expressions. These meanings are metalinguistic or, more strictly, metadiscursive. I will assume that people conceptualize, schematize, and symbolize many aspects of verbal discourse, including its ideological content (thoughts that it evokes in the minds of listeners), phonological shape, situation, interactional structure, and even the intentions of speakers to accomplish pragmatic speech acts.[8] Terms that predicate such things about the discourse itself may be called *discourse indexicals*, or just *discursives* (comparable to nominals, verbals, adjectivals, adverbials, etc.).[9] They may be further characterized as pragmatic, interactional, situational, phonological, etc., according to what they predicate about the discourse, but in most expressions these elements will be mixed. Pragmatic discursives may themselves function as speech acts by virtue of being about speech acts; to redirect the listener's attention to a speech act may be the pragmatic equivalent of repeating the act itself.

The approach of cultural linguistics thus unifies the study of discourse particles with that of other kinds of predications. It also explains a phenomenon that has vexed discourse theorists: that many discourse particles are not particularly well behaved when defined as markers that bracket units of talk (Schiffrin 1987: 31–36). Since they only predicate something about the discourse, rather than govern its interactional structure in a mechanical way, their distribution need not correspond exactly to boundaries of units of talk and their sequential dependence need not be precise. The only discursives that are discourse markers in the strict sense of bracketing the flow of conversation are those that predicate about the sequence of interaction, as opposed to its pragmatic functions, phonology, or ideology.

Haruko Minegishi Cook (1991: 5) provided us with an instructive case study of a pragmatic discursive in her examination of the Japanese particle *yo*, which can sometimes be roughly translated as 'I am telling you,' but at other times takes on a variety of situationally determined meanings, including assertiveness, warning, advice, instructions, announcement, explanation, request, insistence, and contradiction. Consider the following example in which a child attempts to capture the attention of his mother and brother who are engaged in conversation. This is an example of the 'I am telling you' meaning in the first two uses, followed by the more insistent *yoo* in the final use. The arrows point to the expression that the particle is indexing:

> [H is looking at a male insect in a picture book and tries to talk about the insect to the mother and K.]
>
> ((The mother and K are talking))
>
> --->H: Kore osu da *yo*, osu.
>   'This is male, male.'
>
> ((The mother and K are talking))
>
> --->H: Kore osu da *yo*.
>   'This is male.'
>
> ((The mother and K are talking))
>
> --->H: Kore osu da *yoo*.
>   'This is male.'
>
> (1991: 5)

Now consider an assertive use of *yo* in a neighborhood quarrel in which *yo* occurs with very high frequency, 33 times in a text of 824 words, as compared to a normal family conversation of similar length in which *yo* occurs only 8 times:

> Here, Mr. Suzuki, who is an owner of an apartment is angry with one of the tenants, Mr. Kobayashi, who put out his garbage on the wrong day because he is going to move. . . . Mr. Suzuki asserts his points strongly against Mr. Kobayashi's statements in the 1st and 3rd uses of *yo* and points out what could be done in the 2nd use of *yo*.
>
> [Mr. Suzuki and Mr. Kobayashi have been arguing over the garbage that Mr. Kobayashi put out on the wrong day.]
>
> K: Toriaezu hikkoshi dakara koko ni =
>   'Because I'm moving, I put (it) here in haste.'
>
>   S: Un
>   'Uh-huh'
>
> --->S: =Iya, kotchi wa sonna koto shiranai *yo*.
>   'No, I did not know that.'
>
>   Da- dakara otaku mo saa, hikkoshi suru kara kore tanomu tteba
>   ---> ore mo yatte yaru *yo*.

'S- so, if you told me that you'd moved and wanted me to take care of it, I'd do that.'

K: Chotto wakannasugiru no ja nai desu ka?
'Isn't it the case that (you) are too unreasonable?'

-->S: Iya, wakannaku nai *yo*.
'No, (I)'m not unreasonable.'
(1991: 6)

Like the Japanese honorifics and polite forms, *yo* may even be used to assert status relationships. Because of the coercive implications of *yo*, those of lower status must be more circumspect in their usage. Cook (1991: 14) provided an example of a conversation between a woman who is *yome* (married into her husband's family), a position of relatively low status, and her older sister-in-law. In this conversation, the older woman (CH) makes use of *yo*, while the younger woman (AY) uses honorifics (in boldface):

AY: Hansode nanka kite**rashita** mono ne.
'(You) were wearing short-sleeve clothes.'

-->CH: Hansode *yo*.
'(Of course,) short-sleeve clothes.'

Natsufuku no hansode, go-roku-gatsu no.
'Summer short-sleeve clothes, one (one may wear) in May or June.'

From this and other examples, Cook (1991: 14–15) concluded that "the participants in a conversation negotiate their power through the use of language. The use of language can create the social role and the status of the speaker in interactions, while his/her social status in society may restrict particular uses of language."

Native speakers tend to have difficulty in describing the meaning of *yo*, and yet the particles are "important resources for social interaction" (1991: 1). In a view of language in which meaning is embedded in the entities and predicates of propositions, particles such as *yo* fail to contribute to the referential meanings of propositions. Rather, they "signal the structure of the speech context." Cook (1991: 2) argued instead that the meanings of indexicals are unpredictable because they arise from what speakers intend to achieve and from expectations about the reactions and assumptions of listeners.

One possible way of looking at indexicals is to propose that each such

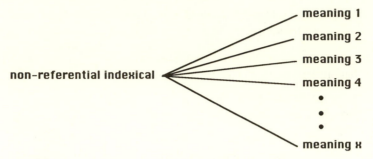

FIGURE 24. Direct linkage of indexical term to meanings acquired in context. From Cook (1991: Fig. 1). Reproduced by permission of Haruko M. Cook.

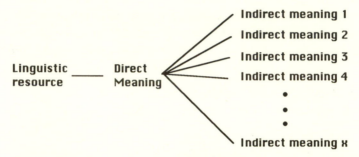

FIGURE 25. Direct and indirect indexical relations. From Cook (1991: Fig. 2). Reproduced by permission of Haruko M. Cook.

term is directly linked to a meaning acquired in context, as in Figure 24, but this model is insufficient because it would not distinguish between different indexicals and because it would not explain why a specific linkage between form and meaning should emerge at all. Why should a use of the term signify any particular component of the situation and not some other?

Citing E. Ochs (1988), Cook suggested an alternative way of modeling the meaning of indexicals. In this model, a term has both a direct and an indirect meaning, as in Figure 25. The direct meaning is abstract and stable. The indirect meaning is situated in the discourse context. The indirect meanings that emerge in discourse can be diagramed for the particle *yo* as in Figure 26.

It is the direct meaning that enables us to distinguish *yo* from other indexicals. But in pointing to the speaker's utterance *yo* also calls attention to the self-described condition of the speaker or the consequences of ignoring the speaker. It calls upon the listener to reexamine the most salient scenarios implicated by the speaker's locution and the situation itself.[10] *Yo* implicitly, but often insistently, calls upon the speaker to make conventional responses to the scenarios that it evokes. *Yo* thereby, indirectly, takes on the character of speech acts (insisting, warning, requesting, etc.) and functions to define social statuses. This model of the functioning of the particle *yo* in discourse seems perfectly consistent with the function of Apache moralistic stories discussed previously. It shows that indexical meaning is not limited to any particular level of discourse.

Do *yo* and other discursives like it have referential meaning in the

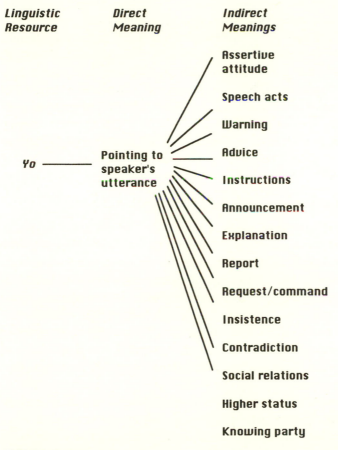

Linguistic Resource

Direct Meaning

Indirect Meanings

Assertive attitude

Speech acts

Warning

Advice

Yo — Pointing to speaker's utterance

Instructions

Announcement

Explanation

Report

Request/command

Insistence

Contradiction

Social relations

Higher status

Knowing party

FIGURE 26. Indexical relations of *yo*. From Cook (1991: Fig. 3). Reproduced by permission of Haruko M. Cook.

sense that they directly symbolize some imagery? *Contra* Silverstein (1976), I believe that they do. A hint as to the nature of this imagery lies in Cook's representation of the "direct meaning" of *yo* as "pointing to speaker's utterance" (1991: 4). I maintain that the grammatical particle *yo* schematically predicates speaker's own most recent locution. The symbol acquires specific semantic and phonological content for each interlocutor from memories of speaker's prior locution reckoned from the moment that *yo* is spoken. The *yo* schema frames these memories. *Yo* acquires pragmatic effects from interlocutors' construals of the current situation as they answer the question of why the speaker wants listeners to recall her prior words.

To summarize, the Japanese particle *yo* provides an example of an expression whose meaning is always situated and subject to interpretation, so that it can perform pragmatic speech acts or it can be used performatively to define social statuses. *Yo* falls at the emergent end of the continuum of conventional to emergent meanings. *Yo* is metalinguistic; it is talk about discourse itself, because its residual conventional sense is to re-evoke an image of the speaker's own previous locution together with its meaning and speaker's intentions. Examination of the stable meaning and grammatical function of *yo* suggests that this and other highly indexical expressions should be regarded as symbolizing abstract imagery of discourse itself.

WHY THE KUNA HOT PEPPER STORY IS DISORGANIZED

According to Hymes and Cazden (1980: 131), "narrative may be an inescapable mode of thought," while Wallace Chafe (1990: 79) saw narratives as "overt manifestations of the mind in action: as windows to both the content of the mind and its ongoing operations." We seem to have a choice of regarding narrative as a liberating window or a confining cell. But if narrative is inescapable, as asserted by Hymes, then what are the forms of narrative that constrain our thinking? If narrative both potentiates and constrains, then an examination of narrative based upon cognitive linguistics may help us to understand the vistas that it presents and limits that it imposes.

Narrative refers to the recitation of stories. Most commonly, narratives describe sequences of events arranged according to time or place, no matter whether the events are judged to be mythical or real. The most simple and prototypical narrative has the form of an independent clause with a concrete subject and object, something like the following:

Coyote threw up his eyes.

A longer narrative could conceivably be made up of many such short narratives, as in the following sequence of three clauses:

A man threw up his eyes. Coyote saw a man. Coyote threw up his eyes.

Austin Hale (1984) called such an elementary sequence the *narrative backbone*. I think of the narrative backbone as a scenario. As we will see, the scenario of a tale does not necessarily surface in its telling; not all tales have such prototypical narrative backbones. But some Amerindian stories seem to have a structure very much like this. The story Coyote Loses His Eyes discussed in Chapter 6 has the quality of a backbone sequence. However, narratives are generally more complex than the backbone scenario. Robert E. Longacre (1981) showed how the narrative backbone and secondary events can be distinguished from setting and background information by verbal tenses and aspects that fall along a continuum from most active to most static.

Obviously, narratives must become more complex as they relate more complex events. Complex narratives must have at least three basic structural features that provide cohesion and interest:[11]

(1) constituent structure;
(2) indices of new and old information; and
(3) profiling of salient content.

Like phrases and clauses, narratives are constructions with constituent structures, but narratives are generally longer, more complex, and more interwoven. Within the constituent structure we find the narrative backbone and other components that specify background and concurrent events. Since narratives often present much more than one or a few basic scenes or scenarios, they require grammatical forms that connect the current position in a given narration to what has preceded it, that is, forms that index and activate old information. Complex narratives must also introduce new characters, new scenes, and new scenarios. Finally, in narratives, as in shorter speech acts, it is necessary to profile the most salient and value-laden components of complex images. Because narratives may be long, the images that they profile may be complex. Narrators use "attention reinforcing devices" to profile images more effectively (Hale 1984: 6). Such devices include repetition, contrast, sequence, foreshadowing, and flashbacks. In Hale's terminology, the three elements of constituent structure, new and old information, and profiling are termed, respectively, *trees, files,* and *focal content.*[12]

The constituent structure of narratives often, but not invariably, coincides with plot structure.[13] For example, here are three common plots that govern the constituent structures of many American Indian folktales and legends:[14]

I. (1) the people experience lack and deprivation; (2) lack is replaced by plenty.
II. (1) a character receives a warning; (2) the character violates the warning; (3) the character experiences unpleasant consequences; (4) the character may attempt to escape.
III. (1) the people (or a hero) are persecuted by enemies or evil characters; (2) the people (or a hero) take revenge.[15]

The imagery that listeners form early in a narrative exerts an influence over subsequent narration. This is the influence of memory, what Hale called *files* and Chafe (1991: 50) placed on a continuum of *given, accessible,* and *new* information. Chafe (1990: 92) proposed that a unit of new information can contain only a single concept, where *concept* is used as a cover term for things, states, and events.

The term *files* provides a concrete metaphor for imagery shared by narrator and audience. Much of this imagery is constructed during the course of a narrative and becomes part of the text world of the performance. Narrators and audiences usually come to narrative events with many common understandings from their cultural heritages, but even this shared information is reactivated. If information that has been mentioned (profiled) in a narrative is used again after a sufficiently brief lapse of time, the narrator can place it in subject position, index it with a pronoun, or delete explicit reference entirely. In the simple narrative, below, National Gizmo is mentioned in the first segment, so the listener "opens a file" on the company. There is no need to mention its name again; instead the narrator can substitute a pronoun (*it*), which directs listener's attention to an open file. Similarly, the second reference to *year* can be dropped because the file is open and the information is active:

In the first *year, National Gizmo* made only 3,000 widgets.

| |
In the second ... , *it* dominated the market.

Some American Indian languages have a device called switch reference, which seems particularly well suited to keeping the proper file highlighted in a narrative, rather like bringing a previously opened window to the foreground of the computer screen while working with a graphic user interface. For example, in Hualapai, an American Indian language of the Yuman family spoken in Arizona, a narrator must specify when the subject of the sentence remains the same or changes by means of the verbal suffixes -*k* and -*m*, respectively. Thus, a narrator mentions the subject, say mythical Wolf, only at the beginning of a passage. Thereafter, the suffix of the same subject, -*k*, on subsequent verbs indexes Wolf as the subject. When the subject switches from Wolf to Coyote, the suffix of the different subject, -*m*, alerts us to it.

Switch reference would be particularly useful as a narrative device wherever characters function as the most common subject headers. Subject headers are symbols that profile salient components shared by multiple story frames. Some common subject headers in American English in the nineties are Michael Jackson, O. J. Simpson, AIDS, drugs, gangs, gun control, the homeless, the environment, education, abortion, taxes, and rap music. Clearly, they have all emerged as subject headers because they evoke controversial social issues. Our understandings of these issues consist largely of expected or alternative social scenarios: Will O. J. be convicted or get off? Will he get a fair trial? Will there be a mistrial? With any luck, you will have the answer by the time you read this.

Instead of presenting a narrative in a sequence of time or space, a narrator may wish instead to present events in order of their relative importance, according to the salience and valuation of their imagery in the narrator's world view. Hale called this dimension of narrative *focal content*. It determines the standard narrative structure of newspaper articles, which normally present the most provocative events first and follow by filling in with characters, sequences, places, and other details. Anthropologists have sometimes observed that narrators in other cultures tell stories in which the necessary temporal order of events appears to be scrambled. In some instances, narrators may be organizing by cultural salience or focal content.

Longacre (1981: 349) observed that a narrator may mark the peak of a story by introducing detail in order to *"pack or extend the event-line."* Non-events are reported as events and characters are crowded onto the narrative stage. At the peak, the narrative may shift from second person to first person, or from third to second. Tense may shift from past to historical present. It seems likely that this marking of person and tense for greater immediacy captures a listener's attention by evoking a more subjective construal of the story, that is, one that imaginatively places listener and/ or narrator closer to the action. There may be more use of pseudodialogue, dialogue, or drama, which Longacre defined as dialogue without the use of quotation formulas. Marking for action and immediacy, crowding, repetition, and dialogue can all be seen as markers of salience or focal content.

Hale's *focal content* and Longacre's *story peaks* seem to depend on some notion of relatively high activation of narrative information. Chafe (1990: 89) proposed that "information can be in any one of three *states of activation* . . . active, semiactive, or inactive." In an analysis of a hiking narrative, Chafe showed how various English expressions operate to either characterize or raise the level of activation of narrated information.

Hale believed that focal content dominates files, trees, and backbone. This can perhaps be seen most clearly in mythology, which dramatizes core values and problematic, but salient, scenarios, seemingly providing a strong but sometimes enigmatic distillation of world view. A Kuna tale shows how constituent structure and natural sequence may be subordinated to focal content.

The text, called the Hot Pepper Story, is narrated by the Kuna Indians of Panama (Sherzer 1987: 303–305). The story apparently tells of a brother, a sister, and their grandmother, who had a pepper plant that was growing near her house. Whenever the boy was beginning to eat he would tell his sister to go and ask the grandmother for some pepper to eat with his food. The grandmother would gather the pepper for her. The boy died and was buried under the pepper plant. One day the girl went to the grandmother to ask for pepper and the grandmother told her to go and gather some. When she did, a person, apparently the spirit of her deceased brother, began to speak from the ground.

That, I think, is the gist of it, but this sequence is difficult to extract from the actual text. It is basically my own construal of the scenario underlying the text. Here is the text itself:

Well one day as they were going to eat.
"While they were beginning to eat" it is said the boy always said to
    his sister "near the grandmother's house then there is something
    growing" he says ah.
"It was growing on top of the ground something very small was
    growing" he says.

Well the grandmother saw that it was getting bigger what-was-it?
Yes.
Well slowly it rises it keeps growing up keeps growing up keeps
    growing up indeed it produced fruit.
Well when it produced fruit its flesh got ripe in fact it was pepper.
Mm, "pepper," see it is said.
Well the grandmother is taking care of, a pepper plant belonged to
    the grandmother ah.
The pepper my friend got-ripe . . . that is what happened to the
    pepper.
And as for the boy who had died, while he was beginning to eat, he
    always said to his baby sister.
"Sister go to that grandmother who is there and ask for some pepper
    for me see I want to eat with pepper ah."
She would always go to ask her.
Well she went there and said to the grandmother "I want some of
    your pepper."
The grandmother says "all right" and the grandmother would always
    go to gather pepper for her.
pepper, gather well the grandmother was there.
Well one day, while eating again, she went to ask again.
And she (the grandmother) says to the girl "you go and gather the
    pepper see."
Well she went to gather the pepper, it is said.
Well, she always went to the grandmother's place to gather it, the
    grandmother is the owner of the pepper plant.
Well a person began to speak from inside the ground to the girl who
    was gathering pepper.[16]

To me the tale seems a bit chaotic. As Sherzer (1987: 305) pointed out,
"One feature of this narration that non-Kuna find particularly strange is
the fact that the pepper plant is growing before the boy dies and that the
boy is later found buried under the plant, as if his burial had caused the
plant to grow." Sherzer offered no Kuna explanation for the order of
recitation.

One reason for the apparent lack of concern with representation of
temporal order could be the fact that most people in a Kuna audience have
heard the story before. The files are already open; the text world is known
to all. It is not necessary to specify just how, when, or where the boy died.

This information may turn up in another tale or at another telling motivated by a different narrative purpose.

A second reason why narrators might depart from normal temporal order would be to dramatize the most salient events, to put forth the focal content by placing it first or last, or by otherwise giving it prominence according to the narrative resources available in the language. Focal content dominates files, trees, and backbone. By repetition of the growth motif and tracking the growth process, this tale seems to profile the growth of pepper. But why should the growth of pepper be of such consuming interest to the Kuna Indians? It helps to know that there is a spirit world populated by several dozen types and subtypes of pepper spirits and that peppers are used in curing rituals and addressed in chants (Sherzer 1983: 32). After the opening line, which places the setting at a meal, and a second line which transfers the setting to the grandmother's house, the following lines, all concerned with growth, appear:

> "It was growing on top of the ground something very small was
>   growing" he says.
> Well the grandmother saw that it was getting bigger what-was-it?
> Yes.
> Well slowly it rises it keeps growing up keeps growing up keeps
>   growing up indeed it produced fruit.
> Well when it produced fruit its flesh got ripe in fact it was pepper.

Following these lines, the brother's death is mentioned, the sister gathers pepper for her brother before he has died, and she discovers the spirit of her brother when it speaks from the ground. The importance of the ground spirit is dramatized by its first appearance in the final line: "a person began to speak from the ground. . . ."

The tale is typical of Amerindian fertility myths that invest important domestic plants or gardens with humanlike spirits that promote growth. It has a two-part structure. First there is the growth of pepper, and second there is the dwelling of a spirit in the ground of the garden where it is discovered by the sister. The dominant story sequence is [GROWTH OF PEPPER, SPIRIT OF PEPPER LIVES IN GROUND]. The more general sequence is [EFFECT-CAUSE]. The story explains how we come to have pepper today and dramatizes the spiritual significance of pepper.

This analysis places the social structure of the tale in the background. Of course, it is certainly no accident that the pepper and the boy's spirit are both located at grandmother's, whatever that may signify to the Kuna. We could speculate on the nurturing and producing roles of grandmothers and brothers in Kuna culture, but in this narration, in my judgment, kinship roles seem more background than foreground, if only slightly so. The dominant frame is organized not in terms of time or location or kinship, but in terms of core values (pepper as curing substance) and salient images (growth, pepper spirit) of Kuna culture. The focal content of the Kuna Hot Pepper Story comes from the Kuna world view.

STORY GRAMMARS

In this section, I will describe an attempt to discover universal constraints on narrative sequences or plots. V. Propp's (1968) *Morphology of the Folktale* serves as a landmark in the twentieth-century attempt to discover the logic of folk narratives and develop story grammars. Since Propp, many other scholars have taken up the problem.[17] Edward M. Bruner (1986b: 9) defined story grammars as "formal descriptions of the minimum structure that yielded stories or storylike sequences." J. Mandler (1984: 18) defined a story grammar as "a rule system devised for the purpose of describing the regularities found in one kind of text." She distinguished the concept of story grammar from *story schema*, which she defined as "a mental structure consisting of sets of expectations about the way in which stories proceed."

The Kuna Hot Pepper Story shows that people can understand stories that have unnatural temporal sequences, so long as the sequences are conventional. The critical importance of convention and cultural values in determining narrative sequences would seem to doom any attempt to provide universal rules by which an underlying plot might be transformed into the surface sequence in a story. Nevertheless, some scholars have attempted to develop story grammars after the pattern of generative grammars. There is thought to be some universal sequence of events that provides the base or the deep structure of all stories. These grammars usually start with some kind of cause-and-effect sequence, an event, or an action followed by a reaction. Transformational rules operate on the base to produce a narration. This supposedly happens in the mind of the narrator and a complementary model that works in reverse must be developed to explain the comprehension of stories by audiences. But John B. Black and Robert Wilensky (1979) evaluated a number of proposed story grammars and concluded that determining whether a story was well formed required understanding the story. The form of stories is determined by semantic processes rather than by syntactic rules. Hence, it would be better to focus on the knowledge that audiences need to understand stories, rather than on the order of occurrence of surface forms (Black and Wilensky 1979).

It is the presuppositions (cultural scenarios) shared by audience and narrator that are crucial to understanding stories as they are intended to be understood.

Robert de Beaugrande and Benjamin N. Colby (1979: 44) grappled with the semantic pole of the story grammar problem by developing a model of story comprehension that starts from the premise that "human actions are controlled by *plans* toward the attainment of *goals*." From this dynamic perspective, they developed a "basic set of plausible STORY-TELLING RULES" that apply to stories with single characters as well as to those having both protagonists and antagonists. For a story to be interesting, they reasoned, the problems of protagonists must be difficult to solve. Here is the *Protagonist-Antagonist Rule Set* for stories that have opposing characters (1979: 46):

RULE 1
> Identify two characters, the protagonist and the antagonist.

RULE 2
> Create a problem state for protagonist which is desired or caused by antagonist.

RULE 3
> Identify a goal state desirable for protagonist and nondesirable for antagonist.

RULE 3.1 (optional)
> Identify a goal state desirable for antagonist and nondesirable for protagonist.

RULE 4
> Initiate a pathway on protagonist's state-action track moving from the problem state toward the goal state.

RULE 5
> Create actions of antagonist that block or deflect protagonist's planned pathway.

RULE 6
> Mark one state transition as decisively enabling or disenabling protagonist's attainment of the goal state evoked by Rule 3 (if Rule 3.1 is applied, define the effects of the state transition for attainment of antagonist's goal state).

RULE 7
> Create a terminal state whose desirability value for protagonist is clearly opposed to that for antagonist, thus matching or not matching their respective goal states.[18]

Beaugrande and Colby's rules represent a basic story scenario. The rules can be applied recursively to subplots and subcharacters as well as to the main scenario. They applied the rules to a delightful old Suffolk tale of Tom Tit Tot, a Rumpelstiltskin character described as "a small little black thing with a long tail" (1979: 52), but the protagonist-antagonist rules seem sufficiently basic to characterize human drama in any culture. However, the rules cannot be used universally to characterize the narrative sequence of stories, because sequences are conventional and culturally determined, as demonstrated by the Kuna Hot Pepper Story. Nevertheless, the protagonist-antagonist scenario may still underlie many stories that have been shaped to other forms by culturally determined conventions of narrative. If the protagonist-antagonist scenario represents a conceptually natural order of events, then the imagery of all cultures must somehow conform. Knowing the narrative conventions of their own cultures, audiences can reconstruct stories in their necessary temporal orders. Each culture instantiates the master scenario with its own specific characters, problems, and goal states.

Mandler (1984: 24) proposed a set of "rewrite rules" for the generation of simple stories. The rules, much more general than the rules of the story scenario of Beaugrande and Colby, comprise categories such as *setting*, *episode*, *beginning*, *development*, *complex reaction*, *goal path*, *outcome*, and *ending*. The problem in writing story grammars, as in defining spatial worlds, is finding the level of schematization that best explains the distribution of linguistic data. In my view, very general schemas such as Mandler's may validly represent psychological reality and carry some linguistic import, but scenarios peopled by intentional actors in conflict, acting in settings and scenes with recognizable objects and events, are more likely to be cognitively salient and linguistically significant.

CHAPTER 8

METAPHOR AND METONYMY

In 1980 Lakoff and Johnson published *Metaphors We Live By*, a book that focused on metaphors in English. The book was remarkable not because it listed a large number of metaphors, but because it seemed to show that language is governed by whole systems of metaphorical thinking organized into hierarchical structures. Metaphorical systems consist of groups of metaphorical expressions that all express some facet of a more general metaphor. For example, the following sentences from Lakoff and Johnson (1980: 98) all express some facet of the metaphor AN ARGUMENT IS A BUILDING:

> We've got the *framework* for a solid argument.
> If you don't *support* your argument with *solid* facts, the whole thing will *collapse*.
> He is trying to *buttress* his argument with a lot of irrelevant facts, but it is still so *shaky* that it will easily *fall apart* under criticism.
> Within the *groundwork* you've got, you can *construct* a pretty strong argument.

These expressions portray verbal arguments as buildings by referring to features of buildings and to actions that are often done to them. Typical buildings have contents; we can monitor the progress of their construction; they have strength and structure; and they are so common and fundamental in our society that they are psychologically basic. In the system of metaphor based on AN ARGUMENT IS A BUILDING, the qualities of buildings become the qualities of arguments. By connecting the discourse of argument to the complex cognitive model of a building the speaker gains access to a range of expressions all linked to a coherent cognitive structure.

We can say that the knowledge of arguments maps onto the schematic cognitive model of a building. Verbal arguments provide the *target domain* of the metaphor—the thing we are talking about—and our schematic knowledge of buildings provides the *source domain*. A connection is established by which the basic structure of buildings is mapped onto the structural features of arguments. In practice, the distinction between target and source domain may break down, as when we are discussing two things at once, each in terms of the other, as often happens in poetry, but it works well enough to characterize most cases of metaphorical speech.

Lakoff and Johnson's treatment of English metaphor is significant because it represents an attempt to explain language on the basis of cognition at a time when semantics was treated by most students of language as ancillary to syntax. *Metaphors We Live By* was at the forefront of the movement in cognitive linguistics to recognize that linguistic usage is governed by complex images, gestalts, or configurations and that the cognitions underlying the use of metaphorical language might be the same as those used in practical reasoning. It was the first book-length essay that clearly belongs to cognitive linguistics.

Lakoff has since pursued the implications of his theory of metaphor for the understanding of human reasoning. He proposed what he calls the *invariance hypothesis*:

> *The Invariance Hypothesis is a proposed general principle intended to characterize a broad range or [sic] regularities in both our conceptual and linguistic systems. Given that all metaphorical mappings are partial, the Invariance Hypothesis claims that the portion of the source domain structure that is mapped preserves cognitive topology (though of course, not all the cognitive topology of the source domain need be mapped).* (1990: 39)

On first approach, this statement appears to be a tautology. The term *map* as used here would seem logically to require the preservation of at least that portion of the source domain that is mapped: the points of correspondence. However, Lakoff appears to mean that the metaphorical mapping preserves not only the points of correspondence, but additionally the image-schematic structure or "topography" of the source domain. We can also think of this schematic structure as all of the entities and relations that connect points of correspondence within the cognitive region that is mapped. The cognitive topology of the source domain constitutes a field of inference. Inferences based upon the source domain are taken to apply to the target domain (Lakoff 1990: 54). In the next section we will examine how Apache Indians name the parts of motor vehicles. This case will bear out aspects of the invariance hypothesis, that the mapping is partial and that metaphor preserves cognitive topology and, to a limited degree, inferential structure.

AUTOMOBILES FROM THE APACHE POINT OF VIEW

In a metaphor, one thing stands for another, or a thing is called by a name for something else. For example, in the Coeur d'Alene Indian language, the tires of a car or truck became 'wrinkled feet,' a reference to the pattern on their treads. The new knowledge of automobiles is likened to the old knowledge of the body. Donald A. Norman believed that the fitting of new knowledge to a framework of old knowledge is a basic process by which people learn complex subject matter such as "learning to play a piano or learning a language" (cited in Evans 1976: 98). Norman was not dealing specifically with metaphor, but metaphor would appear to offer a mechanism by which a complex system of new knowledge in a target domain could theoretically be fit onto the framework of old knowledge in a source domain.

In an article that has been widely read within anthropology and linguistics since its original publication in 1967, Basso (1990b: 15–24) described an entire system of naming the parts of motorized vehicles in the language of the Western Apache of east-central Arizona. The Western Apache have extended the names for the body parts of humans and animals to refer to the parts of automobiles and pickup trucks. In this structural metaphor, the hood became the nose (*bichįh*), the headlights became the eyes (*bidáá*), and the windshield became the forehead (*bita'*). The term for the face (*bínii'*) was extended to the whole area extending from the top of the windshield to the front bumper, so this term included the nose/hood and forehead/windshield as subparts. The front wheels became the hands and arms (*bigan*), while the rear wheels and tires became the feet (*bikee'*). All items under the hood were classified as parts of the innards (*bibiye'*). Under the hood, the battery became the liver (*bizig*); the electrical wiring, the veins (*bits'ǫǫs*); the gas tank, the stomach (*bibid*); the distributor, the heart (*bijíí*); the radiator, the lung (*bijíí'izólé*); the radiator hoses, the intestines (*bich'í'*).

Apparently, when the Western Apache first encountered motorized vehicles, the human body or the horse provided a metaphor by means of which they were able to talk about them.[1] There was an underlying conceptual metaphor, which I will state as MOTOR VEHICLES ARE ANIMATE THINGS, that permitted them to draw correspondences between the parts of living things and the parts of cars and pickup trucks and to name them accordingly.² In the MOTOR VEHICLES ARE ANIMATE THINGS metaphor, the thing of which we speak (the motor vehicle), with its constituent parts and relations (its cognitive topology), is the target domain, while the thing with which we speak (animate beings), with its own constituent parts and relations, is the source domain.

Basso referred to the naming of motorized vehicles in Western Apache as "set extension," suggesting that a set of names from the domain of animate beings had merely been extended in meaning to cover the new set of parts in the domain of motorized vehicles. Foreshadowing Lakoff's invariance hypothesis, Basso argued that set extension preserved the hierarchical cognitive structure of relationships among the parts, so that both the car's body and the human body had "innards" that included the "liver." In other words, the mapping of body part terms onto parts of motor vehicles preserves cognitive topology. While simply assuming complete correspondence in relationships as well as in parts could eventually lead to problems in reasoning about the workings of motorized vehicles, the cognitive efficiency achieved by maintaining a single set of names in place of two does appear to be worthwhile. Perhaps it is just a practical matter of limiting the metaphor to the most superficial levels of appearances and functions in the two domains. As Lakoff (1990: 39) proposed, "not all of the cognitive topology of the source domain need be mapped."

Seeking a better understanding of the naming process, Basso (1990b: 23) discovered that motorized vehicles were classified as animate things, or "'ihi'dahí, a broad category that also includes humans, quadrupeds, birds, reptiles, fish, insects, plants, and several other engine-driven machines (e.g., bulldozers, tractors, steam shovels)." House (n.d.) reported that the Navajo have similar body part terms for automobiles, but no overarching terms that separately categorize animate and inanimate entities.

The Western Apache drew correspondences between their cognitive models of motorized vehicles and the cognitive model, or models, of animate beings. One complex thing has been seen and described in terms of another. The fact that the Apache perceive a schema that subsumes both so that motorized vehicles are assimilated to the class of animate beings does not obviate the metaphor. In fact, the schema might be regarded as necessary to the establishment of metaphor. As Basso (1990b: 22) put it, much as Norman also argued, "Set extension facilitated communication about a totally foreign object in a *familiar frame of reference* and, at least for a while, made it unnecessary for Apaches to contend with an elaborate

English terminology that even native speakers may sometimes find confusing [italics added]."

Apache vehicle names illustrate basic cognitive abilities underlying the
use of metaphor: the ability to analyze complex entities and to compare
the corresponding parts and structures point by point as one complex image is mapped to another. So if one thing stands for another in metaphorical reference, so do the parts of the first stand for the corresponding parts
of the second, as the parts of the body stand for the parts of motor vehicles
in Apache. Furthermore, the parts of the target domain maintain the same
relationships, one to another, as do their named counterparts in the source
domain. Cognitive topology is preserved. But Apache vehicle names also
illustrate our ability to be selective, to abstract just those portions of the
source domain that seem appropriate to the target domain.

ORIENTATIONAL AND ONTOLOGICAL METAPHORS

In Umberto Eco's *Foucault's Pendulum* (1989: 362), the following passage was spoken by Lia:

> And high is better than low, because if you have your head down
> the blood goes to your brain, because feet stink and hair doesn't stink
> as much, because its better to climb a tree and pick fruit than end up
> under ground, food for worms, and because you rarely hurt yourself
> hitting something above—you really have to be in an attic—while
> you often hurt yourself falling. That's why up is angelic and down
> devilish.

Lia's theory is based on *orientational metaphors*, which are metaphors
that are based in our physical and cultural experience and give concepts
spatial orientation. The orientational metaphors discussed by Lakoff and
Johnson (1980: 14–17) are listed below. Only one example of each is
given where the authors listed several:

HAPPY IS UP; SAD IS DOWN
  I'm feeling *up*.
CONSCIOUSNESS IS UP; UNCONSCIOUSNESS IS DOWN
  He *rises* early in the morning.
HEALTH AND LIFE ARE UP; SICKNESS AND DEATH ARE DOWN
  Lazarus *rose* from the dead.
HAVING CONTROL OR FORCE IS UP; BEING SUBJECT TO CONTROL OR
  FORCE IS DOWN
  He's at the *height* of his power.

MORE IS UP; LESS IS DOWN

My income *rose* last year.

FORESEEABLE FUTURE EVENTS ARE UP (and AHEAD)

All *up*coming events are listed in the paper.

HIGH STATUS IS UP; LOW STATUS IS DOWN

He has a *lofty* position.

GOOD IS UP; BAD IS DOWN

Things are looking *up*.

VIRTUE IS UP; DEPRAVITY IS DOWN

I wouldn't *stoop* to that.

RATIONAL IS UP; EMOTIONAL IS DOWN

The discussion *fell to the emotional* level, but I *raised it back up to the rational* plane.

The stock of metaphorical imagery is very rich in any language. While all of the above examples are based on the relation up-down, other spatial metaphors are based on front-back, on-off, center-periphery, and near-far. In addition to orientational metaphors there are *ontological metaphors*, which equate activities, emotions, and ideas to entities and substances. *Her ego is very fragile* is an example of the ontological metaphor THE MIND IS AN ENTITY. In this instance, it is a brittle object (1980: 27–28). Lakoff and Johnson (1980: 8–9) also showed that metaphors have different levels and entailments between levels. For example, the metaphor TIME IS MONEY entails TIME IS A LIMITED RESOURCE, which entails TIME IS A VALUABLE COMMODITY. Such entailments mean that anyone who would understand practical human reasoning would do well to study metaphor, but, as we have seen in the discussion of Quinn's critique of Lakoff and Johnson in Chapter 5, there is more to reasoning than metaphor alone.

We can now use these concepts pertaining to structural, orientational, and ontological metaphors to examine the imagery of some interesting metaphorical expressions in Japanese, English, and Nahuatl.

COMING TO *ATAMA* AND BLOWING YOUR STACK: JAPANESE AND AMERICAN METAPHORS OF ANGER

Each culture models the body according to its own priorities of grouping and differentiation. These models are interesting for their own sake, and knowledge of them enhances appreciation of cultural and linguistic differences, but another reason for paying close attention to cultural anatomical models and maps is that they often serve as the base for figurative

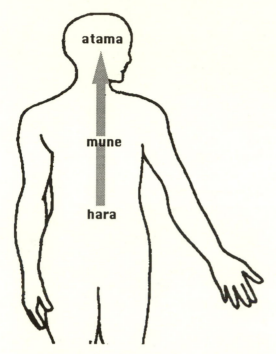

FIGURE 27. Anger rises through bodily containers in Japanese.

language about other topics. A cultural anatomical model can offer insights into the language of behavior and emotions. Let us see how this works in Japanese metaphors for anger. The examples are from Keiko Matsuki (1989).

Figure 27 is a schematic drawing of three regions of the body as they are understood by speakers of Japanese. Each region has a place in Japanese thinking about anger. *Hara* refers to the belly, but it also has extended uses as stomach, center, womb, heart, and intention. Matsuki says that *hara* is the container of the emotions. To express the quality of their anger, Japanese speakers can say **hara** *rises up*, *hold it in* **hara**, or *keep it in* **hara**. *Mune* refers to the chest. When anger can no longer be controlled and held in the *hara*, it rises, like a hot liquid, into *mune*, where it may provide the occasion for statements such as *[I] feel strangled with* **mune** *because of the rise of* **hara**. When a person is about to lose control, anger comes to the head, to *atama*, so we might hear the expression *it came to* **atama** *with a click*, or *finally, it came to* **atama**. *Hara*, *mune*, and *atama* represent three regions of the body where anger is contained, and three stages in the process of getting increasingly angry.

Together with the idea of anger as a hot liquid, *hara*, *mune*, and *atama* provide a schema for the construction of a sequentially ordered metaphorical scenario. To fully understand a statement such as **hara** *rises up*, *strangled with* **mune**, or *it came to* **atama** it is not sufficient to know that *hara* refers to the belly, *mune* to the chest, and *atama* to the head and that pressurized liquid anger may be contained in one of these three regions. We must also know that anger rises up through them in a fixed sequence to create a scale of increasing discomfort and potential for aggression. Just as in school we must know the letter grading schema of F to A in order to understand the statement *I got an A in geometry*, in Japanese we must know the *hierarchy of bodily containers* schema in order to understand language expressing anger. This is why the denotational meaning provided in a terse dictionary definition seldom captures the full meaning of a word. Nor is it enough to provide a list of connotations, if by that term we simply intend other associated meanings, because these may fail to delineate the meaningful schema in which a word is functionally embedded, somewhat as a feather is embedded in the wing of a bird, serving a special function by virtue of its position on the wing as well as its shape.

It is interesting to compare the Japanese schema with that underlying English metaphors of anger. With tensions between the United States and Japan rising over everything from the prices of microchips and Toyotas to the question of Japanese rearmament, it may even become vitally important to make the comparisons. Kövecses (1987: 53–55) proposed that in English the central metaphor for anger is ANGER IS THE HEAT OF A FLUID IN A CONTAINER (an ontological metaphor). This metaphor gives rise to expressions such as the following:

You make my *blood boil*.
Simmer down!
I had reached the *boiling point*.
Let him *stew*.

Like the Japanese case, the basic metaphor involves a scenario that describes what happens when anger becomes more intense: the fluid anger rises; anger produces steam and pressure on the container; when anger becomes too intense, the person explodes; when the person explodes, parts of her go up in the air and whatever was inside comes out. Messy. These scenarios give rise to expressions such as the following:

His pent-up anger *welled up* inside him. (fluid rising)
She got all *steamed up*. (anger produces steam)

He was *bursting with* anger. (anger produces pressure)
She *blew up* at me. (person explodes)
I *blew* my stack. (parts go up in air)
His anger finally *came out*. (what was inside comes out)

In Kövecses's view, the central metaphor for anger is related to the more general English metaphor for the emotions, which says that THE BODY IS A CONTAINER FOR THE EMOTIONS. The fact that anger is a mass noun rather than a count noun gives us a clue to its image. You might say *How much anger does she have pent up inside?* but not *How many angers does she have pent up inside?* Like any mass entity, anger has a scale indicating its amount. In the central metaphor for anger, this is measured by temperature.

Like any metaphor, there is a source domain and a target domain. The source domain is our conception of fluid in a container; the target domain is anger itself. A metaphor sets up a series of correspondences between entities from the two domains. Kövecses (1987: 56–57) called these *ontological correspondences*. Here is how he organized the cognitive model with its ontological correspondences:

Source: HEAT OF FLUID IN CONTAINER
Target: ANGER
Ontological Correspondences:
• the container is the body
• the heat of fluid is the anger
• the heat scale is the anger scale, with end points zero and limit
• container heat is body heat
• pressure in container is internal pressure in the body
• agitation in container is internal pressure in the body
• the limit of the container's capacity to withstand pressure caused by heat is the limit of the anger scale
• explosion is the loss of control
• coolness in the fluid is lack of anger
• calmness of the fluid is lack of agitation

Kövecses apparently regarded knowledge *of* entities as qualitatively different from knowledge *about* entities because he made a distinction between them, calling knowledge *about* entities "epistemic" rather than "ontological." *Epistemic correspondences* arise when the knowledge about entities (fluid, container) in a source domain corresponds to that about entities in a target domain (anger, body). I will give just one of the five epistemic correspondences that he listed:

Source: The effect of intense fluid heat is container heat, internal pressure, and agitation.

Target: The effect of intense anger is body heat, internal pressure, and agitation.

The other four correspondences deal with explosion and loss of control, the damage caused by an explosion of fluid or anger, preventing an explosion by the application of force, and controlling the release of heated fluid (anger). Thus, in Kövecses's view, complete metaphors consist of ontological and epistemic correspondences holding between source and target domains. Though I doubt the ultimate necessity for a rigid distinction between ontological and epistemic (metonymic) correspondences, I accept its utility in separating more central from more peripheral aspects of metaphors.

ANGER IS THE HEAT OF FLUID IN A CONTAINER is not the only metaphor of anger in English. Others are ANGER IS INSANITY, ANGER IS AN OPPONENT, and ANGER IS A DANGEROUS ANIMAL, which give rise to such expressions as *He got so angry, he **went out of his mind**, I'm struggling **with my anger***, and *He has a **ferocious** temper*. Anger is also described in metonymic expressions, in which the part is taken for the whole. With regard to emotions, the general principle of metonymy holds that THE PHYSIOLOGICAL EFFECTS OF AN EMOTION STAND FOR THE EMOTION. Accordingly, a variety of physiological, behavioral, and perceptual events can represent anger: body heat, internal pressure, redness in the face and neck area, agitation, or interference with accurate perception. These metonymies give us such expressions as the following:

Don't get hot under the collar. (BODY HEAT)
Don't get a hernia. (INTERNAL PRESSURE)
She was scarlet with rage. (REDNESS IN FACE AND NECK AREA)
She was shaking with anger. (AGITATION)
She was blind with rage. (INTERFERENCE WITH ACCURATE
    PERCEPTION)

The central English metaphor of anger resembles the Japanese. Both imagine anger as a hot fluid and the body as a container. Because anger is probably everywhere correlated with rising body temperature and blood pressure, it is quite possible that some core images and figurative descriptions of anger are universal. In both English and Japanese, increasing intensity of anger causes fluid to rise. The English metaphor appears to emphasize pressure and explosive escape from the container. In Japanese, loss of control comes with a click rather than an explosion. To understand why, we would need additional information about the Japanese model of the mind and body and a larger collection of Japanese metaphors.

Japanese metaphors of anger show the importance of understanding the native cognitive model of the body, but they also illustrate another important point: that the models underlying terms for emotions include complex scenarios describing how emotions progress sequentially through various states. Definitions of apparently simple terms, such as those for the emotions, may require complex models, as we have already seen in the example of *love*, presented in Chapter 6. Moreover, since emotions have complex conceptual structures, they may give rise to a variety of nontrivial inferences (Kövecses 1987: 50). Therefore, figurative and emotional language may provide insights into reasoning processes. In finding the connections between words and scenarios, we reach a level of language comprehension unattainable through simple translations of words by means of ordinary dictionary definitions.

METONYMICAL THINKING AND EXPRESSION

Much of the scholarly interest in figurative language focuses on metaphor, but equally important is *metonymy*—the relationship of one thing to another within a single conceptual model or scene. Lakoff (1987: 114) defined metonymy as "a function from one element of the model to another." While any kind of association can give rise to metonymy, frequently the part stands for the whole (technically, a synecdoche), as in referring to a friend's new car as a "nice set of wheels." However, metonymy is often based not on physical relationships, but on the content of scenes, as in the following:

> A doctor says, "Is Jones here *the appendectomy* or *the tonsillectomy*?" (OPERATION ON BODY PART FOR PERSON BEING OPERATED ON)
> "One waitress says to another, 'The ham sandwich just spilled beer all over himself.' " (Lakoff 1987: 77) (FOOD ORDERED FOR CUSTOMER)

Notice that there is no metaphorical intention to compare or liken Jones either to his body parts or to the operations, nor is there any intention to compare or liken the customer to a ham sandwich. Rather the hapless Jones and the sloppy customer are identified by something with which they are associated: an operation on a part of the body in the first expression or what the customer ordered in the second. The number of possible metonymical relations in languages of the world is certainly vast and probably indeterminate. Here are some more examples of metonyms:

INCLUDED ACTIVITY FOR ACTIVITY

Who do you *run* with? (RUNNING FOR PLAYING BASKETBALL)

PART FOR WHOLE or CONTAINER FOR CONTENTS

Send me a *card*. (CARD FOR CARD WITH MESSAGE)

ATTRIBUTE FOR THING

Give me *five*. (NUMBER FIVE FOR FIVE FINGERS: FIVE FINGERS FOR GREETING GESTURE WITH HAND)

LOCATION FOR POLITICAL OFFICE

The White House announced a change in policy this morning.

Metonymy has consequences for grammar in that a metonymical expression assumes the grammatical function of its alternative. Consider the following expression from René Dirven (1991: 4): "*Different parts of the country* don't necessarily mean the same thing when they use the same word."

I take this metonymy to be based on the equation DIFFERENT PARTS OF THE COUNTRY = INHABITANTS OF DIFFERENT PARTS OF THE COUNTRY. People and geographical parts of the country are two components of a larger image, and the metonymy is therefore part-to-part. Dirven has called this *ad hoc* metonymy. In Dirven's view, metonymy plays upon the syntagmatic dimension of imagery, that is, the conceptual contiguity, juxtaposition, or clustering of elements in time and space.

The parts of the country metonymy assumes the grammatical function of its conceptual referent. Metonymy violates the normal co-occurrence restrictions that would prevent *different parts of the country . . . mean* if the expression were interpreted literally. The expression makes sense only if the subject of the verb is construed to be human speakers.

Another example with consequences for understanding grammatical constructions is provided by the expression *she heard the piano*. Langacker (1990a: 193–196) argued that in expressions such as these the verb is polysemous. He proposed verbal polysemy in order to avoid deriving the expression from a paraphrase in deep structure, such as *she heard the sound of the piano*.

I think it is right to avoid the deep structure paraphrase solution in favor of polysemy, but the argument for *verbal* polysemy seems unduly complex. A more economical analysis would appeal directly to the metonymy *piano* for *sound of piano*, making the landmark polysemous rather than the verb. The expression profiles only the person, the piano, and the hearing, while implicating the whole base, which is a scene that involves these elements and additionally involves someone playing the piano and the sounds that it emits. Thus, *she heard the piano* is a THING FOR FEATURE metonymy in which the piano stands in for the music it produces.

MERONYMY AND A CASE OF MERONYMOUS MARRIAGE

A technical term for part-whole relations apart from their verbal expression in metonymy is *meronymy*. It happens that in English, and no doubt in all languages, there are quite a number of such meronymic relations. Morton E. Winston, Roger Chaffin, and Douglas Herrmann (1987) identified six types:

1) component–integral object (pedal-bike)
2) member-collection (ship-fleet)
3) portion-mass (slice-pie)
4) stuff-object (steel-car)
5) feature-activity (paying-shopping)
6) place-area (Everglades-Florida).

These types were abstracted from such commonplace expressions as *The head is part of the body*, *Bicycles are partly aluminum*, *Pistons are parts of engines*, and *Dating is a part of adolescence*. The part to whole types themselves can be further distinguished by three other relations according to (1) whether the part-whole relation is functional (pedal-bike), (2) whether the parts are made of the same stuff as their wholes (slice-pie), and (3) whether the parts are separable from their wholes (pedal-bike).

Such part-whole relations have long been subject to debate over whether or not they are transitive. For example, we can say, in English, that the finger is part of the hand and the hand is part of the body, so the finger is part of the body. The relations of finger to hand and to body are clearly transitive. But given that Simpson's arm is part of Simpson's body, and Simpson's body is a member of the philosophy department, we still cannot say that Simpson's arm is either a part of or a member of the philosophy department. Of course this is not necessarily a problem in other cultures. I recall reading of a case in an American Indian culture on the Northwest Coast where a chief who lacked a son of appropriate age arranged a ceremonial marriage of one of his legs to the daughter of another chief. Perhaps the parents of the bride would have been able to characterize the leg as a member of the family. Even in this clear case of social meronymy, the relation is not necessarily transitive. It is something more like the following: a leg is a part of the body; the body is part of the person; a part of the body can stand in for the body. Thus, it was a meronymous marriage.

Meronymic relations are transitive so long as we don't mix any of the six types. The problem of Simpson's body mixes the component-integral object relation with the member-collection relation, and so its transitive use seems anomalous. Maintaining an awareness of the different types of meronymic relations in English, along with perhaps yet uncovered relations in other languages, should assist us in understanding metonymy. They have also given us an interesting research problem: to record and compare transitive and intransitive meronymies in other languages and cultures.

MY HERON FEATHER; MY CORD JACKET: MIXING METAPHORS WITH METONYMS IN CLASSICAL NAHUATL COUPLETS

A colleague of mine, Evan Blythin, recently called my attention to a curious property of Aztec rhetoric: sixteenth-century speakers of Nahuatl, the language of the Aztecs, mixed their metaphors.[3] His interest was aroused by eighty-seven metaphors listed in Book 6 of the thirteen volume of the *Florentine Codex, General History of the Things of New Spain* (1969), written by the Franciscan priest Bernardo de Sahagún. The *Codex* was translated by Sahagún in the year 1577, thirty years after it had been recorded in Nahuatl, or, as Sahagún put it, "in the Mexican language." Since Sahagún's time, the Nahuatl language has incorporated many terms and constructions from Spanish to become what is today called Mexicano, a language with thousands of speakers (Hill and Hill 1986).

My colleague was searching the *Codex* for clues to some puzzling characteristics of contemporary Mexican political rhetoric, particularly the tendency to mix metaphors, which is, of course, a violation of English rhetorical maxims—though not necessarily of common usage. Wayne C. Booth (1979), for example, found that all modern guides to writing seemed to agree that metaphors should be novel and coherent, that is, not mixed. Booth offered several alternative criteria, to which I will return later in this chapter. It is hard to know how the Aztecs felt about novelty in their metaphors, but it was numerous entries such as the following in the *Codex* that caught Blythin's attention: THOU HAST MADE THYSELF INTO A RABBIT; THOU HAST MADE THYSELF INTO A DEER, an expression that appears to mix its metaphors by mixing its animals. According to

Sahagún (1969: 253), it refers to a fugitive from family responsibilities: "This was said of him who no longer lived at home, who no longer obeyed his father, his mother. He just fled when they found it necessary to admonish him."

The pair is coherent in that both the rabbit and the deer are animals that typically flee. The example also typifies the format of Nahuatl metaphors, which come in pairs or groups of pairs. In this respect it is typical of Nahuatl texts in general, which exhibit a variety of couplet structures (Bright 1990), and even more widely of texts from Central America (Sherzer 1983; Tedlock 1985; Hill 1992). Taking a commonly held view in rhetorical studies that the purpose of metaphors is to give us some information about an unknown or *tenor* (i.e., target) by introducing a known or *vehicle* (i.e., source), my colleague reasoned that the function of the double figures was to provide more information about the unknown and, at the same time, perhaps, to introduce even more uncertainty. It is an interesting hypothesis, but, before drawing conclusions about the rhetorical functions of Nahuatl metaphors, it may help to examine their meaning more closely with special attention to imagery and conceptual organization. This will reveal that Nahuatl figures contain more than metaphor alone. Typically, an underlying metaphorical model remains implicit and unnamed, revealed only by explicit mention of two of its parts or, in the case of the rabbit and the deer, two exemplars of the actors in a scenario. Thus, in many cases, an expression combines a metaphor with a metonym, a relation of the part to the whole, an actor to its scenario, an entity to its setting. The resulting figurative couplet is *coherent* in the sense that the two parts have similar entailments, and it is often *consistent*, in the sense that both can be assimilated to the same image or cognitive model (Lakoff and Johnson 1980: 87–96). Consider the following examples:

ONE'S EYE, ONE'S EAR
ONE'S WOMB, ONE'S THROAT
THE TAIL, THE WING

Each of these pairs names two parts of the same image: eye and ear belong to the head, tail and wing to a bird; ONE'S WOMB, ONE'S THROAT is probably best translated as 'one's womb, one's birth canal' (Maxwell and Hanson 1992: 83, 93, 171, 175). All three metaphorical couplets are also metonyms. The pair ONE'S EYE, ONE'S EAR names sensory organs of the head and pertains to a messenger or a spy acting for the emperor. Thus the underlying metaphor is THE EMPEROR IS A HEAD AND HIS SPIES ARE

HIS EYES AND HIS EARS. The corollary to this, what Kövecses (1987) called an epistemic correspondence, is that spies gather information for the emperor just as eyes and ears gather information for the head or brain.

ONE'S WOMB, ONE'S THROAT is said of a member of the royal lineage, that is, one who issues from a royal womb. It is probably a shortened form of HE HATH COME FORTH FROM ONE'S WOMB, FROM ONE'S THROAT. This metaphor could be stated as THE ROYAL LINEAGE IS A MOTHER.

THE TAIL, THE WING refers to peripheral parts of a bird and is said of commoners, that is, HE WHO POSSESSES THE TAIL, HE WHO POSSESSES THE WING (Sahagún 1969: 244). A similar expression, I PROTECT THY HAIR, THY HEAD, also refers to two parts of the body, but in this case there is a second metonymy in that hair may also be construed as a part of the head. It was said to admonish a person to guard his or her honor. The metaphor likens honor to the integrity of a body and its parts.

So Nahuatl metaphors are more coherent, and often consistent, than they might at first appear in that many exhibit a part-whole structure with an implicit coordinating image or cognitive model. Like the expressions discussed above, many other figures refer to concrete entities:

WHERE HAVE I PASSED OVER THE HAIR, THE HEAD OF OUR LORD?
ALREADY IN ANOTHER'S ENCLOSURE, ALREADY IN THE ENTRANCE OF
    ANOTHER'S HOUSE
ONE'S HAIR, ONE'S NAILS, ONE'S SPINES, ONE'S THORNS, ONE'S BEARD,
    ONE'S EYEBROWS, ONE'S CHIP, ONE'S FRAGMENT
HIS FACE IS CAST DOWN: HIS TEETH ARE CAST DOWN
HE STRIKETH OFF OBSIDIAN [POINTS]; HE STRAIGHTENETH ARROW
    SHAFTS
VERILY HE HATH EYES; VERILY HE HATH EARS
HEART, BLOOD
OUR LORD CONTINUETH TO TUG AT OUR FLANK, AT OUR EARS

Some figures recorded by Sahagún pertain to actions or to qualities, rather than to concrete things. Rather than calling to mind an image, they may require a generalization and further require the listener to draw upon his or her knowledge to construe some common meaning in the two parts. This is the case with . . . A RABBIT, . . . A DEER, quoted above, which expresses the idea of the fugitive, rather than parts of a single visual image. Consider also the following figures:

MY HERON FEATHER, MY CORD JACKET
TOMORROW, THE DAY AFTER TOMORROW
ALREADY AT THE EDGE OF THE FIRE, ALREADY AT THE STAIRWAY

The expression MY HERON FEATHER, MY CORD JACKET is rather subtle. It refers concretely to aspects of a slave's dress and metaphorically to one given a task by the city, thereby likening the status of being called to duty to that of slavery. Once again, the imagery—slave's dress—is implicit, while the concrete mention of two items worn by slaves depends upon a part-whole or possessed-possessor relation. Thus, a rather long chain of inference links a part of dress (feather, jacket) to the complete image of slave's dress, to the role of slavery, and finally to onerous duty. The chain of metonym and metaphor, with the target always stated first, is as follows:

ONE GIVEN ONEROUS DUTY IS A SLAVE (metaphor)
A SLAVE WEARS SLAVE'S DRESS (metonymy)
A SLAVE'S DRESS HAS A HERON FEATHER AND A CORD JACKET
  (metonymy)

I am tempted to use MY HERON FEATHER, MY CORD JACKET the next time I am given a bothersome committee assignment, or I may just say, "My chewed pencil, my plastic coffee cup."

The expression TOMORROW, THE DAY AFTER TOMORROW is said to mean "the time toward which we are going—a few days" (Sahagún 1969: 242). In the absence of native language expertise, it is difficult to know whether the translation accurately represents the Aztec conception of time; but if it does, this expression refers to the parts (days) of some more general conception of the future. Or to turn it around, because this expression parallels so many other expressions that are obviously met-onymical, it seems reasonable to postulate a general conception of future time in Aztec world view.

The expression ALREADY AT THE EDGE OF THE FIRE, ALREADY AT THE STAIRWAY was said of persons about to be put to death. It evokes a scene of human sacrifice with a victim poised at the stairway of a temple, at the edge of the sacrificial fire.[4] In evoking a scene with its component setting and scenarios, it differs from figures that call to mind concrete objects (body, bird), abstractions (sustenance, time), or a social status (slave). The complex image presented by a scene contains elements that are both con-crete (stairway, fire) and behavioral (sacrifice). The figure is a metonym, because the sacrificial scene stands for the situation of being condemned to die. It evokes the scene with more metonymy—by mentioning parts of the scene rather than by naming the scene entire.

Nahuatl speakers constructed some metaphors as multiple couplets. For example, the expression ONE'S HAIR, ONE'S NAILS/ONE'S SPINES,

ONE'S THORNS/ONE'S BEARD, ONE'S EYEBROWS/ONE'S CHIP, ONE'S FRAG-MENT has four pairs. It refers to one born into the royal lineage, rather like the English expression *chip off the old block*, with each pair reiterating the theme with subject matter from a different semantic domain: periph-eral body-parts/sharp objects from plant or animal/facial hair/solid mate-rial (bone? obsidian?). The first three couplets suggest great numbers of offspring (compare Maxwell and Hanson 1992: 171). More commonly, we find a pair of pairs in which the second couplet abstracts from the first, as in the explicit metaphor SMOKE, MIST/FAME, HONOR, said of a dead ruler, or LIKE A PRECIOUS GREEN STONE, LIKE A PRECIOUS TURQUOISE/PERFECTLY CYLINDRICAL, WELL ROUNDED, said of excellent discourse. But the second pair may simply reiterate the theme in a different domain, as in I LAY BEFORE THEE THE LIGHT, THE TORCH/THE MODEL, THE MEA-SURE/THE WIDE MIRROR, said of noble instruction. The single final ele-ment of the last phrase (THE WIDE MIRROR) breaks the couplet pattern. Such deviations occur infrequently. The pattern of concrete to abstract is broken again in the double couplet THAT WHICH CAN BE CARRIED, THAT WHICH CAN BE SHOULDERED/THAT WHICH GOETH ON ONE'S LAP, IN THE CRADLE OF THE ARMS, a metaphor for the common folk. Both pairs lie on the same level of specificity. I cannot resist the mention of one last ex-ample, a particularly poetic one, which has the form concrete-concrete/scenario-scenario: THOU ART A CYPRESS, THOU ART A SILK COTTON TREE./BENEATH THEE, THE COMMON FOLK WILL SEEK THE SHADE; THEY WILL SEEK THE SHADOW. The metaphors of the first couplet establish settings for the second.

These examples demonstrate that Nahuatl commonly builds a meta-phor on an image evoked by a metonym. The source of the metaphor is an unnamed cognitive model of which only two of the several possible parts are explicitly verbalized. The content of the underlying models in-cludes concrete objects (body, bird), scenarios (human sacrifice, seeking shade under tree), social statuses (slavery, fugitive), and abstractions (time, fame, cylindrical shape). Longer expressions that stack up two or more pairs are also possible and single elements sometimes occur after pairs. There are many subtle chains of metaphorical reasoning in these figures of speech about which we can know little without further study of the Nahuatl language and the Aztec culture. Hill (1992: 123) reported that the Nahuatl ceremonial couplet *in cuīcatl in xōchitl* 'the song, the flower' makes explicit the Nahuatl linkage of flower and song and that poets were often called "singers of flowers."

Recall Booth's criteria for good metaphors: they should be active, concise, appropriate to their intended target, accommodated to the audience, and constructive to the character of the speaker. Now it seems clear that these criteria are culture bound. Even if we felt justified in applying the rhetorical standards of the English-speaking world to other languages, which I do not, it is still difficult to apply his criteria to the Aztec figures. Nahuatl metaphors are very concise and usually concrete, but they are most often inactive. TO TUG AT OUR FLANK, AT OUR EARS, for example, is more active than ONE'S WOMB, ONE'S THROAT; both pairs are concise and concrete. Sahagún did not record what latitude speakers were allowed or what liberties were taken in offering metaphors appropriate to the situation, the audience, or the speaker, but we can hardly hold him responsible for failing to answer questions posed four centuries later. The very fact that they often refer to social statuses argues that their speakers were sensitive to context of usage.

To summarize, many Nahuatl couplets express a metonymy built on a metaphor, as wing and tail suggest the relation of peripherality and the image of a bird. Nahuatl couplets are metonymical metaphors. They are polytropes (Friedrich 1991). Couplets reveal the intended metaphorical model at the same time that they introduce thought-provoking connotations. Nahuatl speakers of Sahagún's time drew their metaphorical source material from the physical world, scenes of life, social roles, and abstractions. English literary rhetorical standards probably do not apply; but in any case, Nahuatl metaphors were more coherent and consistent than they might appear to be on a casual reading.

TALMY'S FORCE DYNAMICS

Thus far our consideration of metaphor and metonymy has dealt with fairly obvious examples: a car battery is a *liver*, *The **ham sandwich** is waiting for his check*, and *You make my **blood boil*** are typical examples. Even more common expressions such as *I'm feeling **up*** and *It's hard to **get** that idea **across to** him* are also clearly metaphorical, but in these the metaphor may be harder to discern because it lies in well-entrenched senses of common verbs, verb complements, and prepositions. One of the insights of cognitive linguistics is that many expressions that at first seem not to be figurative actually prove to be so when given more systematic study. When all the metaphorical underbrush is cleared from language, it turns out that the residuum is very little. The vast majority of everyday expressions contain metaphorical or metonymical language. As a case in point, consider the following sentences, all of which express some idea involving psychological or social interaction:

I *couldn't help* singing along.
He *resisted accepting* their arguments.
She *refrained from* saying anything impolite.
She *was civil*.
I am *being pressured to* go to the graduation ceremony.
You *must*, you *have to*.
You *can't make* me.
I *guess* I will, *despite* my better judgment.
You *better not try it*.
She *need not trouble herself*.
I *would, but I can't* go.
I know it's *aggravating*, but *try to let it be*.
Keep on keeping on.
I *think I will win, in spite of myself*.

These expressions, for the most part, appear to be quite direct and straightforward, but what is less apparent is that, in addition to registering psychological or social interaction, all of the sentences also fit a cognitive model of *force dynamics* (Talmy 1988). Talmy believed that force dynamics is one of four very basic imaging systems that organize scenes for language. The imagery of force dynamics affects the way we talk about natural events, social pressures, and psychological events. (Notice the metaphor in social pressures.) The other three basic imaging systems pertain to spatial and temporal structure, to the observer's perspective, and to distribution of attention, that is, the scope and focus of attention within a scene. These four imaging systems are thought to be partially independent of one another.

Force dynamics prototypically involves the opposition of two forces in a steady state. One of the two forces is "singled out for focal attention." Talmy called this focal entity in the force schema the *Agonist*, the opposing force the *Antagonist*. As in so many thought experiments in cognitive linguistics, it is not always clear that we can objectively and reliably determine the correct assignments of the roles of *Agonist* and *Antagonist* to entities in a sentence, but let us assume that our subjective judgments will agree. Figure 28 gives us a set of symbols that can be used to represent the entities and their behavior in the schema of force dynamics. Figures 29 to 32, with example sentences, depict the four most basic force schemas in the semantics of English. These four schemas all exist in a steady state: something remains at rest or continues in motion. Other derivative schemas may involve changes of state, as suggested by the sentence *The*

Entities

Agonist

Antagonist

Intrinsic Tendencies

Toward Action

Toward Rest

Balance of Strengths

Stronger Entity +

Weaker Entity −

Resultants of Interaction of Forces

Action

Rest

FIGURE 28. Symbols for force schemas. From Talmy (1988: 54). Reprinted with permission from Ablex Publishing Corporation.

ball's hitting it made the lamp topple from the table, or they may involve scenes where the *Agonist* and *Antagonist* no longer impinge upon one another, as in the sentence *The plug's staying loose let the water drain from the tank*. Talmy developed schematic diagrams for all of the common variations.

The real excitement comes in seeing how the schemas of force dynamics are metaphorically extended to psychological events and social pressures. For example, the two-part schema of *Agonist* and *Antagonist* helps to explain sentences that imply a divided self, as in *I held myself back from responding*. This sentence clearly fits the schema in Figure 30, only the *Agonist* becomes *I* and the *Antagonist* becomes *myself*. The fact that we could also paraphrase the sentence as *I refrained from responding* shows that common verbs of volition can be defined by the schemas of force dynamics. As Talmy (1988: 69) put it, the expression *refrain from* lexicalizes the schema. A phrase is found to dress an idea.

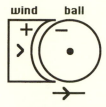

FIGURE 29. Force schema for sentence *The ball kept rolling because of the wind blowing on it. Agonist* (circle) has tendency to remain at rest (•). *Antagonist* has tendency toward action (>). Force of *Antagonist* is stronger (+) than *Agonist* (−). Resultant is *Agonist* remains in motion (−>−−). From Talmy (1988: 55). Reprinted with permission from Ablex Publishing Corporation.

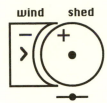

FIGURE 30. Force schema for sentence *The shed kept standing despite the gale wind blowing against it. Agonist* (circle) has tendency to remain at rest (•). *Antagonist* has tendency toward action (>). Force of *Agonist* is stronger (+) than *Antagonist* (−). Resultant is *Agonist* remains at rest (−−•−−). From Talmy (1988: 55). Reprinted with permission from Ablex Publishing Corporation.

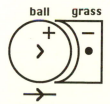

FIGURE 31. Force schema for sentence *The ball kept rolling despite the stiff grass. Agonist* (circle) has tendency to move (>). *Antagonist* has tendency to remain at rest (•). Force of *Agonist* is stronger (+) than *Antagonist* (−). Resultant is *Agonist* continues to move (−>−−). From Talmy (1988: 55). Reprinted with permission from Ablex Publishing Corporation.

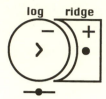

FIGURE 32. Force schema for sentence *The log kept lying on the incline because of the ridge there. Agonist* (circle) has tendency to move (>). *Antagonist* has tendency to remain at rest (•). Force of *Antagonist* is stronger (+) than *Agonist* (−). Resultant is *Agonist* remains at rest (−−•−−). From Talmy (1988: 55). Reprinted with permission from Ablex Publishing Corporation.

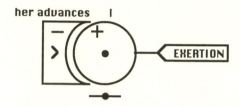

FIGURE 33. Force schema for sentence *I successfully resisted her advances in spite of myself. Agonist* (circle) has tendency to remain at rest (•). *Antagonist* has tendency to move (>). Force of *Agonist* is (assumed) stronger (+) than *Antagonist* (−). Resultant is *Agonist* remains at rest (−−•−−).

Now, suppose we were to say *I successfully resisted her advances **in spite of myself***. We could diagram the scene much as in Figure 30, but the phrase *in spite of myself* suggests that at some level, let us say the libido or the inner self, lexicalized as *myself*, we are willing to give in to the force of the advances acting upon us. We are also resisting that desire with the force of our personality or conscience, so we have a second *Antagonist* (*myself*) acting upon the self with conscience. Talmy would call this the *psychological exertion process*. We could also diagram the conflict of the divided self much as in Figure 30. The two figures can be economically combined to yield a product schema for the sentence by substituting a symbolic shorthand for the psychological exertion process, as in Figure 33. This should be all the symbolic apparatus necessary to depict the force schemas underlying the example sentences, above.

Talmy applied his schema to the semantics and syntax of open class words, showing how the schemas can be used to define common verbs. He also applied them to closed class words, showing how force schemas can be used to unify English helping verbs (*make, let, have,* and *help*) with modal verbs (*can, may, must, should, would, need not, dare not,* and *had better*) into a single syntactic class. Together, they make up what Talmy called the *Greater Modal System*. All of these can take the infinitive form of the verb, without the particle *to*, for a complement, as in the two sets below:

> He can/may/must/should/would/need not/dare not/had better
> I made him/let him/had him/helped (him)
> —push the car to the garage (Talmy 1988: 81)

All of Talmy's examples are taken from English, so we cannot assume that the same four schemas will be prototypical for other languages. For the interested student of language, there awaits an exciting program of semantic research to determine just how other cultures organize schemas of physical, psychological, and social forces and incorporate them into patterns of vocabulary and syntax. Our interest in the imagery underlying figurative language has now taken us from the simple appreciation of some interesting expressions to the more profound realization that much of language is built up by metaphorical correspondences and metonymical analyses from a foundation of cognitive models.

CHAPTER 9

CONSTRUCTING AND DECONSTRUCTING WORD AND SENTENCE GRAMMAR

Perhaps because Western science tends to be analytic and positivistic, rather than synthetic and relativistic, linguists and linguistic anthropologists have most often adopted highly analytical views of word and sentence grammar. We learn, through introductory textbooks or discussions, that all languages have, at least, nouns and verbs and additionally articles, auxiliaries, adjectives, adverbs, and adpositions (prepositions and postpositions). We learn that there are discrete levels of grammatical organization: morpheme, lexeme, phrase, and clause, whose parts snap together cleanly in discrete combinatorial systems.[1] We learn that in their most common systems of constructions languages may be inflectional, with paradigms of affixes whose classes are closed, as is the case with Latin declensions and Bantu noun classifiers; or languages may be synthetic, so that words are typically idiomatic constructions containing several morphemes whose classes are open or large, as is the case with Eskimo; or languages may be isolating, so that each word stands alone as a single morpheme of one or two syllables, as in Mandarin Chinese and, to a lesser degree, English. Our analytic approach gives us the view of language as a set of Legos, a universal set of construction blocks or parameters that can be used to build the great variety of linguistic structures that we find in the languages of the world. Forms of utterance that do not fit the categories are treated as exceptional or quaint aberrations.

In some ways the analytical approach is helpful, because many linguistic expressions can be easily recognized and pigeonholed by simple criteria, so that when we do fieldwork we can efficiently record a significant proportion of the linguistic data. But reifying traditional analytical categories also bears a cost, because it encourages the analyst to ignore a great deal of data that do not conform to *a priori* categories. When ordered in a synthesis appropriate to the language, formally exceptional and intractable data are often more interesting than the analytically well-behaved. They are especially interesting to linguistic anthropologists, who tend to be cultural relativists with as much or more interest in unique systems as in universals.

What does the Legos view of language obscure? For a start, it obscures linguistic continua, prototypes, and networks. For example, members of a verbal paradigm may semantically resemble the third person singular and each other to varying degrees, as Spanish [dwérmo] 'I sleep' and [dormí] 'I slept' resemble [dwérme] 'he sleeps.' A semantic network organized around a prototype, such as [dwérme] 'he sleeps,' may show up in a structure of phonological parallels. In such a symbolic network, some forms may appear to be inflectional (taking affixes from regular paradigms), but others appear to display vowel or consonant alternations (ablaut) or replacement forms (suppletion). In this chapter we will consider an example of such a similarity network from Spanish as described by Joan L. Bybee (1985). Bybee has also shown that within a single language it is possible to arrange nominal and verbal lexical constructions on a scale of relevance, which ranges from inflected forms (having paradigms of affixes) to those that agglutinate roots in compound nouns or verbal incorporations.

Pursuing the synthetic approach further, we find that in some languages grammar fails to distinguish between word roots that can be distinguished semantically as nominal or verbal, so that all roots may take all the verbal and nominal inflections, as is the case with Salish languages such as Coeur d'Alene. In the realm of phonology, we often find phonemes with consistent symbolic values, so that words that at first appear to be suppletive alternatives must be reconsidered as quasi-constructions. A Yuman case is considered in Chapter 10.

But having emphasized the importance of a synthetic approach, the significance of gradients and semantic networks, and the arbitrariness of traditional categories of grammar, I am not advocating the total abandonment of analysis. Every language produces a large, language-specific ensemble of constructions, which are units of grammar constituted by symbolic units. In ideal cases, constituents are clearly defined, giving rise to constructions that are similarly distinct and discrete. But in most, if not all, languages, gradient phenomena and semantic networks intersect with clearly defined symbolic systems to produce intermediate forms and heterogeneous systems, as when we find that the more frequently used forms in a verb paradigm acquire polysemous and idiomatic meanings, while forms used less frequently retain analytically transparent compositional meanings. Both uniform and heterogeneous systems are worthy of study, but a consideration of cognitive principles suggests that, contrary to traditional views, highly uniform systems are probably the exception and heterogeneous systems are the rule. For those who delight in the analogic, synthetic, and heterogeneous qualities of natural phenomena, the approach of cognitive grammar can be liberating. The first example looks at compound nouns in English. Because the meanings of these ubiquitous constructions cannot easily be predicted on the basis of compositional principles, they present a challenge to cognitive and cultural linguistics.

FILLMORE'S *PUMPKIN BUS*: PROFILES AND BASES IN COMPOUNDING

Naming things, in the sense of attaching words to images, is something we all do frequently on the spur of the moment. Names therefore provide us with some of our best clues to linguistic cognition. Many of the things that we name are complex entities—things (such as landscapes and animals), states (such as boredom and kinship), and processes (such as running and emancipation). In the interest of efficient communication, naming typically avoids descriptive detail of the base entity to be named and instead picks out and profiles one or more salient parts or aspects of its imagery. The name is sufficient to evoke the unspoken remainder of the imagery, but only if the term is conventional or the context is known. For example, the term *topless bar* might be taken by a non-native as a bar of iron that is somehow lacking a top. Or, if the hearer understood the word *bar* to be a counter where drinks are served, the term might be taken to mean a bar that lacked a top. Additional knowledge of a social scene would be required to get it right as a commercial establishment where women are employed to dance naked to the waist for the sexual titillation of patrons who drink at a counter called a "bar." This perspective can be applied to the grammar of complex words.

Compound words such as *skyscraper, motor scooter, bookend, top spin, guttersnipe, butter knife, silk purse,* and *ball hog* have a grammatical schema of [noun noun] or [noun verb] and a very abstract semantic schema of [MODIFIER MODIFIED], but knowing that still does not enable us to predict their meaning very well. Besides the fact that at least three of them are metaphorical (*skyscraper, guttersnipe,* and *ball hog*), the two parts of these several compounds play a variety of semantic roles. The terms *skyscraper, butter knife,* and perhaps *bookend* have the more specific semantic relation GOAL-INSTRUMENT; *silk purse* and *motor scooter* are based on the PART-WHOLE relation, though *motor scooter* might also be construed as INSTRUMENT-GOAL; *top spin* and *guttersnipe* are LOCA-TION-PROCESS; and *ball hog* is GOAL-AGENT, or perhaps GOAL-PROCESS. The processes are all nominalized.

Even though compounds seem sensible, characterizing them by their semantics or their syntax does not necessarily enable us to predict the meaning of a new compound. Compounds, whether noun-noun or some other type, are motivated by semantic connections; they have a regular, though abstract, order and a regular pattern of stress falling on the first word; but the specific meanings of compounds are not predictable from syntax. Generative theorists have tried and failed to derive compounds by applying transformations to putative underlying periphrases. Pamela Downing (1977: 840) concluded that noun-noun compounds in English "cannot be characterized in terms of absolute limitations on the semantic or syntactic structures from which they are derived." She found no constraints on the noun-noun compounding process. If language proves to be unpredictable even at this basic level of compound terms, how then can we hope to find predictability in larger constructions, such as phrases and clauses?

While there appears to be little hope of a highly predictive theory of the semantics of compounds, there is no lack of patterning. Since they do make sense to listeners, and since they are apparently semantically motivated, it is worthwhile to explore the meaning of one of these compounds in more detail. The following example is taken from Charles J. Fillmore (1984).[2]

Suppose that only one tour bus in a multi-bus tour is scheduled to stop at a pumpkin farm. This bus could be known for just the duration of the tour by the compound noun *pumpkin bus*. It could be known as the *pumpkin bus* not only by the people on the bus, but also by the other members of the tour on other buses, and, indeed, by anybody having knowledge of the tour. It is tempting to regard the expression as an idiom, because its intended meaning is known but cannot be readily reconstructed from its constituent words alone. But *pumpkin bus* is not an idiom in the usual sense of a grammatically unpredictable but conventional form, because it originated on the spur of the moment. We have to be there to understand it, whereas idioms, such as the similar expression *tour bus*, have a longer history and a more general currency. Most people know what they mean most of the time and they can be interpreted without special knowledge of the situation. Under the right circumstances *pumpkin bus* could eventually become an idiom, but for the time being those who lack all knowl-

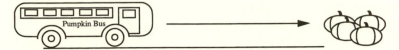

FIGURE 34. *Pumpkin bus* (visiting a pumpkin farm).

FIGURE 35. *Pumpkin bus* (in shape of a pumpkin).

edge of the situation would have no idea what the phrase means. They might think we were speaking of a bus that carries pumpkins or a bus shaped like a pumpkin.

Figures 34 and 35 illustrate possible images named by *pumpkin bus*. Figure 34 shows a bus proceeding along a road to a pumpkin farm. We can think of this as the base image, the scope of the term. The vocabulary frame associated with this particular base concept might include *road*, *highway*, *path*, *visit*, *travel*, *passengers*, *driver*, *farm*, and *countryside*, as well as *bus* and *pumpkin*, each of which evokes some component of the base. Many more terms also come to mind, but only with more effort of reflection. From all the most salient terms, we selected only *pumpkin bus*, thus coining a very economical name. After all, we could call it the *pumpkin farm bus*, the *bus visiting the pumpkin farm*, or, to evoke the wider situation, the *only bus visiting the pumpkin farm*. But we just call it the *pumpkin bus*. The expression is a kind of metonymy that names the bus by profiling an element from the scene in which the bus (conceptually) exists.

Now let's compare a different pumpkin bus. Figure 35 might be understood in the context of a modern version of the Cinderella tale. Perhaps a young girl from the ghetto escapes for an evening in a pumpkin bus with a Prince Charming from the suburbs. Here the term *pumpkin* evokes only the appearance of a pumpkin rather than actual pumpkins as in the previous example. We have narrowed the scope of the meaning of the construction, confining it to the outlines and color of the bus itself rather than a whole travel scene. Thus, the same term seems quite appropriate for two very different images. The selection principle is the same, but the particular base images and selections are different.

A compound name is like an abbreviation of a longer possible description of the situation. However, it is not a true abbreviation of a longer expression in current or previous usage, because many possible longer expressions are bypassed altogether in coining names. We understand *pumpkin bus* as it is intended in Figure 34 because we share the presupposition that we are discussing a bus that is en route to a pumpkin farm. The schematic image represents just the most salient components of the shared presuppositions. But the salience of elements in scenes differs for different speakers and speech communities. That is why it is impossible to predict the content of compounds.

The term *pumpkin bus* illustrates the usual pattern in English compounds: the entire compound profiles the same entity that is profiled in less detail by the second word alone.[3] The first word of the compound is a modifier and the second is the head. In Langacker's (1991: 144) framework, head and modifier are defined in terms of the profile-base relationship: the head of a noun phrase is "the profile determinant at a given level of constituency."[4] In Figure 34, the modifier *pumpkin* evokes the entire pumpkin farm, which is the destination of the bus, and therefore a LOCATION. *Pumpkin*, here, is a part-whole metonym. Since the bus is semantically an instrument used for touring, the semantic relationship underlying pumpkin bus could be stated as LOCATION METONYM to INSTRUMENT, or just LOCATION-INSTRUMENT. This naming of a bus, then, is accomplished by means of composition of linguistic symbols *after* selection of salient elements from images that are shared by interlocutors. Such a selection may, as in the selection of *pumpkin*, be metonymical.

In compounding, the only semantic constraint is that two symbols stand in some relationship of MODIFIER to MODIFIED. We have found the relationships GOAL-INSTRUMENT, PART-WHOLE, INSTRUMENT-GOAL, LOCATION-PROCESS, GOAL-AGENT, GOAL-PROCESS, and LOCATION-INSTRUMENT. The reader can probably discover others. It is doubtful whether these relationships should be regarded as semantic primitives. For example, we have seen that the relation LOCATION-INSTRUMENT schematizes a scene in which agents (people) travel toward a goal (pumpkin farm) by means of an instrument (bus). There appears to be nothing particularly primitive or irreducible about this relation. There probably exists a continuum of expressions that vary from clearly bipolar relations, such as PART-WHOLE, to more complex and indirect relations, such as LOCA-

TION-METONYM TO INSTRUMENT. The examples also show the compounding of metaphors (e.g., *roadhog*). It is likely that compounding works on the same general principles in other natural languages, if not in all.

The conclusion that compound terms designate salient components of scenes fits Pamela Downing's (1977: 842) conclusion that compounds apply to categories that are deemed name-worthy and that this tells us more about the process of categorization than about derivational constraints. In complex images, the components most likely to be designated by compound terms are those that are most salient: *pumpkin bus*, *spin doctor*, *roadhog*. Their forms are determined not by rules operating on underlying sentence paraphrases or constraints on collocations of words, but by conventions based on the strength of imagery.

BYBEE'S CONTINUUM OF MORPHOLOGICAL ABSTRACTION

Joan Bybee (1985) pointed out that the process of noun compounding lies at one end of a semantic continuum, as diagramed in Figure 36. In compounding, the meaning of the modifier term is relevant or integral to that of its head, as black is integral to a blackbird, a motor is integral to a motor scooter, or sky is relevant to the metaphor of the skyscraper. Changing the modifiers of these terms would involve corresponding changes in the essential nature of the designated entity. As a result of the high relevance of these modifiers to their heads, they are likely to be quite restricted in their ability to compound with other terms. The term *motor*, for example, modifies only entities that can have motors (*motor scooter*) or that have something to do with motors (*motor oil*). Such terms can only combine with nouns that have meanings that are somehow complementary, and these are likely to be quite specific and therefore relatively less common than abstract closed-class morphemes.

At the other end of the semantic continuum lie inflected forms. Inflectional morphemes, such as the past tense suffix *-ed*, are very abstract with general application to a great many kinds of things. It may seem odd to see the suffix *-ed* characterized as the head of this term in the diagram. In this, I am following Langacker's approach, which differs from more traditional approaches, which would treat *roast* as a lexical head rather than the modifier of its own suffix. Langacker (1991: 144) argued instead that the element that determines the profile of the construction should be regarded as the head. Since the past tense suffix *-ed* requires instantiation by a process for its realization, it can be thought of as profiling an abstract

Head (profile determinant) is abstract and general; meaning of modifier not particularly relevant to meaning of head; resultant meaning predictable.

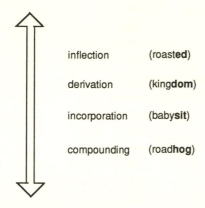

inflection	(roast**ed**)
derivation	(king**dom**)
incorporation	(baby**sit**)
compounding	(road**hog**)

Head (profile determinant) is specific; meaning of modifier highly relevant to meaning of head; resultant meaning idiosyncratic.

FIGURE 36. Continuum of abstraction in morphology (internal grammatical heads in boldface).

process that determines the profile of the verb in which it occurs. A word with a suffix for tense can only be a verb. Therefore, *-ed* should be regarded as the internal head of *roasted.* This somewhat nonintuitive, but logically consistent treatment of inflectional morphology allows for a consistent arrangement of the gamut of constructions on the dimension of relevance, as in Figure 36.

Between compounding and inflection fall (1) the incorporation of nouns into verbs (*hogtie, babysit*),[5] and (2) derivational affixes (*kingdom, obtuse-ly*). Derivations are terms formed by affixes that determine the grammatical class of constructions, as *-dom* requires *kingdom* to be a noun and *-ly* derives an adverb from an adjective. Perhaps because they are semantically more relevant to their modifiers, derivational affixes often occur closer to the root than do inflectional affixes. For nouns, gender and number are derivational because they predicate inherent characteristics of the referent (Bybee 1985: 99).[6] Likewise, in verbs, gender and number of subject or object often affect the inherent nature of the verbal process: one cow may run but a herd can only stampede. Thus, gender and number agreement may be expressed on the verb as lexical replacement (suppletion) as in Navajo, !Kung, and Ainu, or as morphological

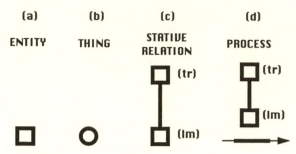

FIGURE 37. Symbols for abstract entity, thing, state, and process. Compare the somewhat more complex diagrams of Langacker (1990a: 128).

reduplication, as in Salish and Wakashan languages (Bybee 1985: 100). These, too, may be regarded as kinds of derivation. Of course, gender and number may also be expressed on the verb by affixation, as in Swahili.

It seems likely that in all languages the constituents of lexical constructions will be found distributed along the continuum from specificity and relevance to abstraction and generality. On this gradient, each language produces its own distribution of constructions that occur with greater frequency, but universal constraints of environment and cognition narrow the types of constructions that occur.

THE COGNITIVE GRAMMAR CONSTRUCTION KIT

Fillmore, Bybee, and Langacker provided some essential perspectives on word compounding. As we move to more complex words, and then to phrases and clause level grammar, it will be useful to have some heuristic diagrams to represent conceptual entities and structures. Langacker (1987: 220) used a simple square to represent the notion of an abstract entity, as in Figure 37(a). A THING, which Langacker represented with a circle, is the semantic basis of nominals. In English, nominals may be profiled by nouns, noun-phrases, or derivational affixes, such as the *-dom* of *kingdom* and *dukedom*. When a concept has more specific content, such as grass, hair, a surface, a hand, or a Nissan, we can represent this specificity with labeling or by drawing the specific object itself.

Langacker (1987: 214) defined a conceptual THING as "a region within some domain." A region is "a set of interconnected entities." In nominal predications (nouns and noun-phrases), a region is profiled collectively; less prominent than the collective profile are the interconnections among its component entities. For example, the eyes, nose, and mouth are all located near each other in predictable relationships on the front of the head, but the term *face* itself does not bring these relations to our attention. Rather, it refers to those parts profiled collectively as a region.

Langacker's definition of THING as designating a set of interconnected entities finds support in two new laws of gestalt formation proposed by Irvin Rock and Stephen Palmer (1990). First, they proposed "a law of enclosure or common region, referring to an observer's tendency to group elements that are *located within* the same perceived region [italics added]" (Rock and Palmer 1990: 86) (see Figure 38). Items grouped because they appear within a region should be accounted for as components of the meaning of the corresponding noun. Thus, the term *archipelago* would have as components of its meaning the islands within its region.

The second law is that of connectedness, which refers to "the powerful tendency of the visual system to perceive any uniform, connected region—such as a spot, line or more extended area—as a single unit" (see Figure 39). Note that Langacker's definition of a noun as a region hangs on the idea of grouping by connectedness. That is, the components of a conceptualized region must be in some way connected, by association or scanning or some other operation.

In our imagery of things, they usually stand in figure-ground relations with other things. It seems to be a characteristic of our thought that there must always be something particularly salient in the foreground of our attention and something less salient in the background: Venus in the night sky or Hillary Clinton on a podium, for example. We can represent a figure-ground relation as a line connecting a trajector and landmark, as in Figure 37(c) and (d). Relations may be either states or processes.

In English, stative relations are often expressed as prepositions, adjectives, or adverbs. For example, a trajector may be *on, beside, over, under,*

FIGURE 38. Grouping by common region. Outer boundary figures impose grouping on pairs of dots. Adapted from Irvin Rock and Stephen Palmer, "The Legacy of Gestalt Psychology." Copyright © 1990 by Scientific American, Inc. All rights reserved.

FIGURE 39. Grouping by connectedness. Adapted from Irvin Rock and Stephen Palmer, "The Legacy of Gestalt Psychology." Copyright © 1990 by Scientific American, Inc. All rights reserved.

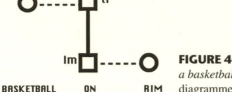

FIGURE 40. Heuristic diagram of construction *a basketball on a rim* (articles not diagrammed).

larger, *smaller*, *darker*, or *brighter* than a landmark. In other languages similar relations may be expressed by postpositions, as in Apache, or prefixes, as in Coeur d'Alene. According to Langacker (1987: 215), the essential difference between a nominal and a relational predication is that "a relational predication puts interconnections in profile (rather than simply presupposing them as part of the base)." Additionally, relations are conceptually dependent. Since relations are connections, they must have something to connect. The bold connecting lines in Figure 37(c) and (d) show that the relation is profiled; but since a relation depends for its meaning on the entities that it connects, these are also shown as profiled. A relational predication profiles both the relation itself and the entities that it connects.

When we put words together, abstract trajectors, landmarks, and relations are elaborated by more specific entities. This requires a correspondence between the specific and abstract entities. Correspondence is the glue that binds symbols together into meaningful constructions. It is what Langacker (1987) called a *valence relation*. In a more formal system, regular patterns of correspondence might be called selection restrictions or constraints. Correspondence is shown with broken lines. To illustrate correspondence in a construction, we can represent the specific idea of *a basketball on a rim* as in Figure 40. The fact that basketballs, rims, and the symbol for a THING are all round has no significance. The same figure, with different labels, would serve to diagram the phrase *a monkey with a banana* or *a politician with a soundbite*.

We need to introduce one more elemental symbol in order to have a useful set of basic tools for representing the most general schemas. This is the symbol for process, which builds upon the schema for a relation. A process is a relation that evolves through time or persists because of some force acting through time. It involves a comparison of states at different points in time. By contrast, a state is any stable configuration.[7] We could diagram a process with a series of relations as in Figure 41.

To diagram a whole series like this every time we want to show a process is cumbersome and tedious, so instead we use a single relation symbol, as in Figure 37(d). The bold arrow shows that time is added to the profile of the connecting relation and its connected entities. Process symbols often surface in language as verbs. In English they may also be suffixes that derive verbs from nouns, such as the *-ize* in *verbalize*.

I will tentatively adopt the premise that the schemas of entity, thing, relation, and process are fundamental and universal, that all languages distinguish between things, relations, and processes, express relations between trajectors and landmarks, and build symbolic constructions by means of correspondences. It is too early in the development of cognitive linguistics to be dogmatic about this position, but it does appear to shed light on a great many specific findings.

PASSING THROUGH A PLAIN: SPATIAL SCHEMAS
IN COEUR D'ALENE INDIAN GEOGRAPHY

The schematic tools that we have developed can now be put to work in the examination of some expressions from Coeur d'Alene, the American Indian language that has been the subject of much of my own research. Coeur d'Alene belongs to the Salish language family, a group composed of twenty-three languages from the American Northwest. These languages differ from English as much as it seems possible for languages to differ. Salish languages are characterized by complex phonologies with large consonant clusters and by the complexity of their words. A variety of reduplications operate on syllables and segments of word roots to signify plurality, repetition, and spatial distribution. Perhaps the most surprising and controversial finding of modern linguistics concerning the Salish languages is their lack of a clear grammatical distinction between nouns and verbs (Kinkade 1983).[8] Roots referring to things, processes, and states may all be modified by the same prefixes and suffixes. An important set of Coeur d'Alene locative prefixes predicate *contiguity*, in the

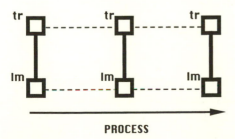

PROCESS

FIGURE 41. Heuristic diagram of a process as a sequence of states.

sense of proximity, contact, or attachment. They are commonly glossed by such terms and phrases as 'on,' 'on something broad,' 'on and part of,' 'in,' 'amidst,' and 'under.'

Coeur d'Alene has a set of nominal suffixes that are particularly important in understanding place-names. Some of the suffixes refer to major parts of the body and may be glossed as 'head,' 'face, eye,' 'hand,' 'arm, hand,' 'leg, foot,' 'belly,' and 'back.' Some of these anatomical suffixes also combine with other suffixes to function as abstract locatives with meanings comparable to English nominal locatives. In these usages, back becomes 'back of,' head becomes 'top of' or 'end of,' mouth becomes 'edge of,' and so on. In complex suffixes, the more abstract uses of the suffixes occur in first position. They should probably be regarded as schematic nominals that lend their nominal profile to the complex suffix. Let us look at how all these elements enter into the construction of the complex word *hənč̓amqínkʷɛʔ*, as follows:

n-	*č̓ɛm*	*-qən*	*-kʷiʔ*
in	surface	head	water
rel	*tr*	*lm*	*lm*

'surface in the head of the (body of) water'

Differences in spelling of morphemes when they are analyzed versus when they are embedded in words arise from Coeur d'Alene phonological processes. The abstract head of the complex suffix functions to confine the location of the trajector, 'surface,' to the smaller region defined by 'head,' as opposed to the entire body of water. Thus, the morphosyntactic structure of a typical Coeur d'Alene place name is as follows:

[locative prefix-stem(-schematic nominal suffix)-substantive nominal suffix]

This can be given the following semantic representation:

[CONTIGUITY/ENTITY/LOCATION_RESTRICTOR/LOCATION]

The grammar of the term can be schematized as follows:

[relation/trajector/restrictive_landmark/landmark]

It is possible to analyze and diagram Coeur d'Alene place-names as grammatical constructions in a way that reveals not only their syntactic structure, but also the schematic imagery of their semantic structure. We can diagram *hənč̓am-qínkʷɛʔ* 'surface in the head of the water' as in Figure 42.

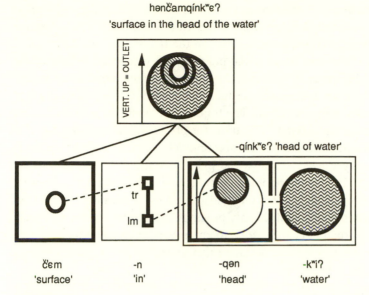

FIGURE 42. Construction of Coeur d'Alene place-name *hənčamqínkʷɛʔ* 'surface in the head of the water.' Boxes indicate concepts which are established or 'entrenched' in the language. Bold lines inside boxes show profiled content for each morpheme. Boxes in bold lines show constituent that determines profile at each level. The profile for the term is inherited from that for 'surface.' Arrow depicts vertical orientation of head at lake outlet to schematic body.

Here 'head' is depicted as a profiled nominal (circle) within and at the top of another nominal. A more iconic representation would depict the semantic base of *-qən* 'head' as a vertical linear form with a demarcated subregion at the top.

hənčamqínkʷɛʔ 'Surface in the Head (of the Water)' is the proper name for the village that formerly existed at the site of the modern town of Coeur d'Alene, Idaho, where the Spokane River flows out of the north end of Lake Coeur d'Alene. The south end of the lake is referred to as *q̓ɛlɛʔíp* 'bottom of the lake.'

Often, Coeur d'Alene place-names predicate an object in motion or a motion relative to a landmark. In these cases, the motion itself may become a trajector for the relation predicated by the prefix. In Coeur d'Alene, one such place-name is *čɛt-čɛgʷš* 'Passing through a Plain,' which is the Coeur d'Alene name for the Big Bend country in eastern Washington state. The root morph is *čɛgʷ* 'extend, pass through.' The stem *čɛgʷš* has a suffix *-š* indicating voluntary action, but here I will just treat the stem as a single unanalyzed verbal unit. The prefix *čɛt-* means 'on something broader than itself.' That is, the landmark is broader than the trajector. It is often translated as 'on the flat.' Thus, the landmark of the prefix apparently refers to the plain, which is a broad feature of the landscape. However, in this term, the landmark of the prefix is not instantiated by a Coeur d'Alene morpheme. The predication of a plain is a tacit entailment of the construction. The trajector of the prefix is the verb stem with the meaning 'extend.' The trajector of the verbal stem itself is also unspecified, but I assume that in this context it is understood as the people who annually traveled through the plain in search of bitterroot in the spring time. The landmark of the verbal stem is also unspecified. I take it to be the point from which the extension (travel or passing through) begins. In fact, the term profiles only passing through and something broad, but the construction is understood to entail human travelers on a plain of the landscape. It represents a kind of metonymy by abstraction. The term is diagramed in Figure 43.

The cognitive grammar of place-names provides a glimpse of Coeur d'Alene imagery of the physical world. It helps us to realize Boas's goal of discovering the psychologies underlying languages. Boas, after all, recorded Kwakiutl Indian place-names with similar trajector and landmark structures, such as the following (1939):[9]

> *magwís* 'round thing on beach,' from *mak^w* 'round thing in somewhere' and *-is* 'on beach';
> *tex^wsamlis* 'green on surface';
> *tlamx^wsam* 'gooseberries, tangled bushes on surface';
> *túbis* 'spot on beach,' from *tup* 'spot' and *-is* 'on beach';

Boas recorded the following suffixes which clearly represent conceptual landmarks:

> *-as* 'place,' *dúy-as* 'place of clam . . .';
> *-ac'* 'receptacle';
> *-is* 'open place surrounded by woods, beach,' *q̉aw-ís* 'pond on beach';
> *-xdam* 'site,' *má-xdams* 'site of killer whales';
> *-a* 'rock, stone,' *múmac'-a* 'old man on rock';
> *-uyu* 'middle,' *łúg-uyu* 'bare in middle.'

These striking similarities between Kwakiutl and Coeur d'Alene can probably not be explained simply as the result of culture contacts. The two are contiguous on the Northwest Coast and share some regional simi-

četčégʷš
'passing through a plain'

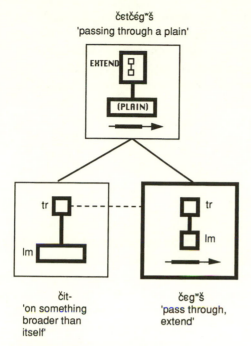

čit-
'on something
broader than
itself'

čegʷš
'pass through,
extend'

FIGURE 43. Diagram of Coeur d'Alene place-name *četčégʷš* 'passing through a plain.'

larities, but Wakashan languages are not thought to bear a close genetic relationship to Salishan languages.

To some degree, the similarities between Salishan and Wakashan languages fit a common American Indian pattern of naming places after features of the landscape, which are perceived to stand in figure-ground (or trajector-landmark) relationships. The figure-ground schema can be used to make wider cross-linguistic comparisons. I will illustrate this with a comparison of Coeur d'Alene to Apache, an Athabascan language with no genetic affinities to Salish languages other than some features of phonology that occur throughout the Northwest, where the Athabascan languages originated. Basso (1990b: 109) characterized Apache place-names as "thoroughly descriptive," "pointedly specific in the physical details they pick out." Let us consider one of his examples:

tse	biká'	tú	ya-	-hi-	-líí
rock	on top of it	water	downward	rep.	it flows
lm	*rel*	*tr*	*rel*		

'water flows down on top of a regular succession of white rocks'

This term has an initial landmark, *tse*, with a postposition, *biká'*. The grammatical frame is [*lm rel tr rel*]. Another example, a name meaning 'white rocks lie above in a compact cluster,' omits mention of the landmark with its locative postposition, though, unlike the previous example, it introduces an adjectival neuter verb, *ɬgai*, and a locative postposition, *dah*, following the noun phrase:

tse	*ɬgai*	*dah*	*sɪdil*
rock	white	above ground level	three or more objects lie in compact cluster
[*tr*	*rel*]	*rel*	*rel*

'white rocks lie above in a compact cluster'

The syntax of schematic elements in this name and others like it is basically [*tr rel*], so the Apache place-name can be represented schematically as [(*lm rel*) *tr rel*], where parentheses signify that a component is optional. With this simple notation, we can compare the grammar of Coeur d'Alene and Apache place-names as follows:

Coeur d'Alene:	[*rel tr* ((*lm*) *lm*)]
Apache:	[(*lm rel*) *tr rel*]

In both languages the component that is most readily omitted from place-names is the landmark, together with its relation to the trajector, as shown by the parentheses. Trajectors, as figures, are by definition more salient than landmarks, which are backgrounds. Consequently, they are more likely to be profiled. It may also follow from the fact that landmarks of relational particles commonly come with some substantive semantic content, such as the 'ground level' in *dah*, so that landmarks may require no further specification to be understood.

The schemas reveal that Apache and Coeur d'Alene reverse the order in which they present figures and grounds in the construction of place-names. Coeur d'Alene presents the trajector before the landmark, but Apache presents the landmark first. Coeur d'Alene and Apache also reverse the order of occurrence of morphs for relations and trajectors. Coeur d'Alene is relation first; Apache is trajector first. These differences are probably related to the fact that Coeur d'Alene has VOS word order while Apache has SOV order. The ease with which we can compare the place-name grammar of these two very different languages suggests that the imagery of trajectors and landmarks has wide applicability in the analysis of the language of spatial relations.

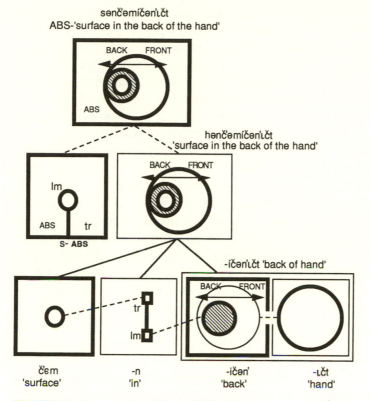

sənčʼəmíčənʼɫčt
ABS-'surface in the back of the hand'

hənčʼəmíčənʼɫčt
'surface in the back of the hand'

-íčənʼɫčt 'back of hand'

čʼem	-n	-íčənʼ	-ɫčt
'surface'	'in'	'back'	'hand'

FIGURE 44. Construction of Coeur d'Alene body-part term *sənčʼəmíčənʼɫčt* 'palm of the hand' or 'surface in the back of the hand.'

COEUR D'ALENE ANATOMY AS GEOGRAPHY

Coeur d'Alene place-names have led us to an understanding of how culturally defined cognitive models are represented in grammar. Another domain where spatial information is important in Salish languages is that of anatomy. Thus, it is no surprise that grammatical constructions that predicate anatomical parts closely resemble those of place names. Consider the word in Figure 44, meaning 'surface in the back of the hand,' which translates to English as 'palm (of the hand).' The structural diagram for this term is very similar to that for the place name *hənčʼamqínkʷɛʔ* 'surface in the head of the water,' discussed above. A minor difference involves the addition of the somewhat unpredictable absolute prefix. (Absolutive case ordinarily applies to nouns that can be either [1] the patient of a state or non-agentive process, or [2] the object of an agentive process.)[10]

In Coeur d'Alene, both place-names and body-parts make use of the same set of anatomical suffixes and anatomy provides the primary metaphor for geography. Figure 45 maps the more commonly used of the seventeen anatomical suffixes onto regions of the body as it is conceived by the Coeur d'Alene. This mapping of the body regions represents an important part of the Coeur d'Alene world view, sufficiently important to warrant a set of at least twenty-seven suffixes and to provide a metaphorical basis for constructions of place-names and verbal predications.[11]

The comparison of schemas from geography and anatomy can yield further insights into Coeur d'Alene world view. Trajectors of geographical terms are drawn from a wide variety of linguistic roots for objects, states, and processes in the natural environment, such as surface, lake, stand, bright, and pass through plain. Landmarks of geographical terms are also quite varied, including some body-part suffixes that signify abstract spatial geometry, such as head (top), mouth (flat edge), waist (narrows), belly (mountainside), tail, forehead (hillside), and ear (covered all over), but also common are suffixes for water, spur (ridge), rock, land, and bottom.

By contrast, trajectors of anatomical terms for exterior parts of the body are more restricted to roots referring to surface and hair, suggesting that skin and hair are highly salient. Landmarks are mostly restricted to suffixes predicating a few regions of the body, specifically, HEAD, FACE, HAND, ARM, and LEG. While we cannot argue from this that the grammar of Coeur d'Alene limits speakers' views of either the environment or the body, we can say that the schemas underlying spatial morphemes afford a glimpse of the Coeur d'Alene construction of conventional meaning in two reasonably complex and important semantic domains. This analysis of Coeur d'Alene geographical and anatomical nomenclature validates Whorf's early interest in figure and ground relationships in Amerindian grammars.

SEEING AROUND CORNERS WITH CORA PREFIXES

Before leaving the realm of physical space, I will briefly describe several studies that illustrate the progress being made in the cognitive grammar of Amerind languages. The first is a recent analysis by Eugene Casad (1993) of directed path schemas as predicated by sequences of prefixes in Cora, a Uto-Aztecan language spoken in the state of Nayarit, Mexico. Casad (1993: 595) defined a prototypical path schema as "the movement of one entity from one location to another within the domain of topography." He showed that a string of prefixes, such as those in the Cora word

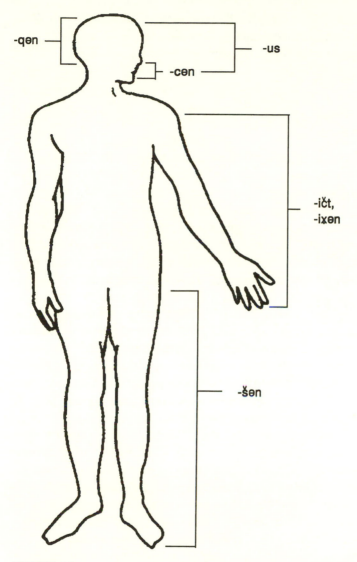

FIGURE 45. Coeur d'Alene anatomical suffixes mapped on the human body. From Palmer and Nicodemus (1985: 344). Reprinted by permission of the American Anthropological Association from *American Ethnologist* 12:2, May 1985. Not for further reproduction.

a-ii-ré'e-*n^{y}eeri-'i* (prefixes in boldface), define a path, much as would the prepositions in the English sentence *Get right back down out of up in that tree!* The Cora word may be analyzed as follows:

a-	*ii-*	*ré'e-*	*n^{y}eeri*	*-'i*
outside-	path-	corner-	visible	-STAT

'By a source coming from behind the house, it is all lit up at the corner of the house.'

To interpret the expression it is necessary to know that the speaker is viewing the scene from a particular perspective and vantage point. Casad puts the speaker's location at one corner of the house, from which she looks along the side toward a back corner. If we then put the light source behind the house, the prefixes trace a path around the corner (*ré'e*), toward the speaker (*ii*), and in the field of vision (*a*). The example shows that in interpreting complex spatial constructions, we may have to consider not only relations that link trajectors and landmarks, but also sequences of relations that define directed paths of observation and construals of speakers' perspectives or vantage points. All three of these considerations are part of the conceptual approach of cognitive grammar but are not normally found in other kinds of linguistic theory.

Spatial prefixes can also be analyzed as complex categories, as Casad and Langacker showed for Cora (Casad and Langacker 1985; Langacker 1990a) and Occhi, Ogawa, and Palmer showed for Coeur d'Alene (Palmer 1990; Occhi, Palmer, and Ogawa 1992; Ogawa and Palmer 1994). Let us see how this works with two contrasting Cora prefixes, *u* 'inside' and *a* 'outside.' Casad and Langacker noticed that in some instances words that contrasted only in these two prefixes were assigned the same translation and could be "employed to describe precisely the same objective situation" (Langacker 1990a: 34). That this is not an isolated linguistic problem can be seen in the fact that M. Dale Kinkade (1975) experienced a similar difficulty in discriminating between two prefixes (*n* and *t*) of Columbian.[12] Such a situation might lead us to conclude that the choice of prefixes is arbitrary, but Casad and Langacker demonstrated that the puzzling usages could be explained if speakers were construing the same objective situation in terms of contrasting imagery. A dog's tail is *u* 'inside' from a perspective behind the dog, because it is construed as inside the viewing area presented by the rump. But the tail is *a* 'outside' when construed as viewed from the dog's side, because it is outside the viewing area in the line of sight.

In addition to the contrast *in line of sight/outside line of sight*, Casad and Langacker also found other variants on the prototypes of *u/a*, such as the specializations *on inner surface/on outer surface* and the extensions *deep penetration to interior/shallow penetration to interior, accessible/ inaccessible*, and *on back side/on face or front*. Such polysemous complexes naturally raise the question of whether any meaning can be discovered that is schematic for all senses of a prefix and that would therefore suffice to define it. Langacker (1990a: 55) concluded that it was "most improbable that a single abstract meaning can be found that would be schematic for all the specific values attested" for either *u* or *a*. Even if a fully schematic sense were found it would not suffice as a definition, because "it would also be schematic for indefinitely many values that *u* and *a* happen not to have" and "it would fail to provide an explicit account of the facts of the language, in particular the range of conventionally established senses and usages characteristic of these morphemes."

By contrast, Occhi, Palmer, and Ogawa (1992) found that a single abstract meaning could reasonably be posited for all of the interesting extensions of the Coeur d'Alene prefix *ne'* 'amidst, among,' which contrasts with several other spatial prefixes having glosses such as 'in,' 'under,' 'on something broad,' 'attached to,' and 'on cylinder.' However, they agreed with Langacker that a description of just the dominant schema would not suffice as a definition of the prefix. Figure 46 presents the prefix as a complex category.

To posit a single dominant schema is not necessarily a wasted effort, even where more specific descriptions do a better job of defining actual usages. It may turn out that the dominant schema defines as yet undiscovered usages, as I found to be the case for the Coeur d'Alene prefix *n* 'in.' [13] Several metaphorical usages that I discovered late in my investigation of this prefix appear to fit the dominant schema but fit none of the subschemas. The prefix appears in all the following terms (in two phonologically conditioned shapes: *hən* and *n*):

s-n-kʷíʔc (NOM-in-dusk) 'at night' (NIGHT IS A SPACE)
hən-kʷín-ɛm (in-sing-MDL) [14] 'he sang' (ACTIVITY IS A SPACE)
hən-x̣íw-ən (in-shameful-place) 'being ashamed' (EMOTION IS A SPACE)

These terms are subsumed only by the dominant schema of diffusely bounded three-dimensional space, essentially, a schematic place, and not by any of the subschemas illustrated in Figure 47.

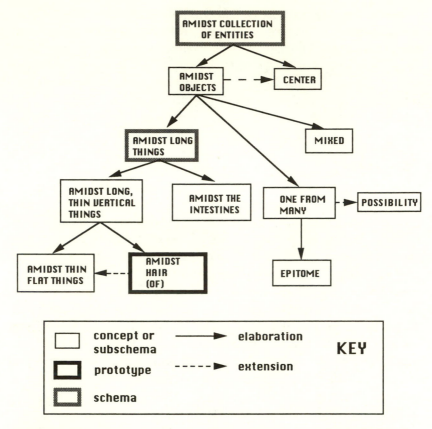

FIGURE 46. Coeur d'Alene prefix *ne'* 'amidst' represented as complex category. From Occhi, Palmer, and Ogawa (1992: 57). Reprinted by permission.

Making detailed investigations of the semantics of spatial prefixes may seem like killing flies with a hammer, but such studies are necessary if we are to understand grammars and the spatial worlds that they predicate. Here, for example, we see that one of the senses of this prefix commonly glossed as 'in' is TOP. If one is talking about a tall object (as opposed to a broad surface), it is not possible to predicate something being 'on' the top with any of the prefixes that are commonly glossed as 'on.' The sense is more like one is 'in' the space at the top. Sense III, SURFACE, may refer to either a horizontal or a vertical surface, so that a rope may hang "in" a wall. Working out definitions of all the various schemas of even a single morpheme can be laborious, but with such an analysis in hand the meaning of many otherwise puzzling usages becomes transparent.

HOW NOT TO LOSE SLEEP OVER DECLENSIONS
AND CONJUGATIONS: PARADIGMS AS COMPLEX CATEGORIES

Among those linguistic phenomena that are most often thought to be governed by rules are the regular paradigms, such as the declensions of Latin nouns and the conjugations of tense and aspect in Spanish verbs. Yet this interpretation has always been troubled by the fact that the most common forms, such as the *to be* verbs of English, often have irregular paradigms. Furthermore, some of the most common forms signal changes in tense by changing their morphological shape, as by vowel alternations or lexical replacements. An example of vowel alternation in English is the alternation between *come* and *came* (rather than *comed*). An example of replacement is the alternation between *go* and *went* (rather than *goed*). Some linguists have tried to solve this problem and preserve their theories of grammar by keeping the grammatical rules where they apply and putting the irregular forms in the lexicon, the mental dictionary of long-term memory. But it seems unnecessarily complicated to suppose that speakers

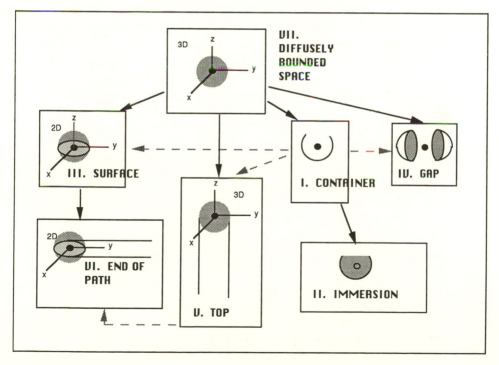

FIGURE 47. Coeur d'Alene prefix *hǝn* 'in' represented as complex category.

derive some words of a paradigm by applying rules but access others in the same paradigm by looking them up in a lexicon, especially since the differences between regular and the irregular forms are often a matter of degree.

Bybee (1985) proposed an ingenious alternative that explains both the regular and the irregular forms. Her explanation makes use of the principles of entrenchment by frequent usage and linkage by similarity. Bybee's term for entrenchment of words is *lexical strength*, which pertains to both the meanings and the sounds of words. She regarded the stronger words as relatively autonomous, providing prototypes for the weaker forms. The weaker words in a paradigm are linked to the prototypes by relations of similarity. Thus, paradigms turn out to be complex categories as defined by Langacker!

Across languages, the most frequently used forms in verb paradigms tend to be the first and third person in preference to second person, the singular in preference to the plural, the present and past in preference to the imperfect, and the indicative in preference to the subjunctive. Therefore, we would expect the singular indicative forms of the present and past tenses to provide prototypes for complex categories. The weaker, less common forms build on the strong forms either by adding affixes to their roots to make paradigms or by changing their vowels or patterns of stress. For example, in the case of the Spanish word *dormir* 'to sleep' the pronunciations of the four most frequently occurring, and therefore prototypical, forms, all singular and indicative, are as follows, in descending order:

[dwérme] (third person, present) [15]
[durmyó] (third person, preterite)
[dwérmo] (first person, present)
[dormí] (first person, preterite)

Since [dwérme] is the strongest form, we can take it as the prototype for all the others, but the other common forms, though they are satellites to [dwérme], may also serve as prototypes for their own satellites. The linkages of similarity between [dwérme] and two other strong forms are shown in Figure 48. The identity linkages are simply the limiting case of similarity. Bybee illustrated similar connections linking each of the strong stems to their own radiants among the weaker forms. She made several important points about her method of representing paradigms, which I paraphrase here. First, some forms have phonological connections to one prototype ("base") and semantic connections to another; second, all the

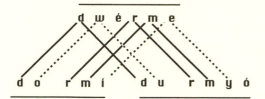

FIGURE 48. Radial structure in partial paradigm for Spanish verb *dormir* 'to sleep'. Solid lines indicate identical segments. Dotted lines indicate relations of similarity, that is, of shared phonetic features. Based on Joan L. Bybee, *Morphology* (1985), p. 126. Reprinted by permission of John Benjamins Publishing Company.

prototypes are actual words (though it would seem that one could abstract a common frame [*d* - back vowel - *rm* - vowel] that could itself function as a central category); third, lesser prototypes are less closely related to the base form than are its own immediate variants.

What does this all mean to the first-year language student struggling to learn paradigms by rote or by system? First, I think it means that you should learn the irregular forms first, as these are likely to occur with greatest frequency. Within a paradigm, you should study the prototypes first, as whole words, until they become habitual, and then look for the similarities that link prototypes in hierarchies or networks. Try to abstract the common frames. Then, with the prototypes and frames under control, you can learn the lesser forms more readily by comparing them either to the frames or to the prototypes. Comparisons should be made on both phonological and semantic dimensions.

CHAPTER 10

CULTURAL PHONOLOGY

The reader who has come this far with me may have noticed a progressive narrowing of the scope of inquiry, which started with world view, proceeded to discourse, figurative language, clause and word grammar, and now concludes with phonology. My hope is that by this time the reader will be so imbued with cultural and cognitive linguistics that it will seem natural to consider phonology as a kind of imagery which, though confined to audition, has many of the same characteristics as other kinds. That is, individual phonemes and sequences of phonemes are governed by auditory schemas (and articulatory routines); they are complex categories; and they are multidimensional. This ensemble constitutes an approach that should be of particular interest to linguistic anthropologists.

But phonology has one more quality that anthropologists may find even more diverting. Contrary to most contemporary views, phonology often reveals a symbolic dimension that is penetrated by the emotive realm of ethos and world view. To give just one example, I would include within the realm of phonology the prosodic shape of the bird-like wailing of the Kaluli people of New Guinea at a mourning ceremony when the bird-soul of the deceased passes into the realm of living birds (Feld 1990, 1991). Grieving for their departed relatives, the Kaluli pattern their songs after the calls of Raggiana birds of paradise, which they visualize in feminine skirts of fluffy, cinnamon-colored plumage, or flightless cassowaries, which appear to them in the silky-textured, black feathers of youth. This is an exotic example, but this link of sound to emotional meaning in song and speech is by no means uncommon. Most linguists would probably place the Kaluli example in a realm of prosody or paralanguage separate from phonology proper. There is some justification for maintaining the distinction, because it is only humans who can rapidly segment speech into consonants and vowels and mesh their combinations into elaborate, multileveled, constructions. But I prefer to take a more inclusive view of phonology as a multidimensional process that may include suprasegmental units of stress and intonation such as those found in the Kaluli representations of birdsongs.

Sound symbolisms provide another justification for taking a broader view of phonology. Commonly, phonology is confined solely to the rules by which phonetic features, phonemes, units of stress, and metrical units such as morae, syllables, and feet interact in non-symbolic systems. It is distinguished from morphology, which links sound to meaning. We commonly think of the morpheme as the smallest linguistic unit that comes complete with its own meaning, while the phoneme is the smallest verbal segment that enables us to distinguish one morpheme from another. We think of the link between phoneme and meaning as indirect. But these convenient distinctions sometimes distort linguistic realities. Phonology and morphology often intersect. This can be seen in sound symbolisms where single segments, not analyzable as morphemes, may signify changes in shape or movement. It can also be seen in syllable reduplications that signify pluralization or diminution. Like other aspects of language, phonology seems intimately connected to image-schemas, cognitive-models, and world views. Phonology is cultural.

PHONEMES AS COMPLEX CATEGORIES

Linguists commonly treat the phoneme as an abstract unit that stands for a small set of similar sounds. The instances of the phoneme may vary freely and unpredictably. For example, speakers of English produce both released and unreleased *p* in word final position, that is, both [p] and [p⌐].[1] Or the instances may vary regularly in correlation to their phonological environments; the variants, or *allophones*, present a pattern of complementary distribution. English aspirated [pʰ] occurs word-initially; unaspirated [p] and [p⌐] occur elsewhere. This seems straightforward, but on closer inspection of the variation we often find that the traditional approach is a bit too clumsy to capture multiple levels of abstraction and prototype effects. These can be captured in the theory of complex categories.

In Langacker's approach to cognitive linguistics, the phoneme schematizes phonetic imagery, profiling only what is common to all instances of usage of a consonant or a vowel.[2] For example, the vowel [a] might follow [p], [t], or [k], each of which would influence it in a particular

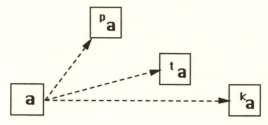

FIGURE 49. Extensions of basic phoneme [a] as variants [ᵖa], [ᵗa], and [ᵏa]. Reprinted from *Foundations of Cognitive Grammar, Volume I: Theoretical Prerequisites* by Ronald W. Langacker with the permission of the publishers, Stanford University Press. © 1987 by the Board of Trustees of the Leland Stanford Junior University.

direction. In standard notation, the abstract phoneme, which represents the schema that all of the instances of [a] have in common, would be represented /a/. Langacker took this point even further, arguing that the allophones are also abstract entities. He noted that "even a low-level (i.e. maximally specific) allophone represents an abstraction from actual articulatory (and auditory) events, each of which is phonetically unique in absolute terms" (1987: 389).

Figure 49 illustrates how allophones are linked in complex categories (i.e., complex phonetic images). A speaker first learns syllables, such as [a], [ka], [pa], and [ta]. A complex category emerges afterward as listeners make categorizing judgments resulting in extensions from the basic allophone [a] to its postconsonantal variants. That is, allophones [ᵖa], [ᵗa], and [ᵏa] are judged to be variants of [a]. The superscripted consonants represent transitions, that is, small variations in pronunciation, induced in the vowels by the preceding consonants. The linking arrows in Figure 49 point to the variants of the "basic allophone" [a]. The basic allophone together with its variants make up a simple prototype category.

So far, the approach is quite similar to structural phonology, but now the real power of Langacker's approach can come into play. The extensions [ᵖa], [ᵗa], and [ᵏa] can be subsumed under a schema that we can call "postconsonantal a," which Langacker represented as [ˣa] (see Figure 50). Here the superscripted ˣ represents what is common to the transitions signified by the superscripted ᵖ, ᵗ, and ᵏ. Finally, the basic allophone [a] and the postconsonantal schema [ˣa] resolve to a higher schema, [⁽ˣ⁾a], where parentheses signify that the consonant before *a* is optional. The higher-level abstractions project over subordinate categories, which they fully sanction. Both [ˣa] and [⁽ˣ⁾a] would correspond to phonemes in traditional phonology, but it is more likely that only one would be recognized. Thus, a phoneme should be regarded as a complex category subsuming both prototype categorization (by extension) and schematic categorization (by elaboration).

Consonants are handled in the same way as vowels. The situation with English /k/ is similar to that of /p/, in that word-initial aspirated forms are in complementary distribution with unaspirated forms, but with /k/ there is also a complementary distribution of palatal forms before front vowels and velar forms before back vowels. Lakoff (1987: 61), following Jaeger (1980), discussed prototype effects in four standard variants of /k/ in English. Table 9 lists the variants, their phonological environments, and an example for each.

Jaeger suggested that the prototype of this group is probably [kʰ].[3] Now, using Langacker's approach, we can diagram the group as a complex category, as in Figure 51. Because the categories of palatization and aspiration intersect in /k/, this network has to be a little more complex than the one for /a/. The diagram nicely captures the added complexity of the category.[4]

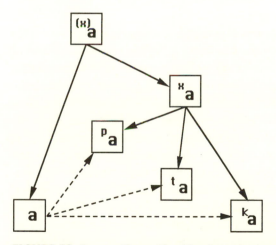

FIGURE 50. Same as Figure 49, with schematic categories [ˣa] and [⁽ˣ⁾a]. Reprinted from *Foundations of Cognitive Grammar, Volume I: Theoretical Prerequisites* by Ronald W. Langacker with the permission of the publishers, Stanford University Press. © 1987 by the Board of Trustees of the Leland Stanford Junior University.

TABLE 9.
COMPLEMENTARY VARIANTS OF ENGLISH PHONEME /k/

Variant	Description	Example
[k]	unaspirated velar	*ch* in *school*
[kʰ]	aspirated velar	*c* in *cool*
[k']	unaspirated palatal	*k* in *ski*
[k'ʰ]	aspirated palatal	*k* in *keel*

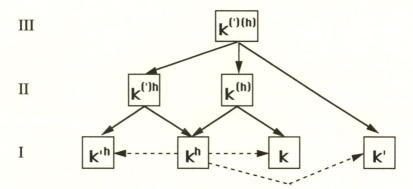

FIGURE 51. English phoneme /k/ represented as a complex category.

Let us now apply this approach to a case that has created problems for traditional phonemic analyses. Mandarin Chinese has two systems of fricative consonants in complementary distribution. In the first system only an alveolopalatal fricative occurs before high front vowels; in the second, three other fricatives contrast distinctively before all other vowels. Geoffrey R. Sampson (1980b) pointed out that traditional phonemic analysis would have difficulty determining which of the three fricatives in the second system to equate with the alveolopalatal fricative in the first system. In a cognitive analysis, we could posit an abstract fricative consonant unit /F2/ that would dominate just system 2, as shown in Figure 52. Then we could also posit a higher-level abstraction /F/ that would dominate both /F2/ and the alveolopalatal fricative in system 1. This would not require that the alveolopalatal be equated with any of the consonants in the second system.

The phonological rules of modern grammars typically identify only the most obvious and regular patterns of abstraction. Of course, writing sim-

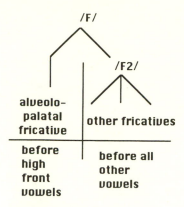

FIGURE 52. Complementary distribution and levels of abstraction in Mandarin Chinese fricative consonants.

plified descriptions of complex phonemes is often justified by practical restrictions, such as limited time or scarce research funds. There may be no need to diagram all the possible variants of a phoneme if the purpose is to devise a practical orthography for an unwritten language, as is often the case for ethnographers working in the field. But practical limitations should not be mistaken for theoretical ones. Since we never know quite what practical problems will emerge in the future, it is best to seek a general understanding of phonology. That understanding is advanced by regarding phonemes as complex categories.

MULTIDIMENSIONAL PHONOLOGY

In some of its endeavors, cultural phonology bears a strong resemblance to what has been called autosegmental phonology in linguistics. *Autosegmental* refers to the fact that segmentation of a stream of speech can take place on different levels or dimensions. For example, tone often segments independently of consonants and vowels so that segments of tone are different in temporal length from those of phonemes. In most cases, they are longer than phonemes, but conceivably they could also be shorter. In either case, we would expect hierarchical relations to develop between the levels, so that a tone segment would extend over a syllable, a word, or a phrase, for example. Without this chunking or nesting of one level into another, the system would soon become hopelessly complex. Syncopation is a good thing, but in moderation. Each level has its own regular temporal patterns of segmentation—its own phonological schemas. The

archipélago

FIGURE 53. Tone contour of *archipélago*. From Goldsmith (1976: 36). Reprinted with permission from *Linguistic Analysis*.

FIGURE 54. Autosegmental description of *archipélago*. From Goldsmith (1976: 36). H = High Tone, L = Low Tone. Reprinted with permission from *Linguistic Analysis*.

task of multidimensional phonology is to describe the schemas for each level and work out the correlations between levels.

The word *archipelago*, whose phonology was analyzed by John Goldsmith (1976), affords a good example of what is meant by levels of segmentation. In Figure 53, the tone pattern is represented below the word. The task is to explain this tone pattern.

Within the framework of autosegmental phonology, we would say that the high tone is associated to the vowel in the stressed syllable and "spreads" to the preceding vowels of the *archi* segment. The low tone is associated with the final two vowels. Thus, at least in rapid speech, words like *infernal*, *interrogative*, and *patrimony* display the same high to low tonal contour, with falling tone after the stressed syllable. The generalization is represented in Figure 54. The lines between the two tiers of the tone and the segmental skeleton represent association (simultaneous expression). The asterisk shows that the high tone is associated with the accented syllable.

Goldsmith (1976: 36) imposed the following "Well-formedness Condition" on his diagram:

(a) All vowels are associated with at least one tone. All tones are associated with at least one vowel.
(b) Association lines do not cross.

The fact that boundaries of units from different levels often coincide is partial justification for Goldsmith's principle that "association lines do not cross." We could also say that time-bounded segments from different dimensions tend to nest in hierarchies. A more complex example of multitiered phonology applied to an example from Mohawk appears in Lakoff (1989). Lakoff (1989: 309) called his approach "constructional phonology," saying, "in constructional phonology, there is no atemporal 'before' and 'after.' There are simply correlations across dimensions." That is, units on dimensions of intonation, morphology, and phonology correlate to one another in time.

The vocal tract is a complex organ. This complexity suggests that the sound imagery that is expressed in the vocal tract must be multidimensional and that for each phonologically significant feature of the vocal tract (e.g., articulations of the tongue and lips, nasal passages, larynx), there must be a dimension of sound imagery that governs it, and these dimensions must be activated in parallel. Douglas Pulleyblank (1989) diagramed the parallel activation of phonological planes for the three segments of the English word *sam*. Reviewing recent developments in phonological theory at the levels of syllables and segments, he concluded that "important results can often be directly traced to the abandonment of linear models of phonology in favor of some version of nonlinear theory" (1989: 225).

Goldsmith pointed the way to a multidimensional phonology of the word; Pulleyblank showed how the same general framework applies to the segment; it is no great leap to suppose that multidimensional perspectives would also work at the level of the syllable and at levels more inclusive than the word. It also seems likely that multidimensionality links phonological schemas of various types to semantic dimensions. One logical way to expand our framework is to see whether minimal phonological categories can be linked to semantic categories to form symbols.

SOUND SYMBOLISM IN YUMAN LANGUAGES

Verbal symbols link conceptual units of sound to units of meaning. In theory, meaning could be attached to a wide variety of sound configurations, including acoustic features, segments, syllables, syllable combinations, suprasegmentals such as tone and stress, and even involuntary exclamations. For example, a male raconteur may use a lisp (an interdental fricative) comically, if chauvinistically, to signify femininity. A rising tone on either the word *Ohhh?* or the phrase *Is it true?* can signify doubt, while a rising-falling tone on *Ohhh?* or the phrase *Of course* signifies recognition or acceptance. These commonplace speech phenomena illustrate the great flexibility in assignment of meanings to sound units at any level of integration. It is hard to escape the conclusion that language is almost infinitely plastic and that its common forms are conventional, the result of habituation and tacit collaborations carried on by communities of speakers and listeners.

Classical structural approaches make a clear break between phonemes—the minimal verbal segments that encode meaning (but have no meanings of their own)—and morphemes—the minimal verbal units that carry their own meanings—placing them at different and distinct levels. At introductory levels of presentation, sound symbolism—the direct association of sound to meaning by analogy—is usually discounted. But linguistic units do not always fit structural models as neatly and crisply as we might like. Between the two poles of the classical phoneme and the classical morpheme there is a range of possibilities where phoneme-like units may become linked to definable meanings. Phenomena that violate the neat *a priori* levels of phonology and morphology are so common that it is almost impossible to ignore them. The cognitive approach would suggest that there can be gradients in which a linguistic unit may more or less resemble a phoneme or a syllabic morpheme. In such an intermediate case, its meaning may provide background or ancillary information that supports the foregrounded information of a full, prototypical morpheme.

To take one example, Margaret Langdon (1971) recorded examples of consonant ablaut (alternation) in Ipai (Northern Diegueño), a Yuman language of southern California. The Ipai data recorded by Langdon have been reanalyzed by Langacker (1987: 399) as instances of sound symbolism. In the examples in Table 10, said to be typical of Yuman languages, there is an alteration between the consonant *ł*, signifying largeness or neutrality with respect to size, and *l*, signifying smallness. In Ipai,

TABLE 10.
IPAI SOUND SYMBOLISM WITH *l* AND *ł*

(a) *cəkułk*	'(large) hole through something'
(b) *cəkulk*	'small hole through something'
(a) *łapəłap*	'to be (large and) flat'
(b) *lapəlap*	'to be small and flat'
(a) *xəkał*	'to have a gap in a row' [e.g., missing tooth]
(b) *xəkal*	'to have a small gap in a row'

the common, or unmarked, form is that with *ł*, signifying larger size. Ipai *l* appears to function very much like the English vowel [ɪ], which gives a diminutive sense to words like *flit*, *twit*, and *nitwit*. The difference is that Ipai also requires phonetic expression of the unmarked form. Such phenomena are widespread and therefore important for both practical and theoretical reasons.

Why should we regard this as sound symbolism? Mainly because the *ł* and *l* cannot be abstracted as morphemes by analogy, for example, to the English past tense suffix *-ed*; that is, we would never encounter instances of *čəkuk* 'hole through something,' *apap* 'to be flat,' or *xəka* 'to have a gap in a row,' or some such, lacking the notions of large and small, nor would we encounter these forms combined with segments other than *ł* and *l*. Morphological analysis leaves forms *čəku . . . k*, *. . . apə . . . ap*, and *xəka . . .* , which Langacker (1987: 400) called "a discontinuous residue that does not itself have morphemic status." Similarly, an analysis of English *flit* would leave the discontinuous form [fl . . . t], which is certainly not a morpheme in the traditional sense. Thus, the Ipai ablaut forms [. . . ł . . ./LARGE] and [. . . l . . ./SMALL] appear to function as symbols by analogy from sound to size.[5] Fricative is to voiced as large is to small.

Yuman languages seem to make good use of sound symbolism for describing motion and physical changes with very compact, efficient expressions. In the Hualapai language of northern Arizona, for example, the word stem *quir* has to do with revolutions. A variety of concepts of shape and motion are symbolized by segmental changes on the stem, as in *quir* 'rolled,' *quid* 'large loops,' and *quin* 'tight, fast spin.'[6] The same process works on many other word stems, a pattern that suggests a cultural and linguistic proclivity for mechanics. What this sound symbolism illustrates, again, is the arbitrariness of the distinction between phoneme and morpheme.

Interest in sound symbolism is by no means new. Whorf (1956b: 75) also noticed that such English words as *flash*, *flicker*, *clash*, *click*, *clack*, *crash*, *lick*, and *lash* could be "resolved into meaningful fractions" and that English demonstrative particles (*the*, *this*, *there*, *than*, etc.) have initial *th*. Whorf's interest was aroused by a reading of Fabret d'Olivet's nineteenth-century study of the grammar of Hebrew, a language in which similar phenomena are fundamental. I would like to extend this topic of sound symbolism with one more case that brings us back full circle to Bybee's symbolic networks. This is the phonology of warm colors in Coeur d'Alene.

Color Terms

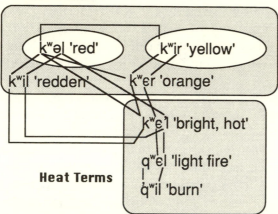

FIGURE 55. Network profiling phonological equivalences in Coeur d'Alene roots pertaining to *red, yellow,* and *heat.* Other lines of correspondence could be drawn to illustrate the similarities of *l* to *r* and *kʷ* to *qʷ*. In this figure, glottalized and non-glottalized forms are taken as equivalent.

THE PHONOLOGY OF WARM COLORS IN COEUR D'ALENE

Bybee (1985) presented strong evidence that phonological similarities imply semantic similarities. As we have seen, she found that verb paradigms in Spanish can be represented as phonological and semantic networks organized around prototypes in the frequently spoken forms. It follows, then, that, for any language, any domain of closely related concepts might be symbolically linked to a vocabulary frame of phonologically related terms and that these may be organized around prototypes. What is true of Spanish verbs could be true, for example, of color terms.

Recall that Wierzbicka (1990) theorized that experiences of fire and the sun are related in that both are warm and light. She related the color *yellow* to the sun and warmth and the color *red* to fire and warmth. We also know that white, red, and yellow occupy adjacent positions on the color chart. Thus there is reason to suspect that brightness, red, yellow, fire, and heat will have close symbolic links in any language. It should therefore be reasonable to expect to find languages that encode this in a set of terms with close phonological relationships. One such language is Coeur d'Alene, whose terms for anatomy and geography have been discussed in previous chapters. Figure 55, which displays the Coeur d'Alene linguistic roots pertaining to *red* and *yellow*, is from Palmer (n.d.b).

Robert Johnson (1975) analyzed the Coeur d'Alene roots $k^w\varepsilon'l$ 'bright, hot,' $k^w\varepsilon r$ 'orange,' $k^w ir$ 'yellow,' $k^w\partial l$ 'red,' $k^w il$ 'redden,' $q^w\varepsilon l$ 'light fire,' and $\dot{q}^w il$ 'burn.' The overall structure of these roots can be described as /{k^w, q^w, $\dot{q}^w$} {∂, ε, i} {r, l, $'l$}/, or more formally as in Figure 56.[7] The initial segment is always a labialized velar or post-velar; the second segment is always a front vowel or a schwa; the final segment is always a liquid r or l, with the l sometimes glottalized. Thus, all of these roots are very similar phonologically.

Assuming that the phonological analysis correctly differentiates the roots in question,[8] then we might also deduce from Figure 55 that a close semantic relationship exists between RED and [BRIGHT, HOT], on the one hand, and YELLOW, ORANGE and [BRIGHT, HOT], on the other. Another interesting feature of this complex is that all the color and heat *states* have initial k^w in contrast to the two *processes* (light fire, burn), which have initial q^w. Similar symbolic clusters are no doubt common in the languages of the world.

DOES BELLA COOLA HAVE WORDS WITHOUT SYLLABLES?

When presented with a transcription of a language new to our experience, and knowing nothing of the meaning of its words, we may first be struck by how differently the language arranges its consonants and vowels into syllables. This is particularly true of languages of the American Northwest, where we may encounter a word such as *xłp'X^włtpłłskʷc'*, which lacks vowels altogether and would therefore be said by some linguists necessarily to lack syllables. Syllables are curious creatures. They are phonological units, so they need not carry any meaning of their own, but often they are co-extensive with morphemes. Some morphemes behave like syllables; indeed, some are syllables at their phonological pole in

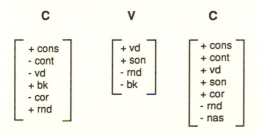

FIGURE 56. Phonological feature description of Coeur d'Alene roots pertaining to *red, yellow,* and *heat.* Vowels and back consonants in Coeur d'Alene are never phonologically nasal.

taking stress or contributing to a language's prosodic rhythm of consonants and vowels, stresses and pitches. For example, the word *recarpeted*
has only three meaningful parts, or morphemes: *re-carpet-ed*; but, in my
pronunciation, it has four syllables: *re-car-pe-ted*. The first syllable, *re-*,
phonetically [ri], is also a morpheme, but the others, *car-pe-ted*, are not.
Some might argue that the last syllable should be *-ed* rather than *-ted*. In
fact, the *t* may be regarded as belonging to both syllables (Clark and Yallop 1990), but either way it would not affect the argument. The syllable is
a phonological and prosodic unit that is independent of the phonological
shape of the morpheme. To say that it is prosodic is to say that it is defined
in terms of pitch, loudness, tempo, or rhythm (Crystal 1985: 249).

At this point I would like to introduce the concept of *dependency* because we need it to understand the syllable and its prototypical constituents: vowels and consonants.[9] Most linguistic constructions, at any level,
can be fairly clearly divided into two units, one autonomous or nuclear,
and the other dependent or peripheral. At the sentence level in symbolic
constructions, we have independent and dependent clauses. At the level
of the syllable in English phonology, vowels provide the nuclear constituents, while consonants are more dependent or peripheral. English syllables must generally have a vowel, but they do not necessarily require a
consonant. Vowels may even function as words, as in the indefinite article
a [ʌ], or as entire utterances, as in the response *oh* [úː]. I can't think of
any instances of English words or utterances made up solely of voiceless
consonants or stop consonants. (Unless we regard the implosive alveolar
affricate in *tsk tsk* as a consonant, but that would be a consonant that
occurs in only one word.) Langacker (1987: 299) described consonants
and vowels as follows:

> consonants presuppose vowels, and require vowels for their full pho-
> netic implementation, but the converse is not true. The most funda-
> mental property of a vowel, I suggest, is a period (however brief) of
> essentially stable sonority. The hallmark of consonants, by contrast,
> is change: consonants can be seen as operations on the sonority pro-
> vided by vowels. The relation between the two is asymmetrical, in
> that the stable sonority of a vowel in no way requires consonantal
> modification for its manifestation, though a consonant does require
> a vowel to provide the sonority it modifies.

Because dependent units, such as consonants, require something more
for their completion, they can be represented as dependency frames with
brackets for the frame and blank slots (elaboration sites) for the abstract

nucleus. In this context, the brackets represent syllable frames, not phonemes as is more usual notation. For example, a frame representation of a syllable based on the consonantal phoneme /r/ might look as follows: [r_], where the slot must be filled by a vowel. We could rewrite it as [rV], where V stands for an abstract vowel. Filling the nuclear slot with [i] to give [ri] describes the first syllable of the word *repeat*; filling it with [e^y] to give [re^y] describes the word *ray*.

In English, and many other languages, the nuclear constituents of syllables are prototypically vowels, but other resonants, such as liquids (*l*, *r*), and nasals (*m*, *n*), often function as vocalic nuclei. When this happens, it is conventional to say that they are *syllabic* and represent them with subscripted dots: ḷ, ṃ, ṇ, ṛ. For example, you could transcribe *apple* as [æpḷ], *atom* as [ætṃ], *platen* as [plætṇ], and *cavern* as [kævṛn]. Examples *platen* and *cavern* show that assignment of dependence is relative to the context: The phoneme /n/ is syllabic in *platen*, but not in *cavern*, where the core of the final syllable is [ṛ].

Degree of dependency may be somewhat indeterminate. Often, two dependent units share a nucleus. For example, if we syllabify *cavern* as [kæv-ṛn], then the first syllable, [kæv], has two consonants, [k_] and [_v], both of which are dependent relative to the nuclear vowel. Perhaps it is best to treat the voiced segments [æv] as forming an autonomous unit with respect to unvoiced [k_], yielding the embedded structure [k[æv]]. This provides a dependency description of the syllable's *onset* (initial consonant or consonants) and *rhyme* (everything following the onset). The consonant-vowel-consonant or CVC syllable structure is a very common structure for word roots in languages of the world, perhaps the most common and prototypical. As a unit with both resonance and boundaries, it provides a good planetary center for prefixes and suffixes, which tend to be CV or VC.

While English may lack words made up solely of consonants, linguists long ago noticed that languages in northwestern North America frequently string consonants together in the complete absence of vowels. What can we say about the syllable structure of words like the following, attested from the Bella Coola language of the central coast of British Columbia and reported by Bruce Bagemihl and Patricia A. Shaw (Shaw 1989; Bagemihl 1991: 627)?

> *xɬp'X^{w}ɬtɬpɬɬsk^{w}c'* 'Then he had had in his possession a bunchberry plant.'
> *k̓xɬcx^{w}sɬX^{w}tɬɬc* 'You had seen that I had gone through the passage.'

BOX 1.

PHONETIC SYMBOLS FOR BELLA COOLA CONSONANTS

This section introduces some rather esoteric phonetic symbols that are in common use by linguists working on languages of northwestern North America. The particular symbols used in the discussion are as follows:

ł	lateral aspiration, rather like pronouncing *shl* out of one side of the mouth
c	an alveolar affricate; pronounced like *ts* in *lets*
ċ, ṗ, t'	glottalizations; these consonants are pronounced with a little explosive puff of air
*x, X, X*ʷ	velar *x* and uvular *X*, *X*ʷ are fricatives, rather like the final consonant in *Bach*; *X*ʷ is labialized; *X* and *X*ʷ are pronounced with the dorsal surface of the tongue articulating farther back in the mouth.

For those brave enough to attempt a pronunciation of either word, a description of the phonetic values of the characters appears in Box 1.

If a syllable structure is signaled by a rhythm of up and down sonority—what Goldsmith (1990: 104) called the sonority view of the syllable—but a word in fact lacks vowels and even sonorant consonants, how can it have syllable nuclei or syllables? Can it be that these words lack syllables altogether? If, on the other hand, we assume that some kind of basic rhythm with units or waves of approximately syllable length (one to five segments) is likely to be found in every language, then another approach must be taken. Perhaps there are consonants that resemble vowels sufficiently closely to provide syllable nuclei. This is the case with syllabic sonorant consonants *l̩*, *r̩*, *m̩*, and *n̩*. Syllabic liquids and nasals are common in Bella Coola, but they don't appear in the examples. Inspection of the two Bella Coola words reveals that not only are there no vowels, but there are no sonorant segments at all!

Another property of vowels is that they are continuant. Since fricatives are also continuant, they might function as syllable nuclei on this basis. Even though they are voiceless, their continuant property gives them a kind of family resemblance to vowels. Because of the resemblance, we could theorize that speakers of Bella Coola may give prosodic license to fricatives, allowing them to act as though they were vowels.[10] The syllable nucleus may be a complex category with vowels as the prototype and voiceless fricatives and obstruents of other kinds as less prototypical variants. Along with stop consonants, fricatives share the property of being obstruents, that is, of obstructing the free passage of air in the vocal tract in varying degrees. Perhaps the Bella Coola ignore that quality in the construction of syllables but pay attention to sibilance, the high-frequency hissing associated with fricatives.

Looking at the word *xłp'X^włtłpłłsk^wc'* again, we find the fricatives *x*, *ł*, *X^w*, and *s*. The *ł* occurs five times. This certainly hints that *ł* performs some important phonological function, perhaps acting as the nucleus for several voiceless syllables. Letting F stand for fricative and O for other obstruents, let us suppose that some possible syllable structures are F, OF, FO, and OFO. In this abstract notation, the word looks like this: FFOFFOFOFFFOO. It is clear that the eight fricatives in this word would provide plenty of material for syllable nuclei, if they can in fact so serve.

This story of prototypical and extended forms of syllable nuclei is attractive, but, as it stands, it oversimplifies Bella Coola phonology. Bagemihl (1991) demonstrated that phonological units containing vowels or resonants (liquids and nasals) undergo a number of phonological processes that do not apply to any units that lack vowels or resonants. For example, stems with vowels or resonants as syllable nuclei can undergo reduplication associated with semantic diminutives and derivation of continuative aspect, as in the following examples:

qayt --> *qaqayt-i*
'hat' --> 'toadstool-diminutive'

yałk- --> *yałyałk*
'do too much' --> 'continuative'

tl̥k^w --> *tl̥tl̥k^w*   [*l*s are syllable nuclei]
'swallow' --> 'continuative'

mn̥łk^wa --> *mn̥mn̥łk^wa-łp*   [*n*s are syllable nuclei]
'bear berry' --> 'plant of the bear berry'

Significantly, there are no forms in which obstruents participate in reduplication as though they were syllable nuclei. For example, the following derivation does not occur:

kł --> **kłkł-*
'fall'

With evidence like this from reduplication processes and further evidence from processes that insert and delete vowels and resonants, Bagemihl concluded that Bella Coola does have syllables, but not all segments need be part of a syllable. He determined that for Bella Coola the "canonical syllable shape" is CRVVC, where R is a resonant, C a consonant, and V a vowel. Clusters of segments that do not belong to a unit that can be subsumed within this shape are simply non-syllabic and consequently do not participate in those phonological processes of Bella Coola that pertain only to syllables. In particular, clusters of obstruents (fricatives, affricates, and stops) do not conform. Of course, for Bagemihl, this means that the words *xɬp'X^wɬtɬpɬtsk^wc'* and *k̓xɬcx^wstX^wtɬc* have no syllables because they are entirely made up of clusters of obstruents. It also means that in Bella Coola an obstruent segment may be part of a word even though it does not belong to a phonological syllable. In Bagemihl's view, Bella Coola licenses (permits the phonetic expression of) any segment having a mora. A mora is "a minimal unit of metrical time equivalent to a short syllable" (Crystal 1985: 198). Other languages only license segments that belong to syllables, which are higher-level units.

Without disputing Bagemihl's evidence, we might adopt a different perspective that is more consistent with the cognitive idea that syllabicity, like other linguistic phenomena, is likely to be found distributed on a gradient, though it will not necessarily be distributed evenly. The Bella Coola prototypical syllable requires a vowel or at least a resonant. But if syllable is a complex or a graded category, then even some obstruent consonants might function as less prototypical syllable cores. Bagemihl dismissed such syllables as "phonetic" as opposed to "phonological," but given that 10 percent of Bella Coola words are formed entirely of obstruents, it seems odd to say that they have *no* phonological or prosodic purposes or functions. From my own experience with the related language Coeur d'Alene, I have an intuitive feeling that such words do have prosodic rhythms that must have some cognitive representation. Even in the absence of resonant segments, prosodic rhythms would be expected on the basis of the grouping well-formedness rules and grouping preference rules postulated by Jackendoff (1986: 132).[11] Even though they do not participate in grammatically significant phonological processes, syllable-level units in Bella Coola made up solely of obstruents might theoretically be discovered by other means. For example, we could examine mistakes or variations in pronunciation, such as that illustrated by the mispronunciation of the English word *sacrosanct* as [séŋkrusækt]. The inversion reveals the phonetic syllables [sæk], [ru], and [seŋk].[12]

Instead of arguing that words made up of obstruents lack syllables, we could argue that Bella Coola has two levels of syllables: (1) prototypical syllables with syllable nuclei consisting of vowels or resonants, and

(2) marginal (and less frequently occurring) syllables with syllable nuclei consisting only of obstruents. Within syllables having sonorant nuclei, vowels are probably more central than liquids and nasals. In those with obstruent nuclei, fricatives are probably more central than affricates and stops. As Bagemihl showed, only prototypical syllables participate in grammatically significant phonological processes. This two-level system of sonorant-phonological and obstruent-prosodic syllables implies, too, that the consonants of Bella Coola are not limited to "operations on the sonority provided by vowels." They may also be thought of as operations on the sibilance of nuclear obstruents. Thus, from the cognitive point of view and the theory of dependence, Bella Coola and other phonologically similar languages in the Northwest differ from most other languages of the world in allowing their obstruents to function with greater autonomy, almost, in some instances, as though they were resonants. If we take this approach, then all Bella Coola words have syllables, but only some Bella Coola words have voiced syllables with phonological functions.

CHAPTER 11

WHERE WE ARE

I have proposed a synthesis of anthropological linguistics with the newly emergent field of cognitive linguistics. The approach centers on linguistic imagery, which is largely defined by culture. Therefore, I call the approach *cultural linguistics*. The term invokes the anthropological tradition that culture is the accumulated knowledge of a community or society, including its stock of cognitive models, schemas, scenarios, and other forms of conventional imagery. I would like to conclude this book, then, by summarizing some basic assumptions of cultural linguistics and offering some general suggestions on how this theoretical framework would affect the practice of ethnography.

SUMMARY OF PRINCIPLES

1. Conventional linguistic meaning is relative to imagery. Images are particular construals of cognitive models, which are largely structured by culture. Cognitive models are activated, and often assembled, as scenes or text models. Images have perspective, figure and ground structure, scope, and emotional values. Imagery is not confined to visual imagery; it may be auditory, kinesthetic, or olfactory as well.

Cognitive models may consist of image-schemas, metaphoric models, metonymic models, folk verbal postulate models, proposition-schemas, or combinations of these. Cognitive models may model things, states, or dynamic processes, or combinations of these; they may originate in more than one of the senses; and they are inextricably interwoven with emotional values and intentions in attitudes, plans, and goals.

2. Language is symbolic. A verbal symbol is the unit formed by a linkage between a phonological unit and a unit of meaning. Grammar refers to the schematic sequential orders and nested structures of linguistic symbols assembled in constructions. Grammatical classes and constructions are themselves schematic linguistic symbols. The constraints

holding between constituents of linguistic constructions are convention-ally motivated by phonological frames, by the imagistic or ideational structures of base models and the correspondences of their parts, by the relative salience of components of the base model (especially figure-ground relationships), and by categorizing relationships.

3. Categorization refers to relationships holding between concepts. Complex categories have a network structure involving relations of schema to instance (elaboration) and prototype to variant (extension). Schemas are gestalts having integrated structures; they are not classical taxonomic categories consisting entirely of collections of features.

Folk systems of linguistic classification appear to favor grammatical classifiers over taxonomies. Systems of grammatical classifiers often de-scribe folk ontologies of shape and substance. Particular classifiers are organized as complex categories that may center on a domain of experi-ence, such as a myth (Dyirbal) or a framework of supernatural belief (Bantu). Classifiers evoke chains of metaphorical and metonymical link-ages as part of their meaning. A classifier highlights general features of its complement nouns and sets up expectations for selection of verbs.

Like the lumpy and fuzzy world that language represents to us, the subsystems of language integrate analytic categories with conceptual continua, thus accounting for the tantalizing mix of regular and irregu-lar alternative and replacement forms in many paradigms of verbal and nominal forms and affixes. In this respect, cultural linguistics responds to Friedrich's (1975) plea for a non-arbitrary treatment of linguistic symbols.

4. Linguistic meaning is subsumed within world view. Linguistic meaning is encyclopedic in the sense that it involves the spreading acti-vation of conceptual networks that are organized chains and hierarchies of cognitive models. Language both expresses and constitutes world view but could only fully determine it in a culture that lacked other means of expression and communication. No such culture exists anywhere (though it may be approximated by academic subcultures).

5. Language resonates in distributed conceptual structures that may be activated in parallel or sequentially. Parallel concurrently active schemas from multiple dimensions, levels, or tiers of phonology, grammar, and world view correlate in time as nested structures (constraints). Cultural phonology and non-linear phonology are based upon this insight. Speak-ing and listening activate the same conceptual networks, so there is no need to postulate a listening process that reverses a sequence of rules in a speaking process.

6. The meaning of discourse is always to some degree both situated and emergent. Situated meaning involves framing meanings as elements of conventional situations. Emergent meaning refers to the schematization (abstraction) of novel experiences (both perceptual and autonomous). Most linguistic usages and discourses exist somewhere on a continuum from conventional, mutually presupposed and traditionally situated meanings to meanings emergent in unique confluences of society, culture, history, and discourse itself. Categorization may be seen as a cognitive process, either spontaneous or directed, by which new schematizations of novel experiences are compared to old schemas.

7. Discourse establishes relationships between interlocutors by instantiating discourse scenarios. Discourse scenarios are cognitive models of verbal interaction consisting of sequences of pragmatic speech act schemas. They interlock with schemas of participation, perspective, and ideation. These categories are intended only as analytic (etic) points of reference for the investigation of folk (emic) discourse scenarios, which may very well be organized along other lines. Discourse is performative in the sense that it enacts cognitive imagery. Narrative can be described along the same lines as other discourse and requires no special theory of its own. Discursives (discourse indexicals) are terms that reflexively predicate aspects of ongoing discourse, including pragmatic, interactional, situational, phonological, and ideational aspects. This approach unifies the study of discourse particles, markers, indices, etc., with that of other kinds of predication.

8. Languages, semantic systems, cognitive models, and world views are all socially constructed. However, cultural linguistics does not require total surrender to unmitigated relativism or "radical alterity" (Keesing 1989). There are several sources of universal constraints on language, including the universal form and functions of the human body and brain (perhaps including physiological components of a few basic affective states), the universal experience of gravity, the earth, the sky, and the sun in the "primal scene," fire, liquid, neurally determined focal color sensations, recognition of human faces, and very general scenarios of human intentions. Lakoff and Johnson called attention to the "emergent" orientational and ontological image-schemas that arise from universal physical experiences. These provide common metaphorical source materials for the framing of much of cultural knowledge.

Another source of universality lies in the functioning of the mind. Several important cognitive functions are relevant here. In general, humans everywhere have the capacity for symbolization and the capacity for language as a rapid verbal form of expression. Humans everywhere have the capacity for imagery: the ability to construe scenes in terms of figure and ground, specificity, perspective, and scope. All humans schematize their experiences and organize their schemas into complex categories, chains, and hierarchies. Humans everywhere have the capacity for figurative language: metaphor and metonymy. Humans everywhere frame their experiences in terms of existing cognitive models and schemas.

Given this common human bedrock of experience and repertoire of cognitive functions, humans everywhere have elaborated rich and unique languages and cultures that are just as remarkable for their tremendous diversity as for any cultural universals. Like image-schemas that emerge from universal physical experiences, cultural categories also provide resources for the framing of experiences. Reversing the metaphorical process, emergent categories themselves may come to be framed by cultural models, as when American Indian cosmologies interpret the cosmos in theological terms. Maya and Ogala Indians, and most other tribes, regard the sun, moon, sky, earth, and cardinal directions as manifestations of deities and address them as kin.

Ultimately, universal emergent categories provide only a kind of cultural anchor, admittedly an important one, because a culture totally adrift from physical and social reality must perish. But, theoretically, each culture on board its own ship may build a world and language of its own. As a practical matter, of course, all contemporary cultures are anchored very close together in that they are mutually accessible via modern media and modes of transportation. They must all learn and assimilate something of each other's worlds.

IMPLICATIONS FOR ETHNOGRAPHIC RESEARCH

Cultural linguistics has implications for how we should study languages, whether the intention is actually to learn to speak them or just to learn about them. Some will want to discover the rules that most reliably predict grammatical usage; others will ask whether cultural linguistics can advance the program to test the Sapir-Whorf hypothesis; and others, like myself, will be most interested in following up Dorothy Lee's interest in gaining insight into the thoughts of native speakers and therefore improving our understanding of texts, performances, and discourse; finally, some will want to improve their understanding of how people pragmatically deploy their linguistic resources in culturally defined situations.

The approach of cultural linguistics suggests that a researcher should ideally become a participant in the culture, because learning to interpret nuances and to speak with the understanding of a native requires empathy that implies a deep and thorough understanding of native cultural models and competence in native patterns of discourse. The more similar our experiences to those of native speakers, the more likely we are to develop the imagery and conceptual bases needed to use and understand languages appropriately. Where possible, we should try to learn the same things in the same perceptual modes as they are learned by natives. In addition to the arts of conversation and narrative, we should pay attention to graphic arts, plastic arts, gastronomic arts, theater, and music; we should follow daily rounds, learn to perform native skills, and learn to recognize conventional social situations. All forms of cultural expression reveal cognitive models that project into linguistic meaning. Similarly, Agar (1994) argued that effective communication requires learning the frames of *languaculture*, that complex entity that includes both language and culture.

With the emphasis on imagery, we are less inclined to use symbolic logic to write a formal description of grammatical forms or genres. In general, it is only necessary to model language with formal logic where native speakers themselves have developed their own highly patterned generative categories, such as elaborate sets of kin terms or regular phonological rules. Ethnographers should make explicit distinctions between verbal postulates and syllogisms that are presented by native speakers and proposition-schemas that are abstracted from language usages or texts and formulated by the ethnographer.

Since language is so pervaded with evidence of metaphorical and metonymical thinking, figurative language should be considered in almost any study of language at any level. It may involve the study of common metaphors or the often unnoticed metaphorical content of grammatical forms, such as the force dynamics model that underlies the English modal system as described by Talmy (1988) or the metaphors and metonyms that link conversations to telephone wires (linear schema) and martial arts contests (turn-taking schema) in the Japanese noun class *hon* (Lakoff 1987). Folk models of meronymy have barely been touched.

I have argued that it is the culturally defined imagery of discourse itself that is predicated by metalinguistic lexemes (such as *lying* and *gabby*) and discursive particles (such as Japanese *yo*). If this is the case, then more efforts should be devoted to trying to discover folk models of communication, as Sweetser (1987) did in her study of lying. Here we can study pragmatic speech acts, participation, sequence, perspective, and ideation as these categories are realized in folk discourse models. Perhaps some of the effort spent studying indexical terms should be shifted from their discourse functions, defined analytically, to their imagery, defined as folk categories. We might ask such questions as "What aspects of previous or upcoming utterances are *predicated* by discourse particle P and what does speaker S think she is accomplishing by uttering P?" Of course, speakers may not be able to verbalize their thoughts, especially about something as automatic as choice of discourse particles, but that is a problem that is common to much of semantics and pragmatics.

Hymes and Sherzer argued convincingly that we should treat discourse as performance that constitutes social relationships. An instance is seen in the status inequality invoked by the honorific language of the Japanese sewing machine salesman. Additionally, we can consider Hymes's categories (*settings, participants, ends, act sequences, keys, instrumentalities, norms,* and *genres*), especially as these are natively conceived. The categories of cultural linguistics and ES do not deal directly with relative status and power, but nothing in the theory precludes including these dimensions in discourse scenarios. Such scenarios would represent how people negotiate or collaborate over linguistic meaning within conventional and emergent structures of political or economic power (as in family arguments, political campaigns, revitalization movements, and legal cases) and how people communicate information about actual and potential political alignments.

In the study of narrative, cultural linguistics dictates no single approach. Conventional plots may be treated as sequences of action schemas, as in the American Indian sequence of Interdiction-Violation-Consequence, or they may be treated as the interplay of Agonists and Antagonists, as in the story of Tom Tit Tom. Folk models of ideational coherence can be applied to the understanding of plots or to the investigation of the sharing and complementarity of knowledge required for narrators and audiences. Conventional phrasings may be treated as pragmatic speech acts or as poetic verbal imagery. Differing cultural values might explain departures from natural or conventional narrative sequences, as described for the Hot Pepper Story of the Kuna. Narrative is so rich, multifaceted, and culturally diverse that cultural linguistics can only hope to illumine bits and facets of specific texts and performances, but in some cases it may do so more incisively than other approaches.

CONCLUSIONS

In a review of schema theory in cognitive anthropology, Casson (1983: 455) noted that he was able to draw together "research and results from many seemingly disparate fields of cognitive study" under a "single, comprehensive and coherent, explanatory framework." He opined that present-day schema theory is "undoubtably overly powerful and too general," but that it has "enormous promise" and offers "a very exciting prospect for future research in cognitive anthropology." This assessment applies equally well to linguistic anthropology as to cognitive anthropology. Much progress has been made since his review, including the founding of the International Cognitive Linguistics Association and its journal *Cognitive Linguistics*, and the publication of theoretical works in cognitive linguistics (Lakoff 1987; Langacker 1987; Kövecses 1990; Langacker 1990a, 1991; Deane 1992). These studies provide fascinating insights into the workings of language, but, Kövecses excepted, they often seem to lack an essential cultural dimension. I hope that cognitive linguists will come to see the need for grounding their theories of models and metaphors in ethnography.

During the same period, cognitive anthropology has seen the publication of several edited collections (Dougherty 1985; Holland and Quinn 1987; Strauss and Quinn 1994), Lucy's (1992a, 1992b) two volumes exploring the validity of the Sapir-Whorf hypothesis, Agar's (1994) popular work on languaculture, D'Andrade's (1995) summing up of cognitive anthropology, and numerous individual articles scattered in journals and edited volumes. Few of these have incorporated recent developments in cognitive linguistics. This book was written in the hope that these authors and others will join me in reconstituting linguistic anthropology as an imagery-centered, cultural theory of language that weaves some bright new cognitive strands into the historical tapestry of our field.

Anthropologists should continue to pursue their traditional interests in language, culture, and world view. However problematic notions of culture and world view may have become, they still provide an essential breadth of interpretive background that is missing from much of contemporary linguistics. The potential scope of application of cultural linguistics to grammar, song, narrative, conversation, figurative speech, speech situations, and many other facets of the world's languages is immense. The studies reviewed in this book have barely set foot on the surface of the new linguistic world opened up by the cultural linguistic perspective. This is not a world to be exploited so much as it is a world to be appreciated, and, since it is our everyday world, it is a world desperately in need of mending and healing by greater cross-cultural understanding and tolerance. Perhaps cultural linguistics can contribute to that process.

NOTES

1. INTRODUCTION

1. For other effective critiques of generative grammar, see Sampson (1980a, 1980b), Doe (1988), and Hockett (1989).

2. Coeur d'Alene is understood and spoken fluently by only a dozen or so elders living in Idaho and understood imperfectly by another two dozen linguists and anthropologists who specialize in languages of northwestern North America. Northwestern American Indian languages are not so difficult, but few people today have the opportunity to learn them. Coeur d'Alene belongs to the Interior Division of the Salish language family. Other closely related languages are Kalispel (including Flathead, Kalispel, and Spokan dialects), Columbian, Okanogan, Shuswap, Thompson, and Lillooet.

3. Coeur d'Alene is written with a practical system developed by native speaker Lawrence Nicodemus in collaboration with linguists and used by the Coeur d'Alene themselves (Nicodemus 1975a, 1975b, 1975c). NOM labels the nominalizing prefix *s-*.

4. Cited in Hoijer (1953: 557). The quote is from Edward Sapir, *Language* (New York: Harcourt, Brace and Co., 1921), 235. I could not find it in my 1949 edition.

5. The phrase is from Givon (1992: 12), who was specifically concerned with the referential accessibility of nominal topics.

2. THREE TRADITIONS IN LINGUISTIC ANTHROPOLOGY

1. This story has been told many times, including most recently by Lucy (1992a), who thoroughly discussed the linguistic relativity of Boas, Sapir, and Whorf.

2. Personal communication (1992).

3. See, for example, Goodwin and Duranti (1992).

3. THE EMERGENCE OF COGNITIVE LINGUISTICS

1. Scheerer (1988) listed computer science, psychology, philosophy, linguistics, anthropology, and neuroscience.

2. For example, Scheerer (1988: 8) said cognitive scientists have a common re-

search objective: "to discover the representational and computational capacities of the mind and their structural and functional representation in the brain."

3. A noted cognitive scientist who takes a different approach is Eleanor Rosch, who collaborated on a work that combines cognitive science, Buddhist philosophy, and phenomenology (Varela, Thompson, and Rosch 1991). In this approach, there are no representations, only *enactions*. Nevertheless, in these enactions there are "cognitive structures," which "emerge from recurrent sensorimotor patterns that enable action to be perceptually guided" (1991: 173). The main effect of the phenomenological move appears to be to redirect attention away from the stability of representational structures and their correspondences to objectively defined entities; attention is redirected toward the dynamic and adaptive emergence of structures in context. In my view, the emphasis in cognitive linguistics on active processes of construal (for example, of figure and ground, perspective, scope, image-schema transformations, etc.) constitutes a more conservative and pragmatic move in the same direction. Whether we speak of representations or cognitive structures does not seem crucial. The former, perhaps mistakenly, retains more of a folk theory of mind; the latter is so abstract as to be nearly empty.

4. Compare Langacker (1990a: 1): "Lexicon, morphology, and syntax form a continuum of symbolic units, divided only arbitrarily into separate components, . . ." (see also 1990a: 115–116 and 343).

5. In my view, this comes very close to saying that language should be viewed as a repertoire of verbal skills.

4. THE SYNTHESIS OF CULTURAL LINGUISTICS

1. I am using the verb *frame* as equivalent to *idealization*, which is the process by which a particular schema is associated with or "applied to" a "full, repletely detailed referent" (Talmy 1983: 258).

2. Opinion, *United States v. Oregon*, Civ. No. 68-513-MA, January 3, 1992. I served as an expert witness for the Colville Confederated Tribes, in which capacity I traced the history of ethnic identities of several Salish-speaking tribes in the Columbia Basin.

3. Ronald Langacker, personal communication (1991).

4. Geertz contrasted interpretive anthropology to cognitive approaches, so it may seem odd to see the assertion that cognitive and cultural linguistics are interpretive, but in 1973 the predominant cognitive approach in anthropology was ethnoscience, which was widely perceived as unduly static. In contemporary cognitive studies, ideas are treated as processes and expectations, rather than frozen structures.

5. Comment on this paper at the 3rd International Cognitive Linguistics Conference.

6. Langacker, personal communication, from a description of cognitive grammar being submitted to the "Instrumentarium" of the handbook being prepared by the International Pragmatics Association, 1993.

7. Ibid.

5. CONCEPTS

1. Tyler (1978: 90) offered a very different view of imagery, based on everyday discourse, that treats it as "subordinated to the unspoken sound of our inner voices" and a "wordless accompaniment to our thought," implying some distinction between imagery and the process of thought itself. He deplored the fact that the languages of psychology and philosophy borrow from ordinary language, but then "attack their common host" (1978: 88).

2. *Oxford English Dictionary*, 2nd ed., prepared by J. A. Simpson and E. S. C. Weiner, vol. 7, Hat–Intervacuum (Oxford: Clarendon Press, 1969), 666.

3. The subscripted dot in ṣ indicates retroflection, that is, the segment is pronounced with the tongue curled toward the roof of the mouth.

4. It is a question of how complex; monkeys are known to recognize kinship relations in unrelated monkeys and to correlate kinship with social status defined as asymmetrical patterns of grooming.

5. I owe this observation to Günter Radden.

6. Fillmore's usage of the term *frame* is widely, but not universally followed. Taylor (1991: 87) defined *frame* as "the knowledge network linking the multiple domains associated with a given linguistic form." He said, "in essence, frames are static configurations of knowledge," giving as an example the *mother* frame: "a mother is a woman who has sexual relations with the father, falls pregnant, gives birth, and then, for the following decade or so, devotes the greater part of her time to nurturing and raising the child, remaining all the while married to the father. In such a situation, all five domains converge" (1991: 88).

Taylor contrasted *frame* with *script*, which he defined as "the temporal sequencing and causal relations which link events and states within certain action frames." But the example appears to contradict his own definition because several of its elements appear to be dynamic, both individually and in their sequencing (having sexual relations, falling pregnant, giving birth, nurturing). I would regard Taylor's *mother* frame as a cognitive model that links scenarios from multiple domains.

7. Casson (1983) provided an excellent review of the concepts of schema, frame, and script.

8. "Symbols, and our understanding of the world, are always unities of fact and feeling" (Tyler 1978: 248).

9. See, for example, Goodenough (1956), Lounsbury (1956), Burling (1964), Lounsbury (1964), and Wallace (1969 [1965]). Wallace attempted to achieve a psychologically valid description of Japanese kinship terms, while Burling argued that componential analyses of kinship terminologies did not necessarily reflect psychological reality.

10. Shakir and Farghal (1991) provided a useful summary of the schema concept.

11. Lakoff used caps to abbreviate trajector and landmark as TR and LM, while Langacker used lowercase letters, *tr* and *lm*. Lakoff's usage suggests that he regarded them as semantic entities, while Langacker's suggests that he regarded them as symbolic entities.

12. In fact, Lakoff presented the terms *instance link* and *similarity link* without defining them and illustrated them in ways that appear to be logically inconsistent.

13. Lakoff depicted the instance link by drawing an arrow from the more specific to the more abstract concept, while Langacker reversed the direction in depicting the relationship of schematicity. See, for example, Langacker (1987: 68) and Lakoff (1987: 424).

14. "Relative arrested in GI's slaying," *Las Vegas Review Journal*, March 26, 1991, 1a, 4a.

15. The schema formulas presented by Agar and Hobbs are a little difficult to read, so I have paraphrased them here.

16. See also Varela, Thompson, and Rosch (1991: 177) and Rosch et al. (1976).

17. But, according to Rosch (1978: 40), "to speak of *a prototype* at all is simply a convenient grammatical fiction; what is really referred to are judgements of degree of prototypicality." In her view, a prototype is not the same as a specific category member or mental structure and is not the same as the use of a mental structure in the processing of information. It is hard for me to see why "the clearest cases of category membership" are not also "specific category member[s]," but Rosch seemed to be objecting to a confusion, in experimental research, of the clearest cases with mental categories. She said, "For natural-language categories, to speak of a single entity that is the prototype is either a gross misunderstanding of the empirical data or a covert theory of mental representation." In my own case, I hope that the theory is not covert.

18. For feature analyses of *bird* and *furniture*, see Bolinger (1992) and Wierzbicka (1992a).

19. Varela, Thompson, and Rosch (1991: 157–171) present an excellent introduction to the psychology and anthropology of basic color terms.

20. See, for example, studies by Berlin (1970) and Brown (1976, 1977, 1979, 1984a, 1984b). See also Eastman (1975) and criticisms of evolutionary semantics in Hunn (1985) and Hunn and Randall (1984).

21. Paul Kay, personal communication (1992).

22. MacLaury (1992: 138–139, footnote) distinguished between a "focus" as "merely the color chip(s) that a consultant chooses as the best example of a color category" and "unique hues," which are "the purest bands of yellow, green, and blue in monochronomatic light, red when the shortwave light cancels its yellowish factor." He avoided the term *focal color*, which confounds focus with unique hue. Strictly speaking, white and black are not unique hues, but they are treated as though they were.

23. See, for example, studies by Frake (1962) and Berlin, Breedlove, and Raven (1973, 1974).

24. See, for example, Bright and Bright (1969), Rosch and Mervis (1975), Randall (1976, 1987), Rosch (1978).

25. Lakoff (1987: 419), I believe inaccurately, described trajector and landmark as "generalizations of the concepts figure and ground," citing Langacker (1986), which is referenced to *Foundations of Cognitive Grammar*, vol. 1, but in *Foundations*

Langacker (1987: 217) defined trajector and landmark as *special cases* of figure and ground—those occurring within a relational profile. Nevertheless, Lakoff's application of the terms to grammatical expressions and schema analysis appears to be consistent with Langacker's practice.

26. NOM = NOMINAL; however, the function of the *s* prefix in Salish is not clearly understood. Kinkade (1983) analyzed it as an aspect marker and recently (1993) found that *s* in Upper Chehalis (Salish) functions to mark imperfectives in directly quoted speech.

27. Bronislaw Malinowski, *Argonauts of the Western Pacific, An Account of Native Enterprise and Adventure in the Archipelagoes of Melanesian New Guinea* (New York: E. P. Dutton and Co., 1961 [1922]), 12.

6. CONNECTING LANGUAGES TO WORLD VIEWS

1. Coyote losing his eyes might be taken as a parable of modern linguistics, which prefers to work only with what it can hear, not with what is seen or imagined.

2. Senate Republican leader Robert Dole is quoted as saying, "We are in the Mideast for three letters—O-I-L," "Three Cheers for Dole," *Las Vegas Review Journal*, October 29, 1990, 9B.

3. Stephen Labash and Emily R. Greenberg, "Misunderstanding Purpose of Free Speech," (Special to the *Baltimore Sun*) *Las Vegas Review Journal*, February 18, 1991, 7B.

4. Heard on Channel 17, Las Vegas, October 15, 1991.

5. I have abbreviated Kövecses's statements.

6. For a more extended treatment of metaphors of love, see Kövecses (1988).

7. Dixon (1986) distinguished between obligatory grammatical *noun classes*, such as those of Bantu languages, Dyirbal, and languages with grammatical gender (e.g., French, German, Latin), and "lexico-syntactic" *noun classifiers*, such as those languages of Southeast Asia and Asia with numeral classifiers. In his scheme, noun classes are closed grammatical systems; classifiers are free forms. Noun classes are concordial, marking other words besides the noun word; classifiers are never concordial outside the noun phrase. Noun classes have fixed meanings; classifiers acquire meanings in context. Navajo and Apache do not fit easily into this system.

In my view, Dixon's observations on class and classifier functions and semantics would be hard to sustain, for reasons that will become apparent in this chapter. I suspect that a continuum stretches between these prototypical notions of class and classifier systems and I would prefer to use the term *classifier* for all such systems, but, in the interest of interdisciplinary discourse, I will follow Dixon's usage where possible.

Colette G. Craig (1986: 4) in fact asserted that Jacaltec lies somewhere in between, "at the fuzzy edges," that Yagua classifiers are "both numeral and concordial and both inflectional and derivational," and, finally, that "a number of North American languages . . . exhibit a secondary type of classification through a process of noun incorporation originally developed as a predicate qualifying system." Setsuko Kiyomi (1992) agreed that it is not possible to divide all classifying languages into two clear-cut prototypes. He proposed instead to use purely morphological criteria, dividing them into languages with free morpheme classifiers (numeral or non-numeral) and bound morpheme classifiers (concordial, predicate, and intra-locative). Predicate classifiers correspond to the classificatory verbs of Navajo. Intra-locative classifiers are affixed to locative expressions that obligatorily co-occur with nouns.

8. In addition to what appears in the table, Creider (1975) included more examples, spellings for Proto-Bantu roots, and lists of exceptions to the classes.

9. If we think of noun classifiers as nominal heads, then Coeur d'Alene lexical suffixes grammatically resemble objects of English prepositions more closely than they resemble noun classifiers. However, if we think of noun classifiers as abstract landmarks in Langacker's (1987, 1990a) sense, whose nouns are connected to them by such relations as PART OF SCENE and SIMILAR TO, as well as INSTANCE OF, then perhaps they are not so different (see Chapter 9).

10. I am indebted to Kennedy G. Ondieki, originally from near Nyaribaii in Kisii, currently a student at the University of Nevada, Las Vegas, for information that led me to the hypothesis of a domain of experience centering around ancestral spirits. Kennedy explained to me that chief and medicine man are roles that require clairvoyance and prophecy, the ability to discern events that lie beyond the reach of ordinary senses. The medicine man, in particular, must diagnose diseases, sometimes by reading the sparks emitted by a fire. He also asserted that the terms for dog and nose belong in the same class with wild animals because wild animals are hunted with dogs and by smell. However, in Kisii, unlike Proto-Bantu, the terms for chief and medicine man belong to the same noun class as other persons; spark remains in the same class with animals.

Many of the ethnographic and linguistic data on Shona on which the following discussion is based are taken from a paper by Dorothea Neal Arin (n.d.). The paper was written for a seminar on cognitive anthropology at the University of Nevada, Las Vegas.

11. I have abbreviated some of his category descriptions and presented only a few representative verb stem glosses. Basso's description of Apache verb classes is much more formal and complete. I have replaced formal specifications, such as "length is at least three times greater than their width or height" (−−> "long"), and omitted negative specifications "nonanimal," "unenclosed in a container," and "length is less than three times as great as their width or height."

12. See note 9 above.

13. I was a student in a class in the Yaqui language conducted at the 1989 Linguistic Institute at the University of Arizona in Tucson. The instructor was Eloise Jelinek. She is not responsible for the conclusions that I draw here.

14. This was my recollection in 1992. Inexplicably, I apparently made no notes on this point. I also have a static description of the duck on the water.

15. The citations are from Sapir in Mandelbaum (1949: 162) and Whorf (1952: 5) in Hoijer (1954b: 92–94).

16. By "the Chinese language" Bloom apparently meant Cantonese and Mandarin or Southern Min, since his research was conducted in Hong Kong and Taiwan.

7. DISCOURSE AND NARRATIVE

1. In Figure 1a, Langacker (1990b: 7) represented the subjective viewer as outside the perceptual field, but he was not attempting to represent the viewer's perception of the discourse itself. I am proposing that observer's perception of discourse in which observer is a participant always involves at least some residual representation of observer.

2. In footnotes Wierzbicka (1992b, n.d.) stated that the natural semantic metalanguage includes the following elements:

[substantives] I, you, someone, something, people
[determiners, quantifiers] this, the same, other, one, two, many (much), all
[mental predicates] know, want, think, feel, say
[actions, events] do, happen
[evaluative] good, bad
[descriptors] big, small
[intensifier] very
[meta-predicates] can, if, because, no (negation), like (how)
[time and place] when, where, after (before), under (above)
[taxonomy, partonymy] kind of, part of

3. "Make your conversational contribution such as is required, at the stage at which it occurs, by the accepted purpose or direction of the talk exchange in which you are engaged" (Grice 1975: 45).

4. Kay and Fillmore appear to regard construction grammar as generative and therefore to regard cognitive and generative approaches as compatible. See Fillmore, Kay, and O'Connor (1988).

5. Sweetser (1987) proposed a more involved answer to the ranking found by Coleman and Kay, based upon a decision tree, but I confess that I find it a bit obscure.

6. Line numbers, pause markers, and interruption markers are omitted.

7. Gumperz (1992: 232) asserted that contextualization cues "function relationally and cannot be assigned context-independent, stable, core lexical meanings." I would argue that honorifics can be assigned stable, conventional meanings, in that they predicate highly schematic social scenarios, though I would agree that much of their meaning comes from their strategic use in framing the context of discourse. The same may be true of many other kinds of contextualization cues. For an example, see Basso (1992: 267), who found that "the Kalapalo evidence contradicts Gumperz' assertion that contextualization cues are 'marginal or semantically insignificant.' "

8. Similarly, Hill and Irvine (1993: 1) observed that "many aspects of linguistic form may usefully be seen as having interactional processes profoundly embedded in them."

9. This usage of *discursive* is a nominalization of the adjectival form of *discourse*, that is, 'pertaining to discourse,' not one of its more conventional dictionary senses of digression, the subject of discourse, or proceeding by reasoning or argument.

10. This is an example of what Silverstein (1976: 33) called "indexical presupposition."

11. Hale, drawing upon the framework of transformational generative grammar, would say that narrative devices operate to transform and distort the backbone.

12. The correspondence is not perfect. Hale is not responsible for my construal of his framework.

13. For a representation of multiple, nonlineal dependencies in plot and subplot, see Palmer (1980).

14. The first two are from Alan Dundes's (1964, 1965) sequences of "Lack-Lack Liquidated" and "Interdiction-Violation-Consequence-Attempted Escape."

15. For a discussion of persecution and revenge motifs, see Palmer (1980).

16. In the original text, a listener makes conventional responses to each line. I have deleted them because they detract from readability and our primary interest is in content rather than performance. However, I have retained spaces, which indicate pauses, and dashes, which indicate prolongations.

17. See, for example, Dundes (1964, 1965), Powlison (1965), Colby (1973), Rumelhart (1975), Beaugrande (1979), Black and Wilensky (1979), Palmer (1980), and Mandler (1984).

18. I have made changes in format in order to improve readability.

8. METAPHOR AND METONYMY

1. While Basso regarded the human body as the primary source of the metaphor, House (n.d.: 5) argued on the basis of Navajo evidence that it was more likely the horse: "While the horse model may be said to be functional, the 'man' model has no functional justification and, to me, appears to be motivated by a purely anthropocentric impulse." House also reported that only 28 of a corpus of 121 Navajo automobile part terms were extensions of anatomical terms. Most of the remaining terms were "descriptive of the appearance or activity of the automobile part"(n.d.: 8).

2. The expression MOTOR VEHICLES ARE ANIMATE THINGS illustrates an orthographic convention: concepts underlying metaphorical or metonymical usages are printed in small caps. More generally, small caps flag meanings, that is, semantic as opposed to phonological values.

3. Blythin is a professor in the School of Communications at the University of Nevada at Las Vegas.

4. Dirven (1991: 5) referred to the combination of elements in a sociocultural context as a *sociocultural syntagm*. He cited the example of *tea*, which may refer in British English to the shrub, to the leaves, or to the meals *afternoon tea* and *high tea*. The extension of the term to meals is metonymy based upon the sociocultural syntagm.

9. CONSTRUCTING AND DECONSTRUCTING WORD AND SENTENCE GRAMMAR

1. "The rules of language are discrete combinatorial systems: phonemes snap cleanly into morphemes, morphemes into words, words into phrases. They do not blend or melt or coalesce . . ." (Pinker 1994: 163).

2. The example was borrowed by Fillmore from K. E. Zimmer.

3. Langacker, personal communication (1972).

4. We could argue that the construction itself, rather than any of its constituents, determines the profile, but Langacker's formula works for English compound nouns.

5. Bybee (1985) noted that "typically, 'incorporation' refers to the inclusion of the nominal patient of the verb within the verb . . . ," but limiting the concept to the patient, as opposed to an agent or oblique object, seems a somewhat arbitrary distinction and not necessary for the purposes of this discussion, which is concerned with general characteristics of constructions rather than *a priori* definitions.

6. Bybee actually wrote "modify inherent characteristics of the referent," but I am using the term *modify* in a different sense here, as the element that adds specific information to a profile determinant.

7. Lakoff (1990: 57) found that states are understood, in English, as bounded regions in space; processes are understood as movements.

8. See also Palmer (1990).

9. I have taken the liberty of substituting a more modern orthography for what I hope are corresponding characters in Boas's difficult notation. Since the substitutions are consistent, it will not affect the point I am making even if I am wrong about the exact phonetic values.

10. In Figure 44 I have represented the absolutive as a relation between an unspecified process or state overall (its landmark) and the patient or object *nčəmíčəɲičt* 'surface in the back of the hand' (its trajector). The interested reader may compare Langacker (1991: 398–408). I have made the perhaps unwarranted assumption that the nominal 'surface' remains in the profile of the absolutive construction at the highest level.

11. For further discussion of Coeur d'Alene anatomical and geographical nomenclature, see Palmer (1990) and Palmer and Nicodemus (1985).

12. The problem is discussed in Palmer (n.d.b). Ogawa and Palmer (1994) presented an analysis of Coeur d'Alene *t*, which is doubtless cognate with Columbian *t*.

13. The diagram of *n* as a complex category is revised from that presented in Palmer (1990).

14. MDL = middle voice.

15. [Dwérme] is also the second person singular of the familiar imperative.

10. CULTURAL PHONOLOGY

1. The example is from Wolfram and Johnson (1982: 45).

2. *Cognitive phonology*, as I use the term, is not to be confused with cognitive phonology as a subfield of generative grammar, as developed by Kaye (1989). In

Kaye's extreme linguistic rationalism, phonological theory contributes to universal grammar, according to which Chinese and English are "nearly identical" languages, with differences which are "relatively minor," nothing more than different values on a set of binary parameters. Kay (1989: 54) said, "One may think of human linguistic capacity as a great printer with a series of dip switches under its cover. Going from English to Chinese to Navajo to Swahili is simply a question of setting of these switches." The digital electronic metaphor for language could hardly be stated more clearly and unequivocally.

3. The prototypicality of [kʰ] was a guess based on the high salience of initial /k/ and the status of [kʰ] as the most distant variant from its voiced counterpart /g/. Jaeger did not present experimental evidence that the prototype of /k/ is [k]. Compare Lakoff (1987: 61).

4. We could draw more dotted arrows to illustrate prototype-variant relations on level II and more solid arrows to show that items on level I elaborate the schema on level III. Of course, we could simplify the diagram by eliminating level II altogether, but Langacker's theory leads us to believe that it has psychological reality.

5. Following Langacker's usage in this context, the brackets signify conceptual frames rather than phonetic values.

6. Margaret Langdon, personal communication (Linguistic Institute, Tucson, Arizona, 1989).

7. /+ consonant, − continuant, − voiced, + back, − coronal, + round/, /+ voiced, + sonorant, − round, − back/, /+ consonant, + continuant, + voiced, + sonorant, + coronal, − round, − nasal/.

8. It is difficult to have complete confidence in the analysis of the vowels, because they are theoretical entities in that they undergo progressive vowel harmony and regressive lowering in the environment of low, back consonants.

9. Langacker (1987: 277) listed "conceptual (as well as phonological) autonomy and dependence" as one of four "valence factors" involved in grammatical constructions. The other three are correspondence, profile determinacy, and constituency. The combination of two or more symbolic structures presupposes a grammatical valence relation of some kind.

10. In Shaw's (1989) terms, the *l* is prosodically licensed at the level of the mora, the lowest level in her framework. For an explanation of metrical phonology, see Hogg and McCully (1987).

11. Jackendoff (1986: 132) argued that Wertheimer's basic principles of grouping, when applied to music, are expressed in "grouping well-formedness rules" and "grouping preference rules," some of which apply locally (to lower level units) and some globally (to higher level units). His grouping well-formedness rules for music are as follows: "a group must be constituted out of a sequence of contiguous events; a piece must be exhaustively segmented into groups; although a group may be completely embedded in another group, it may not overlap a boundary of a group that contains it." It is not clear whether he regarded such rules of musical cognition as

innate human faculties or as specific to Western music. Goldsmith (1976: 36) proposed a similar rule for phonology, stipulating that "all vowels are associated with at least one tone," "all tones are associated with at least one vowel," and "association lines do not cross."

12. Heard by the author in conversation in April 1992.

REFERENCES CITED

Abrahams, Roger D.
  1989 Black Talking on the Streets. In Richard Bauman and Joel Sherzer (eds.), *Explorations in the Ethnography of Speaking*, 240–262. Cambridge: Cambridge University Press.
Abu-Lughod, Lila
  1986 *Veiled Sentiments: Honor and Poetry in a Bedouin Society*. Berkeley: University of California Press.
Adams, Karen L., and Nancy F. Conklin
  1973 Toward a Theory of Natural Classification. In Claudia Corum, T. Cedric Smith-Stark, and Ann Weiser (eds.), *Papers from the Ninth Regional Meeting Chicago Linguistic Society, April 13–15, 1973*, 1–10. Chicago: Chicago Linguistic Society.
Agar, Michael
  1973 *Ripping and Running: A Formal Ethnography of Urban Heroin Addicts*. New York: Seminar Press.
  1994 *Language Shock/Understanding the Culture of Conversation*. New York: William Morrow and Company.
Agar, Michael H., and Jerry R. Hobbs
  1985 How to Grow Schemata out of Interviews. In Janet W. D. Dougherty (ed.), *Directions in Cognitive Anthropology*, 413–431. Urbana and Chicago: University of Illinois Press.
Alverson, Hoyt
  1991 Metaphor and Experience: Looking Over the Notion of Image Schema. In James W. Fernandez (ed.), *Beyond Metaphor: The Theory of Tropes in Anthropology*, 94–117. Stanford: Stanford University Press.
Arin, Dorothea Neal
  n.d. Of Medicine Men, Mediums and Chiefs: Bantu Noun Classes. Unpublished manuscript in possession of the author.
Au, T. K.
  1983 Chinese and English Counterfactuals: The Sapir-Whorf Hypothesis Revisited. *Cognition* 15: 155–187.

Bagemihl, Bruce
    1991   Syllable Structure in Bella Coola. *Linguistic Inquiry* 22: 589–646.

Bartlett, F.
    1932   *Remembering*. Cambridge: Cambridge University Press.

Basso, Ellen B.
    1992   Contextualization in Kalapalo Narratives. In Alessandro Duranti and Charles Goodwin (eds.), *Rethinking Context: Language as an Interactive Phenomenon*, 253–269. Cambridge: Cambridge University Press.

Basso, Keith
    1976   "Wise Words" of the Western Apache: Metaphor and Semantic Theory. In Keith H. Basso and Harry A. Selby (eds.), *Meaning in Anthropology*, 93–121. Albuquerque: University of New Mexico Press.
    1984   "Stalking with Stories": Names, Places, and Moral Narratives among the Western Apache. In Edward M. Bruner (ed.), *Text, Play and Story*, 19–55. Washington, D.C.: AES.
    1990a "To Give Up on Words": Silence in Apache Culture. In Donal Carbaugh (ed.), *Cultural Communication and Intercultural Contact*, 303–320. Hillsdale: Lawrence Erlbaum Associates, Publishers.
    1990b *Western Apache Language and Culture: Essays in Linguistic Anthropology*. Tucson: University of Arizona Press.

Beaugrande, Robert de, and Benjamin N. Colby
    1979   Narrative Models of Action and Interaction. *Cognitive Science* 3: 43–66.

Beaugrande, Robert de, and Wolfgang Dressler
    1981   *Introduction to Text Linguistics*. London and New York: Longman.

Berlin, Brent
    1970   A Universalist-Evolutionary Approach in Ethnographic Semantics. In Ann Fischer (ed.), *Current Directions in Anthropology*, 3–18. Washington, D.C.: American Anthropological Association.
    1972   Speculations on the Growth of Ethnobotanical Nomenclature. *Language in Society* 1: 51–86.
    1992   *Ethnobiological Classification: Principles of Categorization of Plants and Animals in Traditional Societies*. Princeton: N.J.: Princeton University Press.

Berlin, Brent, Dennis E. Breedlove, and Peter H. Raven
    1966   Folk Taxonomies and Biological Classification. *Science* 154: 273–275.
    1973   General Principles of Classification and Nomenclature in Folk Biology. *American Anthropologist* 75: 214–242.
    1974   *Principles of Tzeltal Plant Classification*. New York: Academic Press.

Berlin, Brent, and Paul Kay
    1969   *Basic Color Terms: Their Universality and Evolution*. Berkeley: University of California Press.

Biesele, Megan
   1986 How Hunter-Gatherers' Stories "Make Sense": Semantics and Adaptation. *Cultural Anthropology* 1: 157–170.
Black, John B., and Robert Wilensky
   1979 An Evaluation of Story Grammars. *Cognitive Science* 3: 213–230.
Black, Mary B., and Duane Metzger
   1969 Ethnographic Description and the Study of Law. In Stephen A. Tyler (ed.), *Cognitive Anthropology*, 137–165. New York: Holt, Rinehart, and Winston.
Bloom, Alfred
   1981 *The Linguistic Shaping of Thought: A Study in the Impact of Language on Thinking in China and the West.* Hillsdale, N.J.: Lawrence Erlbaum Associates, Publishers.
Bloom, A. H.
   1984 Caution—The Words You Use May Affect What You Say: A Response to Au. *Cognition* 17: 275–287.
Boas, Franz
   1939 *Geographical Names of the Kwakiutl Indians.* Contributions to Anthropology no. 20. New York: Columbia University.
   1966 *Introduction to Handbook of American Indian Languages.* Lincoln: University of Nebraska Press.
Bolinger, Dwight
   1992 About Furniture and Birds. *Cognitive Linguistics* 3: 111–117.
Booth, Wayne C.
   1979 Metaphor as Rhetoric: The Problem of Evaluation. In Sheldon Sacks (ed.), *On Metaphor*, 47–70. Chicago: University of Chicago Press.
Bregman, Albert S.
   1990 *Auditory Scene Analysis: The Perceptual Organization of Sound.* Cambridge, Mass.: MIT Press.
Bright, Jane O., and William Bright
   1969 Semantic Structures in Northwestern California and the Sapir-Whorf Hypothesis. *American Anthropologist* 67: 249–258.
Bright, William
   1990 "With One Lip, with Two Lips": Parallelism in Nahuatl. *Language* 66: 437–452.
Brody, Jill
   1991 Indirection in the Negotiation of Self in Everyday Tojolabál Women's Conversation. *Journal of Linguistic Anthropology* 1: 78–96.
Brown, Cecil H.
   1976 General Principles of Human Anatomical Partonomy and Speculations on the Growth of Partonomic Nomenclature. *American Ethnologist* 3: 400–424.

1977 Folk Botanical Life-Forms: Their Universality and Growth. *American Anthropologist* 79: 317–342.

1979 Folk Zoological Life-Forms: Their Universality and Growth. *American Anthropologist* 81: 791–817.

1984a The Growth of Ethnobiological Nomenclature. *Current Anthropology* 27: 1–19.

1984b *Language and Living Things: Uniformities in Folk Classification and Naming.* New Brunswick, N.J.: Rutgers University Press.

Brown, Cecil H., and Stanley R. Witkowski

1981 Figurative Language in Universalist Perspective. *American Ethnologist* 8: 596–615.

1983 Polysemy, Lexical Change and Cultural Importance. *Man* n.s. 18: 72–89.

Brugman, Claudia

1983 The Use of Body-Part Terms as Locatives in Chalcatongo Mixtec. In Alice Schlichter, Wallace Chafe, and Leanne Hinton (eds.), *Survey of California and Other Indian Languages*, 235–290. Studies in Mesoamerican Linguistics. Report no. 4. Berkeley: Survey of California and Other Indian Languages.

1988 *The Story of Over: Polysemy, Semantics, and Structure of the Lexicon.* New York: Garland Publishing.

Bruner, Edward M.

1986a Ethnography as Narrative. In Victor W. Turner and Edward M. Bruner (eds.), *The Anthropology of Experience*, 139–155. Urbana: University of Illinois Press.

1986b Experience and Its Expressions. In Victor W. Turner and Edward M. Bruner (eds.), *The Anthropology of Experience*, 3–30. Urbana: University of Illinois Press.

Bruner, Jerome

1986 *Actual Minds, Possible Worlds.* Cambridge, Mass.: Harvard University Press.

1990 *Acts of Meaning.* Cambridge, Mass.: Harvard University Press.

Bullock, Charles

1970 *The Mashona.* Westport, Conn.: Negro Universities Press (reprint of 1928 edition).

Burling, Robbins

1964 Cognition and Componential Analysis: God's Truth or Hocus-Pocus? *American Anthropologist* 66: 20–28.

1970 *Man's Many Voices: Language in Its Cultural Context.* New York: Holt, Rinehart and Winston.

Bybee, Joan L.

1985 *Morphology: A Study of the Relation between Meaning and Form.* Philadelphia: John Benjamins Publishing Company.

Carbaugh, Donal

    1990a *Cultural Communication and Intercultural Contact*. Hillsdale, N.J.: Lawrence Erlbaum Associates, Publishers.

    1990b Culture Talking about Itself. In Donal Carbaugh (ed.), *Cultural Communication and Intercultural Contact*, 1–9. Hillsdale, N.J.: Lawrence Erlbaum Associates, Publishers.

Casad, Eugene

    1993 "Locations," "Paths" and the Cora Verb. In Richard A. Geiger and Brygida Rudzka-Ostyn (eds.), *Conceptualizations and Mental Processing in Language*, 593–645. Berlin: Mouton de Gruyter.

Casad, Eugene, and Ronald Langacker

    1985 "Inside" and "Outside" in Cora Grammar. *International Journal of American Linguistics* 51: 247–281.

Casagrande, J. B., and K. L. Hale

    1967 Semantic Relations in Papago Folk Definitions. In D. Hymes and W. E. Bittle (eds.), *Studies in Southwestern Ethnolinguistics*, 165–196. Mouton: The Hague.

Casson, Ronald W.

    1981 *Language, Culture, and Cognition: Anthropological Perspectives*. New York: Macmillan Publishing Company.

    1983 Schemata in Cognitive Anthropology. In Bernard J. Siegel, Alan R. Beals, and Stephen A. Tyler (eds.), *Annual Review of Anthropology*, 429–462. Palo Alto: Annual Reviews.

Chafe, Wallace

    1990 Some Things That Narratives Tell Us about the Mind. In Bruce K. Britton and A. D. Pellegrini (eds.), *Narrative Thought and Narrative Language*, 79–98. Hillsdale, N.J.: Lawrence Erlbaum Associates.

    1991 Grammatical Subjects in Speaking and Writing. *Text* 11: 45–72.

Cheng, P. W.

    1985 Pictures of Ghosts: A Critique of Alfred Bloom's *The Linguistic Shaping of Thought*. *American Anthropologist* 87: 917–922.

Clark, Herbert H., and Susan E. Haviland

    1977 Comprehension and the Given-New Contract. In Roy O. Freedle (ed.), *Discourse Production and Comprehension*, 1–40. Norwood, N.J.: Ablex Publishing Corporation.

Clark, John, and Colin Yallop

    1990 *An Introduction to Phonetics and Phonology*. Oxford: Basil Blackwell.

Clifford, James

    1986 Introduction: Partial Truths. In James Clifford (ed.), *Writing Culture: The Poetics and Politics of Ethnography*, 1–26. Berkeley: University of California Press.

Colby, B. N.
  1973 A Partial Grammar of Eskimo Folktales. *American Anthropologist* 75: 645–662.

Coleman, Linda, and Paul Kay
  1981 Prototype Semantics. *Language* 57: 26–44.

Comrie, Bernard
  1989 *Language Universals and Linguistic Typology: Syntax and Morphology.* 2nd ed. Chicago: University of Chicago Press.

Conklin, Harold C.
  1964 Hanunóo Color Categories. In Dell Hymes (ed.), *Language in Culture and Society: A Reader in Linguistics and Anthropology,* 189–192. New York: Harper and Row, Publishers.

Cook, Haruko Minegishi
  1991 The Japanese Particle *Yo* as a Non-referential Indexical. Paper presented at the 2nd International Cognitive Linguistics Conference, University of California at Santa Cruz, July 29–August 2, 1991.

Craig, Colette G.
  1986 Introduction. In Colette Craig (ed.), *Noun Classes and Categorization,* 1–10. Amsterdam: John Benjamins.

Creider, Chet A.
  1975 The Semantic System of Noun Classes in Proto-Bantu. *Anthropological Linguistics* 17: 127–138.

Crystal, David
  1985 *A Dictionary of Linguistics and Phonetics.* 2nd ed. Cambridge, Mass.: Basil Blackwell.

D'Andrade, Roy Goodwin
  1981 The Cultural Part of Cognition. *Cognitive Science* 5: 179–195.
  1984 Cultural Meaning Systems. In Richard A. Shweder and Robert A. LeVine (eds.), *Culture Theory: Essays on Mind, Self, and Emotion,* 88–119. Cambridge: Cambridge University Press.
  1995 *The Development of Cognitive Anthropology.* Cambridge: Cambridge University Press.

Deane, Paul
  1992 *Grammar in Mind and Brain: Explorations in Cognitive Syntax.* New York: Mouton de Gruyter.

Denny, J. Peter
  1979 The 'Extendedness' Variable in Classifier Semantics: Universal Features and Cultural Variation. In Madeleine Mathiot (ed.), *Ethnolinguistics: Boas, Sapir, and Whorf Revisited,* 97–119. The Hague: Mouton Publishers.
  1986 The Semantic Role of Noun Classifiers. In Colette Craig (ed.), *Noun Classes and Categorization,* 297–308. Amsterdam: John Benjamins.

Denny, J. Peter, and Chet A. Creider

    1986 The Semantics of Noun Classes in Proto-Bantu. In Colette Craig (ed.), *Noun Classes and Categorization*, 217–239. Amsterdam: John Benjamins.

Dewell, Robert B.

    1993 OVER Again: Image-Schema Transformations in Semantic Analysis. Paper presented at the 3rd International Cognitive Linguistics Conference, Leuven, Belgium, July 18–24, 1993.

Dinneen, Francis P.

    1967 *An Introduction to General Linguistics*. New York: Holt, Rinehart and Winston.

Dirven, René

    1991 Metonymy and Metaphor: Different Mental Strategies of Conceptualization. Paper presented at the 2nd International Cognitive Linguistics Conference, University of California at Santa Cruz, July 29–August 2, 1991.

Dixon, R. M. W.

    1982 *Where Have All the Adjectives Gone?* Berlin: Walter de Gruyter.

    1986 Noun Classes and Noun Classification in Typological Perspective. In Colette Craig (ed.), *Noun Classes and Categorization*, 105–112. Amsterdam: John Benjamins.

Doe, John

    1988 *Speak into the Mirror: A Story of Linguistic Anthropology*. Landham, Md.: University Press of America.

Dougherty, Janet W. E.

    1985 *Directions in Cognitive Anthropology*. Urbana: University of Illinois Press.

Downing, Pamela

    1977 On the Creation and Use of English Compound Nouns. *Language* 53: 810–842.

Driver, H. E.

    1969 *Indians of North America*. 2nd ed. Chicago: University of Chicago Press.

Dundes, Alan

    1964 *The Morphology of American Indian Folktales*. Folklore Fellows Communications 195. Helsinki: Suomalainen Tiedeakatemia.

    1965 Structural Typology in North American Indian Folktales. In Alan Dundes (ed.), *The Study of Folklore*, 206–215. Englewood Cliffs, N.J.: Prentice-Hall.

    1972 Untitled letter. *Current Anthropology* 13: 92–93.

Duranti, Alessandro

    1988 Ethnography of Speaking: Toward a Linguistics of the Praxis. In Frederick J. Newmeyer (ed.), *Linguistics: The Cambridge Survey*, vol. 4: *Language: The Sociocultural Context*, 210–228. Cambridge: Cambridge University Press.

Eastman, Carol
>   1975 *Aspects of Language and Culture*. San Francisco: Chandler and Sharp Publishers.

Eco, Umberto
>   1989 *Foucault's Pendulum*. San Diego: Harcourt, Brace and Jovanovich, Publishers.

Ellis, Donald G.
>   1991 Post-Structuralism and Language: Non-Sense. *Communication Monographs* 58: 213–224.

Ellis, H. D.
>   1986 Introduction to Aspects of Face Processing: Ten Questions in Need of Answers. In Hadyn D. Ellis, Malcolm A. Jeeves, Freda Newcombe, and Andy Young (eds.), *Aspects of Face Processing*, 3–13. Dordrecht: Martinus Nijhoff Publishers.

Evans, R. I.
>   1976 *The Making of Psychology*. New York: Alfred A. Knopf.

Farah, Martha J., Patricia A. McMullen, and Michael M. Meyer
>   1991 Can Recognition of Living Things Be Selectively Impaired? *Neuropsychologia* 29: 185–193.

Feld, Steven
>   1990 *Sound and Sentiment: Birds, Weeping, Poetics, and Song in Kaluli Expression*. Philadelphia: University of Pennsylvania Press.
>   1991 Voices of the Rainforest. 360° Publishing (ASCAP). Audio CD.

Fernandez, James W.
>   1986 *Persuasions and Performances: The Play of Tropes in Culture*. Bloomington: Indiana University Press.

Fillmore, Charles J.
>   1975 Topics in Lexical Semantics. In Roger W. Cole (ed.), *Current Issues in Linguistics*, 76–138. Bloomington: Indiana University Press.
>   1984 Some Thoughts on the Boundaries and Components of Linguistics. In Thomas G. Bever, John M. Carroll, and Lance A. Miller (eds.), *Talking Minds: The Study of Language in Cognitive Science*, 73–108. Cambridge, Mass.: MIT Press.

Fillmore, Charles, Paul Kay, and Mary Catherine O'Connor.
>   1988 Regularity and Idiomaticity in Grammatical Constructions. *Language* 64: 501–538.

Finke, Ronald A.
>   1989 *Principles of Mental Imagery*. Cambridge, Mass.: MIT Press.

Fortune, G.
>   1955 *An Analytical Grammar of SHONA*. London: Longmans, Green and Company.

Frake, Charles O.

1961 The Diagnosis of Disease among the Subanun of Mindanao. *American Anthropologist* 63: 113–132.

1962 The Ethnographic Study of Cognitive Systems. In Stephen A. Tyler (ed.), *Cognitive Anthropology*, 28–41. New York: Holt, Rinehart and Winston. Reprinted from *Anthropology and Human Behavior*. Washington, D.C.: Anthropological Society of Washington.

1969 A Structural Description of Subanun "Religious Behavior." In Stephen A. Tyler (ed.), *Cognitive Anthropology*, 470–487. New York: Holt, Rinehart and Winston.

1981 Plying Frames Can Be Dangerous: Some Reflections on Methodology in Cognitive Anthropology. In Ronald W. Casson (ed.), *Language, Culture, and Cognition*, 366–377. New York: Macmillan Publishing Company.

Friedrich, Paul

1975 The Lexical Symbol and Its Non-arbitrariness. In M. Dale Kinkade, Kenneth L. Hale, and Oswald Werner (eds.), *Linguistics and Anthropology in Honor of C. F. Voegelin*, 199–247. Lisse: Peter De Ridder Press.

1979 *Language, Context, and the Imagination: Essays by Paul Friedrich*. Stanford: Stanford University Press.

1991 Polytropy. In James W. Fernandez (ed.), *Beyond Metaphor: The Theory of Tropes in Anthropology*, 17–55. Stanford: Stanford University Press.

Fry, Peter

1976 *Spirits of Protest*. Cambridge: Cambridge University Press.

Fung Yu-Lan

1966 *A Short History of Chinese Philosophy*. New York: Free Press (Macmillan).

Gardner, Howard

1985 *The Mind's New Science: A History of the Cognitive Revolution*. New York: Basic Books, Publishers.

Geertz, Clifford

1957 Ethos, World-view, and the Analysis of Sacred Symbols. *Antioch Review* 17: 421–437.

1973 *The Interpretation of Cultures*. New York: Basic Books, Publishers.

Gelfand, Michael

1956 *Medicine and Magic of the Mashona*. Cape Town, Wynberg, and Johannesburg: Juta and Company.

1959 *Shona Ritual with Special References to the Chaminuka Cult*. Cape Town, Wynberg, and Johannesburg: Juta and Company.

1964 *Witch Doctor: Traditional Medicine Men of Rhodesia*. Cape Town, Wynberg, and Johannesburg: Juta and Company.

1965 *African Background: The Traditional Culture of the Shona-Speaking People*. Cape Town, Wynberg, and Johannesburg: Juta and Company.

1973 *The Genuine Shona: Survival Values of an African Culture*. Gwelo, Zimbabwe: Mambo Press.

Gibbs, Raymond W.
  1994 *The Poetics of Mind: Figurative Thought, Language, and Understanding.*
        Cambridge: Cambridge University Press.
Gilsenan, Michael
  1976 Lying, Honor, and Contradiction. In Bruce Kapferer (ed.), *Transaction and
        Meaning: Directions in the Anthropology of Exchange and Symbolic Be-
        havior*, 191–219. Philadelphia: Institute for the Study of Human Issues.
Givon, T.
  1992 The Grammar of Referential Coherence as Mental Processing Instructions.
        Linguistics 30: 5–55.
Goldsmith, John
  1976 An Overview of Autosegmental Phonology. *Linguistic Analysis* 2: 23–68.
  1990 *Autosegmental and Metrical Phonology.* Oxford: Basil Blackwell.
Goodenough, Ward H.
  1956 Componential Analysis and the Study of Meaning. *Language* 32: 195–216.
Goodwin, Charles, and Alessandro Duranti
  1992 Rethinking Context: An Introduction. In Alessandro Duranti and Charles
        Goodwin (eds.), *Rethinking Context: Language as an Interactive Phenome-
        non*, 1–42. Cambridge: Cambridge University Press.
Goodwin, Marjorie H.
  1990 *He-Said-She-Said: Talk as Social Organization among Black Children.*
        Bloomington: Indiana University Press.
Grice, H. P.
  1975 Logic and Conversation. In Peter Cole and Jerry L. Morgan (eds.), *Syntax
        and Semantics 3: Speech Acts*, 41–58. New York: Academic Press.
Gumperz, John J.
  1982 *Discourse Strategies.* Cambridge: Cambridge University Press.
  1992 Contextualization and Understanding. In Alessandro Duranti and Charles
        Goodwin (eds.), *Rethinking Context: Language as an Interactive Phenome-
        non*, 229–252. Cambridge: Cambridge University Press.
Gumperz, J. J., and Stephen C. Levinson
  1991 Rethinking Linguistic Anthropology. *Current Anthropology* 32: 613–623.
Guthrie, Malcolm
  1967 *Comparative Bantu: An Introduction to the Comparative Linguistics and
        Prehistory of the Bantu Languages.* Vol. 1. Farnborough, Hants, England:
        Gregg Press.
Haas, Mary R.
  1967 Language and Taxonomy in Northwestern California. *American Anthro-
        pologist* 69: 358–362.
Hale, Austin
  1984 A Discourse Pecking Order. In Robert E. Longacre (ed.), *Theory and Appli-
        cation in Processing Texts in Non-Indoeuropean Languages*, 1–24. Ham-
        burg: Buske.

Hale, Kenneth

    1973 A Note on Subject-Object Inversion in Navajo. In Braj B. Kachru et al. (eds.), *Issues in Linguistics: Papers in Honor of Henry and Renée Kahane*, 300–309. Urbana: University of Illinois Press.

Halle, Morris

    1988 The Immanent Form of Phonemes. In William Hirst (ed.), *The Making of Cognitive Science: Essays in Honor of George A. Miller*, 167–183. Cambridge: Cambridge University Press.

Hanks, W. F.

    1989 Text and Textuality. *Annual Review of Anthropology* 18: 95–127.

    1993 Metalanguage and Pragmatics of Deixis. In John A. Lucy (ed.), *Reflexive Language: Reported Speech and Metapragmatics*, 127–157. Cambridge: Cambridge University Press.

Harris, Randy A.

    1993 *The Linguistics Wars*. New York: Oxford University Press.

Hatano, G.

    1982 Cognitive Barriers in Intercultural Understanding [review of A. H. Bloom, *The Linguistic Shaping of Thought: A Study in the Impact of Language on Thinking in China and the West*, and S. Bochner (ed.), *The Mediating Person: Bridges between Cultures*]. *Contemporary Psychology* 27: 819–820.

Hendrikse, A. P., and G. P. Poulos

    1994 Word Categories—Prototypes and Continua in Southern Bantu. *South African Journal of Linguistics*, Supplement 20: 215–245.

Hill, Jane H.

    1988 Language, Culture, and World View. In Frederick J. Newmeyer (ed.), *Linguistics: The Cambridge Survey*, vol. 4: *Language: The Sociocultural Context*, 14–36. Cambridge: Cambridge University Press.

    1992 The Flower World of Old Uto-Aztecan. *Journal of Anthropological Research* 48: 117–145.

Hill, Jane H., and Kenneth C. Hill

    1986 *Speaking Mexicano: Dynamics of Syncretic Language in Central Mexico*. Tucson: University of Arizona Press.

Hill, Jane H., and Judith T. Irvine

    1993 Introduction. In Jane H. Hill and Judith T. Irvine (eds.), *Responsibility and Evidence in Oral Discourse*, 1–23. Cambridge: Cambridge University Press.

Hill, Jane H., and Bruce Mannheim

    1992 Language and World View. *Annual Review of Anthropology* 21: 381–486.

Hinnebusch, Thomas J.

    1979 Swahili. In Timothy Shopen (ed.), *Languages and Their Status*, 209–293. Cambridge, Mass.: Winthrop Publishers.

Hockett, C. F.
  1989 *Refurbishing Our Foundations: Elementary Linguistics from an Advanced Point of View*. Philadelphia: John Benjamins Publishing Company.

Hoebel, E. Adamson
  1966 *Anthropology: The Study of Man*. 3rd ed. New York: McGraw-Hill Book Company.

Hogg, Richard, and C. B. McCully
  1987 *Metrical Phonology: A Coursebook*. Cambridge: Cambridge University Press.

Hoijer, Harry
  1953 The Relation of Language to Culture. In A. L. Kroeber (ed.), *Anthropology Today*, 554–573. Chicago: University of Chicago Press.
  1954a *Language in Culture: Proceedings of a Conference on the Interrelations of Language and Other Aspects of Culture*. American Anthropologist 56, no. 6, pt. 2, Memoir no. 79. Menasha, Wisc.: American Anthropological Association.
  1954b The Sapir-Whorf Hypothesis. In Harry Hoijer (ed.), *Language in Culture: Proceedings of a Conference on the Interrelations of Language and Other Aspects of Culture*, 92–105. American Anthropologist 56, no. 6, pt. 2, Memoir no. 79. Menasha, Wisc.: American Anthropological Association.
  1964a Cultural Implications of Some Navajo Linguistic Categories. In Dell Hymes (ed.), *Language in Culture and Society: A Reader in Linguistics and Anthropology*, 142–153. New York: Harper and Row, Publishers.
  1964b Linguistic and Cultural Change. In Dell Hymes (ed.), *Language in Culture and Society: A Reader in Linguistics and Anthropology*, 455–462. New York: Harper and Row, Publishers.

Holland, Dorothy, and Naomi Quinn
  1987 *Cultural Models in Language and Thought*. Cambridge: Cambridge University Press.

House, Deborah
  n.d.   An Analysis and Discussion of Chidí hahinidéhígíí t'áadoo le'é bédaháastL'inígíí (A.K.A. Chidí Bi'parts). Unpublished ms.

Hunn, Eugene
  1985 The Utilitarian Factor in Folk Biological Classification. In Janet W. D. Dougherty (ed.), *Directions in Cognitive Anthropology*, 117–140. Urbana and Chicago: University of Illinois Press.

Hunn, Eugene S., and Robert A. Randall
  1984 Do Life-Forms Evolve or Do Uses for Life? Some Doubts about Brown's Universals Hypotheses. *American Ethnologist* 11: 329–349.

Hutchins, E.
  1980 *Culture and Inference: A Trobriand Case Study*. Cambridge: Cambridge University Press.

Hymes, Dell

1962 The Ethnography of Speaking. In T. Gladwin and W. C. Sturtevant (eds.), *Anthropology and Human Behavior*, 13–53. Washington, D.C: Anthropological Society of Washington.

1964a Introduction. In Dell Hymes (ed.), *Language in Culture and Society: A Reader in Linguistics and Anthropology*, 3–14. New York: Harper and Row, Publishers.

1964b A Perspective for Linguistic Anthropology. In Sol Tax (ed.), *Horizons in Anthropology*, 92–107. Chicago: Aldine.

1970 The Ethnography of Speaking. In Joshua A. Fishman (ed.), *Readings in the Sociology of Language*, 99–138. New York: Mouton Publishers.

1971 Sociolinguistics and the Ethnography of Speaking. In Edwin Ardener (ed.), *Social Anthropology and Language*, 47–93. London: Tavistock Publications.

1972 Models of the Interaction of Language and Social Life. In John J. Gumperz and Dell Hymes (eds.), *Directions in Sociolinguistics: The Ethnography of Communication*, 35–71. New York: Holt, Rinehart and Winston.

1974a *Foundations in Sociolinguistics: An Ethnographic Approach*. Philadelphia: University of Pennsylvania Press.

1974b Sociolinguistics and the Ethnography of Speaking. In Ben Blount (ed.), *Language, Culture, and Society*, 335–369. Cambridge, Mass.: Winthrop Publishers.

1981 *"In Vain I Tried to Tell You."* Philadelphia: University of Pennsylvania Press.

1992 The Concept of Communicative Competence Revisited. In Martin Pütz (ed.), *Thirty Years of Linguistic Evolution: Studies in Honor of René Dirven on the Occasion of His Sixtieth Birthday*, 31–57. Philadelphia: John Benjamins Publishing Company.

Hymes, Dell H., and Courtney Cazden

1980 Narrative Thinking and Story-telling Rights: A Folklorist's Clue to a Critique of Education. In Dell H. Hymes (ed.), *Language in Education: Ethnolinguistic Essays*, 126–138. Language and Ethnography Series. Washington, D.C.: Center for Applied Linguistics.

Jackendoff, Ray

1986 *Semantics and Cognition*. Cambridge, Mass.: MIT Press.

Jaeger, Jeri

1980 Categorization in Phonology: An Experimental Approach. Ph.D. dissertation, University of California at Berkeley.

James, William

1961 Principles of Psychology. In Thorne Shipley (ed.), *Classics in Psychology*, 151–223. New York: Philosophical Library.

Johnson, Marcia K.

1991 Reflection, Reality Monitoring, and the Self. In Robert G. Kunzendorf (ed.), *Mental Imagery*, 3–16. New York: Plenum Press.

Johnson, Mark

1987 *The Body in the Mind: The Bodily Basis of Meaning, Imagination, and Reason*. Chicago: University of Chicago Press.

Johnson, Robert

1975 The Role of Phonetic Detail in Coeur d'Alene Phonology. Ph.D. dissertation, Washington State University, Pullman.

Johnson-Laird, P. N.

1983 *Mental Models: Towards a Cognitive Science of Language, Inference, and Consciousness*. Cambridge, England: Cambridge University Press.

Jordan, D. K.

1982 Review of A. Bloom, *The Linguistic Shaping of Thought: A Study in the Impact of Language on Thinking in China and the West. American Anthropologist* 84: 747–748.

Kay, Paul, Brent Berlin, and William Merrifield

1991 Biocultural Implications of Systems of Color Naming. *Journal of Linguistic Anthropology* 1: 12–25.

Kay, Paul, and Chad K. McDaniel

1978 The Linguistic Significance of the Meanings of Basic Color Terms. *Language* 54: 610–646.

Kaye, Jonathan

1989 *Phonology: A Cognitive View*. Hillsdale, N.J.: Lawrence Erlbaum Associates, Publishers.

Kearney, Michael

1992 A Very Bad Disease of the Arms. In Philip R. DeVita (ed.), *The Naked Anthropologist: Tales from around the World*, 47–57. Belmont: Wadsworth Publishing Company.

Keesing, Roger M.

1979 Linguistic Knowledge and Cultural Knowledge. *American Anthropologist* 81: 14–36.

1989 Exotic Readings of Cultural Texts. *Current Anthropology* 30: 459–479.

1992a Anthropology and Linguistics. In Martin Pütz (ed.), *Thirty Years of Linguistic Evolution: Studies in Honor of René Dirven on the Occasion of His Sixtieth Birthday*, 593–609. Philadelphia: John Benjamins Publishing Company.

1992b Not a Real Fish: The Ethnographer as Inside Outsider. In Philip R. DeVita (ed.), *The Naked Anthropologist: Tales from Around the World*, 73–78. Belmont: Wadsworth Publishing Company.

1994 Theories of Culture Revisited. In Robert Borofsky (ed.), *Assessing Cultural Anthropology*, 310–312. New York: McGraw-Hill.

Kenyatta, Jomo

    1966   *Naushangilia Mlima wa Kenya*. Nairobi: East African Institute Press.

Kinkade, M. Dale

    1975   The Lexical Domain of Anatomy in Columbian Salish. In M. Dale Kinkade, Kenneth L. Hale, and Oswald Werner (eds.), *Linguistics and Anthropology in Honor of C. F. Voegelin*, 423–443. Lisse: Peter De Ridder Press.

    1983   Salish Evidence against the Universality of "Noun" and "Verb." *Lingua* 60: 25–40.

    1993   S- Prefixation on Upper Chehalis (Salish) Imperfective Predicates. Paper presented to the SSILA Summer Meeting, Columbus, Ohio, July 2, 1993.

Kiyomi, Setsuko

    1992   Animateness and Shape in Classifiers. *Word* 43: 15–36.

Kluckhohn, Clyde

    1947   Covert Culture and Administrative Problems. *American Anthropologist* 45: 213–229.

Kochman, Thomas

    1981   *Black and White Styles in Conflict*. Chicago: University of Chicago Press.

Koffka, Kurt

    1961   Perception: An Introduction to the Gestalt-Theorie. In Thorne Shipley (ed.), *Classics in Psychology*, 1128–1196. New York: Philosophical Library.

Kosslyn, Stephen M.

    1980   *Image and Mind*. Cambridge, Mass.: Harvard University Press.

Kövecses, Zoltán

    1987   *Metaphors of Anger, Pride and Love*. Philadelphia: John Benjamins.

    1988   *The Language of Love: The Semantics of Passion in Conversational English*. Lewisburg, Pa.: Bucknell University Press.

    1990   *Emotion Concepts*. New York: Springer-Verlag.

    1991a The Fire Metaphor. Paper presented at the 2nd International Cognitive Linguistics Conference, University of California at Santa Cruz, July 29–August 2, 1991.

    1991b A Linguist's Quest for Love. *Journal of Social and Personal Relationships* 8: 77–97.

    1993   American Friendship. Paper presented at the 3rd International Cognitive Linguistics Conference, Leuven, Belgium, published in 1995 as "American Friendship and the Scope of Metaphor," *Cognitive Linguistics* 6(4): 315–346.

Lakoff, George

    1987   *Women, Fire and Dangerous Things: What Categories Reveal about the Mind*. Chicago: University of Chicago Press.

    1988   Cognitive Semantics. In Umberto Eco, Marco Santambrogio, and Patrizia Violi (eds.), *Meaning and Mental Representations*, 119–154. Bloomington and Indianapolis: Indiana University Press.

1989 A Suggestion for a Linguistics with Connectionist Foundations. In David Touretzky, Geoffrey Hinton, and Terrence Sejnowski (eds.), *Proceedings of the 1988 Connectionist Models Summer School*, 301–314. San Mateo, Calif.: Morgan Kaufmann Publishers.

1990 The Invariance Hypothesis: Is Abstract Reason Based on Image-Schemas? *Cognitive Linguistics* 1: 39–74.

1992 Metaphors and War: The Metaphor System Used to Justify War in the Gulf. In Martin Pütz (ed.), *Thirty Years of Linguistic Evolution: Studies in Honor of René Dirven on the Occasion of His Sixtieth Birthday*, 463–481. Philadelphia: John Benjamins Publishing Company.

Lakoff, George, and Mark Johnson

1980 *Metaphors We Live By*. Chicago: University of Chicago Press.

Lakoff, George, and Mark Turner

1989 *More Than Cool Reason: A Field Guide to Poetic Metaphor*. Chicago: University of Chicago Press.

Lan, David

1985 *Guns and Rain: Guerillas and Spirit Mediums in Zimbabwe*. Berkeley: University of California Press.

Langacker, Ronald W.

1986 An Introduction to Cognitive Grammar. *Cognitive Science* 10: 1–40.

1987 *Foundations of Cognitive Grammar*, vol. 1, *Theoretical Prerequisites*. Stanford: Stanford University Press.

1990a *Concept, Image, and Symbol: The Cognitive Basis of Grammar*. Edited by René Dirven and Ronald Langacker. Cognitive Linguistics Research. Berlin: Mouton de Gruyter.

1990b Subjectification. *Cognitive Linguistics* 1: 5–38.

1991 *Foundations of Cognitive Grammar*, vol. 2, *Descriptive Application*. Stanford: Stanford University Press.

1995 Raising and Transparency. *Language* 71 (1): 1–62.

Langdon, Margaret

1971 Sound Symbolism in Yuman Languages. In Jesse Sawyer (ed.), *Studies in American Indian Languages*, 149–173. Berkeley: University of California Press.

Lee, Dorothy

1938 Conceptual Implications of an Indian Language. *Philosophy of Science* 5: 89–102.

1940 Noun Categories in Wintu. *Zeitschrift für Vergleichende Sprachforschung* 67: 197–210.

1944 Categories of the Generic and the Particular in Wintu. *American Anthropologist* 46: 362–369.

1959 *Freedom and Culture*. Englewood Cliffs, N.J.: Prentice-Hall.

Lee, Penny

1993 The Influence of Gestalt Psychology in the work of B. L. Whorf. Paper presented to the 3rd International Cognitive Linguistics Association Conference, Leuven, Belgium, July 18–23, 1993.

Le Gros Clark, W. E.
    1959 *The Antecedents of Man*. New York: Harper Torchbooks.

Liu, L.
    1985 Reasoning and Counterfactuality in Chinese: Are There Any Obstacles? *Cognition* 21: 239–270.

Longacre, Robert E.
    1981 A Spectrum and Profile Approach to Discourse Analysis. *Text* 1: 337–359.

Lounsbury, Floyd G.
    1956 A Semantic Analysis of the Pawnee Kinship Usage. *Language* 32: 158–194.
    1964 A Formal Account of the Crow- and Omaha-Type Kinship Terminologies. In W. H. Goodenough (ed.), *Explorations in Cultural Anthropology*, 351–393. New York: McGraw-Hill. Reprinted in Tyler 1969a, 212–255.

Lucy, John A.
    1992a *Language Diversity and Thought: A Reformulation of the Linguistic Relativity Hypothesis*. Cambridge: Cambridge University Press.
    1992b *Grammatical Categories and Cognition: A Case Study of the Linguistic Relativity Hypothesis*. Cambridge: Cambridge University Press.

Lucy, John A., and Richard A. Shweder
    1981 [1979] Whorf and His Critics: Linguistic and Nonlinguistic Influences on Color Memory. In Ronald W. Casson (ed.), *Language, Culture, and Cognition: Anthropological Perspectives*, 133–163. Originally published in *American Anthropologist* 81: 581–607. New York: Macmillan Publishing Company.

Lutz, Catherine A.
    1988 *Unnatural Emotions: Everyday Sentiments on a Micronesian Atoll and Their Challenge to Western Theory*. Chicago: University of Chicago Press.

MacLaury, Robert E.
    1991 Exotic Color Categories: Linguistic Relativity to What Extent? *Journal of Linguistic Anthropology* 1: 26–51.
    1992 From Brightness to Hue: An Explanatory Model of Color-Category Evolution. *Current Anthropology* 33: 137–186.

Malotki, E.
    1983 *Hopi Time: A Linguistic Analysis of the Temporal Categories in the Hopi Language*. Berlin: Mouton.

Mandelbaum, David G. (ed.)
    1949 *Selected Writings of Edward Sapir*. Berkeley and Los Angeles: University of California Press.

Mandler, J.
    1984 *Stories, Scripts, and Scenes: Aspects of Schema Theory*. Hillsdale, N.J.: Lawrence Erlbaum Associates.

Marcus, George E.
  1994 After the Critique of Ethnography: Faith, Hope, and Charity, But the Great-
        est of These is Charity. In Robert Borofsky (ed.), *Assessing Cultural An-
        thropology*, 40–54. New York: McGraw-Hill.
Marcus, G., and M. Fischer
  1986 *Anthropology as Cultural Critique: An Experimental Moment in the Human
        Sciences*. Chicago: University of Chicago Press.
Martin, J. R.
  1988 Grammatical Conspiracies in Tagalog: Family, Face and Fate—with Regard
        to Benjamin Lee Whorf. In James D. Benson, Michael J. Cummings, and
        William S. Greaves (eds.), *Linguistics in a Systemic Perspective*, 243–300.
        Philadelphia: John Benjamins Publishing Company.
Mathiot, Madeleine
  1979 Overview. In Madeleine Mathiot (ed.), *Ethnolinguistics: Boas, Sapir, and
        Whorf Revisited*, 314–323. The Hague: Mouton Publishers.
  1985 Semantics of Sensory Perception Terms. In Hansjakob Seiler and Gunter
        Brettschneider (eds.), *Language Invariants and Mental Operations: Inter-
        national Interdisciplinary Conference Held at Gummersbach/Cologne,
        Germany, September 18–23, 1983*, 135–161. Tübingen: Gunter Narr
        Verlag.
Matsuki, Keiko
  1989 Metaphors of Anger in Japanese. *Language and Communication*, forth-
        coming.
Maxwell, Judith M., and Craig A. Hanson
  1992 *Of the Manners of Speaking That the Old Ones Had: The Metaphors of
        Andrés Olmos in the TULAL Manuscript "Arte para Aprender la Lengua
        Mexicana 1547."* Salt Lake City: University of Utah Press.
McClelland, James, and David Rumelhart
  1986 *Parallel Distributed Processing*, vol. 2. Cambridge, Mass.: MIT Press.
Nicodemus, Lawrence G.
  1975a *Snchitsu'umshtsn: The Coeur d'Alene Language*. Vol. 1. Spokane: Univer-
        sity Press.
  1975b *Snchitsu'umshtsn: The Coeur d'Alene Language*. Vol. 2. Spokane: Univer-
        sity Press.
  1975c *Snchitsu'umshtsn, the Coeur d'Alene Language: A Modern Course*. Albu-
        querque: Southwest Research Associates.
Noricks, Jay
  1987 Testing for Cognitive Validity: Componential Analysis and the Question of
        Extensions. *American Anthropologist* 89: 424–438.
Norman, Donald A.
  1988 *The Psychology of Everyday Things*. New York: Basic Books, Publishers.
Occhi, Debra, Gary Palmer, and Roy Ogawa
  1992 Like Hair, or Trees: Semantic Analysis of the Coeur d'Alene Prefix ne'

'amidst.' In Margaret Langdon (ed.), *Proceedings of the 1993 Annual Meeting of the Society for the Study of the Indigenous Languages of the Americas, July 2–4, 1993, and the Hokan-Sioux Conference, July 3, 1993, Columbus, Ohio*, 40–58. Report 8. Berkeley: Survey of California and Other Indian Languages.

Ochs, E.
1988 *Culture and Language Development*. Cambridge: Cambridge University Press.

Ogawa, Roy, and Gary Palmer
1994 Three Ways of Being *on*: Coeur d'Alene Prefixes of Contact. Revision of paper presented at the 3rd International Cognitive Linguistics Conference, Leuven, Belgium, July 18–23, 1993.

Ohnuki-Tierney, Emiko
1991 Embedding and Transforming Polytrope: The Monkey as Self in Japanese Culture. In James W. Fernandez (ed.), *Beyond Metaphor: The Theory of Tropes in Anthropology*, 159–189. Stanford: Stanford University Press.

Opler, Morris E.
1946 Themes as Dynamic Forces in Culture. *American Journal of Sociology* 51: 198–206.

Palmer, Gary B.
1980 Persecution, Alliance and Revenge in Shuswap Indian War Legends: A Formal Analysis. In Lucille B. Harten, Claude N. Warren, and Donald N. Touhy (eds.), *Anthropological Papers in Memory of Earl H. Swanson*, 1–7. Pocatello: Idaho Museum of Natural History.
1990 Where There Are Muskrats: The Semantic Structure of Coeur d'Alene Place Names. *Anthropological Linguistics* 32: 263–294.
n.d.a Coeur d'Alene. In Deward E. Walker, Jr. (ed.), *Handbook of North American Indians*, vol. 12, *Plateau*. Washington, D.C.: Smithsonian Institution, forthcoming.
n.d.b Foraging for Patterns in Interior Salish Semantic Domains. In Ewa Czaykowska-Higgins and M. Dale Kinkade (eds.), *Studies in Salish Linguistics: Current Perspectives*. New York and Berlin: Mouton de Gruyter, forthcoming.

Palmer, Gary B., and Lawrence G. Nicodemus
1985 Coeur d'Alene Exceptions to Proposed Universals of Anatomical Nomenclature. *American Ethnologist* 12: 341–359.

Perrott, D. V.
1965 *Teach Yourself Swahili*. London: English Universities Press.

Philips, Susan U.
1989 Warm Springs "Indian Time": How the Regulation of Participation Affects the Progress of Events. In Richard Bauman and Joel Sherzer (eds.), *Explorations in the Ethnography of Speaking*, 92–109. Cambridge: Cambridge University Press.

Pinker, Steven
 1994 *The Language Instinct: How the Mind Creates Language.* New York: William Morrow and Company.
Pinxten, Rik, Ingrid van Dooren, and Frank Harvey
 1983 *Anthropology of Space: Explorations into the Natural Philosophy and Semantics of the Navajo.* Philadelphia: University of Pennsylvania Press.
Powlison, Paul S.
 1965 A Paragraph Analysis of a Yagua Folktale. *International Journal of American Linguistics* 31: 109–118.
Propp, V.
 1968 *Morphology of the Folktale.* Austin and London: University of Texas Press.
Pulleyblank, Douglas
 1989 Nonlinear Phonology. *Annual Review of Anthropology* 18: 203–226.
Quinn, Naomi
 1985 "Commitment" in American Marriage: A Cultural Analysis. In Janet W. Dougherty (ed.), *Directions in Cognitive Anthropology*, 291–320. Champaign: University of Illinois Press.
 1987 Convergent Evidence for a Cultural Model of American Marriage. In Dorothy Holland and Naomi Quinn (eds.), *Cultural Models in Language and Thought*, 173–192. Cambridge: Cambridge University Press.
 1991 The Cultural Basis of Metaphor. In James W. Fernandez (ed.), *Beyond Metaphor: The Theory of Tropes in Anthropology*, 56–93. Stanford: Stanford University Press.
Quinn, Naomi, and Dorothy Holland
 1987 Culture and Cognition. *Cultural Models in Language and Thought*, 3–40. Cambridge: Cambridge University Press.
Randall, Robert A.
 1976 How Tall Is a Taxonomic Tree? Some Evidence for Dwarfism. *American Ethnologist* 3: 543–553.
 1987 The Nature of Highly Inclusive Folk-Botanical Categories. *American Anthropologist* 89: 143–146.
Reddy, Michael
 1979 The Conduit Metaphor. In Andrew Ortony (ed.), *Metaphor and Thought*, 284–324. Cambridge: Cambridge University Press.
Redeker, Gisela
 1991 Linguistic Markers of Discourse Structure: Review of Deborah Schiffrin: *Discourse Markers. Linguistics* 29: 1139–1172.
Reichard, Gladys
 1969 *An Analysis of Coeur d'Alene Indian Myths.* New York: Kraus Reprint Company.
Ridington, Robin
 1991 On the Language of Benjamin Lee Whorf. In Ian Brady (ed.), *Anthropological Poetics*, 241–261. Savage, Md.: Rowman and Littlefield Publishers.

Rock, Irvin, and Stephen Palmer
  1990 The Legacy of Gestalt Psychology. *Scientific American* 263: 84–90.
Rollins, Mark
  1989 *Mental Imagery: On the Limits of Cognitive Science*. New Haven: Yale University Press.
Rosch, Eleanor
  1978 Principles of Categorization. In Eleanor Rosch and B. B. Lloyd (eds.), *Cognition and Categorization*, 27–48. Hillsdale, N.J: Lawrence Erlbaum Associates.
Rosch, Eleanor, and Carolyn B. Mervis
  1975 Family Resemblances: Studies in the Internal Structure of Categories. *Cognitive Psychology* 7: 573–605.
Rosch, E., et al.
  1976 Basic Objects in Natural Categories. *Cognitive Psychology* 8: 382–439.
Rumelhart, D. E.
  1975 Notes on a Schema for Stories. In D. G. Bobrow and A. Collins (eds.), *Representation and Understanding*, 211–236. New York: Academic Press.
Sahagún, Fray Bernardo de
  1969 *Book 6, Rhetoric and Moral Philosophy: Florentine Codex, General History of Things of New Spain*. Translated by Charles E. Dibble and Arthur J. O. Anderson. Monographs of the School of American Research, no. 14, pt. 7. Santa Fe, N.M.: School of American Research.
Sampson, Geoffrey R.
  1980a *Making Sense*. Oxford: Oxford University Press.
  1980b *Schools of Linguistics*. Stanford, Calif.: Stanford University Press.
Sapir, Edward
  1949 [1921] *Language*. New York: Harcourt, Brace and World.
  1964 Conceptual Categories in Primitive Languages. In Dell Hymes (ed.), *Language in Culture and Society: A Reader in Linguistics and Anthropology*, 128. New York: Harper and Row, Publishers.
Sapir, J. David
  1977 *The Social Use of Metaphor: Essays on the Anthropology of Rhetoric*. Philadelphia: University of Pennsylvania Press.
Saunders, Ross, and Philip W. Davis
  1974 Bella Coola Head Bone Nomenclature. *Journal of Anthropological Research* 30: 174–190.
  1975a The Internal Syntax of Lexical Suffixes in Bella Coola. *International Journal of American Linguistics* 41: 106–113.
  1975b Bella Coola Lexical Suffixes. *Anthropological Linguistics* 17: 154–189.
  1975c Bella Coola Referential Suffixes. *International Journal of American Linguistics* 41: 355–368.

Saussure, Ferdinand de
  1966 *Course in General Linguistics.* Translated by Wade Baskin. New York: Mc-
        Graw-Hill Book Company.
Saville-Troike, Muriel
  1989 *The Ethnography of Communication: An Introduction.* 2nd ed. New York:
        Basil Blackwell.
Schank, Roger, and Robert Abelson
  1977 *Scripts, Plans, Goals and Understanding: An Inquiry into Human Knowl-
        edge Structures.* Hillsdale, N.J.: Lawrence Erlbaum Associates, Publishers.
Scheerer, Eckart
  1988 Towards a History of Cognitive Science. *International Social Science Jour-
        nal* 40: 7–19.
Schiefflin, Edward L.
  1976 *The Sorrow of the Lonely and the Burning of the Dancers.* New York:
        St. Martin's Press.
Schiffrin, Deborah
  1987 *Discourse Markers.* Cambridge: Cambridge University Press.
  1993 "Speaking for Another" in Sociolinguistic Interviews: Alignments, Identi-
        ties, and Frames. In Deborah Tannen (ed.), *Framing in Discourse,* 231–
        263. New York: Oxford University Press.
Schlegel, Alice
  1975 Hopi Joking and Castration Threats. In M. Dale Kinkade, Kenneth L. Hale,
        and Oswald Werner (eds.), *Linguistics: An Anthology in Honor of C. F.
        Voegelin,* 521–530. Lisse: Peter De Ridder Press.
Schultz, Emily A.
  1990 *Dialogue at the Margins: Whorf, Bakhtin, and Linguistic Relativity.* Madi-
        son: University of Wisconsin Press.
Scollon, Ronald, and Suzanne Wong-Scollon
  1990 Athabascan-English Interethnic Communication. In Donal Carbaugh (ed.),
        Cultural Communication and Intercultural Contact, 259–286. Hillsdale,
        N.J.: Lawrence Erlbaum Associates, Publishers.
Searle, John R.
  1990 Epilogue to the Taxonomy of Illocutionary Acts. In Donal Carbaugh (ed.),
        Cultural Communication and Intercultural Contact, 409–428. Hillsdale,
        N.J.: Lawrence Erlbaum Associates, Publishers.
Shakir, Abdullah, and Mohammed Farghal
  1991 The Activation of Schemata in Relation to Background Knowledge and
        Markedness. *Text* 11: 201–222.
Shaw, Patricia A.
  1989 On Obstruent Syllabicity. Paper presented at the Linguistic Institute of the
        LSA and the MLA, Tucson, Arizona, July 1989.
Shepard, R. N., and J. Metzler
  1971 Mental Rotation of Three-Dimensional Objects. *Science* 171: 701–703.

Sherzer, Joel

    1983 *Kuna Ways of Speaking: An Ethnographic Perspective*. Austin: University of Texas Press.

    1987 A Discourse-Centered Approach to Language and Culture. *American Anthropologist* 89: 295–309.

Sherzer, Joel, and Greg Urban (eds.)

    1986 *Native South American Discourse*. New York: Mouton de Gruyter. [Includes audiotape cassette, bound separately.]

Shibatani, Masayoshi

    1990 *The Languages of Japan*. Cambridge Language Surveys. Cambridge: Cambridge University Press.

Silverstein, Michael

    1976 Shifters, Linguistic Categories, and Cultural Description. In Keith Basso and Henry Selby (eds.), *Meaning in Anthropology*, 11–55. Albuquerque: University of New Mexico Press.

Simmons, Leo W.

    1942 *Sun Chief: The Autobiography of a Hopi Indian*. New Haven: Yale University Press.

Simon, Herbert A., and Craig A. Kaplan

    1989 Foundations of Cognitive Science. In Michael I. Posner (ed.), *Foundations of Cognitive Science*, 1–47. Cambridge, Mass.: MIT Press.

Spitulnik, Debra A.

    1987 *Semantic Superstructuring and Infrastructuring: Nominal Class Struggle in ChiBemba*. Bloomington: Indiana University Linguistics Club.

Spradley, James P.

    1970 *You Owe Yourself a Drunk: An Ethnography of Urban Nomads*. Boston: Little, Brown.

Spradley, James P., and David W. McCurdy

    1972 *The Cultural Experience: Ethnography in Complex Society*. Chicago: Science Research Associates.

Stocking, George W., Jr.

    1974 The Boas Plan for the Study of American Indian Languages. In Dell Hymes (ed.), *Studies in the History of Linguistics: Traditions and Paradigms*, 454–484. Bloomington: Indiana University Press.

Strauss, Claudia

    1992a Models and Motives. In Roy G. D'Andrade and Claudia Strauss (eds.), *Human Motives and Cultural Models*, 1–20. Cambridge: Cambridge University Press.

    1992b What Makes Tony Run? Schemas as Motives Reconsidered. In Roy G. D'Andrade and Claudia Strauss (eds.), *Human Motives and Cultural Models*, 191–224. Cambridge: Cambridge University Press.

Strauss, Claudia, and Naomi Quinn
   1994 A Cognitive/Cultural Anthropology. In Robert Borofsky (ed.), *Assessing Cultural Anthropology*, 284–300. New York: McGraw-Hill.

Stubbs, Michael
   1983 *Discourse Analysis: The Sociolinguistic Analysis of Natural Language.* Chicago: University of Chicago Press.

Sweetser, Eve E.
   1987 The Definition of Lie: An Examination of the Folk Models Underlying a Semantic Prototype. In Dorothy Holland and Naomi Quinn (eds.), *Cultural Models in Language and Thought*, 43–66. Cambridge: Cambridge University Press.

Talmy, Leonard
   1983 How Language Structures Space. In H. Pick and L. Acredolo (eds.), *Spatial Orientation: Theory, Research and Application*, 225–320. New York: Plenum Press.
   1985 Lexicalization Patterns: Semantic Structure in Lexical Forms. In Timothy Shopen (ed.), *Language Typology and Syntactic Description*, vol. 3, 57–149. Cambridge: Cambridge University Press.
   1988 Force Dynamics in Language and Cognition. *Cognitive Science* 12: 49–100.

Tannen, Deborah
   1989 *Talking Voices: Repetition, Dialogue, and Imagery in Conversational Discourse.* Edited by John J. Gumperz. Studies in Interactional Sociolinguistics 6. Cambridge: Cambridge University Press.

Tannen, Deborah, and Cynthia Wallat
   1993 Interactive Frames and Knowledge Schemas in Interaction: Examples from a Medical Examination/Interview. In Deborah Tannen (ed.), *Framing in Discourse*, 57–76. New York: Oxford University Press.

Tartter, Vivien C.
   1986 *Language Processes.* New York: Holt, Rinehart, and Winston.

Taylor, J. R.
   1991 *Linguistic Categorization: Prototypes in Linguistic Theory.* Oxford: Clarendon Press.

Tedlock, Dennis
   1985 *Popol Vuh: The Mayan Book of the Dawn of Life.* New York: Simon and Schuster.

Tsuda, Aoi
   1984 *Sales Talk in Japan and the United States.* Washington, D.C.: Georgetown University Press.

Turner, Nancy J.
   1974 Plant Taxonomic Systems and Ethnobotany of Three Contemporary Indian Groups of the Pacific Northwest (Haida, Bella Coola, and Lillooet). *Syesis* 7: 1–104.

1989 "All Berries Have Relations": Mid-Range Folk Plant Groupings in Thompson and Lillooet Interior Salish. *Journal of Ethnobiology* 9: 69–110.

n.d.   Salish Plant Names: Pieces of an Intricate Puzzle. In Ewa Czaykowska-Higgins and M. Dale Kinkade (eds.), *Studies in Salish Linguistics: Current Perspectives*. New York and Berlin: Mouton de Gruyter, forthcoming.

Turner, Victor

1967   *The Forest of Symbols*. Ithaca: Cornell University Press.

Tyler, Stephen A.

1969a *Cognitive Anthropology*. New York: Holt, Rinehart and Winston.

1969b Introduction. In Stephen A. Tyler (ed.), *Cognitive Anthropology*, 1–27. New York: Holt, Rinehart and Winston.

1978   *The Said and the Unsaid: Mind, Meaning and Culture*. New York: Academic Press.

Varela, Francisco J., Evan Thompson, and Eleanor Rosch

1991   *The Embodied Mind: Cognitive Science and Human Experience*. Cambridge, Mass.: MIT Press.

Wallace, Anthony F. C.

1969 [1965]   The Problem of the Psychological Validity of Componential Analysis [originally in *American Anthropologist* 67: 229–248]. In Stephen A. Tyler (ed.), *Cognitive Anthropology*, 396–418. New York: Holt, Rinehart and Winston.

1970   *Culture and Personality*. 2nd ed. New York: Random House.

Walrod, Michael R.

1988   *Normative Discourse and Persuasion: An Analysis of Ga'dang Informal Litigation*. Manila: Linguistic Society of the Philippines.

Werth, Paul

1993   Accommodation and the Myth of Presupposition: The View from Discourse. *Lingua* 89: 39–95.

n.d.   Conceptual Structures and Fractal Systems. Unpublished manuscript in possession of the author.

Whorf, Benjamin

1952   *Collected Papers on Metalinguistics*. Washington, D.C.: Foreign Service Institute, Department of State.

1956a Gestalt Technique of Stem Composition in Shawnee. In John B. Carroll (ed.), *Language, Thought, and Reality: Selected Writings of Benjamin Lee Whorf*, 160–172. Cambridge, Mass.: MIT Press.

1956b *Language, Thought, and Reality: Selected Writings of Benjamin Lee Whorf*. Edited by John B. Carroll. Cambridge, Mass.: MIT Press.

1964   A Linguistic Consideration of Thinking. In Dell Hymes (ed.), *Language in Culture and Society: A Reader in Linguistics and Anthropology*, 129–141. New York: Harper and Row, Publishers.

Wierzbicka, Anna

1990 The Meaning of Color Terms: Semantics, Culture, and Cognition. *Cognitive Linguistics* 1: 99–150.

1992a Furniture and Birds: A Reply to Dwight Bolinger. *Cognitive Linguistics* 3: 119–123.

1992b "Cultural Scripts": A Semantic Approach to Cultural Analysis and Cross-Cultural Communication. Paper presented at symposium held in Duisburg, Germany, March 1992.

n.d. "Cultural Scripts": A New Approach to Cross-Cultural Communication. In Martin Pütz (ed.), *Intercultural Communication*. In press.

Williams, Thomas Rhys

1990 *Cultural Anthropology*. Englewood Cliffs: Prentice-Hall.

Winston, Morton E., Roger Chaffin, and Douglas Herrmann

1987 A Taxonomy of Part-Whole Relations. *Cognitive Science* 11: 417–444.

Witherspoon, Gary

1977 *Language and Art in the Navajo Universe*. Ann Arbor: University of Michigan Press.

1980 Language in Culture and Culture in Language. *International Journal of American Linguistics* 46: 1–13.

Wolfram, Walt, and Robert Johnson

1982 *Phonological Analysis, Focus on American English*. Washington, D.C.: Center for Applied Linguistics.

Wu, Cynthia Hsin-feng

1991 If Triangles Were Circles . . . A Study of Chinese Counterfactuals. Paper presented at the 2nd International Cognitive Linguistics Conference, University of California at Santa Cruz, July 29–August 2, 1991.

Young, Robert W., and William Morgan, Sr.

1987 *The Navajo Language: A Grammar and Colloquial Dictionary*. Revised ed. Albuquerque: University of New Mexico Press.

INDEX